The Edinburgh Anthology of Scottish Literature
Volume 2

The Edinburgh Anthology of Scottish Literature

VOLUME 2
SECOND EDITION

Edited by Robert Irvine

Kennedy & Boyd

Kennedy & Boyd
an imprint of
Zeticula
57 St Vincent Crescent
Glasgow
G3 8NQ
Scotland.

http://www.kennedyandboyd.co.uk
admin@kennedyandboyd.co.uk

First published in 2009
Second Edition 2010
Copyright © Zeticula 2009, 2010
Introduction and notes © Robert Irvine 2009, 2010
Cover image: View of the Forth Rail Bridge under construction, from
the north west, by Evelyn Carey (late 1880s) © BRB (Residuary) Ltd.
Reproduced by kind permission.
'Thievie' reproduced by kind permission of Malcolm Hutton.
In Time O' Strife reproduced by kind permission of Morag Corrie.
'Clock-a-doodle-do' reproduced by kind permission of Kenneth Ross.

Every effort has been made to trace possible copyright holders and
to obtain their permission for the use of any copyright material. The
publishers will gladly receive information enabling them to rectify any
error or omission for subsequent editions.

ISBN-13 978-1-84921-079-9 Paperback

Acknowledgements

Many thanks are once more due to Anne Mason for her help in producing this volume. Special thanks are due to Aileen Christianson for her careful preparation of the texts of 'The Pictures', 'Thievie', and 'Clock-a-doodle-do'.

We are very grateful to Malcolm Hutton, Morag Corrie and Kenneth Ross for their gracious permission to allow us to reproduce texts in which they hold copyright; and to Peter Trewin for permission to use the cover image.

A grant from Edinburgh University's School of Languages, Literatures and Cultures supported the preparation of some of these texts.

A note on the texts

Obvious errors have been silently amended.

As well as referring to the *Oxford English Dictionary* (*OED*), footnotes glossing Scots words and phrases (marked Sc.) cite the *Scottish National Dictionary* (*SND*), which can be most conveniently consulted through the Dictionary of the Scots Language website: www.dsl.ac.uk.

Contents

Introduction

When Hugh MacDiarmid (the pseudonym of Christopher Murray Grieve) appropriated the term 'Scottish Renaissance' (from the French critic Denis Saurat, writing in 1925) to name the cultural revival which he led, he was implicitly claiming that Scottish culture, in the 1920s, needed to be 'reborn'. Adopting a series of combative (and sometimes contradictory) stances, MacDiarmid's project was in part to construct a particular type of public persona for himself as a poet. The artist capable of recreating a new and self-consciously modern Scotland had to be a figure of the international *avant-garde*, taking part in the explosion of aesthetic experimentation called Modernism. Modernist art was bound to seem strange and alienating to its readers at first, as it attempted to break with the art of the immediate past, and reinterpret literary and other traditions in radically different terms. The programme of MacDiarmid, as of Virginia Woolf, T.S. Eliot, and James Joyce, was a self-consciously high-cultural one, addressing those well-read in the literary traditions against which their work defined itself, and to which it made complex allusion. The particular persona adopted by MacDiarmid within this context, however, was unambiguously masculine. MacDiarmid's ambitious *A Drunk Man Looks at the Thistle* includes a multiplicity of voices, as does T.S. Eliot's *The Waste Land*, but here they are collected inside the head of a single drunk man, collapsed on his way home from an evening spent in the all-male environment of a traditional Scottish pub. A recurring theme in *A Drunk Man* is the possibility of cultural or spiritual 'rebirth' as the masculine equivalent of (and alternative to) feminine physical procreativity.

The idea of a Scottish Renaissance in the 1920s and early 30s still has currency in studies of twentieth-century Scottish culture. The texts collected in this anthology can be understood as representative of work that tends to be left out or marginalised by this version of literary history: the work of women writers who were MacDiarmid's contemporaries (Findlater, Jacob, Muir); writing that represented the very aspects of Scottish culture he wanted to overcome (Barrie, Macleod, Maclaren); writing that aimed to reach a broad working-class audience for immediate political effect (Corrie); and work by earlier Scottish poets writing in English outside Scotland which could not be easily assimilated to MacDiarmid's cultural nationalism, however much they anticipate his modernism in other ways (Thomson and Davidson).

To pull these writers out from under the shadow cast by the Scottish Renaissance is not to claim that Scotland in the 1920s was not a country in need of renewal. The Great War of 1914–1918 had a disproportionate effect on Scotland, both in terms of the number of men lost (with 10% of the UK population, Scots constituted about 14% of Britons killed), and in the scale on which its economy was turned over to war-production, especially on the Clyde. Social discontent among working people, suffering low wages and terrible housing, simmered throughout the war years, and peace brought further troubles as war-production was scaled back and international markets changed and shifted. Coal-mining, employing around 150,000 men in Scotland in 1924, was particularly badly hit, with many pits producing at a loss. The mine-owners responded with plans to extend the length of a shift from seven to eight hours (a long time underground in the brutal conditions of the time) and a 20% cut in wages. In May 1926, the miners went on strike and initially won the support of the Trade Union Congress, who called Britain's first and last general strike across all unionised industries to force the owners (and their supporters in the British government) to back down. But the T.U.C. called off the General Strike after only nine days; the miners struggled on alone until November, and returned to work under exactly the conditions demanded by their employers. The failure of the strike left the Labour movement dispirited and divided within itself; but it also revealed a country more generally divided, and with economic and social problems which demanded radical solutions.

However, in many ways, the Scottish *cultural* revival that MacDiarmid called for had already happened, in the 1880s and 90s. These were the decades in which Scottish painting was reinvented by the 'Glasgow Boys', under the influence of the Impressionist and Post-impressionist schools in France; in which Charles Rennie Mackintosh and his collaborators made Glasgow one of the centres of *art nouveau* architecture and interior design; and in which mid-Victorian economic individualism and *laissez-faire* were rejected by a renewed civic consciousness, expounded by Idealist philosophers such as Edward Caird in Glasgow, developed in the new science of urban planning invented by Patrick Geddes in Edinburgh, and put into practice by newly-empowered city councils who engaged in various types of improvement and modernisation. In literature, these are also the decades of Robert Louis Stevenson and John Davidson. Taken together, these developments suggest a Scotland that is self-consciously modernising, looking outside itself to connect with and contribute to international developments in ideas and the arts, decades before MacDiarmid aligned his Scottish Renaissance with international Modernism. Caird looked to Berlin and Oxford, Geddes, Mackintosh and the Glasgow Boys to Paris; it is not surprising that Davidson spent most of his career in London, and Stevenson spent most of his almost everywhere else.

Yet the most commercially-successful fictional representations of Scotland in the 1890s portrayed a country of small towns and villages, inward-looking and obsessed with local disputes in politics and religion. These 'kailyard' ('cabbage-patch') fictions were often written by men who had themselves left Scotland, such as J.M. Barrie (for London) and 'Ian Maclaren' (the pseudonym of Rev. John Watson, who became a minister in Liverpool). The idealised or romanticised rural Scotland that they summon up was undoubtedly popular among their fellow Scottish exiles, but they also sold well in the Scottish cities. A story like 'Domsie', from Maclaren's first collection *Beside the Bonnie Briar Bush*, acts out the relation between the village and the city in the journey of its scholar-hero from his Perthshire home to Edinburgh University and back. The narrative voice of the story, too, crosses and re-crosses that divide, sometimes referring to the villagers as 'we' (usually with verbs in the past tense) and sometimes as 'they' or, generally, 'the Scots' (usually with verbs in the present tense). The narrator has been a member of this society; now he is an outsider, and returns, like his readers, as a kind of tourist. But George Howe returns to Drumtochty only to die. He brings with him his academic achievements, received as the city's seal of approval on his community: for all its self-absorption, Drumtochty depends on outside forces (a university, the narrator) to confirm its value in its own eyes. Geordie's death also brings an occasion for the sentimental unification around his grave, not only of his village, but of all Scotland, present in representatives of Highland and Lowland, rich and poor, rural and urban, Liberal and Tory. That the sentiment is so excessive perhaps suggests the vast distance between this fantasy of unification and the real social fragmentation of Scottish life.

The Kailyard provided a useful straw man for MacDiarmid and his allies, representing the Scotland of lowbrow parochial kitsch that they planned to overthrow. Some qualification is in order here. The accusation is often made that stories like Barrie's and Maclaren's are morally culpable in their refusal to face up to the urban, industrial world, with its slum housing and disease, in which most Scots lived. And it is true that, at the time of the 1891 census, just over half of Scots lived in settlements of more than 5,000 people. Yet what is likely to strike a twenty-first century reader about that statistic is that nearly half of Scots did *not* live in urban areas thus defined. What is more, the rural or small-town setting was one that the writers of the '20s and '30s, even MacDiarmid himself and his collaborator Lewis Grassic Gibbon, found it hard to get away from. Perhaps that is one reason why, in stories like Findlater's 'The Pictures' and Jacob's 'Thievie', rural Scottish life appears as a trap, from which any prospect of escape is to be feverishly grasped and doomed to frustration. The narrative voice in both stories remains very close to the protagonist's consciousness. While still a third-person narration, mediating that consciousness in terms not available to the character themselves, this is very different from the ironic distance Maclaren's narrator adopts in relation to the inhabitants of Drumtochty. The narrator of these stories shares with their protagonists, not an origin from which he has escaped and they have not, but a present situation of frustrating marginality in a patriarchal culture.

It was also possible to retreat into a fantasy version of rural Scotland while still remaining in touch with the latest tendencies in international high culture. The 'Celticism' of Fiona Macleod (pseudonym of William Sharp, born in Paisley) is a case in point. In some ways, this did for the Highlands what the Kailyard did for the Lowlands: fabricate a version of rural life to meet the imaginative demands of urban readers. Of course, the Highlands had been used in this way for much longer, since the days of Macpherson and Scott. But where their Gaels were placed very much in the past, those of *Pharais* are at least in the present day; and the novel demonstrates Macleod's genuine interest in surviving Gaelic folklore. The real Gaelic Scotland was at an interesting juncture in the 1890s. On the one hand, a battle had been fought and won over security of tenure for traditional smallholders (crofters) on their land in the eight counties of the Highlands and Islands. After a campaign of protest and civil disobedience modelled on (though less violent than) that carried out for land reform in Ireland, the Crofting Act of 1885 ended the possibility of forced eviction of whole communities ('clearance') that had scarred Highland life for the previous century. On the other hand, emigration continued, indeed accelerated, after the Act, voluntarily and for simple economic reasons. In addition, the Education (Scotland) Act of 1872, in making schooling compulsory for children from 5 to 13, made no provision for teaching in Gaelic. At the time of the 1891 census, over a quarter of a million Scots spoke Gaelic, concentrated in the north-west but spreading east as far as the Highland parts of Perthshire and Aberdeenshire. As generation after generation learned in school that their native tongue was second rate, the language began its steady decline and retreat westward (around 58,000 speak it today, almost all in the islands).

Yet Macleod's Celticism does not offer to defend the Gaelic culture that it portrays. This is in striking contrast to the 'Celtic Revival' in which W.B. Yeats was so active in Ireland. Both Scottish and Irish Celticism find in Gaelic culture aesthetic and spiritual qualities missing from the modern industrialised world, a resource which the Celticist artist can use to revitalise modern culture. But for Yeats and his allies, this was merely the starting point for a political struggle to free Ireland from British rule, and restore Irish Gaelic as a national language. Macleod not only sees the aesthetic resources of the Celtic as devoid of any practical political implication, but understands the commitment of the Celt to the life of beauty and the spirit as rendering her incapable of practical political action; or to put that another way, finds the beauty of Celtic culture precisely in its absolute divorce from political power. In this, she follows the racial thinking of Matthew Arnold from decades before, but is simultaneously in line with contemporary European 'aestheticism' more generally. Such a stance comes close to consigning

Gaelic culture to inevitable real-world extinction, while the Celticist artist sits back and enjoys the pleasurable poignancy of this prospect. *Pharais*, indeed, acts out its own version of 'rebirth' or renaissance, when Lora and Alastair emerge from a womb-like cave after their attempted suicide. But this merely postpones the point at which they die, as inevitably as the Celtic culture that they represent. Macleod indeed goes beyond Arnold in imagining the Celt's responsiveness to natural beauty as a kind of inherited sickness (a consequence of Alastair's 'mind-dark'), drawing both on contemporary medical concerns about 'degeneration', and the interest among 'decadent' modern writers such as Charles Baudelaire and J.K. Huysmans in sickness as facilitating aesthetic experience.

Barrie's representation of small-town Scotland in *A Window in Thrums* is also more complex that it may at first appear. It is, for one thing, comparatively clear-eyed about the physical hardship and material poverty endured by its weaving families. While the petty status-distinctions that structure Thrums society, and the constant and detailed surveillance of one's neighbours that their maintenance demands, are generally played for laughs, they also reveal a community that is claustrophobic as well as supportive. Indeed, one of the most interesting aspects of this story is the extent to which that claustrophobia infects the McQumpha family as well. In the last five chapters, it seems to be required that a young man's relationship with his sister and his mother should not only take priority over, but *take the place of*, any possible heterosexual attachment that he might form elsewhere. And the novel's ending contrives to punish Jamie for forming such an attachment (with 'that woman in London', about whom we learn nothing at all) with the death of his entire family! Such melodrama tends to distract us from the extent to which *A Window in Thrums* is also a historical novel as 'Domsie' is not. Independent hand-loom weavers like Hendry had been wiped out as a class by the introduction of steam-powered looms in factories, a process almost complete by mid-century. Barrie's novel mourns this lost way of life just as Macleod mourns Gaeldom, as Gibbon will mourn the end of Kincardineshire crofting in *Sunset Song* (1932), and as Walter Scott, at the start of the nineteenth century, had mourned the passing of the Highland clans. In 'Domsie', the narrated past is separated from the narrator's present by the 1872 Act. In *A Window in Thrums*, what intervenes is an economic cataclysm, produced by the impersonal and irresistible forces of what Geddes, in 1915, will look back on as the 'Second Industrial Revolution'. But that economic cataclysm is not itself narrated, and in its place, as the explanation for the passing of the McQumphas, we have the story of Jamie's exogamy.

The effects of industrialisation were not the only historical developments to which late nineteenth-century Scottish writers had to respond. A crisis in traditional religious belief was also precipitated by discoveries in natural science: first, the revelation by geologists (Scots like James Hutton and Charles Lyell prominent among them) that the Earth was many millions of years old, and not the few thousand it appeared to be in the biblical account; then Charles Darwin's demonstration, in *On the Origin of Species* (1859), that life on earth had evolved in those millions of years by a process of natural selection, rendering redundant explanations of life with reference to divine creation. James Thomson's poem 'The City of Dreadful Night' can be understood as a portrayal of a world rendered meaningless by the loss of any higher order governing its existence. At several points the poem evokes the Hell of Dante's *Inferno*. But the fate of those in Dante's Hell is the result of a divine ordering of the universe. The wanderers of Thomson's nocturnal metropolis have no explanation for their situation, and no expectation that there might be an explanation, leaving only the 'insufferable inane'

(VI l.24). The Christian virtues of Faith, Hope and Love have simply died (II). Only the communication of their despair from one sufferer to another, such as the poem itself sets out to achieve ('Proem'), seems to offer a thin comfort. Although some commentators suggest otherwise, it is not clear that this is a specifically industrial city, or that the loss of religious faith suffered by the protagonist is part of a more general feeling of alienation and isolation produced by the sheer scale of the modern metropolis. True, it does seem to be a city that has been cut off from its own history, fragments of which only remain as 'Great ruins of an unremembered past' (I.37), in a way that parallels the protagonists' separation from religion as a source of personal meaning. The poem itself, however, remains in touch with *literary* history in a straightforward way, evoking Dante and Blake as its visionary predecessors. The poem turns the city from the scene of a contemporary social and economic trauma into a series of metaphors for the protagonist's state of mind in a way that anticipates *The Waste Land* of 1922. However, in Eliot's poem, the relation to literary history will be part of the problem: rather than offering models to follow, Dante and Shakespeare will appear as fragments themselves, 'great ruins' of a literary past from which the modern world has been cut off by another cataclysm, that of the Great War.

Of the writers included in this anthology, John Davidson is perhaps the one who most successfully addresses *both* the crisis in belief *and* its context in late Victorian society. 'A Ballad in Blank Verse' narrates a poet's abandonment of his parent's religion, not in response to the revelations of science, but out of commitment to a rival vocation, that of poetry itself. Like Jamie in *A Window in Thrums*, the protagonist seems able to establish his own identity only at the cost of killing his parents. But despite this, he experiences his rejection of inherited belief as a new and vital freedom, an opportunity for creation and self-creation, and not as the absolute loss of meaning described by Thomson. But we must not ascribe this optimism to Davidson himself: the young poet's words are carefully bracketed with quotation marks, and framed by a narrator standing aside from his thoughts and setting them in dramatic context. That is, we are invited to read the young poet's response to the new intellectual and spiritual context of the late nineteenth century as the particular response of someone in a particular position in a particular society, the son of a minister in an industrial town in the West of Scotland. From other social positions, the death of God (as Nietzsche referred to it in *The Gay Science*) opens up other possibilities. Two of Davidson's dramatic monologues, included in this anthology, explore the very different ways in which Darwinian and similar ideas are appropriated by their respective speakers. For the Empire Builder, a ruthless colonial entrepreneur in the mould of Cecil Rhodes, the discrediting of conventional Christianity means simply the removal of any moral restraint on his actions. The fading of religious belief produces, not despair as in Thomson, or intellectual freedom as in 'A Ballad in Blank Verse', but the uninhibited celebration of brute power. The world is transformed not into Thomson's Limbo, but into its own version of Heaven and Hell; and in a 'revaluation of all values' (Nietzsche again, in *The Antichrist*), it is the powerful, violent, and lustful who are rewarded, and the weak and well-meaning who are punished.

However, those at the bottom of the social heap might see things very differently. This possibility is vividly imagined in one of Davidson's greatest poems, 'Thirty Bob a Week'. The speaker is a London clerk on this meagre salary, and the poem is written in a verse form that recalls (with its internal rhyme splitting the penultimate line in each stanza) the working-class genre of music-hall song. But in the twelfth stanza, the clerk's voice also becomes that of a life-force which has existed 'A million years before the blooming sun' (1.72) and is now embodied in him. By identifying with this force, the clerk takes absolute responsibility for his own life: 'My weakness and my strength without a doubt / Are mine alone for ever from the first' (ll.81–82). But his realisation that he is himself the product of millions of years of evolution also informs his frustration and anger at the restricted room accorded him to exercise his god-like faculties. The decline of religion may set free a 'hungry wolf' (1.91) like the empire builder, but it also opens to question a social hierarchy that religion had traditionally justified or mitigated, and frees his prey to imagine a social order in which the wolf was put back in his cage.

The clerk does not get as far as such imaginings; he is aware that his predicament is shared 'by many and many a one' (1.95), but does not consider the possibility of uniting with them to change their world for the better. Imaginative freedom does not translate into political agency except through some form of collectivity. In the playwright Joe Corrie we find a writer who assumes that art can have a real and transformative political agency within threatened communities. Corrie was a miner from the pit village of Cardenden, near Bowhill in West Fife: the miner's strike of 1926 turned him into a dramatist as well. During that bitter dispute, Corrie's neighbours and their wives had formed a drama troupe, the Bowhill Players, which toured Fife with sketches and songs to raise money for local soup kitchens and raise morale. Corrie wrote for the group, and when the strike was over wrote his first full-length play, *In Time O' Strife*, which they toured throughout Scotland with great success.

Corrie's play brilliantly explores the greatest industrial conflict of the age within the space of the front room of a miner's cottage. The conduct of the strike here is a matter of personal relationships and loyalties, and not because the family or community is made into an allegory of national politics. Private life is political here, not because of a literary trope, but because of 'the peculiar, self-absorbed and intensely close-knit character of the mining villages of Britain, in which by the early twentieth century unionism had become not just a necessary adjunct of working life, but a social institution with which the identity of the community was bound up' (G.A. Phillips, *The General Strike* [1976]). The village setting, the concern with containment and escape, are in outline not so different from those of the Kailyard. But this is a community in which national divisions are not healed, but reproduced; in which Wull Baxter's escape to Canada represents not a vindication of the people he leaves behind, but their betrayal; and Edinburgh appears not as a university and the prospect of social advancement, but a court, and a jail, and the enforcement of social discipline. Significantly, the forces of solidarity and resistance are embodied here in the women, rather than the mostly feckless men. MacDiarmid too mourned the catastrophe of 1926 (he referred to lines 1119–1218 of *A Drunk Man* as his 'Ballad of the General Strike') and asked in *Second Hymn to Lenin* (1935),

Are my poems spoken in the factories and fields,
In the streets o' the toon?
Gin they're no, than I'm failin' to dae
What I ocht to ha' dune.

The answer to MacDiarmid's question was, of course, no. Corrie's plays, on the other hand, were performed in music halls and miner's institutes, and to that extent he, more than any of the other writers included in this anthology, did what MacDiarmid felt he 'ought to have done'.

James Thomson ('B.V.'), 'The City of Dreadful Night' (1874).[1]

From *The City of Dreadful Night and Other Poems* (London: Reeves and Turner, 1880)

"Per me si va nella città dolente."
—Dante.[2]

"Poi di tanto adoprar, di tanti moti
D'ogni celeste, ogni terrena cosa,
Girando senza posa,
Per tornar sempre là donde son mosse;
Uso alcuno, alcun frutto
Indovinar non so."[3]

"Sola nel mondo eterna, a cui si volve
Ogni creata cosa,
In te, morte, si posa
Nostra ignuda natura;
Lieta no, ma sicura
Dell' antico dolor. . .
Però ch' esser beato
Nega ai mortali e nega a' morti il fato."[4]
—Leopardi.

---

1   The 1880 volume actually gives two dates for the poem: 1870 and 1874. The poem was first published in its entirety in 1874, in instalments in the *National Reformer*, the newspaper of the National Secular Society. But sections I–VII, X, XI, XVIII and XX were written in 1870, the rest in 1873. See William Schaefer, 'The Two Cities of Dreadful Night', *PMLA* 77 (1962): 609–616. 'B.V.' was Thomson's *nom de plume* for the 1874 edition and other poems: it stands for Bysshe Vanolis, borrowing Percy Shelley's middle name and making an anagram of Novalis, the early German Romantic poet (an atheist and a mystic, respectively).

2   'Through me you pass into the city of woe': the first line of the inscription over the entrance to Hell in Canto III of Dante's *Inferno* (1314). The inscription ends with the famous line, 'Lasciate ogne speranza, voi ch'intrate': 'All hope abandon ye who enter here' (trans. H.F. Cary, 1805–1814), quoted below at I.78.

3   From a more recent Italian poet, Giacomo Leopardi (1798–1837), 'Canto notturno di un pastore errante dell'Asia' ('Nocturnal chant of a wandering shepherd of Asia'), XXIII from the *Canti* of 1831, lines 93–98: 'Then out of such endless working, so many movements of everything in heaven and earth, revolving incessantly, only to return to the point from which they were moved: from all this I can imagine neither purpose not gane.'

4   From 'Dialogo di Federico Ruysch e delle sue mummie' ('Dialogue of Ruysch [a famous early anatomist] and his mummies') in Leopardi's *Operette Morali* (1835). The mummies are speaking here, in lines 1–6 and 31–32: 'Eternal alone in the world, receiver of all created things, in you, death, our naked being comes to rest; joyful no, but safe from the age-old pain'; 'for happiness is denied by fate to the living and denied to the dead.'

PROEM

Lo, thus, as prostrate, "In the dust I write
  My heart's deep languor and my soul's sad tears."[5]
Yet why evoke the spectres of black night
  To blot the sunshine of exultant years?
Why disinter dead faith from mouldering hidden?   5
Why break the seals of mute despair unbidden,
  And wail life's discords into careless ears?

Because a cold rage seizes one at whiles
  To show the bitter old and wrinkled truth
Stripped naked of all vesture that beguiles,   10
  False dreams, false hopes, false masks and modes of youth;
Because it gives some sense of power and passion
In helpless impotence to try to fashion
  Our woe in living words howe'er uncouth.

Surely I write not for the hopeful young,   15
  Or those who deem their happiness of worth,
Or such as pasture and grow fat among
  The shows of life and feel nor doubt nor dearth,
Or pious spirits with a God above them
To sanctify and glorify and love them,   20
  Or sages who foresee a heaven on earth.

For none of these I write, and none of these
  Could read the writing if they deigned to try:
So may they flourish, in their due degrees,
  On our sweet earth and in their unplaced sky.   25
If any cares for the weak words here written,
It must be some one desolate, Fate-smitten,
  Whose faith and hope are dead, and who would die.

Yes, here and there some weary wanderer
  In that same city of tremendous night,   30
Will understand the speech, and feel a stir
  Of fellowship in all-disastrous fight;
"I suffer mute and lonely, yet another
Uplifts his voice to let me know a brother
  Travels the same wild paths though out of sight."   35

---

5 From William Shakespeare, *Titus Andronicus* (c.1590), III.i.12–13: 'For these, these, tribunes, in
   the dust I write / My heart's deep languor and my soul's sad tears.' 'These' are Titus's sons,
   sentenced to death by the Roman Republic, for whose lives he now pleads as he did not for
   the previous 22 sons who died honourably in Rome's wars.

O sad Fraternity, do I unfold
    Your dolorous mysteries shrouded from of yore?
Nay, be assured; no secret can be told
    To any who divined it not before:
None uninitiate by many a presage   40
Will comprehend the language of the message,
    Although proclaimed aloud for evermore.

I.

The City is of Night; perchance of Death,
    But certainly of Night; for never there
Can come the lucid morning's fragrant breath
    After the dewy dawning's cold grey air;
The moon and stars may shine with scorn or pity;   5
The sun has never visited that city,
    For it dissolveth in the daylight fair.

Dissolveth like a dream of night away;
    Though present in distempered gloom of thought
And deadly weariness of heart all day.   10
    But when a dream night after night is brought
Throughout a week, and such weeks few or many
Recur each year for several years, can any
    Discern that dream from real life in aught?

For life is but a dream whose shapes return,   15
    Some frequently, some seldom, some by night
And some by day, some night and day: we learn,
    The while all change and many vanish quite,
In their recurrence with recurrent changes
A certain seeming order; where this ranges   20
    We count things real; such is memory's might.[6]

A river girds the city west and south,
    The main north channel of a broad lagoon,
Regurging with the salt tides from the mouth;
    Waste marshes shine and glister to the moon   25

---

6 This is very reminiscent of eighteenth-century philosopher David Hume's argument that much of our knowledge of the world is based, not on our *experience* of underlying laws of necessity, but on the mere *expectation* of uniformity from seeing certain relations in the world constantly repeated (and thus on our memory of what has happened before): see *Treatise of Human Nature* book I, esp. chapter 3, xiv.

For leagues, then moorland black, then stony ridges;
Great piers and causeways, many noble bridges,
    Connect the town and islet suburbs strewn.

Upon an easy slope it lies at large,
    And scarcely overlaps the long curved crest   30
Which swells out two leagues from the river marge.
    A trackless wilderness rolls north and west,
Savannahs, savage woods, enormous mountains,
Bleak uplands, black ravines with torrent fountains;
    And eastward rolls the shipless sea's unrest.   35

The city is not ruinous, although
    Great ruins of an unremembered past,
With others of a few short years ago
    More sad, are found within its precincts vast.
The street-lamps always burn; but scarce a casement   40
In house or palace front from roof to basement
    Doth glow or gleam athwart the mirk air cast.

The street-lamps burn amidst the baleful glooms,
    Amidst the soundless solitudes immense
Of rangèd mansions dark and still as tombs.   45
    The silence which benumbs or strains the sense
Fulfils with awe the soul's despair unweeping:
Myriads of habitants are ever sleeping,
    Or dead, or fled from nameless pestilence!

Yet as in some necropolis you find   50
    Perchance one mourner to a thousand dead,
So there; worn faces that look deaf and blind
    Like tragic masks of stone. With weary tread,
Each wrapt in his own doom, they wander, wander,
Or sit foredone and desolately ponder[7]   55
    Through sleepless hours with heavy drooping head.

Mature men chiefly, few in age or youth,
    A woman rarely, now and then a child:
A child! If here the heart turns sick with ruth
    To see a little one from birth defiled,   60
Or lame or blind, as preordained to languish
Through youthless life, think how it bleeds with anguish
    To meet one erring in that homeless wild.

---

7 Foredone: fordone, exhausted, worn out.

They often murmur to themselves, they speak
 To one another seldom, for their woe   65
Broods maddening inwardly and scorns to wreak
 Itself abroad; and if at whiles it grow
To frenzy which must rave, none heeds the clamour,
Unless there waits some victim of like glamour,
 To rave in turn, who lends attentive show.   70

The City is of Night, but not of Sleep;
 There sweet sleep is not for the weary brain;
The pitiless hours like years and ages creep,
 A night seems termless hell. This dreadful strain
Of thought and consciousness which never ceases, 75
Or which some moments' stupor but increases,
 This, worse than woe, makes wretches there insane.

They leave all hope behind who enter there:
 One certitude while sane they cannot leave,
One anodyne for torture and despair;   80
 The certitude of Death, which no reprieve
Can put off long; and which, divinely tender,
But waits the outstretched hand to promptly render
 That draught whose slumber nothing can bereave.[8]

II.

Because he seemed to walk with an intent
 I followed him; who, shadowlike and frail,
Unswervingly though slowly onward went,
 Regardless, wrapt in thought as in a veil:
Thus step for step with lonely sounding feet   5
We travelled many a long dim silent street.

At length he paused: a black mass in the gloom,
 A tower that merged into the heavy sky;
Around, the huddled stones of grave and tomb:
 Some old God's-acre now corruption's sty:[9] 10
He murmured to himself with dull despair,
Here Faith died, poisoned by this charnel air.

---

8 Though the Garden of thy Life be wholly waste, the sweet flowers withered, the fruit-trees
  barren, over its wall hang ever the rich dark clusters of the Vine of Death, within easy reach
  of thy hand, which may pluck of them when it will. [Thomson's note]
9 God's-acre: graveyard.

Then turning to the right went on once more,
　　And travelled weary roads without suspense;
And reached at last a low wall's open door,　　　　　　　15
　　Whose villa gleamed beyond the foliage dense:
He gazed, and muttered with a hard despair,
Here Love died, stabbed by its own worshipped pair.

Then turning to the right resumed his march,
　　And travelled streets and lanes with wondrous strength,　　20
Until on stooping through a narrow arch
　　We stood before a squalid house at length:
He gazed, and whispered with a cold despair,
Here Hope died, starved out in its utmost lair.

When he had spoken thus, before he stirred,　　　　　　25
　　I spoke, perplexed by something in the signs
Of desolation I had seen and heard
　　In this drear pilgrimage to ruined shrines:
When Faith and Love and Hope are dead indeed,[10]
Can Life still live? By what doth it proceed?　　　　　　30

As whom his one intense thought overpowers,
　　He answered coldly, Take a watch, erase
The signs and figures of the circling hours,
　　Detach the hands, remove the dial-face;
The works proceed until run down; although　　　　　35
Bereft of purpose, void of use, still go.

Then turning to the right paced on again,
　　And traversed squares and travelled streets whose glooms
Seemed more and more familiar to my ken;
　　And reached that sullen temple of the tombs;　　　　　40
And paused to murmur with the old despair,
Here Faith died, poisoned by this charnel air.

I ceased to follow, for the knot of doubt
　　Was severed sharply with a cruel knife:
He circled thus for ever tracing out　　　　　　　　45
　　The series of the fraction left of Life;
Perpetual recurrence in the scope
Of but three terms, dead Faith, dead Love, dead Hope.[11]

10　Faith, Hope and Love (translated as 'Charity' in the King James bible) are that which 'abideth'
　　in Paul's first Epistle to the Corinthians, 13.13.
11　Life divided by that persistent three = LXX/333 = .210 [Thomson's note. The LXX seems to
　　represent the allotted 70 years of a human life. Why Faith, Hope and Love should each be

III.

Although lamps burn along the silent streets;
    Even when moonlight silvers empty squares
The dark holds countless lanes and close retreats;
    But when the night its sphereless mantle wears
The open spaces yawn with gloom abysmal,   5
The sombre mansions loom immense and dismal,
    The lanes are black as subterranean lairs.

And soon the eye a strange new vision learns:
    The night remains for it as dark and dense,
Yet clearly in this darkness it discerns   10
    As in the daylight with its natural sense;
Perceives a shade in shadow not obscurely,
Pursues a stir of black in blackness surely,
    Sees spectres also in the gloom intense.

The ear, too, with the silence vast and deep   15
    Becomes familiar though unreconciled;
Hears breathings as of hidden life asleep,
    And muffled throbs as of pent passions wild,
Far murmurs, speech of pity or derision;
But all more dubious than the things of vision,   20
    So that it knows not when it is beguiled.

No time abates the first despair and awe,
    But wonder ceases soon; the weirdest thing
Is felt least strange beneath the lawless law
    Where Death-in-Life is the eternal king;   25
Crushed impotent beneath this reign of terror,
Dazed with such mysteries of woe and error,
    The soul is too outworn for wondering.

IV.

He stood alone within the spacious square
    Declaiming from the central grassy mound,
With head uncovered and with streaming hair,
    As if large multitudes were gathered round:
A stalwart shape, the gestures full of might,   5
The glances burning with unnatural light: —

represented by the number three (if that is what is happening here), and the significance of
the decimal fraction produced by the division of one number by the other, is anyone's guess.]

As I came through the desert thus it was,
As I came through the desert: All was black,
In heaven no single star, on earth no track;
A brooding hush without a stir or note,   10
The air so thick it clotted in my throat;
And thus for hours; then some enormous things
Swooped past with savage cries and clanking wings:
        But I strode on austere;
        No hope could have no fear.   15

As I came through the desert thus it was,
As I came through the desert: Eyes of fire
Glared at me throbbing with a starved desire;
The hoarse and heavy and carnivorous breath
Was hot upon me from deep jaws of death;   20
Sharp claws, swift talons, fleshless fingers cold
Plucked at me from the bushes, tried to hold:
        But I strode on austere;
        No hope could have no fear.

As I came through the desert thus it was,   25
As I came through the desert: Lo you, there,
That hillock burning with a brazen glare;
Those myriad dusky flames with points a-glow
Which writhed and hissed and darted to and fro;
A Sabbath of the Serpents, heaped pell-mell   30
For Devil's roll-call and some *fête* of Hell:
        Yet I strode on austere;
        No hope could have no fear.

As I came through the desert thus it was,
As I came through the desert: Meteors ran   35
And crossed their javelins on the black sky-span;
The zenith opened to a gulf of flame,
The dreadful thunderbolts jarred earth's fixed frame;
The ground all heaved in waves of fire that surged
And weltered round me sole there unsubmerged: 40
        Yet I strode on austere;
        No hope could have no fear.

As I came through the desert thus it was,
As I came through the desert: Air once more,
And I was close upon a wild sea-shore;   45
Enormous cliffs arose on either hand,

The deep tide thundered up a league-broad strand;
White foambelts seethed there, wan spray swept and flew;
The sky broke, moon and stars and clouds and blue:
         And I strode on austere;   50
         No hope could have no fear.

As I came through the desert thus it was,
As I came through the desert: On the left
The sun arose and crowned a broad crag-cleft;
There stopped and burned out black, except a rim,   55
A bleeding eyeless socket, red and dim;
Whereon the moon fell suddenly south-west,
And stood above the right-hand cliffs at rest:
         Still I strode on austere;
         No hope could have no fear.   60

As I came through the desert thus it was,
As I came through the desert: From the right
A shape came slowly with a ruddy light;
A woman with a red lamp in her hand,
Bareheaded and barefooted on that strand;   65
O desolation moving with such grace!
O anguish with such beauty in thy face!
         I fell as on my bier,
         Hope travailed with such fear.

As I came through the desert thus it was,   70
As I came through the desert: I was twain,
Two selves distinct that cannot join again;
One stood apart and knew but could not stir,
And watched the other stark in swoon and her;
And she came on, and never turned aside,   75
Between such sun and moon and roaring tide:
         And as she came more near
         My soul grew mad with fear.

As I came through the desert thus it was,
As I came through the desert: Hell is mild   80
And piteous matched with that accursèd wild;
A large black sign was on her breast that bowed,
A broad black band ran down her snow-white shroud;
That lamp she held was her own burning heart,
Whose blood-drops trickled step by step apart: 85
         The mystery was clear;
         Mad rage had swallowed fear.

As I came through the desert thus it was,
As I came through the desert: By the sea
She knelt and bent above that senseless me;
Those lamp-drops fell upon my white brow there,
She tried to cleanse them with her tears and hair;
She murmured words of pity, love, and woe,
She heeded not the level rushing flow:
        And mad with rage and fear,
        I stood stonebound so near.

As I came through the desert thus it was,
As I came through the desert: When the tide
Swept up to her there kneeling by my side,
She clasped that corpse-like me, and they were borne
Away, and this vile me was left forlorn;
I know the whole sea cannot quench that heart,
Or cleanse that brow, or wash those two apart:
        They love; their doom is drear,
        Yet they nor hope nor fear;
        But I, what do I here?

V.

How he arrives there none can clearly know;
    Athwart the mountains and immense wild tracts,
Or flung a waif upon that vast sea-flow,
    Or down the river's boiling cataracts:
To reach it is as dying fever-stricken;
To leave it, slow faint birth intense pangs quicken;
    And memory swoons in both the tragic acts.

But being there one feels a citizen;
    Escape seems hopeless to the heart forlorn:
Can Death-in-Life be brought to life again?
    And yet release does come; there comes a morn
When he awakes from slumbering so sweetly
That all the world is changed for him completely,
    And he is verily as if new-born.

He scarcely can believe the blissful change,
    He weeps perchance who wept not while accurst;
Never again will he approach the range
    Infected by that evil spell now burst:

Poor wretch! who once hath paced that dolent city[12]
Shall pace it often, doomed beyond all pity,   20
    With horror ever deepening from the first.

Though he possess sweet babes and loving wife,
    A home of peace by loyal friendships cheered,
And love them more than death or happy life,
    They shall avail not; he must dree his weird;[13]   25
Renounce all blessings for that imprecation,
Steal forth and haunt that builded desolation,
    Of woe and terrors and thick darkness reared.

VI.

I sat forlornly by the river-side,
    And watched the bridge-lamps glow like golden stars
Above the blackness of the swelling tide,
    Down which they struck rough gold in ruddier bars;
And heard the heave and plashing of the flow   5
Against the wall a dozen feet below.

Large elm-trees stood along that river-walk;
    And under one, a few steps from my seat,
I heard strange voices join in stranger talk,
    Although I had not heard approaching feet: 10
These bodiless voices in my waking dream
Flowed dark words blending with the sombre stream: —

And you have after all come back; come back.
I was about to follow on your track.
And you have failed: our spark of hope is black.   15

That I have failed is proved by my return:
The spark is quenched, nor ever more will burn.
But listen; and the story you shall learn.

I reached the portal common spirits fear,
And read the words above it, dark yet clear,   20
"Leave hope behind, all ye who enter here:"

---

12 Dolent: sorrowful, sad. Archaic as an English word, but Thomson is echoing Dante's Italian
    'città dolente' quoted in the first epigraph (in his recent, 1868, translation of the *Inferno*, Henry
    Wadsworth Longfellow had revived the word to translate just this line: 'Through me the way
    is to the city dolent').
13 Dree his weird (Sc.): endure his fate.

And would have passed in, gratified to gain
That positive eternity of pain,
Instead of this insufferable inane.

A demon warder clutched me, Not so fast;   25
First leave your hopes behind! — But years have passed
Since I left all behind me, to the last:

You cannot count for hope, with all your wit,
This bleak despair that drives me to the Pit:
How could I seek to enter void of it?   30

He snarled, What thing is this which apes a soul,
And would find entrance to our gulf of dole
Without the payment of the settled toll?

Outside the gate he showed an open chest:
Here pay their entrance fees the souls unblest;   35
Cast in some hope, you enter with the rest.

This is Pandora's box; whose lid shall shut,[14]
And Hell-gate too, when hopes have filled it; but
They are so thin that it will never glut.

I stood a few steps backwards, desolate;   40
And watched the spirits pass me to their fate,
And fling off hope, and enter at the gate.

When one casts off a load he springs upright,
Squares back his shoulders, breathes with all his might,
And briskly paces forward strong and light: 45

But these, as if they took some burden, bowed;
The whole frame sank; however strong and proud
Before, they crept in quite infirm and cowed.

And as they passed me, earnestly from each
A morsel of his hope I did beseech,   50
To pay my entrance; but all mocked my speech.

---

14 In Greek mythology (e.g. in Hesiod's *Works and Days*), Pandora, the first woman, is given
    a jar by Zeus under strict instructions not to open it. Her curiosity drives her to disobey:
    when she lifts the lid all the evils of the world fly out (note the similarity to Eve's eating the
    forbidden fruit in Genesis). But when she closes it again, Hope remains inside. The story
    Thomson tells in this stanza is his own invention.

Not one would cede a tittle of his store,
Though knowing that in instants three or four
He must resign the whole for evermore.

So I returned. Our destiny is fell;   55
For in this Limbo we must ever dwell,[15]
Shut out alike from Heaven and Earth and Hell.

The other sighed back, Yea; but if we grope
With care through all this Limbo's dreary scope,
We yet may pick up some minute lost hope;   60

And, sharing it between us, entrance win,
In spite of fiends so jealous for gross sin:
Let us without delay our search begin.

VII.

Some say that phantoms haunt those shadowy streets,
    And mingle freely there with sparse mankind;
And tell of ancient woes and black defeats,
    And murmur mysteries in the grave enshrined:
But others think them visions of illusion,   5
Or even men gone far in self-confusion;
    No man there being wholly sane in mind.

And yet a man who raves, however mad,
    Who bares his heart and tells of his own fall,
Reserves some inmost secret good or bad: 10
    The phantoms have no reticence at all:
The nudity of flesh will blush though tameless,
The extreme nudity of bone grins shameless,
    The unsexed skeleton mocks shroud and pall.

I have seen phantoms there that were as men   15
    And men that were as phantoms flit and roam;
Marked shapes that were not living to my ken,
    Caught breathings acrid as with Dead Sea foam:[16]

---

15 In the *Inferno* Canto II, Limbo is the area outside Hell set aside for 'virtuous pagans' such as the
    Roman poet Virgil, Dante's guide: not guilty of sins that would earn them punishment in Hell,
    but shut out of the hope of Heaven by unfortunately being born before the coming of Christ.

16 The Dead Sea is supposed to cover the sites of the sinful 'Cities of the Plain', Sodom and
    Gomorrah, and was imagined to be poisoned by the brimstone with which God destroyed
    them in Genesis 19 (though there is no mention there of the Dead Sea)

The City rests for man so weird and awful,
That his intrusion there might seem unlawful,   20
    And phantoms there may have their proper home.

VIII.

While I still lingered on that river-walk,
    And watched the tide as black as our black doom,
I heard another couple join in talk,
    And saw them to the left hand in the gloom
Seated against an elm bole on the ground,   5
Their eyes intent upon the stream profound.

"I never knew another man on earth
    But had some joy and solace in his life,
    Some chance of triumph in the dreadful strife:
My doom has been unmitigated dearth."   10

"We gaze upon the river, and we note
The various vessels large and small that float,
Ignoring every wrecked and sunken boat."

"And yet I asked no splendid dower, no spoil
    Of sway or fame or rank or even wealth;   15
    But homely love with common food and health,
And nightly sleep to balance daily toil."

"This all-too humble soul would arrogate
Unto itself some signalising hate
From the supreme indifference of Fate!"   20

"Who is most wretched in this dolorous place?
    I think myself; yet I would rather be
    My miserable self than He, than He
Who formed such creatures to His own disgrace.

"The vilest thing must be less vile than Thou   25
    From whom it had its being, God and Lord!
    Creator of all woe and sin! abhorred,
Malignant and implacable! I vow

"That not for all Thy power furled and unfurled,
    For all the temples to Thy glory built,   30
    Would I assume the ignominious guilt
Of having made such men in such a world."

"As if a Being, God or Fiend, could reign,
At once so wicked, foolish, and insane,
As to produce men when He might refrain!   35

"The world rolls round for ever like a mill;
It grinds out death and life and good and ill;
It has no purpose, heart or mind or will.

"While air of Space and Time's full river flow
The mill must blindly whirl unresting so: 40
It may be wearing out, but who can know?

"Man might know one thing were his sight less dim;
That it whirls not to suit his petty whim,
That it is quite indifferent to him.

"Nay, does it treat him harshly as he saith?   45
It grinds him some slow years of bitter breath,
Then grinds him back into eternal death."

                              IX.

It is full strange to him who hears and feels,
      When wandering there in some deserted street,
The booming and the jar of ponderous wheels,
      The trampling clash of heavy ironshod feet:
Who in this Venice of the Black Sea rideth?   5
Who in this city of the stars abideth
      To buy or sell as those in daylight sweet?

The rolling thunder seems to fill the sky
      As it comes on; the horses snort and strain,
The harness jingles, as it passes by;   10
      The hugeness of an overburthened wain:
A man sits nodding on the shaft or trudges
Three parts asleep beside his fellow-drudges:
      And so it rolls into the night again.

What merchandise? whence, whither, and for whom?   15
      Perchance it is a Fate-appointed hearse,
Bearing away to some mysterious tomb
      Or Limbo of the scornful universe
The joy, the peace, the life-hope, the abortions

Of all things good which should have been our portions,　　　20
　　But have been strangled by that City's curse.

X.

The mansion stood apart in its own ground;
　　In front thereof a fragrant garden-lawn,
High trees about it, and the whole walled round:
　　The massy iron gates were both withdrawn;
And every window of its front shed light,　　　5
Portentous in that City of the Night.

But though thus lighted it was deadly still
　　As all the countless bulks of solid gloom:
Perchance a congregation to fulfil
　　Solemnities of silence in this doom,　　　10
Mysterious rites of dolour and despair
Permitting not a breath of chant or prayer?

Broad steps ascended to a terrace broad
　　Whereon lay still light from the open door;
The hall was noble, and its aspect awed,　　　15
　　Hung round with heavy black from dome to floor;
And ample stairways rose to left and right
Whose balustrades were also draped with night.

I paced from room to room, from hall to hall,
　　Nor any life throughout the maze discerned;　　　20
But each was hung with its funereal pall,
　　And held a shrine, around which tapers burned,
With picture or with statue or with bust,
All copied from the same fair form of dust:

A woman very young and very fair;　　　25
　　Beloved by bounteous life and joy and youth,
And loving these sweet lovers, so that care
　　And age and death seemed not for her in sooth:
Alike as stars, all beautiful and bright,
These shapes lit up that mausoléan night.　　　30

At length I heard a murmur as of lips,
　　And reached an open oratory hung
With heaviest blackness of the whole eclipse;
　　Beneath the dome a fuming censer swung;

16

And one lay there upon a low white bed,   35
With tapers burning at the foot and head:

The Lady of the images: supine,
    Deathstill, lifesweet, with folded palms she lay:
And kneeling there as at a sacred shrine
    A young man wan and worn who seemed to pray: 40
A crucifix of dim and ghostly white
Surmounted the large altar left in night:—

The chambers of the mansion of my heart,
In every one whereof thine image dwells,
Are black with grief eternal for thy sake.   45

The inmost oratory of my soul,
Wherein thou ever dwellest quick or dead,
Is black with grief eternal for thy sake.

I kneel beside thee and I clasp the cross,
With eyes for ever fixed upon that face,   50
So beautiful and dreadful in its calm.

I kneel here patient as thou liest there;
As patient as a statue carved in stone,
Of adoration and eternal grief.

While thou dost not awake I cannot move;   55
And something tells me thou wilt never wake,
And I alive feel turning into stone.

Most beautiful were Death to end my grief,
Most hateful to destroy the sight of thee,
Dear vision better than all death or life.   60

But I renounce all choice of life or death,
For either shall be ever at thy side,
And thus in bliss or woe be ever well.—

He murmured thus and thus in monotone,
    Intent upon that uncorrupted face,   65
Entranced except his moving lips alone:
    I glided with hushed footsteps from the place.
This was the festival that filled with light
That palace in the City of the Night.

XI.

What men are they who haunt these fatal glooms,
    And fill their living mouths with dust of death,
And make their habitations in the tombs,
    And breathe eternal sighs with mortal breath,
And pierce life's pleasant veil of various error   5
To reach that void of darkness and old terror
    Wherein expire the lamps of hope and faith?

They have much wisdom yet they are not wise,
    They have much goodness yet they do not well,
(The fools we know have their own Paradise,   10
    The wicked also have their proper Hell);
They have much strength but still their doom is stronger,
Much patience but their time endureth longer,
    Much valour but life mocks it with some spell.

They are most rational and yet insane: 15
    An outward madness not to be controlled;
A perfect reason in the central brain,
    Which has no power, but sitteth wan and cold,
And sees the madness, and foresees as plainly
The ruin in its path, and trieth vainly   20
    To cheat itself refusing to behold.

And some are great in rank and wealth and power,
    And some renowned for genius and for worth;
And some are poor and mean, who brood and cower
    And shrink from notice, and accept all dearth   25
Of body, heart and soul, and leave to others
All boons of life: yet these and those are brothers,
    The saddest and the weariest men on earth.

XII.

Our isolated units could be brought
    To act together for some common end?
For one by one, each silent with his thought,
    I marked a long loose line approach and wend
Athwart the great cathedral's cloistered square,   5
And slowly vanish from the moonlit air.

Then I would follow in among the last:
    And in the porch a shrouded figure stood,
Who challenged each one pausing ere he passed,
    With deep eyes burning through a blank white hood: 10
Whence come you in the world of life and light
To this our City of Tremendous Night? —

From pleading in a senate of rich lords
For some scant justice to our countless hordes
Who toil half-starved with scarce a human right: 15
I wake from daydreams to this real night.

From wandering through many a solemn scene
Of opium visions, with a heart serene
And intellect miraculously bright:
I wake from daydreams to this real night.   20

From making hundreds laugh and roar with glee
By my transcendent feats of mimicry,
And humour wanton as an elfish sprite:
I wake from daydreams to this real night.

From prayer and fasting in a lonely cell,   25
Which brought an ecstasy ineffable
Of love and adoration and delight:
I wake from daydreams to this real night.

From ruling on a splendid kingly throne
A nation which beneath my rule has grown   30
Year after year in wealth and arts and might:
I wake from daydreams to this real night.

From preaching to an audience fired with faith
The Lamb who died to save our souls from death,
Whose blood hath washed our scarlet sins wool-white:[17]   35
I wake from daydreams to this real night.

From drinking fiery poison in a den
Crowded with tawdry girls and squalid men,
Who hoarsely laugh and curse and brawl and fight:
I wake from daydreams to this real night.   40

17 The image of Christ as the Lamb of God is already there in the Gospel of John (1.29, 36), but
    is particularly associated with the apocalyptic pageant of Revelations. The reference here is
    specifically to 7.14, where the saved are those 'which came out of great tribulation, and have
    washed their robes, and made them white in the blood of the Lamb'.

From picturing with all beauty and all grace
First Eden and the parents of our race,
A luminous rapture unto all men's sight:
I wake from daydreams to this real night.

From writing a great work with patient plan   45
To justify the ways of God to man,
And show how ill must fade and perish quite:[18]
I wake from daydreams to this real night.

From desperate fighting with a little band
Against the powerful tyrants of our land,   50
To free our brethren in their own despite:
I wake from daydreams to this real night.

Thus, challenged by that warder sad and stern,
    Each one responded with his countersign,
Then entered the cathedral; and in turn   55
    I entered also, having given mine;
But lingered near until I heard no more,
And marked the closing of the massive door.

XIII.

Of all things human which are strange and wild
    This is perchance the wildest and most strange,
And showeth man most utterly beguiled,
    To those who haunt that sunless City's range;
That he bemoans himself for aye, repeating   5
How Time is deadly swift, how life is fleeting,
    How naught is constant on the earth but change.

The hours are heavy on him and the days;
    The burden of the months he scarce can bear;
And often in his secret soul he prays   10
    To sleep through barren periods unaware,
Arousing at some longed-for date of pleasure;
Which having passed and yielded him small treasure,
    He would outsleep another term of care.

18 At the beginning of his great poem *Paradise Lost* (1667), Milton calls on the Holy Spirit to
    inspire him, 'That to the highth of this great Argument / I may assert Eternal Providence /
    And justifie the wayes of God to men' (I.24–26). In its final book, the Archangel Michael gives
    the fallen Adam a vision of the future coming of Christ that will redeem humankind from sin.

Yet in his marvellous fancy he must make   15
      Quick wings for Time, and see it fly from us;
This Time which crawleth like a monstrous snake,
      Wounded and slow and very venomous;
Which creeps blindwormlike round the earth and ocean,
Distilling poison at each painful motion,   20
      And seems condemned to circle ever thus.

And since he cannot spend and use aright
      The little time here given him in trust,
But wasteth it in weary undelight
      Of foolish toil and trouble, strife and lust,   25
He naturally claimeth to inherit
The everlasting Future, that his merit
      May have full scope; as surely is most just.

O length of the intolerable hours,
      O nights that are as æons of slow pain,   30
O Time, too ample for our vital powers,
      O Life, whose woeful vanities remain
Immutable for all of all our legions
Through all the centuries and in all the regions,
      Not of your speed and variance *we* complain.   35

We do not ask a longer term of strife,
      Weakness and weariness and nameless woes;
We do not claim renewed and endless life
      When this which is our torment here shall close,
An everlasting conscious inanition!   40
We yearn for speedy death in full fruition,
      Dateless oblivion and divine repose.

                         XIV.

Large glooms were gathered in the mighty fane,
      With tinted moongleams slanting here and there;
And all was hush: no swelling organ-strain,
      No chant, no voice or murmuring of prayer;
No priests came forth, no tinkling censers fumed,   5
And the high altar space was unillumed.

Around the pillars and against the walls
      Leaned men and shadows; others seemed to brood
Bent or recumbent in secluded stalls.

Perchance they were not a great multitude   10
Save in that city of so lonely streets
Where one may count up every face he meets.

All patiently awaited the event
    Without a stir or sound, as if no less
Self-occupied, doomstricken, while attent.   15
    And then we heard a voice of solemn stress
From the dark pulpit, and our gaze there met
Two eyes which burned as never eyes burned yet:

Two steadfast and intolerable eyes
    Burning beneath a broad and rugged brow;   20
The head behind it of enormous size.
    And as black fir-groves in a large wind bow,
Our rooted congregation, gloom-arrayed,
By that great sad voice deep and full were swayed: —

O melancholy Brothers, dark, dark, dark!   25
O battling in black floods without an ark!
    O spectral wanderers of unholy Night!
My soul hath bled for you these sunless years,
With bitter blood-drops running down like tears:
    Oh, dark, dark, dark, withdrawn from joy and light!   30

My heart is sick with anguish for your bale;[19]
Your woe hath been my anguish; yea, I quail
    And perish in your perishing unblest.
And I have searched the highths and depths, the scope[20]
Of all our universe, with desperate hope   35
    To find some solace for your wild unrest.

And now at last authentic word I bring,
Witnessed by every dead and living thing;
    Good tidings of great joy for you, for all:
There is no God; no Fiend with names divine   40
Made us and tortures us; if we must pine,
    It is to satiate no Being's gall.

It was the dark delusion of a dream,
That living Person conscious and supreme,
    Whom we must curse for cursing us with life;   45
Whom we must curse because the life He gave

---

19 Bale: evil. *OED*'s several senses include 'mental suffering: misery, sorrow, grief'.
20 Highth is just an archaic spelling of height, as used by Milton in the lines quoted in note 18.

Could not be buried in the quiet grave,
   Could not be killed by poison or by knife.

This little life is all we must endure,
The grave's most holy peace is ever sure,   50
   We fall asleep and never wake again;
Nothing is of us but the mouldering flesh,
Whose elements dissolve and merge afresh
   In earth, air, water, plants, and other men.

We finish thus; and all our wretched race   55
Shall finish with its cycle, and give place
   To other beings, with their own time-doom:
Infinite æons ere our kind began;
Infinite æons after the last man
   Has joined the mammoth in earth's tomb and womb.   60

We bow down to the universal laws,
Which never had for man a special clause
   Of cruelty or kindness, love or hate:
If toads and vultures are obscene to sight,
If tigers burn with beauty and with might,[21]   65
   Is it by favour or by wrath of Fate?

All substance lives and struggles evermore
Through countless shapes continually at war,
   By countless interactions interknit:
If one is born a certain day on earth,   70
All times and forces tended to that birth,
   Not all the world could change or hinder it.

I find no hint throughout the Universe
Of good or ill, of blessing or of curse;
   I find alone Necessity Supreme;   75
With infinite Mystery, abysmal, dark,
Unlighted ever by the faintest spark
   For us the flitting shadows of a dream.

---

21   Alluding to William Blake's famous poem 'The Tyger' from *Songs of Experience* (1794), which
begins, 'Tyger, tyger, burning bright, / In the forests of the night: / What immortal hand
or eye / Could frame thy fearful symmetry?' Since the publication of Charles Darwin's *On
the Origin of Species* in 1859, a new answer was available to Blake's question: no immortal
hand at all, but the operation of the 'universal law' of Natural Selection. This is one of the
sections written in 1873 and thus after Darwin's second book, *The Ascent of Man* (1871) which
made explicit the law's implication that humans, too, have come into existence through this
process, and thus have no special place in the universe of the kind afforded them by revealed
religion (as Thomson observes in this stanza).

O Brothers of sad lives! they are so brief;
A few short years must bring us all relief:
    Can we not bear these years of labouring breath?
But if you would not this poor life fulfil,
Lo, you are free to end it when you will,
    Without the fear of waking after death. —

The organ-like vibrations of his voice
    Thrilled through the vaulted aisles and died away;
The yearning of the tones which bade rejoice
    Was sad and tender as a requiem lay:
Our shadowy congregation rested still
As brooding on that "End it when you will."

XV.

Wherever men are gathered, all the air
    Is charged with human feeling, human thought;
Each shout and cry and laugh, each curse and prayer,
    Are into its vibrations surely wrought;
Unspoken passion, wordless meditation,
Are breathed into it with our respiration;
    It is with our life fraught and overfraught.

So that no man there breathes earth's simple breath,
    As if alone on mountains or wide seas;
But nourishes warm life or hastens death
    With joys and sorrows, health and foul disease,
Wisdom and folly, good and evil labours,
Incessant of his multitudinous neighbours;
    He in his turn affecting all of these.

That City's atmosphere is dark and dense,
    Although not many exiles wander there,
With many a potent evil influence,
    Each adding poison to the poisoned air;
Infections of unutterable sadness,
Infections of incalculable madness,
    Infections of incurable despair.

XVI.

Our shadowy congregation rested still,
  As musing on that message we had heard
And brooding on that "End it when you will;"
  Perchance awaiting yet some other word;
When keen as lightning through a muffled sky   5
Sprang forth a shrill and lamentable cry:—

The man speaks sooth, alas! the man speaks sooth:
  We have no personal life beyond the grave;
There is no God; Fate knows nor wrath nor ruth:
  Can I find here the comfort which I crave?   10

In all eternity I had one chance,
  One few years' term of gracious human life:
The splendours of the intellect's advance,
  The sweetness of the home with babes and wife;

The social pleasures with their genial wit;   15
  The fascination of the worlds of art,
The glories of the worlds of nature, lit
  By large imagination's glowing heart;

The rapture of mere being, full of health;
  The careless childhood and the ardent youth,   20
The strenuous manhood winning various wealth,
  The reverend age serene with life's long truth:

All the sublime prerogatives of Man;
  The storied memories of the times of old,
The patient tracking of the world's great plan   25
  Through sequences and changes myriadfold.

This chance was never offered me before;
  For me the infinite Past is blank and dumb:
This chance recurreth never, nevermore;
  Blank, blank for me the infinite To-come.   30

And this sole chance was frustrate from my birth,
  A mockery, a delusion; and my breath
Of noble human life upon this earth
  So racks me that I sigh for senseless death.

My wine of life is poison mixed with gall,   35
    My noonday passes in a nightmare dream,
I worse than lose the years which are my all:
    What can console me for the loss supreme?

Speak not of comfort where no comfort is,
    Speak not at all: can words make foul things fair?   40
Our life's a cheat, our death a black abyss:
    Hush and be mute envisaging despair. —

This vehement voice came from the northern aisle
    Rapid and shrill to its abrupt harsh close;
And none gave answer for a certain while,   45
    For words must shrink from these most wordless woes;
At last the pulpit speaker simply said,
With humid eyes and thoughtful drooping head: —

My Brother, my poor Brothers, it is thus;
This life itself holds nothing good for us,   50
    But it ends soon and nevermore can be;
And we knew nothing of it ere our birth,
And shall know nothing when consigned to earth:
    I ponder these thoughts and they comfort me.

XVII.

How the moon triumphs through the endless nights!
    How the stars throb and glitter as they wheel
Their thick processions of supernal lights
    Around the blue vault obdurate as steel!
And men regard with passionate awe and yearning   5
The mighty marching and the golden burning,
    And think the heavens respond to what they feel.

Boats gliding like dark shadows of a dream,
    Are glorified from vision as they pass
The quivering moonbridge on the deep black stream;   10
    Cold windows kindle their dead glooms of glass
To restless crystals; cornice, dome, and column
Emerge from chaos in the splendour solemn;
    Like faëry lakes gleam lawns of dewy grass.

With such a living light these dead eyes shine,   15
    These eyes of sightless heaven, that as we gaze
We read a pity, tremulous, divine,
    Or cold majestic scorn in their pure rays:
Fond man! they are not haughty, are not tender;
There is no heart or mind in all their splendour,   20
    They thread mere puppets all their marvellous maze.

If we could near them with the flight unflown,
    We should but find them worlds as sad as this,
Or suns all self-consuming like our own
    Enringed by planet worlds as much amiss: 25
They wax and wane through fusion and confusion;
The spheres eternal are a grand illusion,
    The empyréan is a void abyss.[22]

XVIII.

I wandered in a suburb of the north,
    And reached a spot whence three close lanes led down,
Beneath thick trees and hedgerows winding forth
    Like deep brook channels, deep and dark and lown: [23]
The air above was wan with misty light,   5
The dull grey south showed one vague blur of white.

I took the left-hand lane and slowly trod
    Its earthen footpath, brushing as I went
The humid leafage; and my feet were shod
    With heavy languor, and my frame downbent,   10
With infinite sleepless weariness outworn,
So many nights I thus had paced forlorn.

After a hundred steps I grew aware
    Of something crawling in the lane below;
It seemed a wounded creature prostrate there   15
    That sobbed with pangs in making progress slow,
The hind limbs stretched to push, the fore limbs then
To drag; for it would die in its own den.

But coming level with it I discerned
    That it had been a man; for at my tread   20

---

22 In the old, pre-Galilean cosmology, the empyrean was the outmost of the concentric spheres
    around the earth, composed of fire and imagined as the home of the angels.
23 Lown (Sc.): *SND* gives several relevant senses, but 'peaceful, tranquil, undisturbed, placid'
    probably fits best

It stopped in its sore travail and half-turned,
    Leaning upon its right, and raised its head,
And with the left hand twitched back as in ire
Long grey unreverend locks befouled with mire.

A haggard filthy face with bloodshot eyes,   25
    An infamy for manhood to behold.
He gasped all trembling, What, you want my prize?
    You leave, to rob me, wine and lust and gold
And all that men go mad upon, since you
Have traced my sacred secret of the clue?   30

You think that I am weak and must submit;
    Yet I but scratch you with this poisoned blade,
And you are dead as if I clove with it
    That false fierce greedy heart. Betrayed! betrayed!
I fling this phial if you seek to pass,   35
And you are forthwith shrivelled up like grass.

And then with sudden change, Take thought! take thought!
    Have pity on me! it is mine alone.
If you could find, it would avail you naught;
    Seek elsewhere on the pathway of your own: 40
For who of mortal or immortal race
The lifetrack of another can retrace?

Did you but know my agony and toil!
    Two lanes diverge up yonder from this lane;
My thin blood marks the long length of their soil;   45
    Such clue I left, who sought my clue in vain:
My hands and knees are worn both flesh and bone;
I cannot move but with continual moan.

But I am in the very way at last
    To find the long-lost broken golden thread   50
Which reunites my present with my past,
    If you but go your own way. And I said,
I will retire as soon as you have told
Whereunto leadeth this lost thread of gold.

And so you know it not! he hissed with scorn;   55
    I feared you, imbecile! It leads me back
From this accursed night without a morn,
    And through the deserts which have else no track,
And through vast wastes of horror-haunted time,
To Eden innocence in Eden's clime: 60

And I become a nursling soft and pure,
　　An infant cradled on its mother's knee,
Without a past, love-cherished and secure;
　　Which if it saw this loathsome present Me,
Would plunge its face into the pillowing breast　　65
And scream abhorrence hard to lull to rest.

He turned to grope; and I retiring brushed
　　Thin shreds of gossamer from off my face,
And mused, His life would grow, the germ uncrushed;
　　He should to antenatal night retrace,　　70
And hide his elements in that large womb
Beyond the reach of man-evolving Doom.

And even thus, what weary way were planned,
　　To seek oblivion through the far-off gate
Of birth, when that of death is close at hand!　　75
　　For this is law, if law there be in Fate:
What never has been, yet may have its when;
The thing which has been, never is again.

XIX.

The mighty river flowing dark and deep,
　　With ebb and flood from the remote sea-tides
Vague-sounding through the City's sleepless sleep,
　　Is named the River of the Suicides;
For night by night some lorn wretch overweary,　　5
And shuddering from the future yet more dreary,
　　Within its cold secure oblivion hides.

One plunges from a bridge's parapet,
　　As by some blind and sudden frenzy hurled;
Another wades in slow with purpose set　　10
　　Until the waters are above him furled;
Another in a boat with dreamlike motion
Glides drifting down into the desert ocean,
　　To starve or sink from out the desert world.

They perish from their suffering surely thus,　　15
　　For none beholding them attempts to save,
The while each thinks how soon, solicitous,
　　He may seek refuge in the self-same wave;
Some hour when tired of ever-vain endurance

Impatience will forerun the sweet assurance   20
    Of perfect peace eventual in the grave.
When this poor tragic-farce has palled us long,
    Why actors and spectators do we stay? —
To fill our so-short *rôles* out right or wrong;
    To see what shifts are yet in the dull play   25
For our illusion; to refrain from grieving
Dear foolish friends by our untimely leaving:
    But those asleep at home, how blest are they!

Yet it is but for one night after all:
    What matters one brief night of dreary pain?   30
When after it the weary eyelids fall
    Upon the weary eyes and wasted brain;
And all sad scenes and thoughts and feelings vanish
In that sweet sleep no power can ever banish,
    That one best sleep which never wakes again.   35

                        XX.

I sat me weary on a pillar's base,
    And leaned against the shaft; for broad moonlight
O'erflowed the peacefulness of cloistered space,
    A shore of shadow slanting from the right:
The great cathedral's western front stood there,   5
A wave-worn rock in that calm sea of air.

Before it, opposite my place of rest,
    Two figures faced each other, large, austere;
A couchant sphinx in shadow to the breast,
    An angel standing in the moonlight clear;   10
So mighty by magnificence of form,
They were not dwarfed beneath that mass enorm.

Upon the cross-hilt of a naked sword
    The angel's hands, as prompt to smite, were held;
His vigilant, intense regard was poured   15
    Upon the creature placidly unquelled,
Whose front was set at level gaze which took
No heed of aught, a solemn trance-like look.

And as I pondered these opposèd shapes
    My eyelids sank in stupor, that dull swoon   20

Which drugs and with a leaden mantle drapes
    The outworn to worse weariness. But soon
A sharp and clashing noise the stillness broke,
And from the evil lethargy I woke.

The angel's wings had fallen, stone on stone,   25
    And lay there shattered; hence the sudden sound:
A warrior leaning on his sword alone
    Now watched the sphinx with that regard profound;
The sphinx unchanged looked forthright, as aware
Of nothing in the vast abyss of air.   30

Again I sank in that repose unsweet,
    Again a clashing noise my slumber rent;
The warrior's sword lay broken at his feet:
    An unarmed man with raised hands impotent
Now stood before the sphinx, which ever kept   35
Such mien as if with open eyes it slept.

My eyelids sank in spite of wonder grown;
    A louder crash upstartled me in dread:
The man had fallen forward, stone on stone,
    And lay there shattered, with his trunkless head 40
Between the monster's large quiescent paws,
Beneath its grand front changeless as life's laws.

The moon had circled westward full and bright,
    And made the temple-front a mystic dream,
And bathed the whole enclosure with its light,   45
    The sworded angel's wrecks, the sphinx supreme:
I pondered long that cold majestic face
Whose vision seemed of infinite void space.

XXI.

Anear the centre of that northern crest
    Stands out a level upland bleak and bare,
From which the city east and south and west
    Sinks gently in long waves; and thronèd there
An Image sits, stupendous, superhuman,   5
The bronze colossus of a wingèd Woman,
    Upon a graded granite base foursquare.

Low-seated she leans forward massively,
    With cheek on clenched left hand, the forearm's might

Erect, its elbow on her rounded knee;   10
    Across a clasped book in her lap the right
Upholds a pair of compasses; she gazes
With full set eyes, but wandering in thick mazes
    Of sombre thought beholds no outward sight.

Words cannot picture her; but all men know   15
    That solemn sketch the pure sad artist wrought
Three centuries and threescore years ago,
    With phantasies of his peculiar thought:[24]
The instruments of carpentry and science
Scattered about her feet, in strange alliance   20
    With the keen wolf-hound sleeping undistraught;

Scales, hour-glass, bell, and magic-square above;
    The grave and solid infant perched beside,
With open winglets that might bear a dove,
    Intent upon its tablets, heavy-eyed;   25
Her folded wings as of a mighty eagle,
But all too impotent to lift the regal
    Robustness of her earth-born strength and pride;

And with those wings, and that light wreath which seems
    To mock her grand head and the knotted frown   30
Of forehead charged with baleful thoughts and dreams,
    The household bunch of keys, the housewife's gown
Voluminous, indented, and yet rigid
As if a shell of burnished metal frigid,
    The feet thick-shod to tread all weakness down;   35

The comet hanging o'er the waste dark seas,
    The massy rainbow curved in front of it
Beyond the village with the masts and trees;
    The snaky imp, dog-headed, from the Pit,
Bearing upon its batlike leathern pinions   40
Her name unfolded in the sun's dominions,
    The "MELENCOLIA" that transcends all wit.

Thus has the artist copied her, and thus
    Surrounded to expound her form sublime,
Her fate heroic and calamitous;   45
    Fronting the dreadful mysteries of Time,
Unvanquished in defeat and desolation,

---

24 The 'pure sad artist' is Albrecht Dürer (1471–1528), and the 'solemn sketch' mentioned is his engraving 'Melencolia I' (1514).

Undaunted in the hopeless conflagration
    Of the day setting on her baffled prime.

Baffled and beaten back she works on still,   50
    Weary and sick of soul she works the more,
Sustained by her indomitable will:
    The hands shall fashion and the brain shall pore
And all her sorrow shall be turned to labour,
Till Death the friend-foe piercing with his sabre   55
    That mighty heart of hearts ends bitter war.

But as if blacker night could dawn on night,
    With tenfold gloom on moonless night unstarred,
A sense more tragic than defeat and blight,
    More desperate than strife with hope debarred,   60
More fatal than the adamantine Never
Encompassing her passionate endeavour,
    Dawns glooming in her tenebrous regard:[25]

The sense that every struggle brings defeat
    Because Fate holds no prize to crown success;   65
That all the oracles are dumb or cheat
    Because they have no secret to express;
That none can pierce the vast black veil uncertain
Because there is no light beyond the curtain;
    That all is vanity and nothingness.   70

Titanic from her high throne in the north,
    That City's sombre Patroness and Queen,
In bronze sublimity she gazes forth
    Over her Capital of teen and threne,[26]
Over the river with its isles and bridges,   75
The marsh and moorland, to the stern rock-ridges,
    Confronting them with a coëval mien.

The moving moon and stars from east to west
    Circle before her in the sea of air;
Shadows and gleams glide round her solemn rest.   80
    Her subjects often gaze up to her there:
The strong to drink new strength of iron endurance,
The weak new terrors; all, renewed assurance
    And confirmation of the old despair.

---

25 Tenebrous: full of darkness, dark, or 'obscure, gloomy' (*OED*).
26 Teen: here an archaic term for affliction, suffering; threne: a song of lamentation, a dirge.

J.M. Barrie, *A Window in Thrums*

London: Hodder and Stoughton, 1889

CHAPTER I.

THE HOUSE ON THE BRAE.

ON the bump of green round which the brae twists, at the top of the brae, and within cry of T'nowhead Farm, still stands a one-storey house, whose whitewashed walls, streaked with the discoloration that rain leaves, look yellow when the snow comes. In the old days the stiff ascent left Thrums behind, and where is now the making of a suburb was only a poor row of dwellings and a manse, with Hendry's cot to watch the brae. The house stood bare, without a shrub, in a garden whose paling did not go all the way round, the potato pit being only kept out of the road, that here sets off southward, by a broken dyke of stones and earth. On each side of the slate-coloured door was a window of knotted glass. Ropes were flung over the thatch to keep the roof on in wind.

Into this humble abode I would take any one who cares to accompany me. But you must not come in a contemptuous mood, thinking that the poor are but a stage removed from beasts of burden, as some cruel writers of these days say; nor will I have you turn over with your foot the shabby horse-hair chairs that Leeby kept so speckless, and Hendry weaved for years to buy, and Jess so loved to look upon.

I speak of the chairs, but if we go together into the "room" they will not be visible to you. For a long time the house has been to let. Here, on the left of the doorway, as we enter, is the room, without a shred of furniture in it except the boards of two closed-in beds. The flooring is not steady, and here and there holes have been eaten into the planks. You can scarcely stand upright beneath the decaying ceiling. Worn boards and ragged walls, and the rusty ribs fallen from the fireplace, are all that meet your eyes, but I see a round, unsteady, waxcloth-covered table, with four books lying at equal distances on it. There are six prim chairs, two of them not to be sat upon, backed against the walls, and between the window and the fire-place a chest of drawers, with a snowy coverlet. On the drawers stands a board with coloured marbles for the game of solitaire, and I have only to open the drawer with the loose handle to bring out the dambrod.[1] In the carved wood frame over the window hangs Jamie's portrait; in the only other frame a picture of Daniel in the den of lions, sewn by Leeby in wool. Over the chimney-piece with its shells, in which the roar of the sea can be heard, are strung three rows of birds' eggs. Once again we might be expecting company to tea.

The passage is narrow. There is a square hole between the rafters, and a ladder leading up to it. You may climb and look into the attic, as Jess liked to hear me call my tiny garret-room. I am stiffer now than in the days when I lodged with Jess during the summer holiday I am trying to bring back, and there is no need for me to ascend. Do not laugh at the newspapers with which Leeby papered the garret, nor at the yarn Hendry stuffed into the windy holes. He did it to warm the house for Jess. But the paper must have gone to pieces and the yarn rotted decades ago.

I have kept the kitchen for the last, as Jamie did on the dire day of which I shall have to tell. It has a flooring of stone now, where there used only to be hard earth,

---

1   Dambrod: board for draughts (checkers).

and a broken pane in the window is indifferently stuffed with rags. But it is the other window I turn to, with a pain at my heart, and pride and fondness too, the square foot of glass where Jess sat in her chair and looked down the brae.

Ah, that brae! The history of tragic little Thrums is sunk into it like the stones it swallows in the winter. We have all found the brae long and steep in the spring of life. Do you remember how the child you once were sat at the foot of it and wondered if a new world began at the top? It climbs from a shallow burn, and we used to sit on the brig a long time before venturing to climb. As boys we ran up the brae. As men and women, young and in our prime, we almost forgot that it was there. But the autumn of life comes, and the brae grows steeper; then the winter, and once again we are as the child pausing apprehensively on the brig. Yet are we no longer the child; we look now for no new world at the top, only for a little garden and a tiny house, and a handloom in the house.[2] It is only a garden of kail and potatoes, but there may be a line of daisies, white and red, on each side of the narrow footpath, and honeysuckle over the door. Life is not always hard, even after backs grow bent, and we know that all braes lead only to the grave.

This is Jess's window. For more than twenty years she had not been able to go so far as the door, and only once while I knew her was she ben in the room.[3] With her husband, Hendry, or their only daughter, Leeby, to lean upon, and her hand clutching her staff, she took twice a day, when she was strong, the journey between her bed and the window where stood her chair. She did not lie there looking at the sparrows or at Leeby redding up the house,[4] and I hardly ever heard her complain. All the sewing was done by her; she often baked on a table pushed close to the window, and by leaning forward she could stir the porridge. Leeby was seldom off her feet, but I do not know that she did more than Jess, who liked to tell me, when she had a moment to spare, that she had a terrible lot to be thankful for.

To those who dwell in great cities Thrums is only a small place, but what a clatter of life it has for me when I come to it from my school-house in the glen.[5] Had my lot been cast in a town I would no doubt have sought country parts during my September holiday, but the school-house is quiet even when the summer takes brakes full of sportsmen and others past the top of my footpath, and I was always light-hearted when Craigiebuckle's cart bore me into the din of Thrums. I only once stayed during the whole of my holiday at the house on the brae, but I knew its inmates for many years, including Jamie, the son, who was a barber in London. Of their ancestry I never

---

2 This reference to Hendry's trade evokes a way of life long lost by 1889: the weaving of cotton on hand-operated looms by self-employed artisans, which employed nearly a quarter of a million British workers in 1820, was almost completely replaced by steam-powered looms in factories around 1850. The word 'thrum' itself means 'the end of a warp-thread in a loom, any thread-end in a fabric, esp. where fraying has occurred, a fragment of waste thread or cotton yarn', and in the plural, 'any odds and ends' (SND).

3 The two-room cottage of the nineteenth-century rural poor had its own grammar: to be or go in the kitchen was to be or go 'but the hoose'; to be in the (other) 'room' was to be 'ben the hoose'. Note that the kitchen also has a bed, where Jess sleeps. A common arrangement in weavers' cottages was to house the loom in the 'room', but Hendry keeps his in a shared workshop (see chapters VI and XXI).

4 Redd up (Sc.): tidy up.

5 The fictional Thrums is based on Barrie's own birthplace, Kirriemuir in Angus. Like Kirriemuir, Thrums sits in the fertile low-lying land of Strathmore, but close to the Grampian hills which bound it to the north-west. Of the long 'Angus glens' which run up into the hills, Kirrie is near the entrance to Glen Clova and Glen Prosen: as the narrator goes on to mention, these hills are managed as grouse-moor.

heard. With us it was only some of the articles of furniture, or perhaps a snuff-mull, that had a genealogical tree. In the house on the brae was a great kettle, called the boiler, that was said to be fifty years old in the days of Hendry's grandfather, of whom nothing more is known. Jess's chair, which had carved arms and a seat stuffed with rags, had been Snecky Hobart's father's before it was hers, and old Snecky bought it at a roup in the Tenements.[6] Jess's rarest possession was, perhaps, the christening robe that even people at a distance came to borrow. Her mother could count up a hundred persons who had been baptized in it.

Every one of the hundred, I believe, is dead, and even I cannot now pick out Jess and Hendry's grave; but I heard recently that the christening robe is still in use. It is strange that I should still be left after so many changes, one of the three or four who can to-day stand on the brae and point out Jess's window. The little window commands the incline to the point where the brae suddenly jerks out of sight in its climb down into the town. The steep path up the commonty makes for this elbow of the brae,[7] and thus, whichever way the traveller takes, it is here that he comes first into sight of the window. Here, too, those who go to the town from the south get their first glimpse of Thrums.

Carts pass up and down the brae every few minutes, and there comes an occasional gig. Seldom is the brae empty, for many live beyond the top of it now, and men and women go by to their work, children to school or play. Not one of the children I see from the window to-day is known to me, and most of the men and women I only recognize by their likeness to their parents. That sweet-faced old woman with the shawl on her shoulders may be one of the girls who was playing at the game of palaulays when Jamie stole into Thrums for the last time; the man who is leaning on the commonty gate gathering breath for the last quarter of the brae may, as a barefooted callant, have been one of those who chased Cree Queery past the poor-house. I cannot say; but this I know, that the grandparents of most of these boys and girls were once young with me. If I see the sons and daughters of my friends grown old, I also see the grandchildren spinning the peerie and hunkering at I-dree-I-dree—I-droppit-it—as we did so long ago.[8] The world remains as young as ever. The lovers that met on the commonty in the gloaming are gone, but there are other lovers to take their place, and still the commonty is here. The sun had sunk on a fine day in June, early in the century, when Hendry and Jess, newly married, he in a rich moleskin waistcoat, she in a white net cap, walked to the house on the brae that was to be their home. So Jess has told me. Here again has been just such a day, and somewhere in Thrums there may be just such a couple, setting out for their home behind a horse with white ears instead of walking, but with the same hopes and fears, and the same love light in their eyes. The world does not age. The hearse passes over the brae and up the straight burying-ground road, but still there is a cry for the christening robe.

Jess's window was a beacon by night to travellers in the dark, and it will be so in the future when there are none to remember Jess. There are many such windows still, with loving faces behind them. From them we watch for the friends and relatives who are coming back, and some, alas! watch in vain. Not every one returns who takes the elbow

6 Roup (Sc.): the public auction of effects when a house or farm is vacated. The 'Tenements' in Kirriemuir were the two-story terraced houses in the centre of town, in one of which Barrie himself was born.

7 Commonty (Sc.): the town's common pasture-land.

8 Of the children's games mentioned in these sentences, 'Paulaulays' seems to be a specifically Angus name for hop-scotch, and a 'peerie' is a spinning-top. 'I-dree I-dree I-droppit-it' involves a girl dancing round a ring of other children singing this rhyme, before dropping a hankie (a 'love-letter') at the heels of a boy who then has to chase her.

of the brae bravely, or waves his handkerchief to those who watch from the window with wet eyes, and some return too late. To Jess, at her window always when she was not in bed, things happy and mournful and terrible came into view. At this window she sat for twenty years or more looking at the world as through a telescope; and here an awful ordeal was gone through after her sweet untarnished soul had been given back to God.

CHAPTER II.

ON THE TRACK OF THE MINISTER.

ON the afternoon of the Saturday that carted me and my two boxes to Thrums, I was ben in the room playing Hendry at the dambrod. I had one of the room chairs, but Leeby brought a chair from the kitchen for her father. Our door stood open, and as Hendry often pondered for two minutes with his hand on a "man," I could have joined in the gossip that was going on but the house.

"Ay, weel, then, Leeby," said Jess, suddenly, "I'll warrant the minister 'll no be preachin' the morn."

This took Leeby to the window.

"Yea, yea," she said (and I knew she was nodding her head sagaciously); I looked out at the room window, but all I could see was a man wheeling an empty barrow down the brae.

"That's Robbie Tosh," continued Leeby; "an' there's nae doot 'at he's makkin for the minister's,[9] for he has on his black coat. He'll be to row the minister's luggage to the post-cart. Ay, an' that's Davit Lunan's barrow. I ken it by the shaft's bein' spliced wi' yarn.[10] Davit broke the shaft at the saw-mill."

"He'll be gaen awa for a curran (number of) days," said Jess, "or he would juist hae taen his bag.[11] Ay, he'll be awa to Edinbory, to see the lass."

"I wonder wha'll be to preach the morn—tod, it'll likely be Mr. Skinner, frae Dundee;[12] him an' the minister's chief, ye ken."

"Ye micht gang up to the attic,[13] Leeby, an' see if the spare bedroom vent (chimney) at the manse is gaen. We're sure, if it's Mr. Skinner, he'll come wi' the post frae Tilliedrum the nicht, an' sleep at the manse."[14]

"Weel, I assure ye," said Leeby, descending from the attic, "it'll no be Mr. Skinner, for no only is the spare bedroom vent no gaen, but the blind's drawn doon frae tap to fut, so they're no even airin' the room. Na, it canna be him; an' what's mair, it'll be naebody 'at's to bide a' nicht at the manse."[15]

"I wouldna say that; na, na. It may only be a student; an' Marget Dundas" (the minister's mother and housekeeper) "michtna think it necessary to put on a fire for him."[16]

---

9   'And there's no doubt that he's making for the minister's.' Barrie's north-east Scots routinely contracts 'that' to ''at' when used as a relative pronoun, and sometimes elsewhere.

10   Ken (Sc.): know; 'with' is routinely shortened to 'wi''.

11   Gaen (or ga'en): going (as here) or gone; hae: have; taen (or ta'en): taken (as here) or taking (both Sc.).

12   Wha'll (Sc.): who'll. 'Tod' is a euphemistic alteration of 'God', used as an intensifier, an exclamation. Frae (Sc.): from.

13   Micht gang (Sc.): might go.

14   'Tilliedrum' is a fictional version of Forfar, the county town, about five miles from Kirriemuir.

15   Doon frae tap to fut: down from top to foot; canna: cannot; mair: more; bide a' nicht: stay all night (all Sc.).

16   Michtna (Sc.): night not.

"Tod, I'll tell ye wha it'll be. I wonder I didna think o' 'im sooner. It'll be the lad Wilkie; him 'at's mither mairit on Sam'l Duthie's wife's brither. They bide in Cupar, an' I mind 'at when the son was here twa or three year syne he was juist gaen to begin the diveenity classes in Glesca."[17]

"If that's so, Leeby, he would be sure to bide wi' Sam'l. Hendry, hae ye heard 'at Sam'l Duthie's expeckin' a stranger the nicht?"

"Haud yer tongue," replied Hendry, who was having the worst of the game.[18]

"Ay, but I ken he is," said Leeby triumphantly to her mother, "for ye mind when I was in at Johnny Watt's (the draper's) Chirsty (Sam'l's wife) was buyin' twa yards o' chintz, an' I couldna think what she would be wantin' 't for!"[19]

"I thocht Johnny said to ye 'at it was for a present to Chirsty's auntie?"

"Ay, but he juist guessed that; for, though he tried to get oot o' Chirsty what she wanted the chintz for, she wouldna tell 'im. But I see noo what she was after. The lad Wilkie 'll be to bide wi' them, and Chirsty had bocht the chintz to cover the airm-chair wi'. It's ane o' thae hair-bottomed chairs, but terrible torn, so she'll hae covered it for 'im to sit on."[20]

"I wouldna wonder but ye're richt, Leeby; for Chirsty would be in an oncommon fluster if she thocht the lad's mither was likely to hear 'at her best chair was torn. Ay, ay, bein' a man, he wouldna think to tak aff the chintz an' hae a look at the chair withoot it."

Here Hendry, who had paid no attention to the conversation, broke in—

"Was ye speirin' had I seen Sam'l Duthie?[21] I saw 'im yesterday buyin' a fender at Will'um Crook's roup."

"A fender! Ay, ay, that settles the queistion," said Leeby; "I'll warrant the fender was for Chirsty's parlour. It's preyed on Chirsty's mind, they say, this fower-and-thirty year 'at she doesna hae a richt parlour fender."

"Leeby, look! That's Robbie Tosh wi' the barrow. He has a michty load o' luggage. Am thinkin' the minister's bound for Tilliedrum."[22]

"Na, he's no, he's gaen to Edinbory, as ye micht ken by the bandbox. That'll be his mither's bonnet he's takkin' back to get altered. Ye'll mind she was never pleased wi' the set o' the flowers."

"Weel, weel, here comes the minister himsel, an' very snod he is. Ay, Marget's been puttin' new braid on his coat, an' he's carryin' the sma' black bag he bocht in Dundee last year: he'll hae's nicht-shirt an' a comb in't, I dinna doot. Ye micht rin to' the corner, Leeby, an' see if he cries in at Jess McTaggart's in passin'."[23]

"It's my opeenion," said Leeby, returning excitedly from the corner, " 'at the lad Wilkie's no to be preachin' the morn, after a'. When I gangs to the corner, at ony rate, what think ye's the first thing I see but the minister an' Sam'l Duthie meetin' face to face?[24] Ay, weel, it's gospel am tellin' ye when I say as Sam'l flung back his head an' walkit richt by the minister!"

17 Wha: who; mairit: married; o' 'im: of him; mind: remember; syne: ago (all Sc.). 'Glesca' is Glasgow.
18 Haud (Sc.): hold.
19 Twa (Sc.): two. 'It' is routinely shortened to "'t" when following another word.
20 Ane o' thae (Sc.): one of those.
21 Speirin' (Sc.): asking.
22 'Am thinkin'': I'm thinking. Barrie routinely uses 'am' (more rarely "am') where in more recent Scots we would write 'Ah'm'.
23 Snod: neat, smart; sma': small; bocht: bought; hae's: have his; dinna: don't; rin: run; cries: calls (all Sc.).
24 The morn: tomorrow; at ony rate: in any case (both Sc.).

"Losh keep's a', Leeby; ye say that? They maun hae haen a quarrel."[25]

"I'm thinkin' we'll hae Mr. Skinner i' the poopit the morn after a'."

"It may be, it may be. Ay, ay, look, Leeby, whatna bit kimmer's that wi' the twa jugs in her hand?"[26]

"Eh? Ou, it'll be Lawyer Ogilvy's servant lassieky gaen to the farm o' T'nowhead for the milk. She gangs ilka Saturday nicht. But what did ye say—twa jugs? Tod, let's see! Ay, she has so, a big jug an' a little ane. The little ane 'll be for cream; an', sal, the big ane's bigger na usual."[27]

"There maun be something gaen on at the lawyer's if they're buyin' cream, Leeby. Their reg'lar thing's twopence worth o' milk."

"Ay, but I assure ye that sma' jug's for cream, an' I dinna doot mysel but 'at there's to be fowerpence worth o' milk this nicht."

"There's to be a puddin' made the morn, Leeby. Ou, ay, a' thing points to that; an' we're very sure there's nae puddins at the lawyer's on the Sabbath onless they hae company."

"I dinna ken wha they can hae, if it be na that brither o' the wife's 'at bides oot by Aberdeen."

"Na, it's no him, Leeby; na, na. He's no weel to do, an' they wouldna be buyin' cream for 'im."[28]

"I'll run up to the attic again, an' see if there's ony stir in the lawyer's hoose."

By and by Leeby returned in triumph.

"Ou, ay," she said, "they're expectin' veesitors at the lawyer's, for I could see twa o' the bairns dressed up to the nines, an' Mistress Ogilvy doesnae dress at them in that wy for naething."[29]

"It fair beats me though, Leeby, to guess wha's comin' to them. Ay, but stop a meenute, I wouldnae wonder, no, really I would not wonder but what it'll be —

"The very thing 'at was passin' through my head, mother."

"Ye mean 'at the lad Wilkie 'll be to bide wi' the lawyer i'stead o' wi' Sam'l Duthie? Sal, am thinkin' that's it. Ye ken Sam'l an' the lawyer married on cousins; but Mistress Ogilvy ay lookit on Chirsty as dirt aneath her feet. She would be glad to get a minister, though, to the hoose, an' so I warrant the lad Wilkie'll be to bide a' nicht at the lawyer's."

"But what would Chirsty be doin' gettin' the chintz an' the fender in that case?"

"Ou, she'd been expeckin' the lad, of course. Sal, she'll be in a michty tantrum aboot this. I wouldna wonder though she gets Sam'l to gang ower to the U.P.'s."[30]

Leeby went once more to the attic.

"Ye're wrang, mother," she cried out. "Whaever's to preach the morn is to bide at the manse, for the minister's servant's been at Baker Duffs buyin' short-bread—half a lippy, nae doot."[31]

---

25 Losh keep's a': euphemistic version of 'Lord keep us all'; maun: must; haen (or ha'en): had (as here) or having (all Sc.).

26 'In' is shortened to 'i''; whatna bit kimmer...? (Sc.): 'kimmer' is familiar term for a local woman. This phrase means roughly, 'what kind of woman...?'.

27 Lassieky: lassie, with a second diminutive ending added; ilka: each, every (both Sc.). 'Sal' seems to be another intensifier, like 'tod'.

28 Weel to do: well-off.

29 Doesnae (in Barrie more usually doesna): doesn't; wy: way (both Sc.).

30 Ower (Sc.): over. The United Presbyterian Church was one of several communions produced by secessions from the established Church of Scotland (to which *the* minister of Thrums adheres) over the issue of landowners' role in appointing ministers to parishes.

31 'Half a lippy' probably means half a round, shortbread being made in large flat discs for

"Are ye sure o' that, Leeby?"

"Oh, am certain. The servant gaed in to Duffs the noo, an', as ye ken fine, the manse fowk doesna deal wi' him, except they're wantin' short-bread. He's Auld Kirk." [32]

Leeby returned to the kitchen, and Jess sat for a time ruminating.

"The lad Wilkie," she said at last, triumphantly, " 'll be to bide at Lawyer Ogilvy's; but he'll be gaen to the manse the morn for a tea-dinner."

"But what," asked Leeby, "aboot the milk an' the cream for the lawyer's?"

"Ou, they'll be hae'n a puddin' for the supper the nicht. That's a michty genteel thing, I've heard."

It turned out that Jess was right in every particular.

CHAPTER III.

PREPARING TO RECEIVE COMPANY.

LEEBY was at the fire brandering a quarter of steak on the tongs, when the house was flung into consternation by Hendry's casual remark that he had seen Tibbie Mealmaker in the town with her man.

"The Lord preserve's!" cried Leeby.

Jess looked quickly at the clock.

"Half fower!" she said excitedly.

"Then it canna be dune," said Leeby, falling despairingly into a chair, "for they may be here ony meenute."

"It's most michty," said Jess, turning on her husband, " 'at ye should tak a pleasure in bringin' this hoose to disgrace. Hoo did ye no tell's suner?"

"I fair forgot," Hendry answered, "but what's a' yer steer?" [33]

Jess looked at me (she often did this) in a way that meant, "What a man is this I'm tied to!"

"Steer!" she exclaimed. "Is't no time we was makkin' a steer? They'll be in for their tea ony meenute, an' the room no sae muckle as sweepit. Ay, an' me lookin' like a sweep; an' Tibbie Mealmaker 'at's sae partikler genteel seein' you sic a sicht as ye are!" [34]

Jess shook Hendry out of his chair, while Leeby began to sweep with the one hand, and agitatedly to unbutton her wrapper with the other.

"She didna see me," said Hendry, sitting down forlornly on the table.

"Get aff that table!" cried Jess. "See haud o' the besom," she said to Leeby. [35]

"For mercy's sake, mother," said Leeby, "gie yer face a dicht, an' put on a clean mutch." [36]

"I'll open the door if they come afore you're ready," said Hendry, as Leeby pushed him against the dresser.

---

division into segments.

32 The noo: now; fowk: folk (both Sc.). 'Auld Kirk' probably refers to the Episcopal Church of Scotland, part of the Anglican communion.

33 Hoo: how (here in a Scots sense, meaning why); steer: stir, fuss (both Sc.).

34 Sae muckle as sweepit: so much as swept; sic a sicht; such a sight (all Sc.).

35 See haud o' the besom (Sc.): give me/hand over the broom (haud means hold).

36 Gie: give; dicht: wipe; mutch: the day-cap of white linen or muslin worn by married women (all Sc.).

"Ye daur to speak aboot openin' the door, an' you sic a mess!" cried Jess, with pins in her mouth.

"Havers!" retorted Hendry. "A man canna be aye washin' at 'imsel."[37]

Seeing that Hendry was as much in the way as myself, I invited him upstairs to the attic, whence we heard Jess and Leeby upbraiding each other shrilly. I was aware that the room was speckless; but for all that, Leeby was turning it upside down.

"She's aye ta'en like that," Hendry said to me, referring to his wife, "when she's expectin' company. Ay, it's a peety she canna tak things cannier."[38]

"Tibbie Mealmaker must be some one of importance?" I asked.

"Ou, she's naething by the ord'nar'; but ye see she was mairit to a Tilliedrum man no lang syne, an' they're said to hae a michty grand establishment. Ay, they've a wardrobe spleet new;[39] an' what think ye Tibbie wears ilka day?"

I shook my head.

"It was Chirsty Miller 'at put it through the toon," Hendry continued. "Chirsty was in Tilliedrum last Teisday or Wednesday, an' Tibbie gae her a cup o' tea. Ay, weel, Tibbie telt Chirsty 'at she wears hose ilka day."

"Wears hose?"

"Ay. It's some michty grand kind o' stockin'. I never heard o't in this toon. Na, there's naebody in Thrums 'at wears hose."

"And who did Tibbie get?" I asked; for in Thrums they say, "Wha did she get?" and "Wha did he tak?"

"His name's Davit Curly. Ou, a crittur fu' o' maggots,[40] an' nae great match, for he's juist the Tilliedrum bill-sticker."

At this moment Jess shouted from her chair (she was burnishing the society teapot as she spoke), "Mind Hendry McQumpha, 'at upon nae condition are ye to mention the bill-stickin' afore Tibbie!"

"Tibbie," Hendry explained to me, "is a terrible vain tid,[41] an' doesna think the bill-stickin' genteel. Ay, they say 'at if she meets Davit in the street wi' his paste-pot an' the brush in his hands she pretends no to ken 'im."

Every time Jess paused to think she cried up orders, such as —

"Dinna call her Tibbie, mind ye. Always address her as Mistress Curly."

"Shak' hands wi' baith o' them, an' say ye hope they're in the enjoyment o' guid health."

"Dinna put yer feet on the table."

"Mind, you're no' to mention 'at ye kent they were in the toon."

"When onybody passes ye yer tea say, 'Thank ye.'"

"Dinna stir yer tea as if ye was churnin' butter, nor let on 'at the scones is no our ain bakin'."

"If Tibbie says onything aboot the china yer no' to say 'at we dinna use it ilka day."

"Dinna lean back in the big chair, for it's broken, an' Leeby's gi'en it a lick o' glue this meenute."[42]

"When Leeby gies ye a kick aneath the table that'll be a sign to ye to say grace."

Hendry looked at me apologetically while these instructions came up.

---

37   Daur: dare; havers!: nonsense!; aye: always; 'imsel': himself.
38   Cannier (Sc.): more sensibly.
39   By the ord'nar': out of the ordinary; spleet new: split or splinter-new, brand new (both Sc.).
40   A creature full of maggots: maggots meaning, here, eccentricities, odd ideas.
41   Barrie's use of 'tid' does not correspond to anything in *SND*, but one sense of the word there is 'mood, humour, inclination'.
42   Our ain: our own; gi'en, or gien: giving (as here) or given (both Sc.).

"I winna dive my head wi' sic nonsense,"[43] he said; "it's no' for a man body to be sae crammed fu' o' manners."

"Come awa doon," Jess shouted to him, "an' put on a clean dickey."[44]

"I'll better do't to please her," said Hendry, "though for my ain part I dinna like the feel o' a dickey on week-days. Na, they mak's think it's the Sabbath."[45]

Ten minutes afterwards I went downstairs to see how the preparations were progressing. Fresh muslin curtains had been put up in the room. The grand footstool, worked by Leeby, was so placed that Tibbie could not help seeing it; and a fine cambric handkerchief, of which Jess was very proud, was hanging out of a drawer as if by accident. An antimacassar lying carelessly on the seat of a chair concealed a rent in the horse-hair, and the china ornaments on the mantelpiece were so placed that they looked whole. Leeby's black merino was hanging near the window in a good light,[46] and Jess's Sabbath bonnet, which was never worn, occupied a nail beside it. The tea-things stood on a tray in the kitchen bed, whence they could be quickly brought into the room, just as if they were always ready to be used daily. Leeby, as yet in deshabille, was shaving her father at a tremendous rate, and Jess, looking as fresh as a daisy, was ready to receive the visitors. She was peering through the tiny window-blind looking for them.

"Be cautious, Leeby," Hendry was saying, when Jess shook her hand at him. "Wheesht," she whispered; they're comin'."

Hendry was hustled into his Sabbath coat, and then came a tap at the door, a very genteel tap. Jess nodded to Leeby, who softly shoved Hendry into the room.

The tap was repeated, but Leeby pushed her father into a chair and thrust Barrow's Sermons open into his hand.[47] Then she stole but the house, and swiftly buttoned her wrapper, speaking to Jess by nods the while. There was a third knock, whereupon Jess said, in a loud, Englishy voice—

"Was not that a chap (knock) at the door?"

Hendry was about to reply, but she shook her fist at him. Next moment Leeby opened the door. I was upstairs, but I heard Jess say—

"Dear me, if it's not Mrs. Curly—and Mr. Curly! And hoo are ye? Come in, by. Weel, this is, indeed, a pleasant surprise!"

CHAPTER IV.

WAITING FOR THE DOCTOR.

JESS had gone early to rest, and the door of her bed in the kitchen was pulled to. From her window I saw Hendry buying dulse.[48]

Now and again the dulseman wheeled his slimy boxes to the top of the brae, and sat there stolidly on the shafts of his barrow. Many passed him by, but occasionally some one came to rest by his side. Unless the customer was loquacious, there was no bandying of words, and Hendry merely unbuttoned his east-trouser pocket, giving his

---

43 Winna: will not; dive, usually deave: bother, annoy (both Sc.).
44 Dickey: a shirt-front, worn with a jacket to hide a normal shirt on formal occasions.
45 Mak's (Sc.): make us, i.e. make one.
46 A merino was a shawl made of this type of fine wool.
47 Isaac Barrow (d. 1677) was a seventeenth-century Anglican divine, whose sermons were reprinted well into the nineteenth century. For a list of the printed matter in the McQumpha household, see the start of chapter 10.
48 Dulse is an edible sea-weed, and to judge from this something of a delicacy among the poor.

body the angle at which the pocket could be most easily filled by the dulseman. He then deposited his halfpenny, and moved on. Neither had spoken; yet in the country they would have roared their predictions about to-morrow to a ploughman half a field away.

Dulse is roasted by twisting it round the tongs fired to a red-heat, and the house was soon heavy with the smell of burning sea-weed. Leeby was at the dresser munching it from a broth-plate, while Hendry, on his knees at the fireplace, gingerly tore off the blades of dulse that were sticking to the tongs, and licked his singed fingers.

"Whaur's yer mother?" he asked Leeby.[49]

"Ou," said Leeby, "whaur would she be but in her bed?"

Hendry took the tongs to the door, and would have cleaned them himself, had not Leeby (who often talked his interfering ways over with her mother) torn them from his hands.

"Leeby!" cried Jess at that moment.

"Ay," answered Leeby, leisurely, not noticing, as I happened to do, that Jess spoke in an agitated voice.

"What is't?" asked Hendry, who liked to be told things.

He opened the door of the bed.

"Yer mother's no weel," he said to Leeby.

Leeby ran to the bed, and I went ben the house.

In another two minutes we were a group of four in the kitchen, staring vacantly. Death could not have startled us more, tapping thrice that quiet night on the window-pane.

"It's diphtheria!" said Jess, her hands trembling as she buttoned her wrapper.[50]

She looked at me, and Leeby looked at me.

"It's no, it's no," cried Leeby, and her voice was as a fist shaken at my face. She blamed me for hesitating in my reply. But ever since this malady left me a lonely dominie for life,[51] diphtheria has been a knockdown word for me. Jess had discovered a great white spot on her throat. I knew the symptoms.

"Is't dangerous?" asked Hendry, who once had a headache years before, and could still refer to it as a reminiscence.

"Them 'at has 't never recovers," said Jess, sitting down very quietly. A stick fell from the fire, and she bent forward to replace it

"They do recover," cried Leeby, again turning angry eyes on me.

I could not face her; I had known so many who did not recover. She put her hand on her mother's shoulder.

"Mebbe you would be better in yer bed," suggested Hendry.

No one spoke.

"When I had the headache," said Hendry, "I was better in my bed."

Leeby had taken Jess's hand—a worn old hand that had many a time gone out in love and kindness when younger hands were cold. Poets have sung and fighting men have done great deeds for hands that never had such a record.

"If ye could eat something," said Hendry, "I would gae to the flesher's for 't. I mind when I had the headache, hoo a small steak —"[52]

49 Whaur's (Sc.): where is.

50 Diphtheria is a bacterial infection of the throat, often fatal in the nineteenth century: Barrie's first readers might have recalled the death from diptheria of Queen Victoria's daughter, Princess Alice, and her daughter, 11 years before.

51 Dominie (Sc.): school-master. This is the only glimpse we get of the narrator's personal history.

52 Flesher's: butcher's.

"Gae awa for the doctor, rayther," broke in Leeby.

Jess started, for sufferers think there is less hope for them after the doctor has been called in to pronounce sentence.

"I winna hae the doctor," she said, anxiously.

In answer to Leeby's nods, Hendry slowly pulled out his boots from beneath the table, and sat looking at them, preparatory to putting them on. He was beginning at last to be a little scared, though his face did not show it.

"I winna hae ye," cried Jess, getting to her feet, "ga'en to the doctor's sic a sicht. Yer coat's a' yarn."

"Havers," said Hendry, but Jess became frantic.

I offered to go for the doctor, but while I was upstairs looking for my bonnet I heard the door slam. Leeby had become impatient, and darted off herself, buttoning her jacket probably as she ran. When I returned to the kitchen, Jess and Hendry were still by the fire. Hendry was beating a charred stick into sparks, and his wife sat with her hands in her lap. I saw Hendry look at her once or twice, but he could think of nothing to say. His terms of endearment had died out thirty-nine years before with his courtship. He had forgotten the words. For his life he could not have crossed over to Jess and put his arm round her. Yet he was uneasy. His eyes wandered round the poorly lit room.

"Will ye hae a drink o' watter?" he asked.

There was a sound of footsteps outside.

"That'll be him," said Hendry in a whisper.

Jess started to her feet, and told Hendry to help her ben the house.

The steps died away, but I fancied that Jess, now highly strung, had gone into hiding, and I went after her. I was mistaken. She had lit the room lamp, turning the crack in the globe to the wall. The sheepskin hearthrug, which was generally carefully packed away beneath the bed, had been spread out before the empty fireplace, and Jess was on the arm-chair hurriedly putting on her grand black mutch with the pink flowers.

"I was juist makkin' mysel respectable," she said, but without life in her voice.

This was the only time I ever saw her in the room.

Leeby returned panting to say that the doctor might be expected in an hour. He was away among the hills.

The hour passed reluctantly. Leeby lit a fire ben the house, and then put on her Sabbath dress. She sat with her mother in the room. Never before had I seen Jess sit so quietly, for her way was to work until, as she said herself, she was ready "to fall into her bed."

Hendry wandered between the two rooms, always in the way when Leeby ran to the window to see if that was the doctor at last. He would stand gaping in the middle of the room for five minutes, then slowly withdraw to stand as drearily but the house. His face lengthened. At last he sat down by the kitchen fire, a Bible in his hand. It lay open on his knee, but he did not read much. He sat there with his legs outstretched, looking straight before him. I believe he saw Jess young again. His face was very solemn, and his mouth twitched. The fire sank into ashes unheeded.

I sat alone at my attic window for hours, waiting for the doctor. From the attic I could see nearly all Thrums, but, until very late, the night was dark, and the brae, except immediately before the door, was blurred and dim. A sheet of light canopied the square as long as a cheap Jack paraded his goods there. It was gone before the moon came out. Figures tramped, tramped up the brae, passed the house in shadow and stole silently on. A man or boy whistling seemed to fill the valley. The moon arrived too late to be of service to any wayfarer. Everybody in Thrums was asleep but ourselves, and the doctor who never came.

About midnight Hendry climbed the attic stair and joined me at the window. His hand was shaking as he pulled back the blind. I began to realize that his heart could still overflow.

"She's waur," he whispered, like one who had lost his voice.[53]

For a long time he sat silently, his hand on the blind. He was so different from the Hendry I had known, that I felt myself in the presence of a strange man. His eyes were glazed with staring at the turn of the brae where the doctor must first come into sight. His breathing became heavier, till it was a gasp. Then I put my hand on his shoulder, and he stared at me.

"Nine-and-thirty years come June," he said, speaking to himself.

For this length of time, I knew, he and Jess had been married. He repeated the words at intervals.

"I mind—" he began, and stopped. He was thinking of the spring-time of Jess's life.

The night ended as we watched; then came the terrible moment that precedes the day—the moment known to shuddering watchers by sick beds, when a chill wind cuts through the house, and the world without seems cold in death. It is as if the heart of the earth did not mean to continue beating.

"This is a fearsome nicht," Hendry said, hoarsely.

He turned to grope his way to the stairs, but suddenly went down on his knees to pray. . . .

There was a quick step outside. I arose in time to see the doctor on the brae. He tried the latch, but Leeby was there to show him in. The door of the room closed on him.

From the top of the stair I could see into the dark passage, and make out Hendry shaking at the door. I could hear the doctor's voice, but not the words he said. There was a painful silence, and then Leeby laughed joyously.

"It's gone," cried Jess; "the white spot's gone! Ye juist touched it, an' it's gone! Tell Hendry."

But Hendry did not need to be told. As Jess spoke I heard him say, huskily: "Thank God!" and then he tottered back to the kitchen. When the doctor left, Hendry was still on Jess's arm-chair, trembling like a man with the palsy. Ten minutes afterwards I was preparing for bed, when he cried up the stair—

"Come awa' doon."

I joined the family party in the room: Hendry was sitting close to Jess.

"Let us read," he said, firmly, "in the fourteenth of John."[54]

CHAPTER V.

A HUMORIST ON HIS CALLING.

AFTER the eight o'clock bell had rung, Hendry occasionally crossed over to the farm of T'nowhead and sat on the pig-sty. If no one joined him he scratched the pig, and returned home gradually. Here what was almost a club held informal meetings, at

---

53 Waur (Sc.): worse.
54 Hendry will read out the first three verses of John's Gospel, chapter 14, at the end of chapter XX.

which two or four, or even half a dozen, assembled to debate, when there was any one to start them. The meetings were only memorable when Tammas Haggart was in fettle, to pronounce judgments in his well-known sarcastic way. Sometimes we had got off the pig-sty to separate before Tammas was properly yoked. There we might remain a long time, planted round him like trees, for he was a mesmerising talker.

There was a pail belonging to the pig-sty, which some one would turn bottom upwards and sit upon if the attendance was unusually numerous. Tammas liked, however, to put a foot on it now and again in the full swing of a harangue, and when he paused for a sarcasm I have seen the pail kicked toward him. He had the wave of the arm that is so convincing in argument, and such a natural way of asking questions, that an audience not used to public speaking might have thought he wanted them to reply. It is an undoubted fact that when he went on the platform, at the time of the election, to heckle the Colonel, he paused in the middle of his questions to take a drink out of the tumbler of water which stood on the table. As soon as they saw what he was up to, the spectators raised a ringing cheer.[55]

On concluding his perorations, Tammas sent his snuff-mull round, but we had our own way of passing him a vote of thanks. One of the company would express amazement at his gift of words, and the others would add, "Man, man," or, "Ye cow, Tammas," or, "What a crittur ye are!" all which ejaculations meant the same thing. A new subject being thus ingeniously introduced, Tammas again put his foot on the pail.

"I tak no creedit," he said, modestly, on the evening, I remember, of Willie Pyatt's funeral, "in bein' able to speak wi' a sort o' faceelity on topics 'at I've made my ain."

"Ay," said T'nowhead, "but it's no the faceelity o' speakin' 'at taks me. There's Davit Lunan 'at can speak like as if he had learned it aff a paper, an' yet I canna thole 'im."[56]

"Davit," said Hendry, "doesna speak in a wy 'at a body can follow 'im.[57] He doesna gae even on. Jess says he's juist like a man aye at the cross-roads, an' no sure o' his wy. But the stock has words, an' no ilka body has that."

"If I was bidden to put Tammas's gift in a word," said T'nowhead, "I would say 'at he had a wy. That's what I would say."

"Weel, I suppose I have," Tammas admitted, "but wy or no wy, I couldna put a point on my words if it wasna for my sense o' humour. Lads, humour's what gies the nip to speakin'."

"It's what maks ye a sarcesticist, Tammas," said Hendry; "but what I wonder at is yer sayin' the humorous things sae aisy like.[58] Some says ye mak them up aforehand, but I ken that's no true."

"No only is't no true," said Tammas, "but it couldna be true. Them 'at says sic things, an' weel I ken you're meanin' Davit Lunan, hasna nae idea o' what humour is. It's a thing 'at spouts oot o' its ain accord. Some o' the maist humorous things I've ever said cam oot, as a body may say, by themsels."[59]

"I suppose that's the case," said T'nowhead, "an' yet it maun be you 'at brings them up?"

---

55 Self-employed artisans like Tammas and Hendry prided themselves on their 'independence' from the patronage of landowners; but, despite their attendance at an election meeting here, none of their class had a vote in General Elections until the Second Reform Act (in Scotland, 1868).
56 Thole (Sc.): stand, tolerate.
57 'At a body can follow him (Sc.): that one can follow him.
58 Aisy: easy.
59 Maist: most; cam: came (both Sc.).

"There's no nae doubt aboot its bein' the case," said Tammas, "for I've watched mysel often. There was a vara guid instance occurred sune after I married Easie.[60] The Earl's son met me one day, aboot that time, i' the Tenements, an' he didna ken 'at Chirsty was deid, an' I'd married again. 'Well, Haggart,' he says, in his frank wy, 'and how is your wife?' 'She's vara weel, sir,' I maks answer, 'but she's no the ane you mean.'"

"Na, he meant Chirsty," said Hendry.

"Is that a' the story?" asked T'nowhead.

Tammas had been looking at us queerly.

"There's no nane o' ye lauchin'," he said, "but I can assure ye the Earl's son gaed east the toon lauchin' like onything."[61]

"But what was't he lauched at?"

"Ou," said Tammas, "a humorist doesna tell whaur the humour comes in."

"No, but when you said that, did ye mean it to be humorous?"

"Am no sayin' I did, but as I've been tellin' ye, humour spouts oot by itsel."

"Ay, but do ye ken noo what the Earl's son gaed awa lauchin' at?"

Tammas hesitated.

"I dinna exactly see't," he confessed, "but that's no an oncommon thing. A humorist would often no ken 'at he was ane if it wasna by the wy he maks other fowk lauch. A body canna be expeckit baith to mak the joke an' to see't. Na, that would be doin' twa fowks' wark."

"Weel, that's reasonable enough, but I've often seen ye lauchin'," said Hendry, "lang afore other fowk lauched."

"Nae doubt," Tammas explained, "an' that's because humour has twa sides, juist like a penny piece. When I say a humorous thing mysel I'm dependent on other fowk to tak note o' the humour o't, bein' mysel ta'en up wi' the makkin' o't. Ay, but there's things I see an' hear 'at maks me lauch, an' that's the other side o' humour."

"I never heard it put sae plain afore," said T'nowhead, "an', sal, am no nane sure but what am a humorist too."

" Na, na, no you, T'nowhead," said Tammas, hotly.

"Weel," continued the farmer, "I never set up for bein' a humorist, but I can juist assure ye 'at I lauch at queer things too. No lang syne I woke up i' my bed lauchin' like onything, an' Lisbeth thocht I wasna weel. It was something I dreamed 'at made me lauch, I couldna think what it was, but I lauched richt. Was that no fell like a humorist?"[62]

"That was neither here nor there," said Tammas. "Na, dreams dinna coont, for we're no responsible for them. Ay, an' what's mair, the mere lauchin's no the important side o' humour, even though ye hinna to be telt to lauch.[63] The important side's the other side, the sayin' the humorous things. I'll tell ye what: the humorist's like a man firin' at a target—he doesna ken whether he hits or no till them at the target tells 'im."

"I would be of opeenion," said Hendry, who was one of Tammas's most staunch admirers, " 'at another mark o' the rale humorist was his seein' humour in all things?"[64]

Tammas shook his head—a way he had when Hendry advanced theories.

"I dinna haud wi' that ava," he said. "I ken fine 'at Davit Lunan gaes aboot sayin' he sees humour in everything, but there's nae surer sign at he's no a genuine humorist. Na, the rale humorist kens vara weel 'at there's subjects withoot a spark o' humour in them. When a subject rises to the sublime it should be regairded philosophically, an'

---

60   Vara (Sc.): very.

61   No nane o' ye lauchin' (Sc.): none of you laughing.

62   Fell (Sc.): here, very (*SND* II.2).

63   Hinna to be telt (Sc.): have not to be told, i.e. do not need to be told.

64   Rale (Sc.): real.

no humorously. Davit would lauch 'at the grandest thochts, whaur they only fill the true humorist wi' awe. I've found it necessary to rebuke 'im at times whaur his lauchin' was oot o' place. He pretended aince on this vara spot to see humour i' the origin o' cock-fightin'."[65]

"Did he, man?" said Hendry; "I wasna here. But what is the origin o' cock-fechtin'?"

"It was a' i' the *Cheap Magazine*," said T'nowhead.[66]

"Was I sayin' it wasna?" demanded Tammas. "It was through me readin' the account oot o' the *Cheap Magazine* 'at the discussion arose."

"But what said the *Cheapy* was the origin o' cock-fechtin'?"

"T'nowhead 'll tell ye," answered Tammas; "he says I dinna ken."

"I never said naething o' the kind," returned T'nowhead, indignantly; "I mind o' ye readin't oot fine."

"Ay, weel," said Tammas, "that's a' richt. Ou, the origin o' cock-fightin' gangs back to the time o' the Greek wars, a thoosand or twa years syne, mair or less. There was ane, Miltiades by name, 'at was the captain o' the Greek army, an' one day he led them doon the mountains to attack the biggest army 'at was ever gathered thegither."

"They were Persians," interposed T'nowhead.

"Are you tellin' the story, or am I?" asked Tammas. "I kent fine 'at they were Persians. Weel, Miltiades had the matter o' twenty thoosand men wi' 'im, and when they got to the foot o' the mountain, behold there was two cocks fechtin'."

"Man, man," said Hendry, "an' was there cocks in thae days?"

"Ondoubtedly," said Tammas, "or hoo could thae twa hae been fechtin'?"

"Ye have me there, Tammas," admitted Hendry. "Ye're perfectly richt."

"Ay, then," continued the stone-breaker, "when Miltiades saw the cocks at it wi' a' their micht, he stopped the army and addressed it. 'Behold!' he cried, at the top o' his voice, 'these cocks do not fight for their household gods, nor for the monuments of their ancestors, nor for glory, nor for liberty, nor for their children, but only because the one will not give way unto the other.'"[67]

"It was nobly said," declared Hendry; "na, cocks wouldna hae sae muckle understandin' as to fecht for thae things.[68] I wouldna wonder but what it was some laddies 'at set them at ane another."

"Hendry doesna see what Miltydes was after," said T'nowhead.

"Ye've taen't up wrang, Hendry," Tammas explained. "What Miltiades meant was 'at if cocks could fecht sae weel oot o' mere deviltry, surely the Greeks would fecht terrible for their gods an' their bairns an' the other things."

"I see, I see; but what was the monuments o' their ancestors?"

"Ou, that was the gravestanes they put up i' their kirkyards."

"I wonder the other billies would want to tak them awa. They would be a michty wecht."[69]

---

65 Ava: at all; aince: once (both Sc.).

66 *The Cheap Magazine; or, the Poor Man's Fireside Companion*, published in Haddington, East Lothian, was an early attempt to publish an educational (but not specifically religious) periodical for the working classes. It cost fourpence, but only survived from 1813–1815: it was later in the century that publishers managed to compensate for low unit price with huge print-runs in order to reach this market profitably.

67 This story, about the battle of Marathon in 490 BC, is first told of Miltiades by Alexandrian philosopher Philo (20 BC–50AD); earlier versions ascribed the exortation to another of the Athenian generals, Themistocles.

68 Fecht (Sc.): fight.

69 Wecht (Sc.): weight.

"Ay, but they wanted them, an' nat'rally the Greeks stuck to the stanes they paid for."

"So, so, an' did Davit Lunan mak oot 'at there was humour in that?"

"He do so. He said it was a humorous thing to think o' a hale army lookin' on at twa cocks fechtin'.[70] I assure ye I telt 'im 'at I saw nae humour in't. It was ane o' the most impressive sichts ever seen by man, an' the Greeks was sae inspired by what Miltiades said 'at they sweepit the Persians oot o' their country."

We all agreed that Tammas's was the genuine humour.

"An' an enviable possession it is," said Hendry.

"In a wy," admitted Tammas, "but no in a' wys."

He hesitated, and then added in a low voice—

"As sure as death, Hendry, it sometimes taks grip o' me i' the kirk itsel', an' I can hardly keep frae lauchin'."

CHAPTER VI.

DEAD THIS TWENTY YEARS.

IN the lustiness of youth there are many who cannot feel that they, too, will die. The first fear stops the heart. Even then they would keep death at arm's length by making believe to disown him. Loved ones are taken away, and the boy, the girl, will not speak of them, as if that made the conqueror's triumph the less. In time the fire in the breast burns low, and then, in the last glow of the embers, it is sweeter to hold to what has been than to think of what may be.

Twenty years had passed since Joey ran down the brae to play. Jess, his mother, shook her staff fondly at him. A cart rumbled by, the driver nodding on the shaft. It rounded the corner and stopped suddenly, and then a woman screamed. A handful of men carried Joey's dead body to his mother, and that was the tragedy of Jess's life.

Twenty years ago, and still Jess sat at the window, and still she heard that woman scream. Every other living being had forgotten Joey; even to Hendry he was now scarcely a name, but there were times when Jess's face quivered and her old arms went out for her dead boy.

"God's will be done," she said, "but oh, I grudged Him my bairn terrible sair. I dinna want him back noo, an' ilka day is takkin' me nearer to him, but for mony a lang year I grudged him sair, sair. He was juist five minutes gone, an' they brocht him back deid, my Joey."[71]

On the Sabbath day Jess could not go to church, and it was then, I think, that she was with Joey most. There was often a blessed serenity on her face when we returned, that only comes to those who have risen from their knees with their prayers answered. Then she was very close to the boy who died. Long ago she could not look out from her window upon the brae, but now it was her seat in church. There on the Sabbath evenings she sometimes talked to me of Joey.

"It's been a fine day," she would say, "juist like that day. I thank the Lord for the sunshine noo, but oh, I thocht at the time I couldna look at the sun shinin' again."

"In all Thrums," she has told me, and I know it to be true, "there's no a better man than Hendry. There's them 'at's cleverer in the wys o' the world, but my man, Hendry McQumpha, never did naething in all his life 'at wasna weel intended, an' though his

---

70 Hale (Sc.): whole.

71 Bairn: child; mony: many; sair: sore; brocht: brought (all Sc.).

words is common, it's to the Lord he looks. I canna think but what Hendry's pleasin' to God. Oh, I dinna ken what to say wi' thankfulness to Him when I mind hoo guid He's been to me. There's Leeby 'at I couldna hae done withoot, me bein' sae silly (weak bodily), an' ay Leeby's stuck by me an' gien up her life, as ye micht say, for me. Jamie —"[72]

But then Jess sometimes broke down.

"He's so far awa," she said, after a time, "an' aye when he gangs back to London after his holidays he has a fear he'll never see me again, but he's terrified to mention it, an' I juist ken by the wy he taks haud o' me, an' comes runnin' back to tak haud o' me again. I ken fine what he's thinkin', but I daurna speak.

"Guid is no word for what Jamie has been to me, but he wasna born till after Joey died. When we got Jamie, Hendry took to whistlin' again at the loom, an' Jamie juist filled Joey's place to him. Ay, but naebody could fill Joey's place to me. It's different to a man. A bairn's no the same to him, but a fell bit o' me was buried in my laddie's grave.[73]

"Jamie an' Joey was never nane the same nature. It was aye something in a shop Jamie wanted to be, an' he never cared muckle for his books, but Joey hankered after being a minister, young as he was, an' a minister Hendry an' me would hae done our best to mak him. Mony, mony a time after he came in frae the kirk on the Sabbath he would stand up at this very window an' wave his hands in a reverent way, juist like the minister. His first text was to be 'Thou God seest me.'[74]

"Ye'll wonder at me, but I've sat here in the lang fore-nichts dreamin' 'at Joey was a grown man noo, an' 'at I was puttin' on my bonnet to come to the kirk to hear him preach.[75] Even as far back as twenty years an' mair I wasna able to gang aboot, but Joey would say to me, 'We'll get a carriage to ye, mother, so 'at ye can come and hear me preach on "Thou God seest me."' He would say to me, 'It doesna do, mother, for the minister in the pulpit to nod to ony o' the fowk, but I'll gie ye a look an' ye'll ken it's me.' Oh, Joey, I would hae gien you a look too, an' ye would hae kent what I was thinkin'. He often said, 'Ye'll be proud o' me, will ye no' mother, when ye see me comin' sailin' alang to the pulpit in my gown?' So I would hae been proud o' him, an' I was proud to hear him speakin' o't. 'The other fowk,' he said, 'will be sittin' in their seats wonderin' what my text's to be, but you'll ken, mother, an' you'll turn up to "Thou God seest me," afore I gie oot the chapter.' Ay, but that day he was coffined, for all the minister prayed, I found it hard to say, 'Thou God seest me.' It's the text I like best noo, though, an' when Hendry an' Leeby is at the kirk, I turn't up often, often in the Bible. I read frae the beginnin' o' the chapter, but when I come to 'Thou God seest me,' I stop. Na, it's no 'at there's ony rebellion to the Lord in my heart noo, for I ken He was lookin' doon when the cart gaed ower Joey, an' He wanted to tak my laddie to Himsel. But juist when I come to 'Thou God seest me,' I let the Book lie in my lap, for aince a body's sure o' that they're sure o' all. Ay, ye'll laugh, but I think, mebbe juist because I was his mother, 'at though Joey never lived to preach in a kirk, he's preached frae 'Thou God seest me' to me. I dinna ken 'at I would ever hae been sae sure o' that if it hadna been for him, an' so I think I see 'im sailin' doon to the pulpit juist as he said he would do. I see him gien me the look he spoke o' — ay, he looks my wy first, an' I ken it's him. Naebody sees him but me, but I see him gien me the look he promised. He's so terrible near me, an' him dead, 'at when my time comes I'll be rale willin' to

---

72 Gien (Sc.): given (as here) or giving.
73 Fell (Sc.): here, great or important (*SND* I.6).
74 Genesis 16.13: Hagar's words on being told by an angel that her son by Abraham will 'multiply thy seed exceedingly'.
75 Fore-nichts (Sc.): evenings.

go. I dinna say that to Jamie, because he all trembles; but I'm auld noo, an' I'm no nane loth to gang."

Jess's staff probably had a history before it became hers, for, as known to me, it was always old and black. If we studied them sufficiently we might discover that staves age perceptibly just as the hair turns grey. At the risk of being thought fanciful I dare to say that in inanimate objects, as in ourselves, there is honourable and shameful old age, and that to me Jess's staff was a symbol of the good, the true. It rested against her in the window, and she was so helpless without it when on her feet, that to those who saw much of her it was part of herself. The staff was very short, nearly a foot having been cut, as I think she once told me herself, from the original, of which to make a porridge thieval (or stick with which to stir porridge), and in moving Jess leant heavily on it. Had she stood erect it would not have touched the floor. This was the staff that Jess shook so joyfully at her boy the forenoon in May when he ran out to his death.[76] Joey, however, was associated in Jess's memory with her staff in less painful ways. When she spoke of him she took the dwarf of a staff in her hands and looked at it softly.

"It's hard to me," she would say, "to believe 'at twa an' twenty years hae come and gone since the nicht Joey hod (hid) my staff. Ay, but Hendry was straucht in thae days by what he is noo, an' Jamie wasna born.[77] Twa an' twenty years come the back end o' the year, an' it wasna thocht 'at I could live through the winter. 'Ye'll no last mair than anither month, Jess,' was what my sister Bell said, when she came to see me, and yet here I am aye sittin' at my window, an' Bell's been i' the kirkyard this dozen years.

"Leeby was saxteen month younger than Joey, an' mair quiet like. Her heart was juist set on helpin' aboot the hoose, an' though she was but fower year auld she could kindle the fire an' red up (clean up) the room. Leeby's been my savin' ever since she was fower year auld. Ay, but it was Joey 'at hung aboot me maist, an' he took notice 'at I wasna gaen out as I used to do. Since sune after my marriage I've needed the stick, but there was days 'at I could gang across the road an' sit on a stane. Joey kent there was something wrang when I had to gie that up, an' syne he noticed 'at I couldna even gang to the window unless Hendry kind o' carried me.[78] Na, ye wouldna think 'at there could hae been days when Hendry did that, but he did. He was a sort o' ashamed if ony o' the neighbours saw him so affectionate like, but he was terrible taen up aboot me. His loom was doon at T'nowhead's Bell's father's, an' often he cam awa up to see if I was ony better. He didna lat on to the other weavers 'at he was comin' to see what like I was. Na, he juist said he'd forgotten a pirn, or his cruizey lamp, or onything.[79] Ah, but he didna mak nae pretence o' no carin' for me aince he was inside the hoose. He came crawlin' to the bed no to wauken me if I was sleepin', an' mony a time I made belief 'at I was, juist to please him. It was an awfu' business on him to hae a young wife sae helpless, but he wasna the man to cast that at me. I mind o' sayin' to him one day in my bed, 'Ye made a poor bargain, Hendry, when ye took me.' But he says, 'Not one soul in Thrums 'll daur say that to me but yersel, Jess. Na, na, my dawty, you're the wuman o' my choice;[80] there's juist one wuman i' the warld to me, an' that's you, my ain Jess.' Twa an' twenty years syne. Ay, Hendry called me fond names like thae, no everyday names. What a straucht man he was!

76   Forenoon (Sc.): morning.
77   Straucht (Sc.): straight, i.e. not yet bent-backed by his years at the loom; though at the end of the following paragraph the word seems to have moral connotations as well.
78   Syne (Sc.): here, then.
79   Pirn: 'a weaver's spool for holding his weft yarn in the shuttle' (*SND*); cruizey lamp: old-fashioned iron oil-lamp (both Sc.).
80   Dawty (Sc.): pet.

"The doctor had said he could do no more for me, an' Hendry was the only ane 'at didna gie me up. The bairns, of course, didna understan', and Joey would come into the bed an' play on the top o' me. Hendry would hae ta'en him awa, but I liked to hae 'im. Ye see, we was lang married afore we had a bairn, an' though I couldna bear ony other weight on me, Joey didna hurt me, somehoo. I liked to hae 'im so close to me.

"It was through that 'at he came to bury my staff. I couldna help often thinkin' o' what like the hoose would be when I was gone, an' aboot Leeby an' Joey left so young. So, when I could say it without greetin', I said to Joey 'at I was goin' far awa, an' would he be a terrible guid laddie to his father and Leeby when I was gone?[81] He aye juist said, 'Dinna gang, mother, dinna gang,' but one day Hendry came in frae his loom, and says Joey, 'Father, whaur's my mother gaen to, awa frae us?' I'll never forget Hendry's face. His mooth juist opened an' shut twa or three times, an' he walked quick ben to the room. I cried oot to him to come back, but he didna come, so I sent Joey for him. Joey came runnin' back to me sayin', 'Mother, mother, am awfu' fleid (frightened), for my father's greetin' sair.'

"A' thae things took a haud o' Joey, an' he ended in gien us a fleg (fright). I was sleepin' ill at the time, an' Hendry was ben sleepin' in the room wi' Leeby, Joey bein' wi' me. Ay, weel, one nicht I woke up in the dark an' put oot my hand to 'im, an' he wasna there. I sat up wi' a terrible start, an' syne I kent by the cauld 'at the door maun be open. I cried oot quick to Hendry, but he was a soond sleeper, an' he didna hear me. Ay, I dinna ken hoo I did it, but I got ben to the room an' shook him up. I was near daft wi' fear when I saw Leeby wasna there either. Hendry couldna tak it in a' at aince, but sune he had his trousers on, an' he made me lie down on his bed. He said he wouldna move till I did it, or I wouldna hae dune it. As sune as he was oot o' the hoose crying their names I sat up in my bed listenin'. Sune I heard speakin', an' in a minute Leeby comes runnin' in to me, roarin' an' greetin'. She was barefeeted, and had juist her nichtgown on, an' her teeth was chatterin'. I took her into the bed, but it was an hour afore she could tell me onything, she was in sic a state.

"Sune after Hendry came in carryin' Joey. Joey was as naked as Leeby, and as cauld as lead, but he wasna greetin'. Instead o' that he was awfu' satisfied like, and for all Hendry threatened to lick him he wouldna tell what he an' Leeby had been doin'.[82] He says, though, says he, 'Ye'll no gang awa noo, mother; no, ye'll bide noo.' My bonny laddie, I didna fathom him at the time.

"It was Leeby 'at I got it frae. Ye see, Joey had never seen me gaen ony gait withoot my staff, an' he thocht if he hod it I wouldna be able to gang awa. Ay, he planned it all oot, though he was but a bairn, an' lay watchin' me in my bed till I fell asleep. Syne he creepit oot o' the bed, an' got the staff, and gaed ben for Leeby. She was fleid, but he said it was the only wy to mak me 'at I couldna gang awa. It was juist ower there whaur thae cabbages is 'at he dug the hole wi' a spade, an' buried the staff. Hendry dug it up next mornin'."

CHAPTER VII.

THE STATEMENT OF TIBBIE BIRSE.

ON a Thursday Pete Lownie was buried, and when Hendry returned from the funeral Jess asked if Davit Lunan had been there.

81 Greetin' (Sc.): crying, weeping.
82 Lick: beat (*OED* 6).

"Na," said Hendry, who was shut up in the closet-bed, taking off his blacks, "I heard tell he wasna bidden."

"Yea, yea," said Jess, nodding to me significantly. "Ay, weel," she added, "we'll be hae'n Tibbie ower here on Saturday to deve's (weary us) to death aboot it."

Tibbie, Davit's wife, was sister to Marget, Pete's widow, and she generally did visit Jess on Saturday night to talk about Marget, who was fast becoming one of the most fashionable persons in Thrums. Tibbie was hopelessly plebeian. She was none of your proud kind, and if I entered the kitchen when she was there she pretended not to see me, so that, if I chose, I might escape without speaking to the like of her. I always grabbed her hand, however, in a frank way.

On Saturday Tibbie made her appearance. From the rapidity of her walk, and the way she was sucking in her mouth, I knew that she had strange things to unfold. She had pinned a grey shawl about her shoulders, and wore a black mutch over her dangling grey curls.

"It's you, Tibbie," I heard Jess say, as the door opened.

Tibbie did not knock, not considering herself grand enough for ceremony, and indeed Jess would have resented her knocking. On the other hand, when Leeby visited Tibbie, she knocked as politely as if she were collecting for the precentor's present.[83] All this showed that we were superior socially to Tibbie.

"Ay, hoo are ye, Jess?" Tibbie said.

"Muckle aboot it," answered Jess; "juist aff an' on; ay, an' hoo hae ye been yersel?"

"Ou," said Tibbie.

I wish I could write "ou" as Tibbie said it. With her it was usually a sentence in itself. Sometimes it was a mere bark, again it expressed indignation, surprise, rapture; it might be a check upon emotion or a way of leading up to it, and often it lasted for half a minute. In this instance it was, I should say, an intimation that if Jess was ready Tibbie would begin.

"So Pete Lownie's gone," said Jess, whom I could not see from ben the house. I had a good glimpse of Tibbie, however, through the open doorways. She had the armchair on the south side, as she would have said, of the fireplace.

"He's awa," assented Tibbie, primly.

I heard the lid of the kettle dancing, and then came a prolonged "ou." Tibbie bent forward to whisper, and if she had anything terrible to tell I was glad of that, for when she whispered I heard her best. For a time only a murmur of words reached me, distant music with an "ou" now and again that fired Tibbie as the beating of his drum may rouse the martial spirit of a drummer. At last our visitor broke into an agitated whisper, and it was only when she stopped whispering, as she did now and again, that I ceased to hear her. Jess evidently put a question at times, but so politely (for she had on her best wrapper) that I did not catch a word.

"Though I should be struck deid this nicht," Tibbie whispered, and the sibilants hissed between her few remaining teeth, "I wasna sae muckle as speired to the layin' oot.[84] There was Mysy Cruickshanks there, an' Kitty Wobster 'at was nae friends to the corpse to speak o', but Marget passed by me, me 'at is her ain flesh an' blood, though it mayna be for the like o' me to say it. It's gospel truth, Jess, I tell ye, when I say 'at, for all I ken officially, as ye micht say, Pete Lownie may be weel an' hearty this day. If I

83 The Kirk regarded musical instruments inside the church as sinful; in the absence of an organ, the precentor's job was to lead the singing. This is still the practice in some churches in the islands today.

84 Note that only men attend the funeral itself; women attend the 'laying out' of the body beforehand.

was to meet Marget in the face I couldna say he was deid, though I ken 'at the wricht coffined him;[85] na, an' what's mair, I wouldna gie Marget the satisfaction o' hearin' me say it. No, Jess, I tell ye, I dinna pertend to be on an equalty wi' Marget, but equalty or no equalty, a body has her feelings, an' lat on 'at I ken Pete's gone I will not. Eh? Ou, weel. . . .

"Na faags a; na, na.[86] I ken my place better than to gang near Marget. I dinna deny 'at she's grand by me,[87] an' her keeps a bakehoose o' her ain, an' glad am I to see her doin' sae weel, but let me tell ye this, Jess, 'Pride goeth before a fall.' Yes, it does, it's Scripture; ay, it's nae mak-up o' mine, it's Scripture.[88] And this I will say, though kennin' my place, 'at Davit Lunan is as dainty a man as is in Thrums, an' there's no one 'at's better behaved at a bural, being particularly wise-like (presentable) in's blacks, an' them spleet new. Na, na, Jess, Davit may hae his faults an' tak a dram at times like anither, but he would shame naebody at a bural, an' Marget deleeberately insulted him, no speirin' him to Pete's. What's mair, when the minister cried in to see me yesterday, an' me on the floor washin', says he, 'So Marget's lost her man,' an' I said, 'Say ye so, na?' for let on 'at I kent, an' neither me at the layin' oot nor Davit Lunan at the funeral, I would not.

"'David should hae gone to the funeral,' says the minister, 'for I doubt not he was only omitted in the invitations by a mistake.'

"Ay, it was weel meant, but says I, Jess, says I, 'As lang as am livin' to tak chairge o' 'im, Davit Lunan gangs to nae burals 'at he's no bidden to. An' I tell ye,' I says to the minister, 'if there was one body 'at had a richt to be at the bural o' Pete Lownie,[89] it was Davit Lunan, him bein' my man an' Marget my ain sister. Yes,' says I, though am no o' the boastin' kind, 'Davit had maist richt to be there next to Pete 'imsel.' Ou, Jess. . . .

"This is no a maiter I like to speak aboot; na, I dinna care to mention it, but the neighbours is nat'rally ta'en up aboot it, and Chirsty Tosh was sayin' what would I wager 'at Marget hadna sent the minister to hint 'at Davit's bein' over-lookit in the invitations was juist an accident? Losh, losh, Jess, to think 'at a woman could hae the michty assurance to mak a tool o' the very minister! But, sal, as far as that gangs, Marget would do it, an' gae twice to the kirk next Sabbath, too; but if she thinks she's to get ower me like that, she taks me for a bigger fule than I tak her for. Na, na, Marget, ye dinna draw my leg (deceive me). Ou, no. . . .

"Mind ye, Jess, I hae no desire to be friends wi' Marget. Naething could be farrer frae my wish than to hae helpit in the layin' oot o' Pete Lownie, an', I assure ye, Davit wasna keen to gang to the bural. 'If they dinna want me to their burals,' Davit says, 'they hae nae mair to do than to say sae. But I warn ye, Tibbie,' he says, 'if there's a bural frae this hoose, be it your bural, or be it my bural, not one o' the family o' Lownies casts their shadows upon the corp.' Thae was the very words Davit said to me as we watched the hearse frae the sky-licht. Ay, he bore up wonderfu', but he felt it, Jess — he felt it, as I could tell by his takkin' to drink again that very nicht. Jess, Jess. . . .

"Marget's getting waur an' waur? Ay, ye may say so, though I'll say naething agin her mysel. Of coorse am no on equalty wi' her, especially since she had the bell put up in her hoose. Ou, I hinna seen it mysel, na, I never gang near the hoose, an', as mony a body can tell ye, when I do hae to gang that wy I mak my feet my friend. Ay, but as

85 Wricht (Sc.): wright.
86 'Faags' is Barrie's Angus version of the intensifier fegs (Sc.): indeed, truly.
87 Grand by me (Sc.): grand in comparison to me.
88 Tibbie is right: 'Pride goeth before destruction, and an haughty spirit before a fall' (Proverbs 16.18).
89 Body (Sc.): here, person.

I was sayin', Marget's sae grand noo 'at she has a bell in the hoose. As I understan', there's a rope in the wast room, an' when ye pu' it a bell rings in the east room. Weel, when Marget has company at their tea in the wast room, an' they need mair watter or scones or onything, she rises an' rings the bell. Syne Jean, the auldest lassie, gets up frae the table an' lifts the jug or the plates an' gaes awa ben to the east room for what's wanted. Ay, it's a wy o' doin' 'at's juist like the gentry, but I'll tell ye, Jess, Pete juist fair hated the soond o' that bell, an' there's them 'at says it was the death o' 'im. To think o' Marget ha'en sic an establishment! . . .

"Na, I hinna seen the mournin', I've heard o't. Na, if Marget doesna tell me naething, am no the kind to speir naething, an' though I'll be at the kirk the morn, I winna turn my heid to look at the mournin'. But it's fac as death I ken frae Janet McQuhatty 'at the bonnet's a' crape, an' three yairds o' crape on the dress, the which Marget calls a costume.[90] . . . Ay, I wouldna wonder but what it was hale watter the morn, for it looks michty like rain, an' if it is it'll serve Marget richt, an' mebbe bring doon her pride a wee.[91] No 'at I want to see her humbled, for, in coorse, she's grand by the like o' me. Ou, but . . ."

CHAPTER VIII.

A CLOAK WITH BEADS.

ON weekdays the women who passed the window were meagrely dressed; mothers in draggled winsey gowns, carrying infants that were armfuls of grandeur.[92] The Sabbath clothed every one in her best, and then the women went by with their hands spread out. When I was with Hendry cloaks with beads were the fashion, and Jess sighed as she looked at them. They were known in Thrums as the Eleven and a Bits (threepenny bits), that being their price at Kyowowy's in the square. Kyowowy means finicky, and applied to the draper by general consent. No doubt it was very characteristic to call the cloaks by their market value. In the glen my scholars still talk of their school-books as the tupenny, the fowerpenny, the saxpenny. They finish their education with the tenpenny.

Jess's opportunity for handling the garments that others of her sex could finger in shops was when she had guests to tea. Persons who merely dropped in and remained to tea got their meal, as a rule, in the kitchen. They had nothing on that Jess could not easily take in as she talked to them. But when they came by special invitation, the meal was served in the room, the guests' things being left on the kitchen bed. Jess not being able to go ben the house, had to be left with the things. When the time to go arrived, these were found on the bed, just as they had been placed there, but Jess could now tell Leeby whether they were imitation, why Bell Elshioner's feather went far round the bonnet, and Chirsty Lownie's reason for always holding her left arm fast against her side when she went abroad in the black jacket. Ever since My Hobart's eleven and a bit was left on the kitchen bed Jess had hungered for a cloak with beads. My's was the very marrows of the one T'nowhead's wife got in Dundee for ten-and-sixpence;[93] indeed,

---

90 Fac as death (Sc.): as sure as death.
91 Hale: *SND* lists this as a verb, meaning 'to flow copiously, run down, pour off'. A wee (Sc.): a bit.
92 Winsey was a hard-wearing mixture of linen and wool.
93 The very marrows of (Sc.): the exact match of.

we would have thought that 'Lisbeth's also came from Kyowowy's had not Sanders Elshioner's sister seen her go into the Dundee shop with T'nowhead (who was loth), and hung about to discover what she was after.

Hendry was not quick at reading faces like Tammas Haggart, but the wistful look on Jess's face when there was talk of eleven and a bits had its meaning for him.

"They're grand to look at, no doubt," I have heard him say to Jess, "but they're richt annoyin'. That new wife o' Peter Dickie's had ane on in the kirk last Sabbath, an' wi' her sittin' juist afore us I couldna listen to the sermon for tryin' to count the beads."

Hendry made his way into these gossips uninvited, for his opinions on dress were considered contemptible, though he was worth consulting on material. Jess and Leeby discussed many things in his presence, confident that his ears were not doing their work; but every now and then it was discovered that he had been hearkening greedily. If the subject was dress, he might then become a little irritating.

"Oh, they're grand," Jess admitted; "they set a body aff oncommon."

"They would be no use to you," said Hendry, "for ye canna wear them except ootside."

"A body doesna buy cloaks to be wearin' at them steady," retorted Jess.

"No, no, but you could never wear yours though ye had ane."

"I dinna want ane. They're far ower grand for the like o' me."

"They're no nae sic thing. Am thinkin' ye're juist as fit to wear an eleven and a bit as My Hobart."

"Weel, mebbe I am, but it's oot o' the queistion gettin' ane, they're sic a price."

"Ay, an' though we had the siller, it would surely be an awfu' like thing to buy a cloak 'at ye could never wear?"

"Ou, but I dinna want ane."

Jess spoke so mournfully that Hendry became enraged.

"It's most michty," he said, " 'at ye would gang an' set yer heart on sic a completely useless thing."

"I hinna set my heart on't."

"Dinna blether. Ye've been speakin' aboot thae eleven and a bits to Leeby, aff an' on, for twa month."

Then Hendry hobbled off to his loom, and Jess gave me a look which meant that men are trying at the best, once you are tied to them.

The cloaks continued to turn up in conversation, and Hendry poured scorn upon Jess's weakness, telling her she would be better employed mending his trousers than brooding over an eleven and a bit that would have to spend its life in a drawer. An outsider would have thought that Hendry was positively cruel to Jess. He seemed to take a delight in finding that she had neglected to sew a button on his waistcoat. His real joy, however, was the knowledge that she sewed as no other woman in Thrums could sew. Jess had a genius for making new garments out of old ones, and Hendry never tired of gloating over her cleverness so long as she was not present. He was always athirst for fresh proofs of it, and these were forthcoming every day. Sparing were his words of praise to herself, but in the evening he generally had a smoke with me in the attic, and then the thought of Jess made him chuckle till his pipe went out. When he smoked he grunted as if in pain, though this really added to the enjoyment.

"It doesna matter," he would say to me, "what Jess turns her hand to, she can mak ony mortal thing. She doesna need nae teachin'; na, juist gie her a guid look at onything, be it clothes, or furniture, or in the bakin' line, it's all the same to her. She'll mak another exactly like it. Ye canna beat her. Her bannocks is so superior 'at a Tilliedrum woman took to her bed after tastin' them,[94] an' when the lawyer has company his wife gets Jess to mak some bannocks for her an' syne pretends they're her ain bakin'. Ay, there's a story aboot that. One day the auld doctor, him 'at's deid, was at his tea at the lawyer's, an' says the guidwife, 'Try the cakes, Mr. Riach; they're my own bakin'.' Weel, he was a fearsomely outspoken man, the doctor, an' nae suner had he the bannock atween his teeth, for he didna stop to swallow't, than he says, 'Mistress Geddie,' says he, 'I wasna born on a Sabbath. Na, na, you're no the first grand leddy 'at has gien me bannocks as their ain bakin' 'at was baked and fired by Jess Logan, her 'at's Hendry McQumpha's wife.' Ay, they say the lawyer's wife didna ken which wy to look, she was that mortified. It's juist the same wi' sewin'. There's wys o' ornamentin' christenin' robes an' the like 'at's kent to naebody but herself; an' as for stockin's, weel, though I've seen her mak sae mony, she amazes me yet. I mind o' a furry waistcoat I aince had. Weel, when it was fell dune, do you think she gae it awa to some gaen aboot body (vagrant)? Na, she made it into a richt neat coat to Jamie, wha was a bit laddie at the time. When he grew out o' it, she made a slipbody o't for hersel. Ay, I dinna ken a' the different things it became, but the last time I saw it was ben in the room, whaur she'd covered a footstool wi' 't. Yes, Jess is the cleverest crittur I ever saw. Leeby's handy, but she's no a patch on her mother."

I sometimes repeated these panegyrics to Jess. She merely smiled, and said that men haver most terrible when they are not at their work.[95]

Hendry tried Jess sorely over the cloaks, and a time came when, only by exasperating her, could he get her to reply to his sallies.

"Wha wants an eleven an' a bit?" she retorted now and again.

"It's you 'at wants it," said Hendry, promptly.

"Did I ever say I wanted ane? What use could I hae for't?"

"That's the queistion," said Hendry. "Ye canna gang the length o' the door, so ye would never be able to wear't."

"Ay, weel," replied Jess, "I'll never hae the chance o' no bein' able to wear't, for, hooever muckle I wanted it, I couldna get it."

Jess's infatuation had in time the effect of making Hendry uncomfortable. In the attic he delivered himself of such sentiments as these:

"There's nae understandin' a woman. There's Jess 'at hasna her equal for cleverness in Thrums, man or woman, an' yet she's fair skeered about thae cloaks.[96] Aince a woman sets her mind on something to wear, she's mair onreasonable than the stupidest man. Ay, it micht mak them humble to see hoo foolish they are syne. No, but it doesna do't.

"If it was a thing to be useful noo, I wouldna think the same o't, but she could never wear't. She kens she could never wear't, an' yet she's juist as keen to hae't.

"I dinna like to see her so wantin' a thing, an' no able to get it. But it's an awfu' sum, eleven an' a bit."

He tried to argue with her further.

"If ye had eleven an' a bit to fling awa," he said, "ye dinna mean to tell me 'at ye would buy a cloak instead o' cloth for a gown, or flannel for petticoats, or some useful thing?"

"As sure as death," said Jess, with unwonted vehemence, "if a cloak I could get, a cloak I would buy."

---

94 Bannocks: thick cakes of oatmeal or another grain, baked on a gridle.
95 Haver (Sc.): talk nonsense.
96 Skeered: *SND* only gives this verb the sense of 'scared', which makes no sense here; but as an adjective 'skeer' can mean 'agitated' or 'restive', which is closer to Barrie's usage.

Hendry came up to tell me what Jess had said.

"It's a michty infatooation," he said, "but it shows hoo her heart's set on thae cloaks."

"Aince ye had it," he argued with her, "ye would juist hae to lock it awa in the drawers. Ye would never even be seein' 't."

"Ay, would I," said Jess. "I would often tak it oot an' look at it. Ay, an' I would aye ken it was there."

"But naebody would ken ye had it but yersel," said Hendry, who had a vague notion that this was a telling objection.

"Would they no?" answered Jess. "It would be a' through the toon afore nicht."

"Weel, all I can say," said Hendry, "is 'at ye're terrible foolish to tak the want o' sic a useless thing to heart."

"Am no takkin' 't to heart," retorted Jess, as usual.

Jess needed many things in her days that poverty kept from her to the end, and the cloak was merely a luxury. She would soon have let it slip by as something unattainable had not Hendry encouraged it to rankle in her mind. I cannot say when he first determined that Jess should have a cloak, come the money as it liked, for he was too ashamed of his weakness to admit his project to me. I remember, however, his saying to Jess one day:

"I'll warrant ye could mak a cloak yersel the marrows o' thae eleven and a bits, at half the price?"

"It would cost," said Jess, "sax an' saxpence, exactly. The, cloth would be five shillins, an' the beads a shillin'. I have some braid 'at would do fine for the front, but the buttons would be saxpence."

"Ye're sure o' that?"

"I ken fine, for I got Leeby to price the things in the shop."

"Ay, but it maun be ill to shape the cloaks richt. There was a queer cut aboot that ane Peter Dickie's new wife had on."

"Queer cut or no queer cut," said Jess, "I took the shape o' My Hobart's ane the day she was here at her tea, an' I could mak the identical o't for sax an' sax."

"I dinna believe't," said Hendry, but when he and I were alone he told me, "There's no a doubt she could mak it. Ye heard her say she had taen the shape? Ay, that shows she's rale set on a cloak."

Had Jess known that Hendry had been saving up for months to buy her material for a cloak, she would not have let him do it. She could not know, however, for all the time he was scraping together his pence, he kept up a ring-ding-dang about her folly. Hendry gave Jess all the wages he weaved, except threepence weekly, most of which went in tobacco and snuff. The dulseman had perhaps a halfpenny from him in the fortnight. I noticed that for a long time Hendry neither smoked nor snuffed, and I knew that for years he had carried a shilling in his snuff-mull. The remainder of the money he must have made by extra work at his loom, by working harder, for he could scarcely have worked longer.

It was one day shortly before Jamie's return to Thrums that Jess saw Hendry pass the house and go down the brae when he ought to have come in to his brose.[97] She sat at the window watching for him, and by and by he reappeared, carrying a parcel.

"Whaur on earth hae ye been?" she asked, "an' what's that you're carryin'?"

"Did ye think it was an eleven an' a bit?" said Hendry.

"No, I didna," answered Jess, indignantly.

Then Hendry slowly undid the knots of the string with which the parcel was tied. He took off the brown paper.

---

97 Brose is oatmeal with boiling water poured over it.

"There's yer cloth," he said, "an' here's one an' saxpence for the beads an' the buttons." While Jess still stared he followed me ben the house.

"It's a terrible haver," he said, apologetically, "but she had set her heart on't."

CHAPTER IX.

THE POWER OF BEAUTY.

ONE evening there was such a gathering at the pig-sty that Hendry and I could not get a board to lay our backs against. Circumstances had pushed Pete Elshioner into the place of honour that belonged by right of mental powers to Tammas Haggart, and Tammas was sitting rather sullenly on the bucket, boring a hole in the pig with his sarcastic eye. Pete was passing round a card, and in time it reached me. "With Mr. and Mrs. David Alexander's compliments," was printed on it, and Pete leered triumphantly at us as it went the round.

"Weel, what think ye?" he asked, with a pretence at modesty.

"Ou," said T'nowhead, looking at the others like one who asked a question, "ou, I think; ay, ay."

The others seemed to agree with him, all but Tammas, who did not care to tie himself down to an opinion.

"Ou ay," T'nowhead continued, more confidently, "it is so, deceededly."

"Ye'll no ken," said Pete, chuckling, "what it means?"

"Na," the farmer admitted, "na, I canna say I exac'ly ken that."

"I ken, though," said Tammas, in his keen way.

"Weel, then, what is't?" demanded Pete, who had never properly come under Tammas's spell.

"I ken," said Tammas.

"Oot wi't then."

"I dinna say it's lyin' on my tongue," Tammas replied, in a tone of reproof, "but if ye'll juist speak awa aboot some other thing for a meenute or twa, I'll tell ye syne."

Hendry said that this was only reasonable, but we could think of no subject at the moment, so we only stared at Tammas, and waited.

"I fathomed it," he said at last, "as sune as my een lichted on't.[98] It's one o' the bit cards 'at grand fowk slip 'aneath doors when they mak calls, an' their friends is no in. Ay, that's what it is."

"I dinna say ye're wrang," Pete answered, a little annoyed. "Ay, weel, lads, of course David Alexander's oor Dite as we called 'im, Dite Elshioner, an' that's his wy o' signifyin' to us 'at he's married."

"I assure ye," said Hendry, "Dite's doin' the thing in style."

"Ay, we said that when the card arrived," Pete admitted.

"I kent," said Tammas, " 'at that was the wy grand fowk did when they got married. I've kent it a lang time. It's no nae surprise to me."

"He's been lang in marryin'," Hookey Crewe said.

"He was thirty at Martinmas," said Pete.

"Thirty, was he?" said Hookey. "Man, I'd buried twa wives by the time I was that age, an' was castin' aboot for a third."

"I mind o' them," Hendry interposed.

---

98   Een (Sc.): eyes.

"Ay," Hookey said, "the first twa was angels." There he paused. "An' so's the third," he added, "in many respects."

"But wha's the woman Dite's ta'en?" T'nowhead or some one of the more silent members of the company asked of Pete.

"Ou, we dinna ken wha she is," answered Pete; "but she'll be some Glasca lassie, for he's there noo. Look, lads, look at this. He sent this at the same time; it's her picture." Pete produced the silhouette of a young lady, and handed it round.

"What do ye think?" he asked.

"I assure ye!" said Hookey.

"Sal," said Hendry, even more charmed, "Dite's done weel."

"Lat's see her in a better licht," said Tammas.

He stood up and examined the photograph narrowly, while Pete fidgeted with his legs.[99]

"Fairish," said Tammas at last. "Ou, ay; no what I would selec' mysel, but a dainty bit stocky![100] Ou, a tasty crittury! ay, an' she's weel in order. Lads, she's a fine stoot kimmer."

"I conseeder her a beauty," said Pete, aggressively.

"She's a' that," said Hendry.

"A' I can say," said Hookey, "is 'at she taks me most michty."

"She's no a beauty," Tammas maintained; "na, she doesna juist come up to that; but I dinna deny but what she's weel faured."[101]

"What faut do ye find wi' her, Tammas?" asked Hendry.

"Conseedered critically," said Tammas, holding the photograph at arm's length, "I would say 'at she—let's see noo; ay, I would say 'at she's defeecient in genteelity."

"Havers," said Pete.

"Na," said Tammas, "no when conseedered critically. Ye see she's drawn lauchin'; an' the genteel thing's no to lauch, but juist to put on a bit smirk. Ay, that's the genteel thing."

"A smile, they ca' it," interposed T'nowhead.

"I said a smile," continued Tammas. "Then there's her waist. I say naething agin her waist, speakin' in the ord'nar meanin'; but, conseedered critically, there's a want o' suppleness, as ye micht say, aboot it. Ay, it doesna compare wi' the waist o'—" (Here Tammas mentioned a young lady who had recently married into a local county family.)

"That was a pretty tiddy,"[102] said Hookey. "Ou, losh, ay! it made me a kind o' queery to look at her."

"Ye're ower kyow-owy (particular), Tammas," said Pete.

"I may be, Pete," Tammas admitted; "but I maun say I'm fond o' a bonny-looken wuman, an' no aisy to please: na, I'm nat'rally ane o' the critical kind."

---

99 Commercial photographic studios were working in Glasgow in the 1840s, but these offered expensive portraits in larger formats, using the Daguerreotype process from which multiple copies could not be easily produced: it is unlikely that Mr David Alexander has sent his country cousin one of *these*. The purpose for which this picture is being used instead recalls the craze for photographic *carte de visite* which swept the British middle classes in the 1860s, made possible by new techniques which allowed the cheap multiplication of small prints. But this is significantly later than the period suggested by other aspects of the narrative: see notes 2 and 135.

100 According to *SND*, a 'stock' or 'stocky' is usually a bloke; only in Angus can it also apply to women.

101 Weel faured (Sc.): well-favoured, good-looking.

102 Tiddy (Sc.): 'having a good figure, shapely, plump, buxom' (*SND*).

"It's extror'nar," said T'nowhead, "what a poo'er beauty has. I mind when I was a callant readin' aboot Mary Queen o' Scots till I was fair mad, lads;[103] yes, I was fair mad at her bein' deid. Ou, I could hardly sleep at nichts for thinking o' her."

"Mary was spunky as weel as a beauty," said Hookey, "an' that's the kind I like. Lads, what a persuasive tid she was!"

"She got roond the men," said Hendry, "ay, she turned them roond her finger. That's the warst o' thae beauties."

"I dinna gainsay," said T'nowhead, "but what there was a little o' the deevil in Mary, the crittur."

Here T'nowhead chuckled, and then looked scared.

"What Mary needed," said Tammas, "was a strong man to manage her."

"Ay, man, but it's ill to manage thae beauties. They gie ye a glint o' their een, an' syne whaur are ye?"

"Ah, they can be managed," said Tammas, complacently. "There's naebody nat'rally safter wi' a pretty stocky o' a bit wumany than mysel;[104] but for a' that, if I had been Mary's man I would hae stood nane o' her tantrums. 'Na, Mary, my lass,' I would hae said, 'this winna do; na, na, ye're a bonny body, but ye maun mind 'at man's the superior; ay, man's the lord o' creation, an' so ye maun juist sing sma'.' That's hoo I would hae managed Mary, the speerity crittur 'at she was."

"Ye would hae haen yer wark cut oot for ye, Tammas."

"Ilka mornin'," pursued Tammas, "I would hae said to her, 'Mary,' I would hae said, 'wha's to wear thae breeks the day, you or me?' Ay, syne I would hae ordered her to kindle the fire, or if I had been the king, of coorse I would hae telt her instead to ring the bell an' hae the cloth laid for the breakfast. Ay, that's the wy to mak the like o' Mary respec ye."

Pete and I left them talking. He had written a letter to David Alexander, and wanted me to "back" it.[105]

CHAPTER X.

A MAGNUM OPUS.

TWO Bibles, a volume of sermons by the learned Dr. Isaac Barrow, a few numbers of the *Cheap Magazine*, that had strayed from Dunfermline, and a "Pilgrim's Progress," were the works that lay conspicuous ben in the room. Hendry had also a copy of Burns, whom he always quoted in the complete poem, and a collection of legends in song and prose, that Leeby kept out of sight in a drawer.

The weight of my box of books was a subject Hendry was very willing to shake his head over, but he never showed any desire to take off the lid. Jess, however, was more curious; indeed, she would have been an omnivorous devourer of books had it not been for her conviction that reading was idling. Until I found her out she never allowed to me that Leeby brought her my books one at a time. Some of them were novels, and Jess took about ten minutes to each. She confessed that what she read was only the last chapter, owing to a consuming curiosity to know whether "she got him."

---

103 Callant (Sc.): young man, lad.
104 Safter (Sc.): softer.
105 That is, address it.

She read all the London part, however, of "The Heart of Midlothian," because London was where Jamie lived, and she and I had a discussion about it which ended in her remembering that Thrums once had an author of its own.

"Bring oot the book," she said to Leeby, "it was put awa i' the bottom drawer ben i' the room sax year syne, an' I sepad it's there yet."[106]

Leeby came but with a faded little book, the title already rubbed from its shabby brown covers. I opened it, and then all at once I saw before me again the man who wrote and printed it and died. He came hobbling up the brae, so bent that his body was almost at right angles to his legs, and his broken silk hat was carefully brushed as in the days when Janet, his sister, lived. There he stood at the top of the brae, panting.

I was but a boy when Jimsy Duthie turned the corner of the brae for the last time, with a score of mourners behind him. While I knew him there was no Janet to run to the door to see if he was coming. So occupied was Jimsy with the great affair of his life, which was brewing for thirty years, that his neighbours saw how he missed his sister better than he realized it himself. Only his hat was no longer carefully brushed, and his coat hung awry, and there was sometimes little reason why he should go home to dinner. It is for the sake of Janet who adored him that we should remember Jimsy in the days before she died.

Jimsy was a poet, and for the space of thirty years he lived in a great epic on the Millennium. This is the book presented to me by Jess, that lies so quietly on my topmost shelf now. Open it, however, and you will find that the work is entitled "The Millennium: an Epic Poem, in Twelve Books: by James Duthie." In the little hole in his wall where Jimsy kept his books there was, I have no doubt—for his effects were rouped before I knew him except by name—a well-read copy of "Paradise Lost." Some people would smile, perhaps, if they read the two epics side by side, and others might sigh, for there is a great deal in "The Millennium" that Milton could take credit for. Jimsy had educated himself, after the idea of writing something that the world would not willingly let die came to him, and he began his book before his education was complete. So far as I know, he never wrote a line that had not to do with "The Millennium." He was ever a man sparing of his plural tenses, and "The Millennium" says "has" for "have"; a vain word, indeed, which Thrums would only have permitted as a poetical licence. The one original character in the poem is the devil, of whom Jimsy gives a picture that is startling and graphic, and received the approval of the Auld Licht minister.[107]

By trade Jimsy was a printer, a master-printer with no one under him, and he printed and bound his book, ten copies in all, as well as wrote it. To print the poem took him, I dare say, nearly as long as to write it, and he set up the pages as they were written, one by one. The book is only printed on one side of the leaf, and each page was produced separately like a little hand-bill. Those who may pick up the book—but who will care to do so? — will think that the author or his printer could not spell—but they would not do Jimsy that injustice if they knew the circumstances in which it was produced. He had but a small stock of type, and on many occasions he ran out of a letter. The letter *e* tried him sorely. Those who knew him best say that he tried to think of words without an *e* in them, but when he was baffled he had to use a little *a* or an *o*

---

106 *SND* explains that 'I sepad' is Barrie's version of 'I'se uphaud' (Sc.), literally 'I should uphold', that is 'I'll warrant' or 'I'm sure that'. *A Window in Thrums* is *SND*'s only source for this spelling.

107 The 'Auld Licht' faction were the fundamentalist wing of the Kirk, given in their sermons to vivid descriptions of Hell and its master. The McQumphas are Auld Licht in their strict observation of the Sabbath: see chapter XVIII.

instead. He could print correctly, but in the book there are a good many capital letters in the middle of words, and sometimes there is a note of interrogation after "alas" or "Woes me," because all the notes of exclamation had been used up.

Jimsy never cared to speak about his great poem even to his closest friends, but Janet told how he read it out to her, and that his whole body trembled with excitement while he raised his eyes to heaven as if asking for inspiration that would enable his voice to do justice to his writing. So grand it was, said Janet, that her stocking would slip from her fingers as he read—and Janet's stockings, that she was always knitting when not otherwise engaged, did not slip from her hands readily. After her death he was heard by his neighbours reciting the poem to himself, generally with his door locked. He is said to have declaimed part of it one still evening from the top of the commonty like one addressing a multitude, and the idlers who had crept up to jeer at him fell back when they saw his face. He walked through them, they told, with his old body straight once more, and a queer light playing on his face. His lips are moving as I see him turning the corner of the brae. So he passed from youth to old age, and all his life seemed a dream, except that part of it in which he was writing, or printing, or stitching, or binding "The Millennium." At last the work was completed.

"It is finished," he printed at the end of the last book. "The task of thirty years is over."

It is indeed over. No one ever read "The Millennium." I am not going to sentimentalize over my copy, for how much of it have I read? But neither shall I say that it was written to no end.

You may care to know the last of Jimsy, though in one sense he was blotted out when the last copy was bound. He had saved one hundred pounds by that time, and being now neither able to work nor to live alone, his friends cast about for a home for his remaining years. He was very spent and feeble, yet he had the fear that he might be still alive when all his money was gone. After that was the workhouse. He covered sheets of paper with calculations about how long the hundred pounds would last if he gave away for board and lodgings ten shillings, nine shillings, seven and sixpence a week. At last, with sore misgivings, he went to live with a family who took him for eight shillings. Less than a month afterwards he died.

CHAPTER XI.

THE GHOST CRADLE.

OUR dinner-hour was twelve o'clock, and Hendry, for a not incomprehensible reason, called this meal his brose. Frequently, however, while I was there to share the expense, broth was put on the table, with beef to follow in clean plates, much to Hendry's distress, for the comfortable and usual practice was to eat the beef from the broth-plates. Jess, however, having three whole white plates and two cracked ones, insisted on the meals being taken genteelly, and her husband, with a look at me, gave way.

"Half a pound o' boiling beef, an' a penny bone," was Leeby's almost invariable order when she dealt with the flesher, and Jess had always neighbours poorer than herself who got a plateful of the broth. She never had anything without remembering some old body who would be the better of a little of it.

Among those who must have missed Jess sadly after she was gone was Johnny Proctor, a halfwitted man who, because he could not work, remained straight at a time of life when most weavers, male and female, had lost some inches of their stature. For as far back as my memory goes, Johnny had got his brose three times a week from Jess, his custom being to walk in without ceremony, and, drawing a stool to the table, tell Leeby that he was now ready. One day, however, when I was in the garden putting some rings on a fishing-wand, Johnny pushed by me, with no sign of recognition on his face. I addressed him, and, after pausing undecidedly, he ignored me. When he came to the door, instead of flinging it open and walking in, he knocked primly, which surprised me so much that I followed him.

"Is this whaur Mistress McQumpha lives?" he asked, when Leeby, with a face ready to receive the minister himself, came at length to the door.

I knew that the gentility of the knock had taken both her and her mother aback.

"Hoots, Johnny," said Leeby, "what haver's this? Come awa in."

Johnny seemed annoyed.

"Is this whaur Mistress McQumpha lives?" he repeated.

"Say 'at it is," cried Jess, who was quicker in the uptake than her daughter.

"Of course this is whaur Mistress McQumpha lives," Leeby then said, "as weel ye ken, for ye had yer dinner here no twa hours syne."

"Then," said Johnny, "Mistress Tully's compliments to her, and would she kindly lend the christenin' robe, an' also the tea-tray, if the same be na needed?"

Having delivered his message as instructed, Johnny consented to sit down until the famous christening robe and the tray were ready, but he would not talk, for that was not in the bond. Jess's sweet face beamed over the compliment Mrs. Tully, known on ordinary occasions as Jean McTaggart, had paid her, and, after Johnny had departed laden, she told me how the tray, which had a great bump in the middle, came into her possession.

"Ye've often heard me speak aboot the time when I was a lassie workin' at the farm o' the Bog? Ay, that was afore me an' Hendry kent ane anither, an' I was as fleet on my feet in thae days as Leeby is noo. It was Sam'l Fletcher 'at was the farmer, but he maun hae been gone afore you was mair than born. Mebbe, though, ye ken 'at he was a terrible invalid, an' for the hinmost years o' his life he sat in a muckle chair nicht an' day. Ay, when I took his denner to 'im, on that very tray 'at Johnny cam for, I little thocht 'at by an' by I would be sae keepit in a chair mysel.

"But the thinkin' o' Sam'l Fletcher's case is ane o' the things 'at maks me awfu' thankfu' for the lenient wy the Lord has aye dealt wi' me; for Sam'l couldna move oot o' the chair, aye sleepin' in't at nicht, an' I can come an' gang between mine an' my bed. Mebbe, ye think I'm no much better off than Sam'l, but that's a terrible mistak. What a glory it would hae been to him if he could hae gone frae one end o' the kitchen to the ither. Ay, I'm sure o' that.

"Sam'l was rale weel liked, for he was saft-spoken to everybody, an' fond o' ha'en a gossip wi' ony ane 'at was aboot the farm. We didna care sae muckle for the wife, Eppie Lownie, for she managed the farm, an' she was fell hard an' terrible reserved we thocht, no even likin' ony body to get friendly wi' the mester, as we called Sam'l. Ay, we made a richt mistak."

As I had heard frequently of this queer, mournful mistake made by those who considered Sam'l unfortunate in his wife, I turned Jess on to the main line of her story.

"It was the ghost cradle, as they named it, 'at I meant to tell ye aboot. The Bog was a bigger farm in thae days than noo, but I daursay it has the new steadin' yet. Ay, it winna be new noo, but at the time there was sic a commotion aboot the ghost cradle, they were juist puttin' the new steadin' up. There was sax or mair masons at it, wi' the lads on the farm helpin', an' as they were all sleepin' at the farm, there was great stir aboot the place. I couldna tell ye hoo the story aboot the farm's bein' haunted rose, to begin wi', but I mind fine hoo fleid I was; ay, an' no only me, but every man-body an' woman-body on the farm. It was aye late 'at the soond began, an' we never saw naething, we juist heard it. The masons said they wouldna hae been sae fleid if they could hae seen't, but it never was seen. It had the soond o' a cradle rockin', an' when we lay in our beds hearkenin', it grew louder an' louder till it wasna to be borne, an' the women-folk fair skirled wi' fear.[108] The mester was intimate wi' a' the stories aboot ghosts an' water-kelpies an' sic like, an' we couldna help listenin' to them. But he aye said 'at ghosts 'at was juist heard an' no seen was the maist fearsome an' wicked. For all there was sic fear ower the hale farm-toon 'at naebody would gang ower the door alane after the gloamin' cam,[109] the mester said he wasna fleid to sleep i' the kitchen by 'imsel. We thocht it richt brave o' 'im, for ye see he was as helpless as a bairn.

"Richt queer stories rose aboot the cradle, an' travelled to the ither farms. The wife didna like them ava, for it was said 'at there maun hae been some awful murder o' an infant on the farm, or we wouldna be haunted by a cradle. Syne folk began to mind 'at there had been nae bairns born on the farm as far back as onybody kent, an' it was said 'at some lang syne crime had made the Bog cursed.

"Dinna think 'at we juist lay in our beds or sat round the fire shakkin' wi' fear. Everything 'at could be dune was dune. In the daytime, when naething was heard, the masons explored a' place i' the farm, in the hope o' findin' oot 'at the sound was caused by sic a thing as the wind playin' on the wood in the garret. Even at nichts, when they couldna sleep wi' the soond, I've kent them rise in a body an' gang all ower the house wi' lichts. I've seen them climbin' on the new steadin', crawlin' alang the rafters haudin' their cruizey lamps afore them, an' us women-bodies shiverin' wi' fear at the door. It was on ane o' thae nichts 'at a mason fell off the rafters an' broke his leg. Weel, sic a state was the men in to find oot what it was 'at was terrifyin' them sae muckle, 'at the rest o' them climbed up at aince to the place he'd fallen frae, thinkin' there was something there 'at had fleid 'im. But though they crawled back an' forrit there was naething ava.[110]

"The rockin' was louder, we thocht, after that nicht, an' syne the men said it would go on till somebody was killed. That idea took a richt haud o' them, an' twa ran awa back to Tilliedrum, whaur they had come frae. They gaed thegither i' the middle o' the nicht, an' it was thocht next mornin' 'at the ghost had spirited them awa.

"Ye couldna conceive hoo low-spirited we all were after the masons had gien up hope o' findin' a nat'ral cause for the soond. At ord'nar times there's no ony mair lichtsome place than a farm after the men hae come in to their supper, but at the Bog we sat dour an' sullen; an' there wasna a mason or a farm-servant 'at would gang by 'imsel as far as the end o' the hoose whaur the peats was keepit. The mistress maun hae saved some siller that spring through the Egyptians (gypsies) keepin' awa,[111] for the farm had got sic an ill name, 'at nae tinkler would come near't at nicht. The tailorman an' his laddie, 'at should hae bidden wi' us to sew things for the men, walkit off fair skeered one mornin', an' settled doon at the farm o' Cragiebuckle fower mile awa, whaur our lads had to gae to them. Ay, I mind the tailor's sendin' the laddie for the money owin' him; he hadna the speerit to venture again within soond o' the cradle

---

108 Skirl (Sc.): scream or shriek.
109 Farm-toon: that is, the farm buildings; gloamin': twilight (all Sc.).
110 Forrit (Sc.): forward.
111 Siller (Sc.): silver, i.e. money.

'imsel. The men on the farm, though, couldna blame 'im for that. They were juist as flichtered themsels,[112] an' mony a time I saw them hittin' the dogs for whinin' at the soond. The wy the dogs took on was fearsome in itsel, for they seemed to ken, aye when nicht cam on, 'at the rockin' would sune begin, an' if they werena chained they cam runnin' to the hoose. I hae heard the hale glen fu, as ye micht say, wi' the whinin' o' dogs, for the dogs on the other farms took up the cry, an' in a glen ye can hear soonds terrible far awa at nicht.

"As lang as we sat i' the kitchen, listenin' to what the mester had to say aboot the ghosts in his young days, the cradle would be still, but we were nae suner awa speeritless to our beds than it began, an sometimes it lasted till mornin'. We lookit upon the mester almost wi' awe, sittin' there sae helpless in his chair, an' no fleid to be left alane. He had lang white hair, an' a saft bonny face 'at would hae made 'im respeckit by onybody, an' aye when we speired if he wasna fleid to be left alane, he said, 'Them 'at has a clear conscience has naething to fear frae ghosts.'

"There was some 'at said the curse would never leave the farm till the house was razed to the ground, an' it's the truth I'm tellin' ye when I say there was talk among the men aboot settin' t on fire. The mester was richt stern when he heard o' that, quotin' frae Scripture in a solemn wy 'at abashed the masons, but he said 'at in his opeenion there was a bairn buried on the farm, an' till it was found the cradle would go on rockin'. After that the masons dug in a lot o' places lookin' for the body, an' they found some queer things, too, but never nae sign o' a murdered litlin'.[113] Ay, I dinna ken what would hae happened if the commotion had gaen on muckle langer. One thing I'm sure o' is 'at the mistress would hae gaen daft, she took it a' sae terrible to heart.

"I lauch at it noo, but I tell ye I used to tak my heart to my bed in my mooth. If ye hinna heard the story, I dinna think ye'll be able to guess what the ghost cradle was."

I said I had been trying to think what the tray had to do with it.

"It had everything to do wi't," said Jess "an' if the masons had kent hoo that cradle was rockit, I think they would hae killed the mester. It was Eppie 'at found oot, an' she telt naebody but me, though mony a ane kens noo. I see ye canna mak it oot yet, so I'll tell ye what the cradle was. The tray was keepit against the kitchen wall near the mester, an' he played on't wi' his foot. He made it gang bump bump, an' the soond was juist like a cradle rockin'. Ye could hardly believe sic a thing would hae made that din, but it did, an' ye see we lay in our beds hearkening for't. Ay, when Eppie telt me, I could scarce believe 'at that guid devout-lookin' man could hae been sae wicked. Ye see, when he found hoo terrified we a' were, he keepit it up. The wy Eppie found out i' the tail o' the day was by wonderin' at 'im sleepin' sae muckle in the daytime. He did that so as to be fresh for his sport at nicht. What a fine releegious man we thocht 'im, too!

"Eppie couldna bear the very sicht o' the tray after that, an' she telt me to break it up; but I keepit it, ye see. The lump i' the middle's the mark, as ye may say, o' the auld man's foot."

CHAPTER XII.

THE TRAGEDY OF A WIFE.

WERE Jess still alive to tell the life-story of Sam'l Fletcher and his wife, you could not hear it and sit still. The ghost cradle is but a page from the black history of a woman who

---

112 Flichtered (Sc.): frightened.
113 Litlin (Sc.): infant.

married, to be blotted out from that hour. One case of the kind I myself have known, of a woman so good mated to a man so selfish that I cannot think of her even now with a steady mouth. Hers was the tragedy of living on, more mournful than the tragedy that kills. In Thrums the weavers spoke of "lousing" from their looms, removing the chains, and there is something woeful in that. But pity poor Nanny Coutts, who took her chains to bed with her.

Nanny was buried a month or more before I came to the house on the brae, and even in Thrums the dead are seldom remembered for so long a time as that. But it was only after Sanders was left alone that we learned what a woman she had been, and how basely we had wronged her. She was an angel, Sanders went about whining when he had no longer a woman to ill-treat. He had this sentimental way with him, but it lost its effect after we knew the man.

"A deevil couldna hae deserved waur treatment," Tammas Haggart said to him; "gang oot o' my sicht, man."

"I'll blame mysel till I die," Jess said, with tears in her eyes, "for no understandin' puir Nanny better."

So Nanny got sympathy at last, but not until her forgiving soul had left her tortured body. There was many a kindly heart in Thrums that would have gone out to her in her lifetime, but we could not have loved her without upbraiding him, and she would not buy sympathy at the price. What a little story it is, and how few words are required to tell it! He was a bad husband to her, and she kept it secret. That is Nanny's life summed up. It is all that was left behind when her coffin went down the brae. Did she love him to the end, or was she only doing what she thought her duty? It is not for me even to guess. A good woman who suffers is altogether beyond man's reckoning. To such heights of self-sacrifice we cannot rise. It crushes us; it ought to crush us on to our knees. For us who saw Nanny, infirm, shrunken, and so weary, yet a type of the noblest womanhood, suffering for years, and misunderstood her to the end, what expiation can there be? I do not want to storm at the man who made her life so burdensome. Too many years have passed for that, nor would Nanny take it kindly if I called her man names.

Sanders worked little after his marriage. He had a sore back, he said, which became a torture if he leant forward at his loom. What truth there was in this I cannot say, but not every weaver in Thrums could "louse" when his back grew sore. Nanny went to the loom in his place, filling as well as weaving,[114] and he walked about, dressed better than the common, and with cheerful words for those who had time to listen. Nanny got no approval even for doing his work as well as her own, for they were understood to have money, and Sanders let us think her merely greedy. We drifted into his opinions.

Had Jess been one of those who could go about, she would, I think, have read Nanny better than the rest of us, for her intellect was bright, and always led her straight to her neighbours' hearts. But Nanny visited no one, and so Jess only knew her by hearsay. Nanny's standoffishness, as it was called, was not a popular virtue, and she was blamed still more for trying to keep her husband out of other people's houses. He was so frank and full of gossip, and she was so reserved. He would go everywhere, and she nowhere. He had been known to ask neighbours to tea, and she had shown that she wanted them away, or even begged them not to come. We were not accustomed to go behind the face of a thing, and so we set down Nanny's inhospitality to churlishness or greed. Only after her death, when other women had to attend him, did we get to know what a tyrant Sanders was at his own hearth. The ambition of Nanny's life was that we

---

114 This is obscure: 'filling' is another name for the weft, the thread passed through the warp in the process of weaving; but Barrie seems to imply an activity in addition to this.

should never know it, that we should continue extolling him, and say what we chose about herself. She knew that if we went much about the house and saw how he treated her, Sanders would cease to be a respected man in Thrums.

So neat in his dress was Sanders, that he was seldom seen abroad in corduroys. His blue bonnet for everyday wear was such as even well-to-do farmers only wore at fair-time, and it was said that he had a handkerchief for every day in the week. Jess often held him up to Hendry as a model of courtesy and polite manners.

"Him an' Nanny's no weel matched," she used to say, "for he has grand ideas, an' she's o' the commonest. It maun be a richt trial to a man wi' his fine tastes to hae a wife 'at's wrapper's never even on, an' wha doesna wash her mutch aince in a month."

It is true that Nanny was a slattern, but only because she married into slavery. She was kept so busy washing and ironing for Sanders that she ceased to care how she looked herself. What did it matter whether her mutch was clean? Weaving and washing and cooking, doing the work of a breadwinner as well as of a housewife, hers was soon a body prematurely old, on which no wrapper would sit becomingly. Before her face, Sanders would hint that her slovenly ways and dress tried him sorely, and in company at least she only bowed her head. We were given to respecting those who worked hard, but Nanny, we thought, was a woman of means, and Sanders let us call her a miser. He was always anxious, he said, to be generous, but Nanny would not let him assist a starving child. They had really not a penny beyond what Nanny earned at the loom, and now we know how Sanders shook her if she did not earn enough. His vanity was responsible for the story about her wealth, and she would not have us think him vain.

Because she did so much, we said that she was as strong as a cart-horse. The doctor who attended her during the last week of her life discovered that she had never been well. Yet we had often wondered at her letting Sanders pit his own potatoes when he was so unable.

"Them 'at's strong, ye see," Sanders explained, "doesna ken what illness is, an' so it's nat'ral they shouldna sympathize wi' onweel fowk. Ay, I'm rale thankfu' 'at Nanny keeps her health. I often envy her."

These were considered creditable sentiments, and so they might have been had Nanny uttered them. Thus easily Sanders built up a reputation for never complaining. I know now that he was a hard and cruel man who should have married a shrew; but while Nanny lived I thought he had a beautiful nature. Many a time I have spoken with him at Hendry's gate, and felt the better of his heartiness.

"I mauna complain,"[115] he always said; "na, we maun juist fecht awa."

Little, indeed, had he to complain of, and little did he fight away.

Sanders went twice to church every Sabbath, and thrice when he got the chance. There was no man who joined so lustily in the singing or looked straighter at the minister during the prayer. I have heard the minister say that Sanders's constant attendance was an encouragement and a help to him. Nanny had been a great church-goer when she was a maiden, but after her marriage she only went in the afternoons, and a time came when she ceased altogether to attend. The minister admonished her many times, telling her, among other things, that her irreligious ways were a distress to her husband. She never replied that she could not go to church in the forenoon because Sanders insisted on a hot meal being waiting him when the service ended. But it was true that Sanders, for appearances' sake, would have had her go to church in the afternoons. It is now believed that on this point alone did she refuse to do as she was bidden. Nanny was very far from perfect, and the reason she forsook the kirk utterly was because she had no Sabbath clothes.

115 Mauna (Sc.): must not.

She died as she had lived, saying not a word when the minister, thinking it his duty, drew a cruel comparison between her life and her husband's.

"I got my first glimpse into the real state of affairs in that house," the doctor told me one night on the brae, "the day before she died. 'You're sure there's no hope for me?' she asked wistfully, and when I had to tell the truth she sank back on the pillow with a look of joy."

Nanny died with a lie on her lips. "Ay," she said, "Sanders has been a guid man to me."

CHAPTER XIII.

MAKING THE BEST OF IT.

HENDRY had a way of resuming a conversation where he had left off the night before. He would revolve a topic in his mind, too, and then begin aloud, "He's a queer ane," or, "Say ye so?" which was at times perplexing. With the whole day before them, none of the family was inclined to waste strength in talk; but one morning when he was blowing the steam off his porridge, Hendry said, suddenly —

"He's hame again."[116]

The women-folk gave him time to say to whom he was referring, which he occasionally did as an after-thought. But he began to sup his porridge, making eyes as it went steaming down his throat.

"I dinna ken wha ye mean," Jess said; while Leeby, who was on her knees rubbing the hearthstone a bright blue, paused to catch her father's answer.

"Jeames Geogehan," replied Hendry, with the horn spoon in his mouth.

Leeby turned to Jess for enlightenment.

"Geogehan," repeated Jess; "what, no little Jeames 'at ran awa?"

"Ay, ay, but he's a muckle stoot man noo, an' gey grey."[117]

"Ou, I dinna wonder at that. It's a guid forty year since he ran off."

"I waurant ye couldna say exact hoo lang syne it is?"

Hendry asked this question because Jess was notorious for her memory, and he gloried in putting it to the test.

"Let's see," she said.

"But wha is he?" asked Leeby. "I never kent nae Geogehans in Thrums."

"Weel, it's forty-one years syne come Michaelmas," said Jess.

"Hoo do ye ken?"

"I ken fine. Ye mind his father had been lickin' 'im, an' he ran awa in a passion, cryin' oot 'at he would never come back? Ay, then, he had a pair o' boots on at the time, an' his father ran after 'im an' took them aff 'im. The boots was the last 'at Davie Mearns made, an' it's fully ane-an-forty years since Davie fell ower the quarry on the day o' the hill-market. That settles't. Ay, an' Jeames 'll be turned fifty noo, for he was comin' on for ten year auld at that time. Ay, ay, an' he's come back. What a state Eppie 'll be in!"

"Tell's wha he is, mother."

"Od, he's Eppie Guthrie's son. Her man was William Geogehan, but he died 'afore

116 Hame (Sc.): home.
117 Muckle stoot: big stout; gey: quite, with the same ambiguity as the English word between 'completely' and 'a bit' (both Sc.).

you was born, an' as Jeames was their only bairn, the name o' Geogehan's been a kind o' lost sicht o'. Hae ye seen him, Hendry? Is't true 'at he made a fortune in thae far-awa countries? Eppie 'll be blawin' aboot him richt?"[118]

"There's nae doubt aboot the siller," said Hendry, "for he drove in a carriage frae Tilliedrum, an' they say he needs a closet to hing his claes in, there's sic a heap o' them. Ay, but that's no a' he's brocht, na, far frae a'."

"Dinna gang awa till ye've telt's a' aboot 'im. What mair has he brocht?"

"He's brocht a wife," said Hendry, twisting his face curiously.

"There's naething surprisin' in that."

"Ay, but there is, though. Ye see, Eppie had a letter frae 'im no mony weeks syne, sayin' 'at he wasna deid, an' he was comin' hame wi' a fortune. He said, too, 'at he was a single man, an' she's been boastin' aboot that, so ye may think 'at she got a surprise when he hands a wuman oot o' the carriage."

"An' no a pleasant ane," said Jess. "Had he been leein'?"[119]

"Na, he was single when he wrote, an' single when he got the length o' Tilliedrum. Ye see, he fell in wi' the lassie there, an' juist gaed clean aff his heid aboot her. After managin' to withstand the women o' foreign lands for a' thae years, he gaed fair skeer aboot this stocky at Tilliedrum. She's juist seventeen year auld, an' the auld fule sits wi' his airm round her in Eppie's hoose, though they've been mairit this fortnicht."

"The doited fule," said Jess.

Jeames Geogehan and his bride became the talk of Thrums, and Jess saw them from her window several times. The first time she had only eyes for the jacket with fur round it worn by Mrs. Geogehan, but subsequently she took in Jeames.

"He's tryin' to carry't aff wi' his heid in the air," she said, "but I can see he's fell shamefaced, an' nae wonder. Ay, I sepad he's mair ashamed o't in his heart than she is. It's an awful like thing o' a lassie to marry an auld man. She had dune't for the siller. Ay, there's pounds' worth o' fur aboot that jacket."

"They say she had siller hersel," said Tibbie Birse.

"Dinna tell me," said Jess. "I ken by her wy o' carryin' hersel 'at she never had a jacket like that afore."

Eppie was not the only person in Thrums whom this marriage enraged. Stories had long been alive of Jeames's fortune, which his cousins' children were some day to divide among themselves, and as a consequence these young men and women looked on Mrs. Geogehan as a thief.

"Dinna bring the wife to our hoose, Jeames," one of them told him, "for we would be fair ashamed to hae her. We used to hae a respect for yer name, so we couldna look her i' the face."

"She's mair like yer dochter than yer wife," said another.

"Na," said a third, "naebody could mistak her for yer dochter. She's ower young-like for that."

"Wi' the siller you'll leave her, Jeames," Tammas Haggart told him, "she'll get a younger man for her second venture."

All this was very trying to the newly-married man, who was thirsting for sympathy. Hendry was the person whom he took into his confidence.

"It may hae been foolish at my time o' life," Hendry reported him to have said, "but I couldnae help it. If they juist kent her better they couldna but see 'at she's a terrible takkin' crittur."[120]

118 Blawing (Sc.): boasting.
119 Leein' (Sc.): lying.
120 Takkin' (Sc.): taking, i.e. attractive.

Jeames was generous; indeed he had come home with the intention of scattering largess. A beggar met him one day on the brae, and got a shilling from him. She was waving her arms triumphantly as she passed Hendry's house, and Leeby got the story from her.

"Eh, he's a fine man tha, an' a saft ane," the woman said. "I juist speired at 'im hoo his bonny wife was, an' he oot wi' a shillin'!"

Leeby did not keep this news to herself, and soon it was through the town. Jeames's face began to brighten.

"They're comin' round to a mair sensible wy o' lookin' at things," he told Hendry. "I was walkin' wi' the wife i' the buryin' ground yesterday, an' we met Kitty McQueen. She was ane o' the warst agin me at first, but she telt me i' the buryin' ground 'at when a man mairit he should please 'imsel. Oh, they're comin' round."

What Kitty told Jess was—

"I minded o' the tinkler wuman 'at he gae a shillin' to, so I thocht I would butter up at the auld fule too. Weel, I assure ye, I had nae suner said 'at he was rale wise to marry wha he likit than he slips a pound note into my hand. Ou, Jess, we've taen the wrang wy wi' Jeames. I've telt a' my bairns 'at if they meet him they're to praise the wife terrible, an' I'm far mista'en if that doesna mean five shillins to ilka ane o' them."

Jean Whamond got a pound note for saying that Jeames's wife had an uncommon pretty voice, and Davit Lunan had ten shillings for a judicious word about her attractive manners. Tibbie Birse invited the newly-married couple to tea (one pound).

"They're takkin' to her, they're takkin' to her," Jeames said, gleefully. "I kent they would come round in time. Ay, even my mother, 'at was sae mad at first, sits for hours noo aside her, haudin' her hand. They're juist inseparable."

The time came when we had Mr. and Mrs. Geogehan and Eppie to tea.

"It's true enough," Leeby ran ben to tell Jess, " 'at Eppie an' the wife's fond o' ane another. I wouldna hae believed it o' Eppie if I hadna seen it, but I assure ye they sat even at the tea-table haudin' ane another's hands. I waurant they're doin't this meenute."

"I wasna born on a Sabbath," retorted Jess. "Na, na, dinna tell me Eppie's fond o' her. Tell Eppie to come but to the kitchen when the tea's ower."

Jess and Eppie had half an hour's conversation alone, and then our guests left.

"It's a richt guid thing," said Hendry, " 'at Eppie has ta'en sic a notion o' the wife."

"Ou, ay," said Jess.

Then Hendry hobbled out of the house.

"What said Eppie to ye?" Leeby asked her mother.

"Juist what I expeckit," Jess answered. "Ye see she's dependent on Jeames, so she has to butter up at 'im."

"Did she say onything aboot haudin' the wife's hand sae fond-like?"

"Ay, she said it was an awfu' trial to her, an' 'at it sickened her to see Jeames an' the wife baith believin' 'at she likit to do't."

CHAPTER XIV.

VISITORS AT THE MANSE.

ON bringing home his bride, the minister showed her to us, and we thought she would do when she realized that she was not the minister. She was a grand lady from Edinburgh, though very frank, and we simple folk amused her a good deal, especially when we were sitting cowed in the manse parlour drinking a dish of tea with her, as happened to Leeby, her father, and me, three days before Jamie came home.

Leeby had refused to be drawn into conversation, like one who knew her place, yet all her actions were genteel and her monosyllabic replies in the Englishy tongue, as of one who was, after all, a little above the common. When the minister's wife asked her whether she took sugar and cream, she said politely, "If you please" (though she did not take sugar), a reply that contrasted with Hendry's equally well-intended answer to the same question. "I'm no partikler," was what Hendry said.

Hendry had left home glumly, declaring that the white collar Jess had put on him would throttle him; but her feikieness ended in his surrender, and he was looking unusually perjink. [121] Had not his daughter been present he would have been the most at ease of the company, but her manners were too fine not to make an impression upon one who knew her on her everyday behaviour, and she had also ways of bringing Hendry to himself by a touch beneath the table. It was in church that Leeby brought to perfection her manner of looking after her father. When he had confidence in the preacher's soundness, he would sometimes have slept in his pew if Leeby had not had a watchful foot. She wakened him in an instant, while still looking modestly at the pulpit; however reverently he might try to fall over, Leeby's foot went out. She was such an artist that I never caught her in the act. All I knew for certain was that, now and then, Hendry suddenly sat up.

The ordeal was over when Leeby went upstairs to put on her things. After tea Hendry had become bolder in talk, his subject being ministerial. He had an extraordinary knowledge, got no one knew where, of the matrimonial affairs of all the ministers in these parts, and his stories about them ended frequently with a chuckle. He always took it for granted that a minister's marriage was womanhood's great triumph, and that the particular woman who got him must be very clever. Some of his tales were even more curious than he thought them, such as the one Leeby tried to interrupt by saying we must be going.

"There's Mr. Pennycuick, noo," said Hendry, shaking his head in wonder at what he had to tell; "him 'at's minister at Tilliedrum. Weel, when he was a probationer he was michty poor, an' one day he was walkin' into Thrums frae Glen Quharity,[122] an' he tak's a rest at a little housey on the road. The fowk didna ken him ava, but they saw he was a minister, an' the lassie was sorry to see him wi' sic an auld hat. What think ye she did?"

"Come away, father," said Leeby, re-entering the parlour; but Hendry was now in full pursuit of his story.

"I'll tell ye what she did," he continued. "She juist took his hat awa, an' put her father's new ane in its place, an' Mr. Pennycuick never kent the differ till he landed in Thrums. It was terrible kind o' her. Ay, but the auld man would be in a michty rage when he found she had swappit the hats."

---

121 *SND* does not list 'feikieness', but gives as one sense of the verb 'fyke' 'to exert oneself [...] take trouble or pains'; and as another, 'to make a fuss or pother about nothing very much'. Perjink: exact, precise (all Sc.).

122 A probationer is a divinity graduate, licenced to preach but not yet ordained into a parish. 'Quharity' is the only place-name that Barrie borrows from the real Kirriemuir area: the Quharity Burn runs to the north of the town. But its shallow catchment could hardly be called a glen, and with its own postie (chapter XV) and school (the narrator's, as is confirmed in the final chapter), it seems Barrie is evoking something on the scale of the adjacent glens Prosen or Clova.

"Come away," said Leeby, still politely, though she was burning to tell her mother how Hendry had disgraced them.

"The minister," said Hendry, turning his back on Leeby, "didna forget the lassie. Na; as sune as he got a kirk, he married her. Ay, she got her reward. He married her. It was rale noble o' 'im."

I do not know what Leeby said to Hendry when she got him beyond the manse gate, for I stayed behind to talk to the minister. As it turned out, the minister's wife did most of the talking, smiling good-humouredly at country gawkiness the while.

"Yes," she said, "I am sure I shall like Thrums, though those teas to the congregation are a little trying. Do you know, Thrums is the only place I was ever in where it struck me that the men are cleverer than the women."

She told us why.

"Well, to-night affords a case in point. Mr. McQumpha was quite brilliant, was he not, in comparison with his daughter? Really she seemed so put out at being at the manse that she could not raise her eyes. I question if she would know me again, and I am sure she sat in the room as one blindfolded. I left her in the bedroom a minute, and I assure you, when I returned she was still standing on the same spot in the centre of the floor."

I pointed out that Leeby had been awestruck.

"I suppose so," she said; "but it is a pity she cannot make use of her eyes, if not of her tongue. Ah, the Thrums women are good, I believe, but their wits are sadly in need of sharpening. I daresay it comes of living in so small a place."

I overtook Leeby on the brae, aware, as I saw her alone, that it had been her father whom I passed talking to Tammas Haggart in the Square. Hendry stopped to have what he called a tove with any likely person he encountered,[123] and, indeed, though he and I often took a walk on Saturdays, I generally lost him before we were clear of the town.

In a few moments Leeby and I were at home to give Jess the news.

"Whaur's yer father?" asked Jess, as if Hendry's way of dropping behind was still unknown to her.

"Ou, I left him speakin' to Gavin Birse," said Leeby. "I daursay he's awa to some hoose."

"It's no very silvendy (safe) his comin' ower the brae by himsel," said Jess, adding in a bitter tone of conviction, "but he'll gang in to no hoose as lang as he's so weel dressed. Na, he would think it boastfu'."

I sat down to a book by the kitchen fire; but, as Leeby became communicative, I read less and less. While she spoke she was baking bannocks with all the might of her, and Jess, leaning forward in her chair, was arranging them in a semicircle round the fire.

"Na," was the first remark of Leeby's that came between me and my book, "it is no new furniture."

"But there was three cart-loads o't, Leeby, sent on frae Edinbory. Tibbie Birse helpit to lift it in and she said the parlour furniture beat a'."

"Ou, it's substantial, but it is no new. I sepad it had been bocht cheap second-hand, for the chair I had was terrible scratched like, an', what's mair, the airm-chair was a heap shinnier than the rest."

"Ay, ay, I wager it had been new stuffed. Tibbie said the carpet cowed for grandeur!"

"Oh, I dinna deny it's a guid carpet; but if it's been turned once it's been turned half a dozen times, so it's far frae new. Ay, an' forby, it was rale threadbare aneath the table, so ye may be sure they've been cuttin't an' puttin' the worn pairt whaur it would be least seen."

---

123 Tove (Sc.): chat or gossip.

"They say 'at there's twa grand gas brackets i' the parlour, an' a wonderfu' gasoliery i' the dinin'-room?"[124]

"We wasna i' the dinin'-room, so I ken naething aboot the gasoliery; but I'll tell ye what the gas brackets is. I recognized them immeditly. Ye mind the auld gasoliery i' the dinin'-room had twa lichts? Ay, then, the parlour brackets is made oot o' the auld gasoliery."

"Weel, Leeby, as sure as ye're standin' there, that passed through my head as sune as Tibbie mentioned them!"

"There's nae doot about it. Ay, I was in ane o' the bedrooms, too!"

"It would be grand?"

"I wouldna say 'at it was partikler grand, but there was a great mask (quantity) o' things in't, an' near everything was covered wi' cretonne.[125] But the chairs dinna match. There was a very bonny-painted cloth alang the chimley — what they call a mantelpiece border, I warrant."

"Sal, I've often wondered what they was."

"Weel, I assure ye they winna be ill to mak, for the border was juist nailed upon a board laid on the chimley. There's naething to hender's makin' ane for the room."

"Ay, we could sew something on the border instead o' paintin't. The room lookit weel, ye say?"

"Yes, but it was economically furnished. There was nae carpet below the wax-cloth; na, there was nane below the bed either."

"Was't a grand bed?"

"It had a fell lot o' brass aboot it, but there was juist one pair o' blankets. I thocht it was gey shabby, hae'n the ewer a different pattern frae the basin; ay, an' there was juist a poker in the fireplace, there was nae tangs."

"Yea, yea; they'll hae but one set o' bedroom fireirons. The tangs'll be in anither room. Tod, that's no sae michty grand for Edinbory. What like was she hersel?"

"Ou, very ladylike and saft spoken. She's a canty body an' frank.[126] She wears her hair low on the left side to hod (hide) a scar, an' there's twa warts on her richt hand."

"There hadna been a fire i' the parlour?"

"No, but it was ready to licht. There was sticks and paper in't. The paper was oot o' a dressmaker's journal."

"Ye say so? She'll mak her ain frocks, I sepad."

When Hendry entered to take off his collar and coat before sitting down to his evening meal of hot water, porter, and bread mixed in a bowl, Jess sent me off to the attic. As I climbed the stairs I remembered that the minister's wife thought Leeby in need of sharpening.

CHAPTER XV.

HOW GAVIN BIRSE PUT IT TO MAG LOWNIE.

IN a wet day the rain gathered in blobs on the road that passed our garden. Then it crawled into the cart-tracks until the road was streaked with water. Lastly, the water gathered in heavy yellow pools. If the on-ding still continued, clods of earth toppled from the garden dyke into the ditch.

---

124 A gasoliery was a gas-light chandelier.
125 Cretonne was a strong printed cotton fabric used to cover soft furnishings.
126 Canty (Sc.): lively, cheerful.

On such a day, when even the dulseman had gone into shelter, and the women scudded by with their wrappers over their heads, came Gavin Birse to our door. Gavin, who was the Glen Quharity post, was still young, but had never been quite the same man since some amateurs in the glen ironed his back for rheumatism. I thought he had called to have a crack with me.[127] He sent his compliments up to the attic, however, by Leeby, and would I come and be a witness?

Gavin came up and explained. He had taken off his scarf and thrust it into his pocket, lest the rain should take the colour out of it. His boots cheeped, and his shoulders had risen to his ears. He stood steaming before my fire.

"If it's no' ower muckle to ask ye," he said, "I would like ye for a witness."

"A witness! But for what do you need a witness, Gavin?"

"I want ye," he said, "to come wi' me to Mag's, and be a witness."

Gavin and Mag Birse had been engaged for a year or more. Mag was the daughter of Janet Ogilvy, who was best remembered as the body that took the hill (that is, wandered about it) for twelve hours on the day Mr. Dishart, the Auld Licht minister, accepted a call to another church.

"You don't mean to tell me, Gavin," I asked, "that your marriage is to take place to-day?"

By the twist of his mouth I saw that he was only deferring a smile.

"Far frae that," he said.

"Ah, then, you have quarrelled, and I am to speak up for you?"

"Na, na," he said, "I dinna want ye to do that above all things. It would be a favour if ye could gie me a bad character."

This beat me, and, I daresay, my face showed it.

"I'm no' juist what ye would call anxious to marry Mag noo," said Gavin, without a tremor.

I told him to go on.

"There's a lassie oot at Craigiebuckle," he explained, "workin' on the farm—Jeanie Luke by name. Ye may hae seen her?"

"What of her?" I asked, severely.

"Weel," said Gavin, still unabashed, "I'm thinkin' noo 'at I would rather ha'e her."

Then he stated his case more fully.

"Ay, I thocht I liked Mag oncommon till I saw Jeanie, an' I like her fine yet, but I prefer the other ane. That state o' matters canna gang on for ever, so I came into Thrums the day to settle 't one wy or another."

"And how," I asked, "do you propose going about it? It is a somewhat delicate business."

"Ou, I see nae great difficulty in 't. I'll speir at Mag, blunt oot, if she'll let me aff. Yes, I'll put it to her plain."

"You're sure Jeanie would take you?"

"Ay; oh, there's nae fear o' that."

"But if Mag keeps you to your bargain?"

"Weel, in that case there's nae harm done."

"You are in a great hurry, Gavin?"

"Ye may say that; but I want to be married. The wifie I lodge wi' canna last lang, an' I would like to settle doon in some place."

"So you are on your way to Mag's now?"

"Ay, we'll get her in atween twal' and ane."[128]

---

127 Crack (Sc.): chat, entertaining conversation.
128 Twal' (Sc.): twelve.

"Oh, yes; but why do you want me to go with you?"

"I want ye for a witness. If she winna let me aff, weel and guid; and if she will, it's better to hae a witness in case she should go back on her word."

Gavin made his proposal briskly, and as coolly as if he were only asking me to go fishing; but I did not accompany him to Mag's. He left the house to look for another witness, and about an hour afterwards Jess saw him pass with Tammas Haggart. Tammas cried in during the evening to tell us how the mission prospered.[129]

"Mind ye," said Tammas, a drop of water hanging to the point of his nose, "I disclaim all responsibility in the business. I ken Mag weel for a thrifty, respectable woman, as her mither was afore her, and so I said to Gavin when he came to speir me."

"Ay, mony a pirn has 'Lisbeth filled to me," said Hendry, settling down to a reminiscence.

"No to be ower hard on Gavin," continued Tammas, forestalling Hendry, "he took what I said in guid part; but aye when I stopped speakin' to draw breath, he says, 'The queistion is, will ye come wi' me?' He was michty made up in 's mind."

"Weel, ye went wi' him," suggested Jess, who wanted to bring Tammas to the point.

"Ay," said the stone-breaker, "but no in sic a hurry as that."

He worked his mouth round and round, to clear the course, as it were, for a sarcasm.

"Fowk often say," he continued, " 'at 'am quick beyond the ordinar' in seein' the humorous side o' things."

Here Tammas paused, and looked at us.

"So ye are, Tammas," said Hendry. "Losh, ye mind hoo ye saw the humorous side o' me wearin' a pair o' boots 'at wisna marrows! No, the ane had a toe-piece on, an' the other hadna."

"Ye juist wore them sometimes when ye was delvin',"[130] broke in Jess, "ye have as guid a pair o' boots as ony in Thrums."

"Ay, but I had worn them," said Hendry, "at odd times for mair than a year, an' I had never seen the humorous side o' them. Weel, as fac as death (here he addressed me), Tammas had juist seen them twa or three times when he saw the humorous side o' them. Syne I saw their humorous side, too, but no till Tammas pointed it oot."

"That was naething," said Tammas, "naething ava to some things I've done."

"But what aboot Mag?" said Leeby.

"We wasna that length, was we?" said Tammas. "Na, we was speakin' aboot the humorous side. Ay, wait a wee, I didna mention the humorous side for naething."

He paused to reflect.

"Oh, yes," he said at last, brightening up, "I was sayin' to ye hoo quick I was to see the humorous side o' onything. Ay, then, what made me say that was 'at in a clink (flash) I saw the humorous side o' Gavin's position."

"Man, man," said Hendry, admiringly, "and what is 't?"

"Oh, it's this, there's something humorous in speirin' a woman to let ye aff so as ye can be married to another woman."

"I daursay there is," said Hendry, doubtfully.

"Did she let him aff?" asked Jess, taking the words out of Leeby's mouth.

"I'm comin' to that," said Tammas. "Gavin proposes to me after I had haen my laugh—"

"Yes," cried Hendry, banging the table with his fist, "it has a humorous side. Ye're richt again, Tammas."

"I wish ye wadna blatter (beat) the table," said Jess, and then Tammas proceeded.

---

129 Cried in (Sc.): called in.
130 Delvin': i.e., digging over the garden.

"Gavin wanted me to tak' paper an' ink an' a pen wi' me, to write the proceedins doon, but I said, 'Na, na, I'll tak paper, but no nae ink nor nae pen, for there'll be ink an' a pen there.' That was what I said."

"An' did she let him aff?" asked Leeby.

"Weel," said Tammas, "aff we goes to Mag's hoose, an' sure enough Mag was in. She was alane, too; so Gavin, no to waste time, juist sat doon for politeness' sake, an' syne rises up again; an' says he, 'Marget Lownie, I ha'e a solemn question to speir at ye, namely this, Will you, Marget Lownie, let me, Gavin Birse, aff?'"

"Mag would start at that?"

"Sal, she was braw an' cool.[131] I thocht she maun ha'e got wind o' his intentions aforehand, for she juist replies, quiet-like, 'Hoo do ye want aff, Gavin?'

"'Because,' says he, like a book, 'my affections has undergone a change.'

"'Ye mean Jean Luke,' says Mag.

"'That is wha I mean,' says Gavin, very straitforrard."

"But she didna let him aff, did she?"

"Na, she wasna the kind. Says she, 'I wonder to hear ye, Gavin, but 'am no goin' to agree to naething o' that sort.'

"'Think it ower,' says Gavin.

"'Na, my mind's made up,' said she.

"'Ye would sune get anither man,' he says, earnestly.

"'Hoo do I ken that?' she speirs, rale sensibly, I thocht, for men's no sae easy to get.

"' 'Am sure o' 't,' Gavin says, wi' michty conviction in his voice, 'for ye're bonny to look at, an' weel-kent for bein' a guid body.'

"'Ay,' says Mag, "I'm glad ye like me, Gavin, for ye have to tak me.'"

"That put a clincher on him," interrupted Hendry.

"He was loth to gie in," replied Tammas, "so he says, 'Ye think 'am a fine character, Marget Lownie, but ye're very far mista'en. I wouldna wonder but what I was lossin' my place some o' thae days,[132] an' syne whaur would ye be? — Marget Lownie,' he goes on, ' 'am nat'rally lazy an' fond o' the drink. As sure as ye stand there, 'am a reglar devil!'"

"That was strong language," said Hendry, "but he would be wantin' to fleg (frighten) her?"

"Juist so, but he didna manage 't, for Mag says, 'We a' ha'e oor faults, Gavin, an' deevil or no deevil, ye're the man for me!'

"Gavin thocht a bit," continued Tammas, "an' syne he tries her on a new tack. 'Marget Lownie,' he says, 'ye're father's an auld man noo, an' he has naebody but yersel to look after him. I'm thinkin' it would be kind o' cruel o' me to tak ye awa frae him?'"

"Mag wouldna be ta'en in wi' that; she wasna born on a Sawbath," said Jess, using one of her favourite sayings.

"She wasna," answered Tammas. "Says she, 'Hae nae fear on that score, Gavin; my father's fine willin' to spare me!'"

"An' that ended it?"

"Ay, that ended it."

"Did ye tak it doon in writin'?" asked Hendry.

"There was nae need," said Tammas, handing round his snuff-mull. "No, I never touched paper. When I saw the thing was settled, I left them to their coortin'. They're to tak a look at Snecky Hobart's auld hoose the nicht. It's to let."

---

131 Braw an' cool (Sc.): fine and cool, i.e. very cool.
132 Lossin' my place (Sc.): losing my place (as a postman).

CHAPTER XVI.

THE SON FROM LONDON.

IN the spring of the year there used to come to Thrums a painter from nature whom Hendry spoke of as the drawer. He lodged with Jess in my attic, and when the weavers met him they said, "Weel, drawer," and then passed on, grinning. Tammas Haggart was the first to say this.

The drawer was held a poor man because he straggled about the country looking for subjects for his draws, and Jess, as was her way, gave him many comforts for which she would not charge. That, I daresay, was why he painted for her a little portrait of Jamie. When the drawer came back to Thrums he always found the painting in a frame in the room. Here I must make a confession about Jess. She did not in her secret mind think the portrait quite the thing, and as soon as the drawer departed it was removed from the frame to make way for a calendar. The deception was very innocent, Jess being anxious not to hurt the donor's feelings.

To those who have the artist's eye, the picture, which hangs in my school-house now, does not show a handsome lad, Jamie being short and dapper, with straw-coloured hair, and a chin that ran away into his neck. That is how I once regarded him, but I have little heart for criticism of those I like, and, despite his madness for a season, of which, alas, I shall have to tell, I am always Jamie's friend. Even to hear any one disparaging the appearance of Jess's son is to me a pain.

All Jess's acquaintances knew that in the beginning of every month a registered letter reached her from London. To her it was not a matter to keep secret. She was proud that the help she and Hendry needed in the gloaming of their lives should come from her beloved son, and the neighbours esteemed Jamie because he was good to his mother. Jess had more humour than any other woman I have known, while Leeby was but sparingly endowed; yet, as the month neared its close, it was the daughter who put on the humorist, Jess thinking money too serious a thing to jest about. Then if Leeby had a moment for gossip, as when ironing a dickey for Hendry, and the iron was a trifle too hot, she would look archly at me before addressing her mother in these words:

"Will he send, think ye?"

Jess, who had a conviction that he would send, affected surprise at the question.

"Will Jamie send this month, do ye mean? Na, oh, losh no! it's no to be expeckit. Na, he couldna do't this time."

"That's what ye aye say, but he aye sends. Yes, an' vara weel ye ken 'at he will send."

"Na, na, Leeby; dinna let me ever think o' sic a thing this month."

"As if ye wasna thinkin' o't day an' nicht!"

"He's terrible mindfu', Leeby, but he doesna hae't. Na, no this month; mebbe next month."

"Do you mean to tell me, mother, 'at ye'll no be up oot o' yer bed on Monunday an hour afore yer usual time, lookin' for the post?"

"Na, no this time. I may be up, an' tak a look for 'im, but no expeckin' a registerdy; na, na, that wouldna be reasonable."

"Reasonable here, reasonable there, up you'll be, keekin' (peering) through the blind to see if the post's comin', ay, an' what's mair, the post will come, and a registerdy in his hand wi' fifteen shillings in't at the least."

"Dinna say fifteen, Leeby; I would never think o' sic a sum. Mebbe five —"

"Five! I wonder to hear ye. Vera weel you ken 'at since he had twenty-twa shillings in the week he's never sent less than half a sovereign."

"No, but we canna expeck —"

"Expeck! No, but it's no expeck, it's get."

On the Monday morning when I came downstairs, Jess was in her chair by the window, beaming, a piece of paper in her hand. I did not require to be told about it, but I was told. Jess had been up before Leeby could get the fire lit, with great difficulty reaching the window in her bare feet, and many a time had she said that the post must be by.

"Havers," said Leeby, "he winna be for an hour yet. Come awa' back to your bed."

"Na, he maun be by," Jess would say in a few minutes; "ou, we couldna expeck this month."

So it went on until Jess's hand shook the blind. "He's comin', Leeby, he's comin'. He'll no hae naething, na, I couldna expeck — He's by!"

"I dinna believe it," cried Leeby, running to the window, "he's juist at his tricks again."

This was in reference to a way our saturnine post had of pretending that he brought no letters and passing the door. Then he turned back. "Mistress McQumpha," he cried, and whistled. "Run, Leeby, run," said Jess, excitedly.

Leeby hastened to the door, and came back with a registered letter.

"Registerdy," she cried in triumph, and Jess, with fond hands, opened the letter. By the time I came down the money was hid away in a box beneath the bed, where not even Leeby could find it, and Jess was on her chair hugging the letter. She preserved all her registered envelopes.

This was the first time I had been in Thrums when Jamie was expected for his ten days' holiday, and for a week we discussed little else. Though he had written saying when he would sail for Dundee, there was quite a possibility of his appearing on the brae at any moment, for he liked to take Jess and Leeby by surprise. Hendry there was no surprising, unless he was in the mood for it, and the coolness of him was one of Jess's grievances. Just two years earlier Jamie came north a week before his time, and his father saw him from the window. Instead of crying out in amazement or hacking his face, for he was shaving at the time, Hendry calmly wiped his razor on the window-sill, and said —

"Ay, there's Jamie."

Jamie was a little disappointed at being seen in this way, for he had been looking forward for four and forty hours to repeating the sensation of the year before. On that occasion he had got to the door unnoticed, where he stopped to listen. I daresay he checked his breath, the better to catch his mother's voice, for Jess being an invalid, Jamie thought of her first. He had Leeby sworn to write the truth about her, but many an anxious hour he had on hearing that she was "complaining fell (considerably) about her back the day," Leeby, as he knew, being frightened to alarm him. Jamie, too, had given his promise to tell exactly how he was keeping, but often he wrote that he was "fine" when Jess had her doubts. When Hendry wrote he spread himself over the table, and said that Jess was "juist about it", or "aff and on," which does not tell much. So Jamie hearkened painfully at the door, and by and by heard his mother say to Leeby that she was sure the teapot was running out. Perhaps that voice was as sweet to him as the music of a maiden to her lover, but Jamie did not rush into his mother's arms. Jess had told me with a beaming face how craftily he behaved. The old man, of lungs that shook Thrums by night, who went from door to door selling firewood, had a way of shoving doors rudely open and crying —

"Ony rozetty roots?" and him Jamie imitated.[133]

"Juist think," Jess said, as she recalled the incident, "what a startle we got. As we think, Pete kicks open the door and cries oot, 'Ony rozetty roots?' and Leeby says 'No', and gangs to shut the door. Next minute she screeches, 'What, what, what!' and in walks Jamie!"

Jess was never able to decide whether it was more delightful to be taken aback in this way or to prepare for Jamie. Sudden excitement was bad for her according to Hendry, who got his medical knowledge second-hand from persons under treatment, but with Jamie's appearance on the threshold Jess's health began to improve. This time he kept to the appointed day, and the house was turned upside down in his honour. Such a polish did Leeby put on the flagons which hung on the kitchen wall, that, passing between them and the window, I thought once I had been struck by lightning. On the morning of the day that was to bring him, Leeby was up at two o'clock, and eight hours before he could possibly arrive Jess had a night-shirt warming for him at the fire. I was no longer anybody, except as a person who could give Jamie advice. Jess told me what I was to say. The only thing he and his mother quarrelled about was the underclothing she would swaddle him in, and Jess asked me to back her up in her entreaties.

"There's no a doubt," she said, "but what it's a hantle caulder here than in London,[134] an' it would be a terrible business if he was to tak the cauld."

Jamie was to sail from London to Dundee, and come on to Thrums from Tilliedrum in the post-cart.[135] The road at that time, however, avoided the brae, and at a certain point Jamie's custom was to alight, and take the short cut home, along a farm road and up the commonty. Here, too, Hookey Crewe, the post, deposited his passenger's box, which Hendry wheeled home in a barrow. Long before the cart had lost sight of Tilliedrum, Jess was at her window.

"Tell her Hookey's often late on Monundays," Leeby whispered to me, "for she'll gang oot o' her mind if she thinks there's onything wrang."

Soon Jess was painfully excited, though she sat as still as salt.

"It maun be yer time," she said, looking at both Leeby and me, for in Thrums we went out and met our friends.

"Hoots," retorted Leeby, trying to be hardy, "Hookey canna be oot o' Tilliedrum yet."

"He maun hae startit lang syne."

"I wonder at ye, mother, puttin' yersel in sic a state. Ye'll be ill when he comes."

"Na, am no in nae state, Leeby, but there'll no be nae accident, will there?"

"It's most provokin' 'at ye will think 'at every time Jamie steps into a machine there'll be an accident. Am sure if ye would tak mair after my father, it would be a blessin'. Look hoo cool he is."

"Whaur is he, Leeby ?"

"Oh, I dinna ken. The henmost time I saw him he was layin' doon the law aboot something to T'nowhead."[136]

---

133 Rozetty (Sc.): resinous. Such roots were useful as firelighters: the regular fuel would be coal.
134 Hantle caulder (Sc.): good deal colder.
135 The sea journey from London to Scotland, though much longer and less comfortable, remained a much cheaper option than the train into the second half of the nineteenth century. There was, in any case, no connection between the Scottish and English rail networks until 1848. Branch lines reached Forfar in 1839 and Kirriemuir in 1854: like the general employment in hand-loom weaving, the absence of any mention of railways in the life of Tilliedrum and Thrums invites us to place the action in the first half of the century.
136 Henmost: hindmost, last; this seems to be a specifically Angus version of hindmaist (Sc.).

"It's an awfu' wy that he has o' ga'en oot withoot a word. I wouldna wonder 'at he's no bein' in time to meet Jamie, an' that would be a pretty business."

"Od, ye're sure he'll be in braw time."

"But he hasna ta'en the barrow wi' him, an' hoo is Jamie's luggage to be brocht up withoot a barrow?"

"Barrow! He took the barrow to the saw-mill an hour syne to pick it up at Rob Angus's on the wy."

Several times Jess was sure she saw the cart in the distance, and implored us to be off.

"I'll tak no settle till ye're awa," she said, her face now flushed and her hands working nervously.

"We've time to gang and come twa or three times yet," remonstrated Leeby; but Jess gave me so beseeching a look that I put on my hat. Then Hendry dandered in to change his coat deliberately, and when the three of us set off, we left Jess with her eye on the door by which Jamie must enter. He was her only son now, and she had not seen him for a year.

On the way down the commonty, Leeby had the honour of being twice addressed as Miss McQumpha, but her father was Hendry to all, which shows that we make our social position for ourselves. Hendry looked forward to Jamie's annual appearance only a little less hungrily than Jess, but his pulse still beat regularly. Leeby would have considered it almost wicked to talk of anything except Jamie now, but Hendry cried out comments on the tatties, yesterday's roup, the fall in jute, to everybody he encountered.[137] When he and a crony had their say and parted, it was their custom to continue the conversation in shouts until they were out of hearing.

Only to Jess at her window was the cart late that afternoon. Jamie jumped from it in the long great-coat that had been new to Thrums the year before, and Hendry said calmly —

"Ay, Jamie."

Leeby and Jamie made signs that they recognized each other as brother and sister, but I was the only one with whom he shook hands. He was smart in his movements and quite the gentleman, but the Thrums ways took hold of him again at once. He even inquired for his mother in a tone that was meant to deceive me into thinking he did not care how she was.

Hendry would have had a talk out of him on the spot, but was reminded of the luggage. We took the heavy farm road, and soon we were at the saw-mill. I am naturally leisurely, but we climbed the commonty at a stride. Jamie pretended to be calm, but in a dark place I saw him take Leeby's hand, and after that he said not a word. His eyes were fixed on the elbow of the brae, where he would come into sight of his mother's window. Many, many a time, I know, that lad had prayed to God for still another sight of the window with his mother at it. So we came to the corner where the stile is that Sam'l Dickie jumped in the race for T'nowhead's Bell, and before Jamie was the house of his childhood and his mother's window, and the fond, anxious face of his mother herself. My eyes are dull, and I did not see her, but suddenly Jamie cried out, "My mother!" and Leeby and I were left behind. When I reached the kitchen Jess was crying, and her son's arms were round her neck. I went away to my attic.

There was only one other memorable event of that day. Jamie had finished his tea, and we all sat round him, listening to his adventures and opinions. He told us how the country should be governed, too, and perhaps put on airs a little. Hendry asked the

---

137 The mechanical processing of Indian jute, the raw material for making hessian cloth, had been Dundee's major industry since the 1830s.

questions, and Jamie answered them as pat as if he and his father were going through the Shorter Catechism. When Jamie told anything marvellous, as how many towels were used at the shop in a day, or that twopence was the charge for a single shave, his father screwed his mouth together as if preparing to whistle, and then instead made a curious clucking noise with his tongue, which was reserved for the expression of absolute amazement. As for Jess, who was given to making much of me, she ignored my remarks, and laughed hilariously at jokes of Jamie's which had been received in silence from me a few minutes before.

Slowly it came to me that Leeby had something on her mind, and that Jamie was talking to her with his eyes. I learned afterwards that they were plotting how to get me out of the kitchen, but were too impatient to wait. Thus it was that the great event happened in my presence. Jamie rose and stood near Jess—I daresay he had planned the scene frequently. Then he produced from his pocket a purse, and coolly opened it. Silence fell upon us as we saw that purse. From it he took a neatly-folded piece of paper, crumpled it into a ball, and flung it into Jess's lap.

I cannot say whether Jess knew what it was. Her hand shook, and for a moment she let the ball of paper lie there.

"Open't up," cried Leeby, who was in the secret.

"What is't ?" asked Hendry, drawing nearer.

"It's juist a bit paper Jamie flung at me," said Jess, and then she unfolded it.

"It's a five-pound note!" cried Hendry.

"Na, na; oh keep us, no," said Jess; but she knew it was.

For a time she could not speak.

"I canna tak it, Jamie," she faltered at last.

But Jamie waved his hand, meaning that it was nothing, and then, lest he should burst, hurried out into the garden, where he walked up and down whistling. May God bless the lad, thought I. I do not know the history of that five-pound note, but well aware I am that it grew slowly out of pence and silver, and that Jamie denied his passions many things for this great hour. His sacrifices watered his young heart and kept it fresh and tender. Let us no longer cheat our consciences by talking of filthy lucre. Money may always be a beautiful thing. It is we who make it grimy.

CHAPTER XVII.

A HOME FOR GENIUSES.

FROM hints he had let drop at odd times I knew that Tammas Haggart had a scheme for geniuses, but not until the evening after Jamie's arrival did I get it out of him. Hendry was with Jamie at the fishing, and it came about that Tammas and I had the pig-sty to ourselves.

"Of course," he said, when we had got a grip of the subject, "I dount pretend as my ideas is to be followed withoot deeviation, but ondootedly something should be done for geniuses, them bein' aboot the only class as we do naething for. Yet they're fowk to be prood o', an' we shouldna let them overdo the thing, nor run into debt; na, na. There was Robbie Burns, noo, as real a genius as ever —"

At the pig-sty, where we liked to have more than one topic, we had frequently to tempt Tammas away from Burns.

"Your scheme," I interposed, "is for living geniuses, of course?"

"Ay," he said, thoughtfully, "them 'at's gone canna be brocht back. Weel, my idea is 'at a Home should be built for geniuses at the public expense, whaur they could all live thegither, an' be decently looked after. Na, no in London; that's no my plan, but I would hae't within an hour's distance o' London, say five mile frae the market-place, an' standin' in a bit garden, whaur the geniuses could walk aboot arm-in-arm, composin' their minds."

"You would have the grounds walled in, I suppose, so that the public could not intrude?"

"Weel, there's a difficulty there, because, ye'll observe, as the public would support the institootion, they would hae a kind o' richt to look in. How-some-ever, I daur say we could arrange to fling the grounds open to the public once a week on condition 'at they didna speak to the geniuses. I'm thinkin' 'at if there was a small chairge for admission the Home could be made self-supportin'. Losh! to think 'at if there had been sic an institootion in his time a man micht hae sat on the bit dyke and watched Robbie Burns danderin' roond the —"[138]

"You would divide the Home into suites of rooms, so that every inmate would have his own apartments?"

"Not by no means; na, na. The mair I read aboot geniuses the mair clearly I see as their wy o' living alane ower muckle is ane o' the things as breaks doon their health, and makes them meeserable. I' the Home they would hae a bedroom apiece, but the parlour an' the other sittin'-rooms would be for all, so as they could enjoy ane another's company. The management? Oh, that's aisy. The superintendent would be a medical man appointed by Parliament, and he would hae men-servants to do his biddin'."

"Not all men-servants, surely?"

"Every one o' them. Man, geniuses is no to be trusted wi' womenfolk. No, even Robbie Bu —"

"So he did; but would the inmates have to put themselves entirely in the superintendent's hands?"

"Nae doubt; an' they would see it was the wisest thing they could do. He would be careful o' their health, an' send them early to bed as weel as hae them up at eight sharp. Geniuses' healths is always breakin' doon because of late hours, as in the case o' the lad wha used often to begin his immortal writin's at twal' o'clock at nicht, a thing 'at would ruin ony constitootion. But the superintendent would see as they had a tasty supper at nine o'clock — something as agreed wi' them. Then for half an hour they would quiet their brains readin' oot aloud, time about, frae sic a book as the "Pilgrim's Progress," an' the gas would be turned aff at ten precisely."

"When would you have them up in the morning?"

"At sax in summer an' seven in winter. The superintendent would see as they were all properly bathed every mornin', cleanliness bein' most important for the preservation o' health."

"This sounds well; but suppose a genius broke the rules — lay in bed, for instance, reading by the light of a candle after hours, or refused to take his bath in the morning?"

"The superintendent would hae to punish him. The genius would be sent back to his bed, maybe. An' if he lay lang i' the mornin' he would hae to gang withoot his breakfast."

"That would be all very well where the inmate only broke the regulations once in a way; but suppose he were to refuse to take his bath day after day (and, you know, geniuses are said to be eccentric in that particular), what would be done? You could not starve him; geniuses are too scarce."

---

138 Dander, dauner (Sc.): stroll or saunter.

"Na, na; in a case like that he would hae to be reported to the public. The thing would hae to come afore the Hoose of Commons. Ay, the superintendent would get a member o' the Opposeetion to ask a queistion such as 'Can the honourable gentleman, the Secretary of State for Home Affairs, inform the Hoose whether it is a fac that Mr. Sic-a-one,[139] the well-known genius, at present resident in the Home for Geniuses, has, contrairy to regulations, perseestently and obstinately refused to change his linen; and, if so, whether the Government proposes to take ony steps in the matter?' The newspapers would report the discussion next mornin', an' so it would be made public withoot onnecessary ootlay."

"In a general way, however, you would give the geniuses perfect freedom? They could work when they liked, and come and go when they liked?"

"Not so. The superintendent would fix the hours o' wark, an' they would all write, or whatever it was, thegither in one large room. Man, man, it would mak a grand draw for a painter-chield,[140] that room, wi' all the geniuses working awa' thegither."

"But when the labours of the day were over the genius would be at liberty to make calls by himself or to run up, say, to London for an hour or two?"

"Hoots no, that would spoil everything. It's the drink, ye see, as does for a terrible lot o' geniuses. Even Rob —"

"Alas! yes. But would you have them all teetotalers?"

"What do ye tak me for? Na, na; the superintendent would allow them one glass o' toddy every nicht, an' mix it himsel; but he would never let the keys o' the press,[141] whaur he kept the drink, oot o' his hands. They would never be allowed oot o' the gairden either, withoot a man to look after them; an' I wouldna burthen them wi' ower muckle pocket-money. Saxpence in the week would be suffeecient."

"How about their clothes?"

"They would get twa suits a year, wi' the letter G sewed on the shoulders, so as if they were lost they could be recognized and brocht back."

"Certainly it is a scheme deserving consideration, and I have no doubt our geniuses would jump at it; but you must remember that some of them would have wives."

"Ay, an' some o' them would hae husbands. I've been thinkin' that oot, an' I daur say the best plan would be to partition aff a pairt o' the Home for female geniuses."

"Would Parliament elect the members?"

"I wouldna trust them. The election would hae to be by competitive examination.[142] Na, I canna say wha would draw up the queistions. The scheme's juist growin' i' my mind, but the mair I think o't the better I like it."

---

139 Fac (Sc.): fact.

140 Chield, chiel (Sc.): fellow, chap.

141 Press (Sc.): cupboard.

142 Tammas is in tune with the progressive thinking of his time. Before the mid-nineteenth century jobs in government service were acquired through the applicant's (usually family or local) contacts in the institution in question ('patronage'). Over the second half of the century this was replaced by entry through competitive examination, starting with the Indian Civil Service in 1853.

CHAPTER XVIII.

LEEBY AND JAMIE.

BY the bank of the Quharity on a summer day I have seen a barefooted girl gaze at the running water until tears filled her eyes. That was the birth of romance. Whether this love be but a beautiful dream I cannot say, but this we see, that it comes to all, and colours the whole future life with gold. Leeby must have dreamt it, but I did not know her then. I have heard of a man who would have taken her far away into a country where the corn is yellow when it is still green with us, but she would not leave her mother, nor was it him she saw in her dream. From her earliest days, when she was still a child staggering round the garden with Jamie in her arms, her duty lay before her, straight as the burying-ground road. Jess had need of her in the little home at the top of the brae, where God, looking down upon her as she scrubbed and gossipped and sat up all night with her ailing mother, and never missed the prayer-meeting, and adored the minister, did not perhaps think her the least of His handmaids. Her years were less than thirty when He took her away, but she had few days that were altogether dark. Those who bring sunshine to the lives of others cannot keep it from themselves.

The love Leeby bore for Jamie was such that in their younger days it shamed him. Other laddies knew of it, and flung it at him until he dared Leeby to let on in public that he and she were related.

"Hoo is your lass?" they used to cry to him, inventing a new game.

"I saw Leeby lookin' for ye," they would say; "she's wearyin' for ye to gang an' play wi' her."

Then if they were not much bigger boys than himself, Jamie got them against the dyke and hit them hard until they publicly owned to knowing that she was his sister, and that he was not fond of her.

"It distressed him mair than ye could believe, though," Jess has told me; "an' when he came hame he would greet an' say 'at Leeby disgraced him."

Leeby, of course, suffered for her too obvious affection.

"I wonder 'at ye dinna try to control yersel," Jamie would say to her, as he grew bigger.

"Am sure," said Leeby, "I never gie ye a look if there's onybody there."

"A look! You're ay lookin' at me sae fond-like 'at I dinna ken what wy to turn."

"Weel, I canna help it," said Leeby, probably beginning to whimper.

If Jamie was in a very bad temper he left her, after this, to her own reflections; but he was naturally soft-hearted.

"Am no tellin' ye no to care for me," he told her, "but juist to keep it mair to yersel. Naebody would ken frae me 'at am fond o' ye."

"Mebbe yer no?" said Leeby.

"Ay, am I, but I can keep it secret. When we're in the hoose am juist richt fond o' ye."

"Do ye love me, Jamie?"

Jamie waggled his head in irritation.

"Love," he said, "is an awful like word to use when fowk's weel. Ye shouldna speir sic annoyin' queistions."

"But if ye juist say ye love me I'll never let on again afore fowk 'at yer onything to me ava."

"Ay, ye often say that."

"Do ye no believe my word?"

"I believe fine ye mean what ye say, but ye forget yersel when the time comes."

"Juist try me this time."

"Weel, then, I do."

"Do what?" asked the greedy Leeby.

"What ye said."

"I said love."

"Weel," said Jamie, "I do't."

"What do ye do? Say the word."

"Na," said Jamie, "I winna say the word. It's no a word to say, but I do't."

That was all she could get out of him, unless he was stricken with remorse, when he even went the length of saying the word.

"Leeby kent perfectly weel," Jess has said, " 'at it was a trial to Jamie to tak her ony gait, an' I often used to say to her 'at I wondered at her want o' pride in priggin' wi' him.[143] Ay, but if she could juist get a promise wrung oot o' him, she didna care hoo muckle she had to prig. Syne they quarrelled, an' ane or baith o' them grat (cried) afore they made it up. I mind when Jamie went to the fishin' Leeby was aye terrible keen to get wi' him, but ye see he wouldna be seen gaen through the toon wi' her. 'If ye let me gang,' she said to him, 'I'll no seek to go through the toon wi' ye. Na, I'll gang roond by the Roods an' you can tak the buryin'-ground road,[144] so as we can meet on the hill.' Yes, Leeby was willin' to agree wi' a' that, juist to get gaen wi' him. I've seen lassies makkin' themsels sma' for lads often enough, but I never saw ane 'at prigged so muckle wi' her ain brother. Na, it's other lassies' brothers they like as a rule."

"But though Jamie was terrible reserved aboot it," said Leeby, "he was as fond o' me as ever I was o' him. Ye mind the time I had the measles, mother?"

"Am no likely to forget it, Leeby," said Jess, "an' you blind wi' them for three days. Ay, ay, Jamie was richt taen up aboot ye. I mind he broke open his pirly (money-box), an' bocht a ha'penny worth o' something to ye every day."

"An' ye hinna forgotten the stick?"

" 'Deed no, I hinna. Ye see," Jess explained to me, "Leeby was lyin' ben the hoose, an' Jamie wasna allowed to gang near her for fear o' infection. Weel, he got a lang stick—it was a pea-stick—an' put it 'aneath the door an' waggled it. Ay, he did that a curran times every day, juist to let her see he was thinkin' o' her."

"Mair than that," said Leeby, "he cried oot 'at he loved me."

"Ay, but juist aince," Jess said; "I dinna mind o't but aince. It was the time the doctor came late, an' Jamie, being waukened by him, thocht ye was deein'. I mind as if it was yesterday hoo he cam runnin' to the door an' cried oot, 'I do love ye, Leeby; I love ye richt.' The doctor got a start when he heard the voice, but he laughed loud when he unerstood."

"He had nae business, though," said Leeby, "to tell onybody."

"He was a rale clever man, the doctor," Jess explained to me, "ay, he kent me as weel as though he'd gaen through me wi' a lichted candle. It got oot through him, an' the young billies took to sayin' to Jamie, 'Ye do love her, Jamie; ay, ye love her richt.' The only reglar fecht I ever kent Jamie hae was wi' a lad 'at cried that to him. It was Bowlegs Christy's laddie. Ay, but when she got better Jamie blamed Leeby."

"He no only blamed me," said Leeby, "but he wanted me to pay him back a' the bawbees he had spent on me."[145]

---

143 Tak her ony gait: acknowledge her in any manner (for this sense see *SND* 'tak' 13); priggin': pleading (all Sc.).

144 'The Roods' is the name of a neighbourhood, originally town common-land made available for building on (*SND* 'ruid' 4).

145 Bawbees (Sc.): ha'pennies.

"Ay, an' I sepad he got them too," said Jess.

In time Jamie became a barber in Tilliedrum, trudging many heavy miles there and back twice a day that he might sleep at home, trudging bravely I was to say, but it was what he was born to, and there was hardly an alternative. This was the time I saw most of him, and he and Leeby were often in my thoughts. There is as terrible a bubble in the little kettle as on the cauldron of the world, and some of the scenes between Jamie and Leeby were great tragedies, comedies, what you will, until the kettle was taken off the fire. Hers was the more placid temper; indeed, only in one way could Jamie suddenly rouse her to fury. That was when he hinted that she had a large number of frocks. Leeby knew that there could never be more than a Sabbath frock and an everyday gown for her, both of her mother's making, but Jamie's insinuations were more than she could bear. Then I have seen her seize and shake him. I know from Jess that Leeby cried herself hoarse the day Joey was buried, because her little black frock was not ready for wear.

Until he went to Tilliedrum Jamie had been more a stay-at-home boy than most. The warmth of Jess's love had something to do with keeping his heart aglow, but more, I think, he owed to Leeby. Tilliedrum was his introduction to the world, and for a little it took his head. I was in the house the Sabbath day that he refused to go to church.

He went out in the forenoon to meet the Tilliedrum lads, who were to take him off for a holiday in a cart. Hendry was more wrathful than I remember ever to have seen him, though I have heard how he did with the lodger who broke the Lord's Day. This lodger was a tourist who thought, in folly surely rather than in hardness of heart, to test the religious convictions of an Auld Licht by insisting on paying his bill on a Sabbath morning. He offered the money to Jess, with the warning that if she did not take it now she might never see it. Jess was so kind and good to her lodgers that he could not have known her long who troubled her with this poor trick. She was sorely in need at the time, and entreated the thoughtless man to have some pity on her.

"Now or never," he said, holding out the money.

"Put it on the dresser," said Jess at last, "an' I'll get it the morn."

The few shillings were laid on the dresser, where they remained unfingered until Hendry, with Leeby and Jamie, came in from church.

"What siller's that?" asked Hendry, and then Jess confessed what she had done.

"I wonder at ye, woman," said Hendry, sternly; and lifting the money he climbed up to the attic with it.

He pushed open the door, and confronted the lodger.

"Take back yer siller," he said, laying it on the table, "an' leave my hoose. Man, you're a pitiable crittur to tak the chance, when I was oot, o' playin' upon the poverty o' an onweel woman."

It was with such unwonted severity as this that Hendry called upon Jamie to follow him to church; but the boy went off, and did not return till dusk, defiant and miserable. Jess had been so terrified that she forgave him everything for sight of his face, and Hendry prayed for him at family worship with too much unction. But Leeby cried as if her tender heart would break. For a long time Jamie refused to look at her, but at last he broke down.

"If ye go on like that," he said, 'I'll gang awa oot an' droon mysel, or be a sojer."

This was no uncommon threat of his, and sometimes, when he went off, banging the door violently, she ran after him and brought him back. This time she only wept the more, and so both went to bed in misery. It was after midnight that Jamie rose and crept to Leeby's bedside. Leeby was shaking the bed in her agony. Jess heard what they said.

"Leeby," said Jamie, "dinna greet, an' I'll never do't again."

He put his arms round her, and she kissed him passionately.

"Oh, Jamie," she said, "hae ye prayed to God to forgie ye?"

Jamie did not speak.

"If ye was to die this nicht," cried Leeby, "an' you no made it up wi' God, ye wouldna gang to heaven. Jamie, I canna sleep till ye've made it up wi' God."

But Jamie still hung back. Leeby slipped from her bed, and went down on her knees.

"O God, O dear God," she cried, "mak Jamie to pray to you!"

Then Jamie went down on his knees too, and they made it up with God together.

This is a little thing for me to remember all these years, and yet how fresh and sweet it keeps Leeby in my memory.

Away up in the glen, my lonely schoolhouse lying deep, as one might say, in a sea of snow, I had many hours in the years long by for thinking of my friends in Thrums and mapping out the future of Leeby and Jamie. I saw Hendry and Jess taken to the churchyard, and Leeby left alone in the house. I saw Jamie fulfil his promise to his mother, and take Leeby, that stainless young woman, far away to London, where they had a home together. Ah, but these were only the idle dreams of a dominie. The Lord willed it otherwise.

CHAPTER XIX.

A TALE OF A GLOVE.

SO long as Jamie was not the lad, Jess twinkled gleefully over tales of sweethearting. There was little Kitty Lamby who used to skip in of an evening, and, squatting on a stool near the window, unwind the roll of her enormities. A wheedling thing she was, with an ambition to drive men crazy, but my presence killed the gossip on her tongue, though I liked to look at her. When I entered, the wag at the wa' clock had again possession of the kitchen.[146] I never heard more than the end of a sentence:

"An' did he really say he would fling himsel into the dam, Kitty?"

Or – "True as death, Jess, he kissed me."

Then I wandered away from the kitchen, where I was not wanted, and marvelled to know that Jess of the tender heart laughed most merrily when he really did say that he was going straight to the dam. As no body was found in the dam in those days, whoever he was he must have thought better of it.

But let Kitty, or any other maid, cast a glinting eye on Jamie, then Jess no longer smiled. If he returned the glance she sat silent in her chair till Leeby laughed away her fears.

"Jamie's no the kind, mother," Leeby would say. "Na, he's quiet, but he sees through them. They dinna draw his leg (get over him)."

"Ye never can tell, Leeby. The laddies 'at's maist ill to get sometimes gangs up in a flame a' at aince, like a bit o' paper."

"Ay, weel, at ony rate Jamie's no on fire yet."

Though clever beyond her neighbours, Jess lost all her sharpness if they spoke of a lassie for Jamie.

"I warrant," Tibbie Birse said one day in my hearing, " 'at there's some leddy in London he's thinkin' o'. Ay, he's been a guid laddie to ye, but i' the coorse o' nature he'll be settlin' dune soon."

---

146 A 'wag-at-the-wa'' clock is a wall-mounted one with an unencased pendulum.

Jess did not answer, but she was a picture of woe. "Yer lettin' what Tibbie Birse said lie on yer mind," Leeby remarked, when Tibbie was gone. "What can it maiter what she thinks?"

"I canna help it, Leeby," said Jess. "Na, an' I canna bear to think o'Jamie bein' mairit. It would lay me low to loss my laddie. No yet, no yet."

"But, mother," said Leeby, quoting from the minister at weddings, "ye wouldna be lossin' a son, but juist gainin' a dochter."

"Dinna haver, Leeby," answered Jess, "I want nane o' thae dochters; na, na."

This talk took place while we were still awaiting Jamie's coming. He had only been with us one day when Jess made a terrible discovery. She was looking so mournful when I saw her, that I asked Leeby what was wrong.

"She's brocht it on hersel," said Leeby. "Ye see she was up sune i' the mornin' to begin to the darnin' o' Jamie's stockins an' to warm his sark at the fire afore he put it on. He woke up, an' cried to her 'at he wasna accustomed to ha'en his things warmed for him. Ay, he cried it oot fell thrawn, so she took it into her head 'at there was something in his pouch he didna want her to see.[147] She was even onaisy last nicht."

I asked what had aroused Jess's suspicions last night.

"Ou, ye would notice 'at she sat devourin' him wi' her een, she was so lifted up at ha'en 'im again. Weel, she says noo 'at she saw 'im twa or three times put his hand in his pouch as if he was findin' to mak sure 'at something was safe. So when he fell asleep again this mornin' she got haud o' his jacket to see if there was onything in't. I advised her no to do't, but she couldna help hersel. She put in her hand, an' pu'd it oot. That's what's makkin' her look sae ill."

"But what was it she found?"

"Did I no tell ye? I'm ga'en dottle, I think. It was a glove, a woman's glove, in a bit paper. Ay, though she's sittin' still she's near frantic."

I said I supposed Jess had put the glove back in Jamie's pocket.

"Na," said Leeby, " 'deed no. She wanted to fling it on the back o' the fire, but I woudna let her. That's it she has aneath her apron."

Later in the day I remarked to Leeby that Jamie was very dull.

"He's missed it," she explained.

"Has any one mentioned it to him," I asked, "or has he inquired about it?"

"Na," said Leeby, "there hasna been a syllup (syllable) aboot it. My mother's fleid to mention't, an' he doesna like to speak aboot it either."

"Perhaps he thinks he has lost it?"

"Nae fear o' him," Leeby said. "Na, he kens fine wha has't."

I never knew how Jamie came by the glove, nor whether it had originally belonged to her who made him forget the window at the top of the brae. At the time I looked on as at play-acting, rejoicing in the happy ending. Alas! in the real life how are we to know when we have reached an end?

But this glove, I say, may not have been that woman's, and if it was, she had not then bedevilled him. He was too sheepish to demand it back from his mother, and already he cared for it too much to laugh at Jess's theft with Leeby. So it was that a curious game at chess was played with the glove, the players a silent pair.

Jamie cared little to read books, but on the day following Jess's discovery, I found him on his knees in the attic, looking through mine. A little box, without a lid, held them all, but they seemed a great library to him.

"There's readin' for a lifetime in them," he said. "I was juist takkin' a look through them."

---

147 Thrawn: stubborn, determined; pouch: pocket (both Sc.).

His face was guilty, however, as if his hand had been caught in a money-bag, and I wondered what had enticed the lad to my books. I was still standing pondering when Leeby ran up the stair; she was so active that she generally ran, and she grudged the time lost in recovering her breath.

"I'll put yer books richt," she said, making her word good as she spoke. "I kent Jamie had been ransackin' up here, though he cam up rale canny. Ay, ye would notice he was in his stockin' soles."

I had not noticed this, but I remembered now his slipping from the room very softly. If he wanted a book, I told Leeby, he could have got it without any display of cunning.

"It's no a book he's lookin' for," she said, "na, it's his glove."

The time of day was early for Leeby to gossip, but I detained her for a moment.

"My mother's hodded (hid) it," she explained, "an' he winna speir nae queistions. But he's lookin' for't. He was ben in the room searchin' the drawers when I was up i' the toon in the forenoon. Ye see he pretends no to be carin' afore me, an' though my mother's sittin' sae quiet-like at the window she's hearkenin' a' the time. Ay, an' he thocht I had hod it up here."

But where, I asked, was the glove hid.

"I ken nae mair than yersel," said Leeby. "My mother's gi'en to hoddin' things. She has a place aneath the bed whaur she keeps the siller, an' she's no speakin' aboot the glove to me noo, because she thinks Jamie an' me's in comp (company). I speired at her whaur she had hod it, but she juist said, 'What would I be doin' hoddin't?' She'll never admit to me 'at she hods the siller either."

Next day Leeby came to me with the latest news.

"He's found it," she said, "ay, he's got the glove again. Ye see, what put him on the wrang scent was a notion 'at I had put it some gait. He kent 'at if she'd hod it, the kitchen maun be the place, but he thocht she'd gi'en it to me to hod. He cam upon't by accident. It was aneath the paddin' o' her chair."

Here, I thought, was the end of the glove incident, but I was mistaken. There were no presses or drawers with locks in the house, and Jess got hold of the glove again. I suppose she had reasoned out no line of action. She merely hated the thought that Jamie should have a woman's glove in his possession.

"She beats a' wi' 'cuteness,"[148] Leeby said to me. "Jamie didna put the glove back in his pouch. Na, he kens her ower weel by this time. She was up, though, lang afore he was wauken, an' she gaed almost strecht to the place whaur he had hod it.[149] I believe she lay waukin a' nicht thinkin' oot whaur it would be. Ay, it was aneath the mattress. I saw her hodden't i' the back o' the drawer, but I didna let on."

I quite believed Leeby when she told me afterwards that she had watched Jamie feeling beneath the mattress.

"He had a face," she said, "I assure ye, he had a face, when he discovered the glove was gone again."

"He maun be terrible ta'en up aboot it," Jess said to Leeby, "or he wouldna keep it aneath the mattress."

"Od," said Leeby," it was yersel 'at drove him to't."

Again Jamie recovered his property, and again Jess got hold of it. This time he looked in vain. I learnt the fate of the glove from Leeby.

"Ye mind 'at she keepit him at hame frae the kirk on Sabbath, because he had a cauld?" Leeby said. "Ay, me or my father would hae a gey ill cauld afore she would

---

148 'cuteness: that is, acuteness.
149 Strecht (Sc.): straight.

let's bide at hame frae the kirk; but Jamie's different. Weel, mair than aince she's been near speakin' to 'im aboot the glove, but she grew fleid aye. She was sae terrified there was something in't.

"On Sabbath, though, she had him to hersel, an' he wasna so bright as usual. She sat wi' the Bible on her lap, pretendin' to read, but a' the time she was takkin' keeks (glances) at him. I dinna ken 'at he was broodin' ower the glove, but she thocht he was, an' juist afore the kirk came oot she couldna stand it nae langer. She put her hand in her pouch, an' pu'd oot the glove,[150] wi' the paper round it, juist as it had been when she came upon't.

"'That's yours, Jamie,' she said; 'it was ill-dune o' me to tak it, but I couldna help it.'

"Jamie put oot his hand, an' syne he drew't back. 'It's no a thing o' nae consequence, mother,' he said.

"'Wha is she, Jamie?' my mother said.

"He turned awa his heid — so she telt me. 'It's a lassie in London,' he said, 'I dinna ken her muckle."

"'Ye maun ken her weel,' my mother persisted, 'to be carryin' aboot her glove; I'm dootin' yer gey fond o' her, Jamie?'

"'Na', said Jamie, 'am no. There's no naebody I care for like yersel, mother.'

"Ye wouldna carry aboot onything o' mine, Jamie,' my mother said; but he says, 'Oh, mother, I carry aboot yer face wi' me aye; an' sometimes at nicht I kind o' greet to think o' ye.'

"Ay, after that I've nae doot he was sittin' wi' his airms aboot her. She didna tell me that, but weel he kens it's what she likes, an' she maks nae pretence o' it's no bein'. But for a' he said an' did, she noticed him put the glove back in his inside pouch.

"'It's wrang o' me, Jamie,' she said, 'but I canna bear to think o' ye carryin' that aboot sae carefu'. No, I canna help it.'

"Weel, Jamie, the crittur, took it oot o' his pouch, an' kind o' hesitated. Syne he lays't on the back o' the fire, an' they sat thegither glowerin' at it.

"'Noo, mother,' he says, 'you're satisfied, are ye no?'

"Ay," Leeby ended her story, "she said she was satisfied. But she saw 'at he laid it on the fire fell fond-like."

CHAPTER XX.

THE LAST NICHT.

"JUIST another sax nichts, Jamie," Jess would say, sadly. "Juist fower nichts noo, an' you'll be awa." Even as she spoke seemed to come the last night.

The last night! Reserve slipped unheeded to the floor. Hendry wandered ben and but the house, and Jamie sat at the window holding his mother's hand. You must walk softly now if you would cross that humble threshold. I stop at the door. Then, as now, I was a lonely man, and when the last night came the attic was the place for me.

This family affection, how good and beautiful it is. Men and maids love, and after many years they may rise to this. It is the grand proof of the goodness in human nature, for it means that the more we see of each other the more we find that is lovable. If you would cease to dislike a man, try to get nearer his heart.

Leeby had no longer any excuse for bustling about. Everything was ready — too

---

150 Pu'd (Sc.): pulled.

soon. Hendry had been to the fish-cadger in the square to get a bervie for Jamie's supper, and Jamie had eaten it, trying to look as if it made him happier.[151] His little box was packed and strapped, and stood terribly conspicuous against the dresser. Jess had packed it herself.

"Ye mauna trachle (trouble) yersel, mother," Jamie said, when she had the empty box pulled toward her.

Leeby was wiser.

"Let her do't," she whispered, "it'll keep her frae broodin'."

Jess tied ends of yarn round the stockings to keep them in a little bundle by themselves. So she did with all the other articles.

"No 'at it's ony great affair," she said, for on the last night they were all thirsting to do something for Jamie that would be a great affair to him.

"Ah, ye would wonder, mother," Jamie said, "when I open my box an' find a'thing tied up wi' strings sae careful, it a' comes back to me wi' a rush wha did it, an' 'am as fond o' thae strings as though they were a grand present. There's the pocky (bag) ye gae me to keep sewin' things in. I get the wifie I lodge wi' to sew to me, but often when I come upon the pocky I sit an' look at it."

Two chairs were backed to the fire, with underclothing hanging upside down on them. From the string over the fireplace dangled two pairs of much-darned stockings.

"Ye'll put on baith thae pair o'stockin's, Jamie," said Jess, "juist to please me?"

When he arrived he had rebelled against the extra clothing.

"Ay, will I, mother?" he said now.

Jess put her hand fondly through his ugly hair. How handsome she thought him.

"Ye have a fine brow, Jamie," she said. "I mind the day ye was born sayin' to mysel 'at ye had a fine brow."

"But ye thocht he was to be a lassie, mother," said Leeby.

"Na, Leeby, I didna. I kept sayin' I thocht he would be a lassie because I was fleid he would be; but a' the time I had a presentiment he would be a laddie. It was wi' Joey deein' sae sudden, an' I took on sae terrible aboot 'im 'at I thocht a' alang the Lord would gie me another laddie."

"Ay, I wanted 'im to be a laddie myself," said Hendry, "so as he could tak Joey's place."

Jess's head jerked back involuntarily, and Jamie may have felt her hand shake, for he said in a voice out of Hendry's hearing—

"I never took Joey's place wi' ye, mother."

Jess pressed his hand tightly in her two worn palms, but she did not speak.

"Jamie was richt like Joey when he was a bairn," Hendry said.

Again Jess's head moved, but still she was silent.

"They were sae like," continued Hendry, " 'at often I called Jamie by Joey's name."

Jess looked at her husband, and her mouth opened and shut.

"I canna mind 'at you ever did that?" Hendry said.

She shook her head.

"Na," said Hendry, "you never mixed them up. I dinna think ye ever missed Joey sae sair as I did."

Leeby went ben, and stood in the room in the dark; Jamie knew why.

"I'll just gang ben an' speak to Leeby for a meenute," he said to his mother; "I'll no be lang."

"Ay, do that, Jamie," said Jess. "What Leeby's been to me nae tongue can tell. Ye canna bear to hear me speak, I ken, o' the time when Hendry an' me'll be awa, but, Jamie, when that time comes ye'll no forget Leeby?"

151 A bervie is a smoked haddock, as made in the fishing village of Inverbervie on the east coast.

"I winna, mother, I winna," said Jamie. "There'll never be a roof ower me 'at's no hers too."

He went ben and shut the door. I do not know what he and Leeby said. Many a time since their earliest youth had these two been closeted together, often to make up their little quarrels in each other's arms. They remained a long time in the room, the shabby room of which Jess and Leeby were so proud, and whatever might be their fears about their mother they were not anxious for themselves. Leeby was feeling lusty and well, and she could not know that Jamie required to be reminded of his duty to the folk at home. Jamie would have laughed at the notion. Yet that woman in London must have been waiting for him even then. Leeby, who was about to die, and Jamie, who was to forget his mother, came back to the kitchen with a happy light on their faces. I have with me still the look of love they gave each other before Jamie crossed over to Jess.

"Ye'll gang anower, noo, mother," Leeby said, meaning that it was Jess's bed-time.

"No yet, Leeby," Jess answered, "I'll sit up till the readin's ower."

"I think ye should gang, mother," Jamie said, an' I'll come an' sit aside ye after ye're i' yer bed."

"Ay, Jamie, I'll no hae ye to sit aside me the morn's nicht, an' hap (cover) me wi' the claes."

"But ye'll gang suner to yer bed, mother."

"I may gang, but I winna sleep. I'll aye be thinkin' o' ye tossin' on the sea. I pray for ye a lang time ilka nicht, Jamie."

"Ay, I ken."

"An' I pictur ye ilka hour o' the day. Ye never gang hame through thae terrible streets at nicht but I'm thinkin' o' ye."

"I would try no to be sae sad, mother," said Leeby. "We've ha'en a richt fine time, have we no?"

"It's been an awfu' happy time," said Jess. "We've ha'en a pleasantness in oor lives 'at comes to few. I ken naebody 'at's ha'en sae muckle happiness one wy or another."

"It's because ye're sae guid, mother," said Jamie.

"Na, Jamie, 'am no guid ava. It's because my fowk's been sae guid, you an' Hendry an' Leeby an' Joey when he was livin'. I've got a lot mair than my deserts."

"We'll juist look to meetin' next year again, mother. To think o' that keeps me up a' the winter."

"Ay, if it's the Lord's will, Jamie, but am gey dune noo, an' Hendry's fell worn too."

Jamie, the boy that he was, said, "Dinna speak like that, mother," and Jess again put her hand on his head.

"Fine I ken, Jamie," she said, " 'at all my days on this earth, be they short or lang, I've you for a staff to lean on."

Ah, many years have gone since then, but if Jamie be living now he has still those words to swallow.

By and by Leeby went ben for the Bible, and put it into Hendry's hands. He slowly turned over the leaves to his favourite chapter, the fourteenth of John's Gospel. Always, on eventful occasions, did Hendry turn to the fourteenth of John.

"Let not your heart be troubled; ye believe in God, believe also in Me."

"In My Father's house are many mansions; if it were not so I would have told you. I go to prepare a place for you."

As Hendry raised his voice to read there was a great stillness in the kitchen. I do not know that I have been able to show in the most imperfect way what kind of man Hendry was. He was dense in many things, and the cleverness that was Jess's had been denied to him. He had less book-learning than most of those with whom he passed his days, and he had little skill in talk. I have not known a man more easily taken in by persons whose speech had two faces. But a more simple, modest, upright man, there never was in Thrums, and I shall always revere his memory.

"And if I go and prepare a place for you, I will come again, and receive you unto Myself; that where I am there ye may be also."

The voice may have been monotonous. I have always thought that Hendry's reading of the Bible was the most solemn and impressive I have ever heard. He exulted in the fourteenth of John, pouring it forth like one whom it intoxicated while he read. He emphasized every other word; it was so real and grand to him.

We went upon our knees while Hendry prayed, all but Jess, who could not. Jamie buried his face in her lap. The words Hendry said were those he used every night. Some, perhaps, would have smiled at his prayer to God that we be not puffed up with riches nor with the things of this world. His head shook with emotion while he prayed, and he brought us very near to the throne of grace. "Do thou, O our God," he said, in conclusion, "spread Thy guiding hand over him whom in Thy great mercy Thou hast brought to us again, and do Thou guard him through the perils which come unto those that go down to the sea in ships. Let not our hearts be troubled, neither let them be afraid, for this is not our abiding home, and may we all meet in Thy house, where there are many mansions, and where there will be no last night. Amen."

It was a silent kitchen after that, though the lamp burned long in Jess's window. By its meagre light you may take a final glance at the little family; you will never see them together again.

CHAPTER XXI.

JESS LEFT ALONE.

THERE may be a few who care to know how the lives of Jess and Hendry ended. Leeby died in the back-end of the year I have been speaking of, and as I was snowed up in the school-house at the time, I heard the news from Gavin Birse too late to attend her funeral. She got her death on the commonty one day of sudden rain, when she had run out to bring in her washing, for the terrible cold she woke with next morning carried her off very quickly. Leeby did not blame Jamie for not coming to her, nor did I, for I knew that even in the presence of death the poor must drag their chains. He never got Hendry's letter with the news, and we know now that he was already in the hands of her who played the devil with his life. Before the spring came he had been lost to Jess.

"Them 'at has got sae mony blessin's mair than the generality," Hendry said to me one day, when Craigiebuckle had given me a lift into Thrums, "has nae shame if they would pray aye for mair. The Lord has gi'en this hoose sae muckle, 'at to pray for mair looks like no bein' thankfu' for what we've got. Ay, but I canna help prayin' to Him 'at in His great mercy he'll tak Jess afore me. Noo 'at Leeby's gone, an' Jamie never lets us hear frae him, I canna gulp doon the thocht o' Jess bein' left alane."

This was a prayer that Hendry may be pardoned for having so often in his heart, though God did not think fit to grant it. In Thrums, when a weaver died, his womenfolk had to take his seat at the loom, and those who, by reason of infirmities, could not do so, went to a place, the name of which, I thank God, I am not compelled to write in this chapter. I could not, even at this day, have told any episodes in the life of Jess had it ended in the poorhouse.[152]

Hendry would probably have recovered from the fever had not this terrible dread darkened his intellect when he was still prostrate. He was lying in the kitchen when I saw him last in life, and his parting words must be sadder to the reader than they were to me. "Ay, richt ye are," he said, in a voice that had become a child's; "I hae muckle, muckle, to be thankfu' for, an' no the least is 'at baith me an' Jess has aye belonged to a bural society.[153] We hae nae cause to be anxious aboot a' thing bein' dune respectable aince we're gone. It was Jess 'at insisted on oor joinin': a' the wisest things I ever did I was put up to by her."

I parted from Hendry, cheered by the doctor's report, but the old weaver died a few days afterwards. His end was mournful, yet I can recall it now as the not unworthy close of a good man's life. One night poor worn Jess had been helped ben into the room, Tibbie Birse having undertaken to sit up with Hendry. Jess slept for the first time for many days, and as the night was dying Tibbie fell asleep too. Hendry had been better than usual, lying quietly, Tibbie said, and the fever was gone. About three o'clock Tibbie woke and rose to mend the fire. Then she saw that Hendry was not in his bed.

Tibbie went ben the house in her stocking-soles, but Jess heard her.

"What is't, Tibbie?" she asked, anxiously.

"Ou, it's no naething," Tibbie said, "he's lyin' rale quiet."

Then she went up to the attic. Hendry was not in the house.

She opened the door gently and stole out. It was not snowing, but there had been a heavy fall two days before, and the night was windy. A tearing gale had blown the upper part of the brae clear, and from T'nowhead's fields the snow was rising like smoke. Tibbie ran to the farm and woke up T'nowhead.

For an hour they looked in vain for Hendry. At last some one asked who was working in Elshioner's shop all night. This was the long earthen-floored room in which Hendry's loom stood with three others.

"It'll be Sanders Whamond likely," T'nowhead said, and the other men nodded.

But it happened that T'nowhead's Bell, who had flung on a wrapper, and hastened across to sit with Jess, heard of the light in Elshioner's shop.

"It's Hendry," she cried, and then every one moved toward the workshop.

The light at the diminutive, yarn-covered window was pale and dim, but Bell, who was at the house first, could make the most of a cruizey's glimmer.

"It's him," she said, and then, with swelling throat, she ran back to Jess.

The door of the workshop was wide open, held against the wall by the wind. T'nowhead and the others went in. The cruizey stood on the little window. Hendry's back was to the door, and he was leaning forward on the silent loom. He had been dead for some time, but his fellow-workers saw that he must have weaved for nearly an hour.

So it came about that for the last few months of her pilgrimage Jess was left alone. Yet I may not say that she was alone. Jamie, who should have been with her, was undergoing his own ordeal far away; where, we did not now even know. But though

---

152 That Thrums has a poorhouse we know from chapter I. Traditionally, financial support for the very poor, including the sick, old and unemployed, had been raised and distributed by local parishes and magistrates. The Poor Law Amendment Act of 1834 made poor-relief increasingly conditional on entering new, designedly unpleasant, institutions such as this, with the intention of forcing the unemployed to migrate to where work might be available.

153 Burial societies were co-operatives that offered insurance, for a minimal premium, to cover the cost of a decent funeral.

the poorhouse stands in Thrums, where all may see it, the neighbours did not think only of themselves.

Than Tammas Haggart there can scarcely have been a poorer man, but Tammas was the first to come forward with offer of help. To the day of Jess's death he did not once fail to carry her water to her in the morning, and the luxuriously living men of Thrums, in these present days of pumps at every corner, can hardly realize what that meant. Often there were lines of people at the well by three o'clock in the morning, and each had to wait his turn. Tammas filled his own pitcher and pan, and then had to take his place at the end of the line with Jess's pitcher and pan, to wait his turn again. His own house was in the Tenements, far from the brae in winter time, but he always said to Jess it was "naething ava."

Every Saturday old Robbie Angus sent a bag of sticks and shavings from the saw-mill by his little son Rob, who was afterwards to become a man for speaking about at nights. Of all the friends that Jess and Hendry had, T'nowhead was the ablest to help, and the sweetest memory I have of the farmer and his wife is the delicate way they offered it. You who read will see Jess wince at the offer of charity. But the poor have fine feelings beneath the grime, as you will discover if you care to look for them, and when Jess said she would bake if any one would buy, you would wonder to hear how many kindly folk came to her door for scones.

She had the house to herself at nights, but Tibbie Birse was with her early in the morning, and other neighbours dropped in. Not for long did she have to wait the summons to the better home.

"Na," she said to the minister, who has told me that he was a better man from knowing her, "my thochts is no nane set on the vanities o' the world noo. I kenna hoo I could ever hae ha'en sic an ambeetion to hae thae stuff-bottomed chairs."

I have tried to keep away from Jamie, whom the neighbours sometimes upbraided in her presence. It is of him you who read would like to hear, and I cannot pretend that Jess did not sit at her window looking for him.

"Even when she was bakin'," Tibbie told me, "she aye had an eye on the brae. If Jamie had come at ony time when it was licht she would hae seen 'im as sune as he turned the corner."

"If he ever comes back, the sacket (rascal)," T'nowhead said to Jess, "we'll show 'im the door gey quick."

Jess just looked, and all the women knew how she would take Jamie to her arms.

We did not know of the London woman then, and Jess never knew of her. Jamie's mother never for an hour allowed that he had become anything but the loving laddie of his youth.

"I ken 'im ower weel," she always said, "my ain Jamie."

Toward the end she was sure he was dead. I do not know when she first made up her mind to this, nor whether it was not merely a phrase for those who wanted to discuss him with her. I know that she still sat at the window looking at the elbow of the brae.

The minister was with her when she died. She was in her chair, and he asked her, as was his custom, if there was any particular chapter which she would like him to read. Since her husband's death she had always asked for the fourteenth of John, "Hendry's chapter," as it is still called among a very few old people in Thrums. This time she asked him to read the sixteenth chapter of Genesis.

"When I came to the thirteenth verse," the minister told me, "'And she called the name of the Lord that spake unto her, Thou God seest me,' she covered her face with her two hands, and said, 'Joey's text, Joey's text. Oh, but I grudged ye sair, Joey.'"

"I shut the book," the minister said, "when I came to the end of the chapter, and then I saw that she was dead. It is my belief that her heart broke one-and-twenty years ago."

CHAPTER XXII.

JAMIE'S HOME-COMING.

ON a summer day, when the sun was in the weavers' workshops, and bairns hopped solemnly at the game of palaulays, or gaily shook their bottles of sugarelly water into a froth, Jamie came back. The first man to see him was Hookey Crewe, the post.

"When he came frae London," Hookey said afterwards at T'nowhead's pig-sty, "Jamie used to wait for me at Zoar, i' the north end o' Tilliedrum. He carried his box ower the market muir, an' sat on't at Zoar, waitin' for me to catch 'im up. Ay, the day afore yesterday me an' the powny was clatterin' by Zoar, when there was Jamie standin' in his identical place. He hadna nae box to sit upon, an' he was far frae bein' weel in order, but I kent 'im at aince, an' I saw 'at he was waitin' for me. So I drew up, an' waved my hand to 'im."

"I would hae drove straucht by 'im," said T'nowhead; "them 'at leaves their auld mother to want doesna deserve a lift."

"Ay, ye say that sittin' there," Hookey said; "but, lads, I saw his face, an' as sure as death it was sic an' awfu' meeserable face 'at I couldna but pu' the powny up. Weel, he stood for the space o' a meenute lookin' straucht at me, as if he would like to come forrit but dauredna, an' syne he turned an' strided awa ower the muir like a huntit thing. I sat still i' the cart, an' when he was far awa he stoppit an' lookit again, but a' my cryin' wouldna bring him a step back, an' i' the end I drove on. I've thocht since syne 'at he didna ken whether his fowk was livin' or deid, an' was fleid to speir."

"He didna ken," said T'nowhead, "but the faut was his ain. It's ower late to be ta'en up aboot Jess noo."

"Ay, ay, T'nowhead," said Hookey, "it's aisy to you to speak like that. Ye didna see his face."

It is believed that Jamie walked from Tilliedrum, though no one is known to have met him on the road. Some two hours after the post left him he was seen by old Rob Angus at the sawmill.

"I was sawin' awa wi' a' my micht," Rob said, "an' little Rob was haudin' the booards, for they were silly but things, when something made me look at the window. It couldna hae been a tap on't, for the birds has used me to that, an' it would hardly be a shadow, for little Rob didna look up. Whatever it was I stoppit i' the middle o' a booard, an' lookit up, an' there I saw Jamie McQumpha. He joukit back when our een met, but I saw him weel;[154] ay, it's a queer thing to say, but he had the face o' a man 'at had come straucht frae hell."

"I stood starin' at the window," Angus continued, "after he'd gone, an' Robbie cried oot to ken what was the maiter wi' me. Ay, that brocht me back to mysel, an' I hurried oot to look for Jamie, but he wasna to be seen. That face gae me a turn."

From the saw-mill to the house at the top of the brae, some may remember, the road is up the commonty. I do not think any one saw Jamie on the commonty, though there were those to say they met him. "He gae me sic a look," a woman said, " 'at I was fleid an' ran hame," but she did not tell the story until Jamie's home-coming had become a legend.

---

154 Joukit back (Sc): jerked back (as if to avoid a blow).

There were many women hanging out their washing on the commonty that day, and none of them saw him. I think Jamie must have approached his old home by the fields, and probably he held back until gloaming.

The young woman who was now mistress of the house at the top of the brae both saw and spoke with Jamie.

"Twa or three times," she said, "I had seen a man walk quick up the brae an' by the door. It was gettin' dark, but I noticed 'at he was short an' thin, an' I would hae said he wasna nane weel if it hadna been 'at he gaed by at sic a steek.[155] He didna look our wy—at least no when he was close up, an' I set 'im doon for some ga'en aboot body. Na, I saw naething aboot 'im to be fleid at.

"The aucht o'clock bell was ringin' when I saw 'im to speak to. My twa-year-auld bairn was standin' aboot the door, an' I was makkin' some porridge for my man's supper when I heard the bairny skirlin'. She cam runnin' in to the hoose an' hung i' my wrapper, an' she was hingin' there, when I gaed to the door to see what was wrang.

"It was the man I'd seen passin' the hoose. He was standin' at the gate, which, as a'body kens, is but sax steps frae the hoose, an' I wondered at 'im neither runnin' awa nor comin' forrit. I speired at 'im what he meant by terrifyin' a bairn, but he didna say naething. He juist stood. It was ower dark to see his face richt, an' I wasna nane ta'en aback yet, no till he spoke. Oh, but he had a fearsome word when he did speak. It was a kind o' like a man hoarse wi' a cauld, an' yet no that either."

"'Wha bides i' this hoose?' he said, ay standin' there.

"'It's Davit Patullo's hoose,' I said, 'an' am the wife.'

"'Whaur's Hendry McQumpha?' he speired.

"'He's deid,' I said.

"He stood still for a fell while.

"'An' his wife, Jess?' he said.

"'She's deid, too,' I said.

"I thocht he gae a groan, but it may hae been the gate.

"'There was a dochter, Leeby?' he said.

"'Ay,' I said, 'she was ta'en first.'

"I saw 'im put up his hands to his face, an' he cried oot, 'Leeby too!' an' syne he kind o' fell agin the dyke. I never kent 'im nor nane o' his fowk, but I had heard aboot them, an' I saw 'at it would be the son frae London. It wasna for me to judge 'im, an' I said to 'im would he no come in by an' tak a rest. I was nearer 'im by that time, an' it's an awfu' haver to say 'at he had a face to frichten fowk. It was a rale guid face, but no ava what a body would like to see on a young man. I felt mair like greetin' mysel when I saw his face than drawin' awa frae 'im.

"But he wouldnae come in. 'Rest,' he said, like ane speakin' to 'imsel, 'na, there's nae mair rest for me.' I didna weel ken what mair to say to 'im, for he aye stood on, an' I wasna even sure 'at he saw me. He raised his heid when he heard me tellin' the bairn no to tear my wrapper.

"'Dinna set yer heart ower muckle on that bairn,' he cried oot, sharp like. 'I was aince like her, an' I used to hing aboot my mother, too, in that very roady. Ay, I thocht I was fond o' her, an' she thocht it too. Tak' a care, wuman, 'at that bairn doesna grow up to murder ye.'

"He gae a lauch when he saw me tak haud o' the bairn, an' syne a' at aince he gaed awa quick. But he wasna far doon the brae when he turned an' came back.

"'Ye'll, mebbe, tell me,' he said, richt low, 'if ye hae the furniture 'at used to be my mother's?'

---

155 Steek (Sc.): a quick rate or pace (*SND* 4: a specifically Angus usage).

"'Na,' I said, 'It was roupit, an' I kenna whaur the things gaed, for me an' my man comes frae Tilliedrum.'

"'Ye wouldna hae heard,' he said, 'wha got the muckle airm-chair 'at used to sit i' the kitchen i' the window 'at looks ower the brae?'

"'I couldna be sure,' I said, 'but there was an armchair 'at gaed to Tibbie Birse. If it was the ane ye mean, it a' gaed to bits, an' I think they bumed it. It was gey dune.'

"'Ay,' he said. 'It was gey dune.'

"'There was the chairs ben i' the room,' he said, after a while.

"I said I thocht Sanders Elshioner had got them at a bargain because twa o' them was mended wi' glue, an' gey silly.

"'Ay, that's them,' he said, 'they were richt neat mended. It was my mother 'at glued them. I mind o' her makkin' the glue, an' warnin' me an' my father no to sit on them. There was the clock too, an' the stool 'at my mother got oot an' into her bed wi', an' the basket 'at Leeby carried when she gaed the errands. The straw was aff the handle, an' my father mended it wi' strings.'

"'I dinna ken,' I said, 'whaur nane o' thae gaed; but did yer mother hae a staff?'

"'A little staff,' he said; 'it was near black wi' age. She couldna gang frae the bed to her chair withoot it. It was broadened oot at the foot wi' her leanin' on't sae muckle.'

"'I've heard tell,' I said, ' 'at the dominie up i' Glen Quharity took awa the staff.'

"He didna speir for nae other thing. He had the gate in his hand, but I dinna think he kent 'at he was swingin't back an' forrit. At last he let it go.

"'That's a',' he said, 'I maun awa. Good-nicht, an' thank ye kindly.'

"I watched 'im till he gaed oot o' sicht. He gaed doon the brae."

We learnt afterwards from the gravedigger that some one spent great part of that night in the graveyard, and we believe it to have been Jamie. He walked up the glen to the school-house next forenoon, and I went out to meet him when I saw him coming down the path.

"Ay," he said, "it's me come back."

I wanted to take him into the house and speak with him of his mother, but he would not cross the threshold.

"I came oot," he said, "to see if ye would gie me her staff—no 'at I deserve't."

I brought out the staff and handed it to him, thinking that he and I would soon meet again. As he took it I saw that his eyes were sunk back into his head. Two great tears hung on his eyelids, and his mouth closed in agony. He stared at me till the tears fell upon his cheeks, and then he went away.

That evening he was seen by many persons crossing the square. He went up the brae to his old home, and asked leave to go through the house for the last time. First he climbed up into the attic, and stood looking in, his feet still on the stair. Then he came down and stood at the door of the room, but he went into the kitchen.

"I'll ask one last favour o' ye," he said to the woman: "I would like ye to leave me here alane for juist a little while."

"I gaed oot," the woman said, "meanin' to leave 'im to 'imsel', but my bairn wouldna come, an' he said, 'Never mind her,' so I left her wi' 'im an' closed the door. He was in a lang time, but I never kent what he did, for the bairn juist aye greets when I speir at her.

"I watched 'im frae the corner window gang doon the brae till he came to the corner. I thocht he turned round there an' stood lookin' at the hoose. He would see me better than I saw him, for my lamp was i' the window, whaur I've heard tell his mother keepit her cruizey. When my man came in I speired at 'im if he'd seen onybody standin' at the corner o' the brae, an' he said he thocht he'd seen somebody wi' a little staff in his hand. Davit gaed doon to see if he was aye there after supper-time, but he was gone."

Jamie was never again seen in Thrums.

From Matthew Arnold,
"On the Study of Celtic Literature" (1866).[1]

[Politics vs. "Literature":]

[...] The fusion of all the inhabitants of these islands into one homogeneous, English-speaking whole, the breaking down of barriers between us, the swallowing up of separate provincial nationalities, is a consummation to which the natural course of things irresistibly tends; it is a necessity of what is called modern civilisation, and modern civilisation is a real, legitimate force; the change must come, and its accomplishment is a mere affair of time. The sooner the Welsh language disappears as an instrument of the practical, political, social life of Wales, the better; the better for England, the better for Wales itself. [...]

[HOWEVER,] I regard the Welsh literature, — or rather, dropping the distinction between Welsh and Irish, Gaels and Cymris, let me say Celtic literature, — as an object of very great interest. My brother Saxons have, as is well known, a terrible way with them of wanting to improve everything but themselves off the face of the earth; I have no such passion for finding nothing but myself everywhere; I like variety to exist and to show itself to me, and I would not for the world have the lineaments of the Celtic genius lost. But I know my brother Saxons, I know their strength, and I know that the Celtic genius will make nothing of trying to set up barriers against them in the world of fact and brute force, of trying to hold its own against them as a political and social counter-power, as the soul of a hostile nationality. [...]

[The Celtic Genius as Sentiment:]

Sentiment is [...] the word which marks where the Celtic races really touch and are one; sentimental, if the Celtic nature is to be characterised by a single term, is the best term to take. An organisation quick to feel impressions, and feeling them very strongly; a lively personality therefore, keenly sensitive to joy and to sorrow; this is the main point. If the downs of life too much outnumber the ups, this temperament, just because it is so quickly and nearly conscious of all impressions, may no doubt be seen shy and wounded; it may be seen in wistful regret, it may be seen in passionate, penetrating melancholy; but its essence is to aspire ardently after life, light, and emotion, to be expansive, adventurous, and gay. [...]

Sentimental, — *always ready to react against the despotism of fact;* that is the description a great friend of the Celt gives of him;[2] and it is not a bad description of the sentimental temperament; it lets us into the secret of its dangers and of its habitual want of success. Balance, measure, and patience, these are the eternal conditions, even supposing the happiest temperament to start with, of high success; and balance, measure, and patience are just what the Celt has never had. Even in the world of spiritual creation, he has never, in spite of his admirable gifts of quick perception and warm emotion, succeeded perfectly, because he never has had steadiness, patience, sanity enough to comply with the conditions under which alone can expression be perfectly given to the finest perceptions and emotions. [...]

---

1   This essay was based on a series of lectures advocating the establishment of a chair of Celtic at Oxford. For the complete text see R.H. Super (ed.), *Lectures and Essays in Criticism. The Complete Prose Works of Matthew Arnold* vol. III (Ann Arbor: University of Michigan Press, 1962). Extract headings in square brackets are the present editor's addition.
2   The 'great friend' is the historian Henri Martin (1810–83) in his *Histoire de France*, which had appeared in an expanded 16-volume version in 1861–65.

And as in material civilisation he has been ineffectual, so has the Celt been ineffectual in politics. This colossal, impetuous, adventurous wanderer, the Titan of the early world, who in primitive times fills so large a place on the earth's scene, dwindles and dwindles as history goes on, and at last is shrunk to what we now see him. For ages and ages the world has been constantly slipping, ever more and more, out of the Celt's grasp. "They went forth to war," Ossian says most truly, "*but they always fell.*"[3]

[The Celtic, Nature, and the Feminine:]
And yet, if one sets about constituting an ideal genius, what a great deal of the Celt does one find oneself drawn to put into it! [...] Sensibility gives genius its materials; one cannot have too much of it, if one can but keep its master and not be its slave. Do not let us wish that the Celt had had less sensibility, but that he had been more master of it. Even as it is, if his sensibility has been a source of weakness to him, it has been a source of power too, and a source of happiness. Some people have found in the Celtic nature and its sensibility the main root out of which chivalry and romance and the glorification of a feminine ideal spring; [...] [In any case,] no doubt the sensibility of the Celtic nature, its nervous exaltation, have something feminine in them, and the Celt is thus particularly disposed to feel the spell of the feminine idiosyncrasy; he has an affinity to it; he is not far from its secret. Again, his sensibility gives him a particularly near and intimate feeling of nature and the life of nature; here, too, he seems in a special way attracted by the secret before him, the secret of natural beauty and natural magic, and to be close to it, to half-divine it.

[The Celtic element in the English race and English poetry:]
Here, then, if commingling there is in our [i.e. English] race, are two very unlike elements to commingle: the steady-going Saxon temperament and the sentimental Celtic temperament. [...]
It is in our poetry that the Celtic part in us has left its trace clearest [sic], and in our poetry I must follow it before I have done.
If I were asked where English poetry got these three things, its turn for style, its turn for melancholy, and its turn for natural magic, for catching and rendering the charm of nature in a wonderfully near and vivid way, — I should answer, with some doubt, that it got much of its turn for style from a Celtic source; with less doubt, that it got much of its melancholy from a Celtic source; and with no doubt at all, that from a Celtic source it got nearly all its natural magic.

[The Function of the Celtic at the Present Time:]
So long as this mixed constitution of our nature possesses us, we pay it tribute and serve it [...] So long as we are blindly and ignorantly rolled around by the forces of our nature, their contradiction baffles us and lames us; so soon as we have clearly discerned what they are, and begun to apply to them a law of measure, control, and guidance, they may be made to work to our good and to carry us forward. [...] But this they have not yet been; we ride one force of our nature to death; we will be nothing but Anglo-Saxons in the Old World or in the New; and when our race has built Bold Street, Liverpool, and pronounced it very good, it hurries across the Atlantic, and builds Nashville, and Jacksonville, and Milledgeville, and thinks it is fulfilling the designs of Providence in an incomparable manner. But true Anglo-Saxons, simply and sincerely rooted in the German nature, we are not and cannot be [...].

'They came forth to war, but they always fell.' From 'Cath-Loda', Duan Second, in *The Works of Ossian, the Son of Fingal, translated from the Galic Language by James Macpherson*. In Two Volumes. Vol. I (London 1773).

From Fiona Macleod (William Sharp), "Celtic" (1900).[1]

[...] I am somewhat tired of an epithet [Celtic] that, in a certain association, is become jejune, through use and misuse. [...]

The "Celtic Movement," in the first place, is not, as is so often confusingly stated, an arbitrary effort to reconstruct the past; though it is, in part, an effort to discover the past. [...] I do not seek merely to reproduce ancient Celtic presentments of tragic beauty and fate, but do seek in nature and in life, and in the swimming thought of the timeless imagination, for the kind of beauty that the old Celtic poets discovered and uttered. There were poets and mythmakers in those days; and today we may be sure that a new Mythus is being woven; though we may no longer regard with the old wonder, or in the old wonder imaginatively shape and colour the forces of Nature and her silent and secret processes; for the mythopoeic faculty is not only a primitive instinct but a spiritual need.

*****

The ideal of art should be to represent beautiful life. If we want a vision of life that is not beautiful, we can have it otherwise: a multitude can depict the ignoble; the lens can replicate the usual.

It should be needless to add that our vision of the beautiful must be deep and wide and virile, as well as high and ideal. When we say that art should represent beautiful life, we do not say that it should represent only the beautiful in life, which would be to ignore the roots and the soil and the vivid sap, and account the blossom only. [...] There is no "art" saved by a moral purpose, though all true art is subtly informed of the spirit; but I know none, with pen or brush, with chisel or score, which, ignobly depicting the ignoble, survives in excellence.

In this, one cannot go well astray. Not do I seek an unreal Ideal [...]. I do not, with Blake, look upon this world as though it were at best a basis for transcendental vision, while in itself "a hindrance and a mistake," but rather, as a wiser has said, to an Earth spiritualised, not a Heaven naturalised. [...].

*****

Let me say at once, then, that I am not a great believer in "movements," and still less in "renascences" [...]. So far as I understand the "Celtic Movement," it is a natural outcome, the natural expression of a freshly inspired spiritual and artistic energy. That this expression is coloured by racial temperament is its distinction; that it is controlled to novel usage is its opportunity. When we look for its source we find it in the usufruct of an ancient and beautiful treasure of national tradition. One may the more aptly speak thus collectively of a mythology and a literature, and a vast and wonderful legendary folklore, since to us now, it is in great part hidden behind veils of an all but forgotten tongue, and of a system of life and customs, ideals and thoughts, that no longer obtains.

I am unable, however, to see that it has sustenance in continuity of revolt. A new movement need not be a revolt, but rather a sortie to carry a fresh position. [...]

There is no racial road to beauty, nor to any excellence. Genius, which leads thither, beckons neither to tribe not clan, neither to school nor movement, but only to one soul here and to another there. [...]

Even those characteristics which distinguish Celtic literature – intimate natural vision; a swift emotion that is sometimes a spiritual ecstasy, but sometimes is also a mere intoxication of the senses; a peculiar sensitiveness to the beauty of what is remote

---

1   First published in *Contemporary Review*, 1900; reprinted in *The Winged Destiny* (1904).

and solitary; a rapt pleasure in what is ancient and in the contemplation of what holds an indwelling melancholy; a visionary passion for beauty, which is of the immortal things, beyond the temporal beauty of what is mutable and mortal – even in these characteristics it does not stand alone, and perhaps not preeminent. [...]

There is no law set upon beauty. It has no geography. It is the domain of the spirit. [...]

*****

[...] What is a Celtic writer? If the word is to have any exact acceptance, it must denote an Irish or a Scottish Gael, a Cymric or Breton Celt, who writes in the language of his race. It is obvious that if one would write English literature, one must write in English and in the English tradition.

[. . .]

But above all else it is time for a prevalent pseudo-nationalism should be dissuaded. [...] If I were Irish, I would be proud, but I would not lower my pride by marrying it to a ceaseless ill-will, an irreconcilable hate, for there can be a nobler pride in unvanquished acquiescence than in futile revolt. [...] And proud as I might be to be Highland, or Scottish, or Irish, or Welsh, or English, I would be more proud to be British — for, there at least, we have a bond to unite us all, and to give us space for every ideal, whether communal or individual, whether national or spiritual.

As for literature, there is, for us all, only English literature. All else is provincial or dialectic.

*****

The Celtic element in our national life has a vital and great part to play. We have a most noble ideal if we will but accept it. And that is [...] so to live, so to pray, so to hope, so to work, so to achieve, that we, what is left of the Celtic races, of the Celtic genius, may permeate the greater race of which we are a vital part, so that with this Celtic emotion, Celtic love of beauty, and Celtic spirituality a nation greater than any the world has seen may issue, a nation refined and strengthened by the wise relinquishings and steadfast ideal of Celt and Saxon, united in a common fatherland, and in singleness of pride and faith.

*****

Perhaps the most significant sentence in M. Renan's remarkable study of the Poetry of the Celtic Races is that where he speaks of the Celtic race as having worn itself out in mistaking dreams for realities.[2] I am not certain that this is true, but it holds so great a part of the truth that it should make us think upon where we stand.

I think that our people have most truly loved their land, and their country, and their songs, and their ancient traditions, and that the word of bitterest savour is that sad word exile. But it is also true that in that love we love vaguely another land, a rainbow-land, and that our most desired country is not the real Ireland, the real Scotland, the real Brittany, but the vague Land of Youth, the shadowy Land of Heart's Desire. And it is also true, that deep in the songs we love above all other songs is a lamentation for what is gone away from the world, rather than merely from us as a people. [...] And true, too, that no tradition from of old is so compelling as the tradition that is from within; and that the long sorrow of our exile is in part because we have driven from us that company of hopes and dreams which were once realities, but are now among beautiful idle words.

---

2   Ernest Renan (1823–92), French philosopher, born in Brittany, and author of *Poesie des Races Celtiques* (1854).

In a word, we dwell overmuch among desired illusions: beautiful, when, like the rainbow, they are the spiritual reflection of certainties; but worthless as the rainbow-gold with which the Shee deceive the unwary, when what is a phantom of a spiritual desire is taken to be the reality of material fact.[1]

*****

Sometimes I fear that we who as a people do so habitually companion ourselves with dreams may fall into that abyss where the realities are become shadows, and shadows alone live and move. And then I remember that dreamers and visionaries are few; that we are no such people; that no such people has ever been; and that of all idle weaving of sand and foam none is more idle than this, the strange instinctive dread of the multitude, that the few whose minds and imaginations dwell among noble memories and immortal desires shall supersede the many who are content with lesser memories and ignoble desires.

---

1 Shee: faeries.

PHARAIS A ROMANCE OF THE ISLES BY FIONA MACLEOD

PRINTED BY HARPUR AND MURRAY
AT THE MORAY PRESS IN DERBY
MAY 1894 AND SOLD BY FRANK
MURRAY AT HIS BOOKSHOPS IN
DERBY LEICESTER AND NOTTINGHAM

"Mithich domh triall gu tigh Pharais."
(It is time for me to go up unto the House of Paradise.)
Muireadhach Albannach[1]

*"How many beautiful things have come to us
from Pharais."*
"Bileag-na-Toscùil."

To
E. W. R..[2]

Dear friend, – While you gratify me by your pleasure in this inscription, you modestly deprecate the dedication to you of this story of alien life – of that unfamiliar island-life so alien in all ways from the life of cities, and, let me add, from that of the great mass of the nation to which, in the communal sense, we both belong. But in the Domhan-Tòir[3] of friendship there are resting-places where all barriers of race, training, and circumstance fall away in dust. At one of these places of peace we met, a long while ago, and found that we loved the same things, and in the same way. You have been in the charmed West yourself: have seen the gloom and shine of the mountains that throw their shadow on the sea: have heard the wave whisper along that haunted shore which none loves save with passion, and none, loving, can bear to be long parted from. You, unlike so many who delight only in the magic of sunshine and cloud, love this dear land when the mists drive across the hillsides, and the brown torrents are in spate, and the rain and the black wind make a gloom upon every loch, and fill with the dusk of storm every strath, and glen, and corrie. Not otherwise can one love it aright: "Tir nam Beann 's nan glean 's nan ghaisgach," as one of our ancient poets calls it – "The land of hills, and glens, and heroes."[4] You, too, like Deirdre of old, have looked back on "Alba,"[5] and, finding it passing fair and dear, have, with the Celtic Helen, said in your heart –

---

1 Muireadhach Albannach Ó Dálaigh, 13th-century Gaelic bard.
2 Mrs Edith Wingate Rinder, Celticist and translator of Breton folk tales. Sharp met her in Rome in 1890: 'she appears to have been the wellspring for the emergence of Fiona MacLeod, who began to take form in his mind in 1891' (*DNB*).
3 Literally, 'world-quest'.
4 I cannot find an 'ancient poet' who came up with this phrase: it seems to be proverbial.
5 Alba is the Gaelic name for Scotland.

Inmain tir in tir ud thoir,
Alba cona lingantaibh ! . . .
["Beloved is that eastern land,
Alba of the lochs."][6]

In the mythology of the Gael are three forgotten deities, children of Delbaith-Dana. These are Seithoir, Teithoir, and Keithoir. One dwells throughout the sea, and beneath the soles of the feet of another are the highest clouds; and these two may be held sacred for the beauty they weave for the joy of eye and ear. But now that, as surely none may gainsay, Keithoir is blind and weary, let us worship at his fane[7] rather than give all our homage to the others. For Keithoir is the god of the earth; dark-eyed, shadowy brother of Pan; and his fane is among the lonely glens and mountains and lonelier isles of "Alba cona lingantaibh." *It is because you and I are of the children of Keithoir that I wished to grace my book with your name.*

The most nature-wrought of the English poets hoped he was not too late in transmuting into his own verse something of the beautiful mythology of Greece. But while Keats spun from the inexhaustible loom of his own genius, and I am but an obscure chronicler of obscure things, is it too presumptuous of me to hope that here, and mayhap elsewhere, I, the latest comer among older and worthier celebrants and co-enthusiasts, likewise may do something, however little, to win a further measure of heed for, and more intimate sympathy with, that old charm and stellar beauty of Celtic thought and imagination, now, alas, like so many other lovely things, growing more and more remote, discoverable seldom in books, and elusive amid the sayings and oral legends and fragmentary songs of a passing race?

A passing race: and yet, mayhap not so. Change is inevitable; and even if we could hear the wind blowing along Magh Mell – the Plain of Honey – we might list to a new note, bitter sweet: and, doubtless, the waves falling over the green roof of Tir-na-Thonn[8] murmur drowsily of a shifting of the veils of circumstance, which Keithoir weaves blindly in his dark place. But what was, surely is; and what is, surely may yet be. The form changes; the essential abides. As the saying goes among the islefolk: The shadow fleets beneath the cloud driven by the wind, and the cloud falls in rain or is sucked of the sun, but the wind sways this way and that for ever. It may well be that the Celtic Dream is not doomed to become a memory merely. Were it so, there would be less joy in all Springs to come, less hope in all brown Autumns; and the cold of a deathlier chill in all Winters still dreaming by the Pole. For the Celtic joy in the life of Nature – the Celtic vision – is a thing apart: it is a passion; a visionary rapture. There is none like it among the peoples of our race.

Meanwhile, there are a few remote spots, as yet inviolate. Here, Anima Celtica[9] still lives and breathes and hath her being. She dreams; but if she awake, it may not necessarily be to a deepening twilight, or to a forlorn passage to Tir Tairngire – that Land of Promise whose borders shine with the loveliness of all forfeited, or lost, or banished dreams and realities of Beauty. It may be that she will arise to a wider sway, over a disfrontiered realm. Blue are the hills that are far from us. Dear saying of the Gael, whose soul as well as whose heart speaks

---

6 These lines come from 'The Lament of Deirdre' in a medieval Scottish Gaelic manuscript of the old Irish story. Deirdre elopes from Ireland to Scotland with her lover Naoise, but they are lured back by their enemies, who murder Naoise; Deirdre then kills herself. Deirdre's story was made into plays by W.B. Yeats (1907) and J.M. Synge (1910). Sharp compares her to Homer's Helen of Troy in *The Iliad.*
7 Fane: temple, as of a household god.
8 Sharp refers to two otherworlds referred to in the old Irish mythology, the latter one lying under the sea.
9 That is, the Celtic spirit.

therein. Far hills recede, recede! Dim veils of blue, woven from within and without, haunt us, allure us, always, always!

But now, before I send you my last word of greeting, let me add (rather for other readers than for you, who already know of them) a word concerning the Gaelic runes interpolated in *Pharais*.[10] The "**Urnuigh Smalaidh Teine**" (p.124) and "**Altachadh Leapa**" (p.125) respectively a prayer to be said at covering up the peat-fire at bed-time and a Rest-blessing — are relics of ancient Celtic folklore which were sent to the Rev. Dr. Alexander Stewart, of "Nether Lochaber" fame,[11] by Mr. A. A. Carmichael, of South Uist, who took them down from the recitation of a man living at Iocar of Uist. From the same Hebridean source came the "**Rann Buachailleachd**," or rune to be said over cattle when led to pasture at morn, introduced at p.128. The English versions, by Dr. Stewart, appeared first in "The Inverness Courier," over twenty years ago. There are several versions current of the authentic incident of the innocent old woman held to be a witch, and of her prayer. I weave into my story the episode as I heard it many years ago, though with the rune rescued from oblivion by Dr. Stewart, rather than with the longer and commonly corrupted version still to be heard by the croft-fire in many localities, all "the far cry" from the Ord of Sutherland to the Rhinns of Islay.[12] The "**Laoidh Mhnathan**" — the Chant of Women, at pp.146-7 — is not ancient in the actual form here given, which is from an unpublished volume of "Oràin Spioradail."[13]

The sweetest-voiced of the younger Irish singers of to-day has spoken of the Celtic Twilight.[14] A twilight it is; but, if night follow gloaming, so also does dawn succeed night. Meanwhile, twilight voices are sweet, if faint and far, and linger lovingly in the ear.

There is another *Pàras* than that seen of Alastair of Innisròn — the Tir-na-h'Oigh of friendship. Therein we both have seen beautiful visions and dreamed dreams. Take, then, out of my heart, this book of vision and dream.

FIONA MACLEOD.

> "O bileag-geal,
> O bileag-na-Toscùil, bileag Pharais,
> O tha e boidheach!
> Tha e boidheach!"[15]

---

10 A slightly anglicised lection of the Gaelic word *Paras* = *Paradise*, Heaven. "*Pharais*," properly, is the genitive and dative case of *Pàras*, as in the line from Muireadhach Albannach, quoted after the title page, "*Mithich domh triall gu tigh Pharais*" — "It is time for me to go up unto the House of Paradise." [Sharp's note]. By 'rune' Sharp just means charm or incantation.

11 Alexander Stewart, *Nether Lochaber: The Natural History, Legends and Folk-lore of the West Highlands* (1883).

12 That is, all across the Gaelic-speaking Highlands, from the north to the south-west.

13 'Spiritual Songs'. There are at least two collections of Gaelic hymns and prayers with this title from the early nineteenth century.

14 Yeats's *The Celtic Twilight*, a collection of Irish folklore, was published the year before *Pharais*, in 1893.

15 'O white petal of Pharais [...] It is beautiful!'

I.

IT was midway in the seventh month of her great joy that the child moved, while a rapture leaped to her heart, within the womb of Lora, daughter of the dead Norman Maclean, minister of Innisròn, in the Outer Isles.

On the same eve the cruel sorrow came to her that had lain waiting in the dark place beyond the sunrise.

Alastair, her so dearly beloved, had gone, three days earlier, by the Western Isles steamer to the port of Greenock, thence to fare to Glasgow, to learn from a great professor of medicine concerning that which so troubled him — both by reason of what the islesmen whispered among themselves, and for what he felt of his own secret pain and apprehension.

There was a rocky spur on Innisròn whence the watcher could scan the headland round which the *Clansman* would come on her thrice-weekly voyage: in summer, while the isles were still steeped in the yellow shine; in autumn, when the sky seaward was purple, and every boulder in each islet was as transparent amber amid a vapour of amethyst rising from bases and hollow caverns of a cold day-dawn blue.

Hither Lora had come in the wane of the afternoon. The airs were as gentle and of as sweet balmy breath as though it were Summersleep rather than only the extreme of May. The girl looked, shading her eyes, seaward; and saw the blue of the midmost sky laid as a benediction upon the face of the deep, but paler by a little, as the darkest turquoise is pale beside the lightest sapphire. She lifted her eyes from the pearl-blue of the horizon to the heart of the zenith, and saw there the soul of Ocean gloriously arisen. Beneath the weedy slabs of rock whereon she stood, the green of the sea-moss lent a yellow gleam to the slow-waving dead-man's-hair which the tide laved to and fro sleepily, as though the bewitched cattle of Sheumais the seer were drowsing there unseen, known only of their waving tails, swinging silently as the bulls dreamed of the hill-pastures they should see no more. Yellow-green in the sunlit spaces as the sea-hair was, it was dark against the shifting green light of the water under the rocks, and till so far out as the moving blue encroached.

To Lora's right ran a curved inlet, ending in a pool fringed with dappled fronds of sea-fern, mare's-tails, and intricate bladder-wrack. In the clear hollow were visible the wave-worn stones at the bottom, many crowned with spreading anemones, with here and there a star-fish motionlessly agleam, or a cloud of vanishing shrimps above the patches of sand, or hermit crabs toiling cumbrously from perilous shelter to more sure havens. Looking down she saw herself, as though her wraith had suddenly crept therein and was waiting to whisper that which, once uttered and once heard, would mean disunion no more.

Slipping softly to her knees, she crouched over the pool. Long and dreamily she gazed into its depths. What was this phantasm, she wondered, that lay there in the green-gloom as though awaiting her? Was it, in truth, the real Lora, and she but the wraith?

How strangely expressionless was that pale face, looking upward with so straightforward a mien, yet with so stealthy an understanding, with dark abysmal eyes filled with secrecy and dread, if not, indeed, with something of menace.

A shrill of fear went to the girl's heart. A mass of shadow had suddenly obscured her image in the water. Her swift fancy suggested that her wraith had abruptly shrouded herself, fearful of revelation. The next moment she realised that her own wealth of dark hair had fallen down her neck and upon her shoulders — hair dusky as twilight, but interwrought with threads of bronze that, in the shine of fire or sun, made an evasive golden gleam.

She shuddered as she perceived the eyes of her other self intently watching her through that cloudy shadow. A breath came from the pool, salt and shrewd, and cold as though arisen from those sea-sepulchres whence the fish steal their scales of gold and silver. A thin voice was in her ears that was not the lap of the tide or the cluck of water gurgling in and out of holes and crannies.

With a startled gesture she shrank back.

"What is it? What is it?" she cried; but the sound of her own awed voice broke the spell: and almost at the same moment an eddy of wind came circling over the rock-bastions of the isle, and, passing as a tremulous hand over the pool, ruffled it into a sudden silvery sheen.

With a blithe laugh, Lora rose to her feet. The sunlight dwelt about her as though she were the sweetest flower in that lost garden of Aodh the poet,[16] where the streams are unspanned rainbows flowing to the skiey cauldrons below the four quarters, and where every white flower has at dusk a voice, a whisper, of surpassing sweetness.

"O Alastair, Alastair!" she cried, "will the boat never be coming that is to bring you back to me!"

Not a black spot anywhere, of wherry or steamer, caught the leaping gaze. Like a bird it moved across the sea, and found no object whereon to alight.

The *Clansman* was often late; but her smoke could be seen across Dunmore Head nigh upon quarter of an hour before her prow combed the froth from the Sound.

With a sigh, the girl moved slowly back by the way she had come. Over and over, as she went, she sang, crooningly, lines from a sweet song of the Gael, *O, Till, a Leannain!*

As she passed a place of birchen undergrowth and tall bracken, she did not see an old man, seated, grey and motionless as a heron. He looked at her with the dull eyes of age, though there was pity in them and something of a bewildered awe.

"Aye," he muttered below his breath, "though ye sing for your dear one to return, ye know not what I know. Have I not had the vision of him with the mist growin' up an' up, an' seen the green grass turn to black mools[17] at his feet?"

Lora, unwitting, passed; and he heard her voice wax and wane, as falling water in a glen where the baffled wind among the trees soughs now this way and now that: —

"*Mo chridhe-sa! 's tusa 'bhios truagh, 'bhios truagh,
Mur pill is' 'thog oirre gu cluaidh, gu cluaidh!*"[18]

She went past the boulder on the path that hid the clachan[19] from view, and within a net-throw of which was the byre of Mrs. Maclean's cottage, where, since her father's death, she had dwelt.

A tall, gaunt, elderly woman, with hair of the ivory white of the snowberry, was about to pass from behind the byre with a burthen of fresh bracken for Ian Maclean's bed — for the old islesman abode by the way of his fathers, and was content to sleep on a deerskin spread upon fresh-gathered fern — when she caught sight of Lora. She stopped, and with an eager glance looked at the girl: then beyond, and finally seaward, with her long, thin, brown arm at an angle, and her hand curved over her eyes against the glare of the water.

---

16 Aodh: presumably a reference to the poet-god of Irish mythology.
17 Mools: the soil used to fill a grave.
18 These are lines from the song 'O Till a Leannain' already mentioned: Sharp might have come across it in the collection *The Celtic Lyre: A Collection of Gaelic Songs with English Translations* published in Edinburgh, Glasgow and Oban in 1883.
19 Clachan: township.

Silence was about her as a garment. Every motion of her, even, suggested a deep calm. Mrs. Maclean spoke seldom, and when she said aught it was in a low voice, sweet and serene, but as though it came from a distance and in the twilight. She was of the shadow, as the islemen say; and strangers thought her to be austere in look and manner, though that was only because she gazed long before she replied to one foreign to her and her life: having the Gaelic, too, so much more natively than the English, that oftentimes she had to translate the one speech into the other nearer to her: that, and also because the quiet of the sea was upon her, as often with hill-folk there is a hushed voice and mien.

Lora knew what was in her mind when she saw her gaze go seaward and then sweep hither and thither like a hawk ere it settles.

"The boat is not yet in sight, Mary; she is late," she said simply: adding immediately, "I have come back to go up Cnoc-an-Iolair; from there I'll see the smoke of the *Clansman* sooner. She is often as late as this."

Mrs. Maclean looked compassionately at the girl.

"Mayhap the *Clansman* will not be coming this way at all to-night, Lora. She may be going by Kyle-na-Sith."

A flush came into Lora's face. Her eyes darkened, as a tarn under rain.

"And for why should she not be sailing this way to-night, when Alastair is coming home, and is to be here before sundown?"

"He may have been unable to leave. If he does not come to-day, he will doubtless be here to-morrow."

"To-morrow! O Mary, Mary, have you ever loved that you can speak like that? Think what Alastair went away for! Surely you do not know how the pain is at my heart?"

"Truly, *mùirnean*.[20] But it is not well to be sure of that which may easily happen otherwise."

"To-morrow, indeed! Why, Mary, if the *Clansman* does not come by this evening, and has gone as you say by Kyle-na-Sith, she will not be here again till the day *after* to-morrow!"

"Alastair could come by the other way, by the Inverary boat, and thence by the herring-steamer from Dunmore, after he had reached it from Uan Point or by way of Craig-Sionnach."

"That may be, of course; but I think not. I cannot believe the boat will not be here to-night."

Both stood motionless, with their hands shading their eyes, and looking across the wide Sound, where the tide bubbled and foamed against the slight easterly wind-drift. The late sunlight fell full upon them, working its miracle of gold here and there, and making the skin like a flower. The outline of each figure stood out darkly clear as against a screen of amber.

For a time neither spoke. At last, with a faint sigh, Mrs. Maclean turned.

"Did you see Ian on your way, *Lora-mo-ghràidh*?"[21]

"No."

"Do not have speech with the old man to-night, dear one. He is not himself."

"Has he had the sight again?"

"Ay, Lora."

Again a silence fell. The girl stood moodily, with her eyes on the ground: the elder watched her with a steadfast, questioning look.

"Mary!"

20 Mùirnean (G.): darling.
21 'Lora my love' (though this should be *a ghràidh*).

Mrs. Maclean made no reply, but her eyes brought Lora's there with the answer that was in them.

"Ian has never had the sight again upon . . . upon Alastair, has he?"

"How can I say, *Lora-gaolaiche*?"[22]

"But do you know if he has? If you do not tell me, I will ask him."

"I asked him that only yester-morning. He shook his head."

"Do you believe he can foresee all that is to happen?"

"No. Those who have the vision do not read all that is in the future. Only God knows. They can see the thing of peril, ay, and the evil of accident, and even Death — and what is more, the nearness and sometimes the way of it. But no man sees more than this — unless, indeed, he has been to Tir-na-h'Oigh."

Mrs. Maclean spoke the last words almost in a whisper, and as though she said them in a dream.

"Unless he has been to Tir-na-h'Oigh, Mary?"

"So it is said. Our people believe that the Land of Eternal Youth lies far yonder across the sea; but Aodh, the poet, is right when he tells us that that land is lapped by no green waves such as we know here, and that those who go thither do so in sleep, or in vision, or when God has filled with dusk the house of the brain."

"And when a man has been to Tir-na-h'Oigh in sleep, or in dream, or in mind-dark, does he see there what shall soon happen here?"

"It is said."

"Has Ian been beyond the West?"

"No."

"Then what he sees when he has the sight upon him is not *beannaichte*: is not a thing out of heaven?"

"I cannot say. I think not."

"Mary, is it the truth you are now telling me?"

A troubled expression came into the woman's face, but she did not answer.

"And is it the truth, Mary, that Ian has not had the sight upon Alastair since he went away — that he did not have it last night or this morning?"

Lora leaned forward in her anxiety. She saw that in her companion's eyes which gave her the fear. But the next moment Mrs. Maclean smiled.

"I too have the sight, *Lora-ghaolache*; and shall I be telling you that which it will be giving you joy to hear?"

"Ay, surely, Mary!"

"Then I think you will soon be in the arms of him you love" — and, with a low laugh, she pointed across the sea to where a film of blue-grey smoke rose over the ridge of Dunmore headland.

"Ah, the *Clansman*!" cried Lora, with a gasp of joy; and the next moment she was moving down the path again towards the little promontory. The wind had risen slightly. The splash, splash, of the sunny green waves against each other, the lapping of the blue water upon the ledges to the east, the stealthy whisper where the emerald-green tide-flow slipped under the hollowed sandstone, the spurtle of the sea-wrack, the flashing fall and foam-send of the gannets, the cries of the gulls, the slap of wind as it came over the forehead of the isle and struck the sea a score of fathoms outward — all gave her a sense of happiness. The world seemed suddenly to have grown young. The exultant Celtic joy stood over against the brooding Celtic shadow, and believed the lances of the sunlight could keep at bay all the battalions of gloom.

---

22 'Darling Lora'.

The breeze was variable, for the weft of blue smoke which suddenly curled round the bend of Dunmore had its tresses blown seaward, though where Lora stood the wind came from the west, and even caused a white foam along the hither marge of the promontory.

With eager eyes she watched the vessel round the point. After all, it was just possible she might not be the *Clansman*.

But the last sunglow shone full against Dunmore and upon the bows of the steamer as she swung to the helm; and the moment the red funnel changed from a dusky russet into a flame of red, Lora's new anxiety was assuaged. She knew every line of the boat, and already she felt Alastair's kisses on her lips. The usual long summer-gloaming darkened swiftly — for faint films of coming change were being woven across the span of the sky from mainland oceanward. Even as the watcher on Innisròn stood, leaning forward in her eager outlook, she saw the extreme of the light lift upward as though it were the indrawn shaft of a fan. The contours of the steamer grew confused: a velvety duskiness overspread Dunmore foreland.

The sky overhead had become a vast lift[23] of perishing yellow — a spent wave of daffodil by the north and by the south; westward, of lemon, deepening into a luminous orange glow shot with gold and crimson, and rising as an exhalation from hollow cloud-sepulchres of amethyst, straits of scarlet, and immeasurable spaces of dove-grey filled with shallows of the most pale sea-green.

Lora stood as though wrought in marble. She had seen that which made the blood leap from her heart, and surge in her ears, and clamour against her brain.

No pennon flew at the peak of the steamer's foremast. This meant there was neither passenger nor freight to be landed at Innisròn, so that there was no need for the ferry.

She could scarcely believe it possible that the *Clansman* could come, after all, and yet not bring Alastair back to her. It seemed absurd: some ill-timed by-play; nay, a wanton cruelty. There must be some mistake, she thought, as she peered hungrily into the sea-dusk.

Surely the steamer was heading too much to the northward! With a cry, Lora instinctively stretched her arms towards the distant vessel; but no sound came from her lips, for at that moment a spurt of yellow flame rent the grey gloom, as a lantern was swung aloft to the mast-head.

In a few seconds she would know all; for whenever the *Clansman* was too late for her flag-signal to be easily seen, she showed a green light a foot or so beneath the yellow.

Lora heard the heavy pulse of the engines, the churn of the beaten waves, even the delirious surge and suction as the spent water was driven along the hull and poured over and against the helm ere it was swept into the wake that glimmered white as a snow-wreath. So wrought was she that, at the same time, she was keenly conscious of the rapid *tweet-tweet-tweet-tweet-tweet — o-o-h sweet! — sweet!* of a yellowhammer among the whin close by, and of the strange, mournful cry of an oyster-opener as it flew with devious swoops towards some twilight eyrie.

The throb of the engines — the churn of the beaten waves — the sough of the swirling yeast — even the churning, swirling, under-tumult, and through it and over it the heavy pulse, the deep panting rhythmic throb: this she heard, as it were the wrought surge of her own blood.

Would the green light never swing up to that yellow beacon?

A minute passed: two minutes: three! It was clear that the steamer had no need to call at Innisròn. She was coming up the mid of the Sound, and, unless the ferry-light signalled to her to draw near, she would keep her course north-westward.

---

23 Lift (Sc.): sky.

Suddenly Lora realised this. At the same time there flashed into her mind the idea that perhaps Alastair was on board after all, but that he was ill, and had forgotten to tell the captain of his wish to land by the island ferry.

She turned, and, forgetful or heedless of her condition, moved swiftly from ledge to ledge, and thence by the path to where, in the cove beyond the clachan, the ferry-boat lay on the tide-swell, moored by a rope fastened to an iron clank fixt in a boulder.

"Ian! Ian!" she cried, as she neared the cove; but at first she saw no one, save Mrs. Maclean, black against the fire-glow from her cottage. "Ian! Ian!"

A dark figure rose from beside the ferry-shed.

"Is that you, Ian? *Am bheil am bhàta deas?* Is the boat ready? *Bi ealamh! bi ealamh! mach am bhàta:* quick! quick! out with the boat!"

In her eager haste she spoke both in the Gaelic and the English: nor did she notice that the old man did not answer her, or make any sign of doing as she bade him.

"*Oh, Ian, bi ealamh! bi ealamh! Faigh am bhàta deas! rach a stigh do'n bhàta!*"

Word for word, as is the wont of the people, he answered her: —

"Why is it that I should be quick? Why should I be getting the boat ready? For what should I be going into the boat?"

"The *Clansman!* Do you not see her? *Bi ealamh! bi ealamh!* or she will go past us like a dream."

"She has flown no flag, she has no green light at the mast. No one will be coming ashore, and no freight; and there is no freight to go from here, and no one who wants the ferry unless it be yourself, *Lora nighean Tormaid!*"[24]

"Alastair is there: he was to come by the steamer to-day! Be quick, Ian! Do you hear me?"

"I hear," said the old man, as he slowly moved toward the boulder to his left, unloosed the rope from the iron clank, and drew the boat into the deep water alongside the landing-ledge.

"There is no good in going out, *Lora bhàn!*[25] The wind is rising: ay, I tell you, the wind goes high: we may soon hear the howling of the sea-dogs."

But Lora, taking no notice, had sprung into the boat, and was already adjusting the long oars to the old-fashioned wooden thole-pins. Ian followed, grumblingly repeating, "*Tha gaoth ruhòr am! Tha cultas stairm' air!*"

Once, however, that the wash of the sea caught the wherry, and the shrewd air sent the salt against their faces, the old man appeared to realise that the girl was in earnest. Standing, he laid hold of the sloped mast, to steady himself against the swaying as the tide sucked at the keel and the short waves slapped against the bows, and then gave a quick calculating glance seaward and at the advancing steamer.

Rapidly he gave his directions to Lora to take the helm and to keep the boat to windward:

"*Gabh an stiuir, Lora: cum ris a' ghàoth i!*"

The next moment the long oars were moving slowly, but powerfully, through the water, and the ferry-boat drove into the open, and there lay over a little with the double swing of wind and tide.

The gloaming was now heavy upon the sea; for a mist had come up with the dipping of the sun, and thickened the dusk.

Suddenly Ian called to Lora to hold the oars. As soon as she had caught them, and was steadying the boat in the cross surge of the water, he lifted a lantern from under the

---

24 'Lora daughter of Norman'.
25 'Fair Lora'.

narrow fore-deck, lighted the wick below the seat (after the wind had twice blown the flame into the dark), and then, gripping the mast, waved the signal to and fro overhead.

It was well he thought of this, for the steamer was going at full speed, and would not have slackened.

In a few minutes thereafter the heavy stertorous throb and splash was close to them, while the screw revolved now at quarter-speed.

A hoarse voice came from the *Clansman:*

"Ferry ahoy!"

"Ay, ay, ta ferry she will pe," called back Ian in the quaint English of which he was so proud: though he thought the language a poor, thin speech, and fit only for folk who never leave the mainland.

"What are ye oot for, Ian? Ha' ye ony body comin' aboard?"

"We've come out for Mr. Alastair Macleod," Lora broke in eagerly: "we've come to take him off."

"Hoots, my girl, what for d'ye fash yersel an' us too for the like o' sic havers.[26] There's no one aboard who wants to land at Innisròn: an' as for Alastair Macleod, he was na' on the *Clansman* when we left Greenock, so he couldna' well be on her the now! As for you, Ian Maclean, are ye doited,[27] when, wi' neither flag nor green light aloft, ye stop the steamer like this, a' for a lassie's haverin'! Ye'll hear o' this yet, my man, I'se telling ye! Auld fule that ye are, awa' wi' ye! keep aff the wash o' the steamer . . . an' by the Lord, I'll . . ."

But already the *Clansman* was forging ahead, and the second officer's menace was swallowed up in the tumult of churned seas.

A minute later the steamer was a dark mass to the nor'-west, with a sheet of white writhing after her, and a swirl of flaming cinders from her funnel riding down the night like a shoal of witch-lights.

The wherry rocked heavily, caught as she was in the surge from the screw, and lying adrift in the sliding hollows and rough criss-cross of the waves.

Lora sat motionless and speechless. The old man stared down into the darkness of the boat: but though his lips moved continuously, no sound came from them.

For a time it was as though a derelict were the sport of the sea, which had a dull moan in it, that partly was from the stifled voice of the tide as it forced its way from the cauldrons of the deep, and partly from the fugitive clamour of breaking waves, and mostly from the now muffled, now loud and raucous sough of the wind as it swung low by the surge, or trailed off above the highest reach of the flying scud.

At last, in a whisper, the girl spoke.

"Ian, has aught of evil come to Alastair?"

"God forbid!"

"Do you know anything to his undoing?"

"No, *Lora bhàn."*

"You have not had the sight upon him lately?"

The islesman hesitated a moment. Raising his eyes at last he glanced first at his companion and then out into the dusk across the waves, as though he expected to see some one or something there in answer to his quest.

"I dreamt a dream, Lora, wife of Alastair. I saw you and him and another go away into a strange place. You and the other were as shadows; but Alastair was a man, as now, though he walked through mist, and I saw nothing of him but from the waist upward."

26 Fash: trouble; havers: nonsense (both Sc.).
27 Doited (Sc.): dim-witted, confused, senile.

Silence followed this, save for the wash of the sea, the moan of wind athwart wave, and the soft rush of the breeze overhead.

Ian rose, and made as though he were going to put out the oars; but as he saw how far the boat had drifted from the shore, and what a jumble of water lay between them and the isle, he busied himself with hoisting the patched brown sail.

As if no interval had occurred, Lora abruptly called him by name.

"Ian," she added, "what does the mist mean? . . . the mist that you saw about the feet and up to the waist of Alastair?"

There was no reply. Ian let go the sail, secured it, and then seated himself a few feet away from Lora.

She repeated the question; but the old man was obstinately silent, nor did he speak word of any kind till the wherry suddenly slackened, as she slipped under the lee of the little promontory of the landing-place.

"The tide will be on turning now," he exclaimed in his awkward English, chosen at the moment because he did not dare to speak in the Gaelic, fearful as he was of having any further word with his companion; "and see, after all, the wind she will soon pe gone."

Lora, who had mechanically steered the boat to its haven, still sat in the stern, though Ian had stepped on to the ledge and was holding the gunwale close to it so that she might step ashore with ease. She looked at him as though she did not understand. The old man shifted uneasily. Then his conscience smote him for having used the cold, unfriendly English instead of the Gaelic so dear to them both: for was not the girl in the shadow of trouble, and did he not foresee for her more trouble to come? So, in a gentle, apologetic voice, he repeated in Gaelic what he had said about the tide and the wind:

"*Thill an sruth: Dh' fhalbh a' ghàoth.*"

"There will be peace to-night," he added. "It was but a sunset breeze, after all. There will be no storm. I think now there will be a calm. It will be bad for the herring-boats. It is a long pull and a hard pull when the water sleeps against the keel. A dark night, too, most likely."

Lora rose, and slowly stepped on shore. She took no notice of Ian's sudden garrulity. She did not seem to see him even. He looked at her with momentary resentment: but almost simultaneously a pitiful light came into his eyes.

"He will be here to-morrow," he murmured, "and if not, then next day for sure."

Lora moved up the ledge in silence.

In the middle of the cove she stopped, waved her hand, and, in a dull voice bidding good-night, wished sound steep to him:

"*Beannachd leibh! Cadal math dhiubh!*"

Ian answered simply, "*Beannachd leibh!*" and turned to fasten the rope to the iron clank.

The dew was heavy, even on the rough salt spear-grass which fringed the sand above the cove. On the short sheep-grass, on the rocky soil beyond, it was dense, and shone white as a shroud in a dark room. A bat swung this way and that, whirling silently. The fall of the wind still sighed in the bent rowan trees to the west of the clachan, where the pathway diverged from the shore. Against the bluff of Cnoc-an-Iolair it swelled intermittently: its voice in the hollows and crevices of the crag broken up in moans and short gasps, fainter and fainter.

Lora noted all this wearily as she advanced. She was conscious, also, of the nibbling of the sheep, quenching their thirst with the wet grass: of the faint swish of her feet going through the dew: of the dark track, like a crack in black ice, made wherever she walked in the glisten. But though she saw and unwittingly noted, her thoughts were all with Alastair and with what had kept him.

In her remote life there was scarce room for merely ordinary vicissitudes. It was not a thing to ponder as ominous that one should go out to sea after herring or mackerel and not return that night or the morrow, or even by the next gloaming, or second dawn; or that a man should go up among the hills and not come back for long after his expected hour. But that one could miss the great steamer was a thing scarce to believe in. To Lora, who had been so little on the mainland, and whose only first-hand knowledge of the feverish life of towns was derived from her one winter of school-life at Rothesay and brief visits to Greenock and Oban, it was difficult to realise how any one could fail to leave by the steamer, unless ill or prevented by some serious mischance. The periodical coming of the *Clansman* symbolised for her, to a certain extent, the inevitable march of time and fate. To go or come by that steam-driven, wind-heedless vessel was to be above the uncertainties and vicissitudes to which ordinary wayfaring mortals are subject. The girl thought she knew so much that to her all of what town-life meant must be bare, because of her reading: knowing not that, with a woman whose heart aches, a tear will drown every word writ in any book, a sigh scatter the leaves into nothingness.

Deep was the puzzle to her as she slowly ascended the path which led to Mary Maclean's cottage. She stopped once or twice, half-unconsciously, to smell the fragrance of the bog-myrtle where the gale[28] grew in tufts out of the damper patches, or of the thyme as it was crushed under her feet and made over-sweet, over-poignant by the dew.

The peat-reek reached her nostrils from the cottage, blent with the breaths of the cows that still loitered afoot, munching the cool wilding fodder. Her gaze, too, fell upon the fire-lit interior, with a table overspread by a white cloth, flushed by the glow that wavered from betwixt the red-hot bars; and, later, upon the figure of Mrs. Maclean, who had come out to meet her, or, more likely, had been there ever since the ferry-boat had gone off upon its useless errand.

"Are you wet, Lora? Are you cold?" she asked, as the girl drew near. There was no need to say aught of the bitter disappointment, any more than to speak of the glooming of the dusk: both were obvious facts beyond the yea or nay of speech.

"I am very tired, Mary."

"Come in, dear, and have your tea. It will do you good. *Lora-mo-ghràidh,* you should not have gone out in the ferry-boat. It was no use, and the sea was rough, and you might have come to harm; and what would Alastair Macleod be saying, to-morrow, if he found his heart's-delight ill, and that I had stood by and seen her do so foolish a thing?"

"Oh, Mary, do you really think he will be here, to-morrow?"

"Surely."

"But I fear he will wait now till the next sailing of the *Clansman.*"

"We cannot say. Come in, my fawn, out of the chill."

"It is going to be a lovely night. The wind falls fast; even now it is almost still. The purple peace will be upon everything to-night. I am restless; I do not wish to go in-doors."

"No, no, Lora dear to me! Come in and have your tea, and then rest. You can rise at daybreak, if you will, and go round the island, lest he should be coming in any of the herring-smacks."

"I want to speak to Ian."

"Ian has gone across to Ivor Maquay's; he will not be here to-night."

Lora looked suspiciously at the speaker. Had she not left Ian a few minutes ago,

---

28   Gale is another name for bog-myrtle.

and was he not even now following her? She stared about her, but saw no one. In the gloaming she could just descry the black mass of the wherry. Ian was nowhere visible. She did not think of scrutinising the shadow of the beached and long disused coble which lay a few yards away. Had she done so, she might have perceived the old islesman standing rigid. He had overheard his kinswoman, and understood. As soon as the two women had entered the cottage, he moved swiftly and silently away, and, traversing the clachan, was soon swallowed up of the darkness.

After the meal was ended, Lora found herself overworn with excitement. All wish to go out again went from her. From where she lay resting, she watched Mrs. Maclean put away the things and then seat herself by the fire.

For a long time neither woman spoke. A drowsy peace abode upon the threshold.

The hot red glow of the peats shone steadily.

At first there had been a little lamp on the table, but after a time Mrs. Maclean had extinguished it. Instead, she had thrown upon the fire a log of pinewood. The dry crackle, the spurt of the sap as it simmered in the heat, the yellow tongues and sudden red fangs and blue flames, gave the sound and glow whereof a sweeter silence can be wrought into what has been but stillness before.

An hour went by. With brief snatches of talk, all made up of fears and hopes, another hour passed. Then a long quietness again, broken at the last by a low crooning song from the elder woman, as she leaned to the fire and stared absently into its heart. The song was old: older than the oldest things, save the summits of the mountains, the granite isles, and the brooding pain of the sea. Long ago it had been sung by wild Celtic voices, before ever spoken word was writ in letters — before that again, mayhap, and caught perhaps from a wailing Pictish[29] mother — so ancient was the moving old-world strain, so antique the words of the lullaby that was dim with age when it soothed to sleep the child Ossian, son of Fingal.

When the crooning died away, Lora slept. With soft step Mrs. Maclean moved across the room, and lightly dropped a plaid over the girl's figure, recumbent in beautiful ease upon the low bed-couch.

She returned slowly to her place by the fire. After a while she was about to seat herself, when she started violently. Surely that was a face pressed for a moment against the window?

With a strange look in her eyes, she reproved herself for her nervous folly. She sat down, with gaze resolutely fixed on the glowing peats: nor would she have stirred again, but for a sound as of a low moan.

The blood ran chill in her veins; her mouth twitched; and the intertwisted fingers of her hands were white and lifeless with the fierce grip that came of her fear.

But she was not a woman to be mastered by terror. With a quivering sigh she rose, looked round the room, forced herself to stare fixedly at the window, and then moved quietly to the door. As soon as she felt the air upon her brows she became calm, and all dread left her.

"Is that you, Ian?" she whispered.

There was no one visible: no sound.

"Is that you, Alastair Macleod?"

So low was the utterance that, if any one had been there, he could scarce have heard it.

To her strained ears it was as though she heard a light susurrus of brushed dew; but

29 The Picts were the inhabitants of northern Scotland at the time of Roman contact, pre-dating the arrival of the Gaels from Ireland.

it might be a wandering breath of air among the gale, or an adder moving through the grass, or a fern-owl hawking under the rowan-trees.

She waited a little; then, with a sigh of relief, re-entered the cottage and closed the door.

A glance at Lora showed her that the girl was sleeping unperturbed. For some time there after she sat by the fire, brooding over many things. Weary, at last, she rose, cast a farewell glance at the sleeper, and then slipt quietly to her bed in the adjoining room.

Night lay passively upon the sea, upon the isle, upon the clachan. Not a light lingered in any cottage, save the fire-glow in that of Mary Maclean: a hollow, attenuating beam that stared through the dark unwaveringly.

Neither star nor moon was visible. The clouds hung low, but without imminence of rain for the isles, drawn inland as the vapours were by the foreheads of the bens.

An hour later the door of the cottage opened and closed again, silently. It was Lora who came forth.

She walked hesitatingly at first, and then more swiftly, not pausing till she reached the little boulder-pier. There she stood motionless, listening intently.

The water lapped among the hollows, above which the ebb-left shellfish gaped thirstily. There was a lift among the dulse-heaps,[30] as though a finger stirred them and let loose their keen salt smells. The bladder-wrack moved with strange noises, sometimes startlingly loud, oftenest as if sea-things were being stifled or strangled.

From the promontory came a cry: abrupt, strident—the hunger-note of a skua. The thin pipe of the dotterel[31] fell into the darkness beyond the shallows where the sea-mist lay. In the Kyle a muffled, stertorous breath, near and twice as far away, told that two whales were in the wake of the mackerel.

From the isle, no sound. The sheep lay on the thyme, or among the bracken, still as white boulders. The kye crouched, with misty nostrils laid low to the damp grass, rough with tangled gale. The dogs were silent. Even the tufted canna[32] hung straight and motionless. The white moths had, one by one, fallen like a falling feather. The wind-death lay upon all: at the last, too, upon the sea.

II.

SLOWLY, as though a veil were withdrawn, the cloudy dusk passed from the lift. The moon, lying in violet shadow, grew golden: while the sheen of her pathway, trailed waveringly across the sea and athwart the isle, made Innisròn seem as a beautiful body motionlessly adrift on the deep.

One by one the stars came forth—solemn eyes watching for ever the white procession move onward orderly where there is neither height, nor depth, nor beginning, nor end.

In the vast stellar space the moon-glow waned until it grew cold, white, ineffably remote. Only upon our little dusky earth, upon our restless span of waters, the light descended in a tender warmth. Drifting upon the sea, it moved tremulously onward, weaving the dark waters into a weft of living beauty.

Strange murmur of ocean, even when deep calm prevails, and not the most homeless wind lifts a weary wing from wave-gulf to wave-gulf. As a voice heard in dream; as a whisper in the twilight of one's own soul; as a breath, as a sigh from one knows not

30 Dulse: a type of sea-weed.
31 Skua: a predatory sea-bird; dotterel: a kind of plover.
32 Canna (Sc.): bog-cotton.

whence, heard suddenly and with recognising awe; so is this obscure, troublous echo of a tumult that is over, that is not, but that may be, that awaiteth.

To Lora it was almost inaudible. Rather, her ears held no other sound than the babbling repetitive chime and whisper of the lip of the sea moving to and fro the pebbles on the narrow strand just beyond her.

Her eyes saw the lift of the dark, the lovely advance of the lunar twilight, the miracle of the yellow bloom — golden here and here white as frost-fire — upon sea and land: they saw, and yet saw not. Her ears heard the muffled voice of ocean and the sweet recurrent whispering of the foam-white runnels beside her: they heard, and yet heard not.

Surely, in the darkness, in the loneliness, she would have knowledge of Alastair. Surely, she thought, he would come to her in the spirit. In deep love there is a living invisible line from soul to soul whereby portent of joy or disaster, or passion of loneliness, or passion of fear, or passion of longing may be conveyed with terrifying surety.

How beyond words dreadful was this remoteness which environed her, as the vast dome of night to a single white flower growing solitary in a waste place.

Inland upon the isle, seaward, skyward, Lora looked with aching eyes. The moonlight wounded her with its peace. The shimmering sea beat to a rhythm atune to a larger throb than that of a petty human life. In the starry infinitude her finitude was lost, absorbed, as a grain of sand wind-blown a few yards across an illimitable desert.

That passionate protest of the soul against the absolute unheed of nature was hers: that already defeated revolt of the whirling leaf against the soaring, far-come, far-going wind that knows nothing of what happens beneath it in the drift of its inevitable passage.

With a sob, she turned, vaguely yearning for the human peace that abode in the cottage. As she moved, she saw a shadow, solidly clear-cut in the moonlight, sweep from a rock close by, as though it were a swinging scythe.

Instinctively she glanced upward, to see if the cloud-counterpart were overhead. The sky was now cloudless: neither passing vapour nor travelling wild-swan had made that shadow leap from the smooth boulder into the darkness.

She trembled: for she feared she had seen the Watcher of the Dead. At the wane of the last moon, an old islesman had passed into the white sleep. Lora knew that his spirit would have to become the Watcher of Graves till such time as another soul should lapse into the silence. Was this he, she wondered with instinctive dread — was this Fergus, weary of his vigil, errant about the isle which had been the world to him, a drifting shadow from graveyard to byre and sheiling, from fold to dark fold, from the clachan-end to the shore-pastures, from coble to havened coble, from the place of the boats to the ferry-rock? Did he know that he would soon have one to take over from him his dreadful peace? Or was he in no satiate peace, but an-hungered as a beast of prey for the death of another? And then . . . and then . . . who was this other? Who next upon the isle would be the Watcher of the Dead?

With a low, shuddering breath, she sighed, "*Fergus!*"

The fall of her voice through the silence was an echo of terror. She clasped her hands across her breast. Her body swayed forward as a bulrush before the wind.

"*Ah, Dia! Dia!*" broke from her lips; for, beyond all doubt, she saw once again the moving of a darkness within the dark. Yet what she saw was no shadow-man weary of last vigil, but something that for a moment filled her with the blindness of dread. Was it possible? Was she waylaid by one of those terrible dwellers in twilight-water of which she had heard so often from the tellers of old tales?

"*Toradh nu féudalach gun am faicinn,*" she muttered with cold lips: "the offspring of the cattle that have not been seen!"

"Ah, no, no!" she cried. The next moment, and with a sob of relief, she saw a moonbeam steal upon the hollow and reveal its quietude of dusk. She would have moved at once from boulder to boulder, eager for that lost sanctuary whence she had come — when the very pulse of her heart sprang to the burst of a human sob close by.

She stood still, as though frozen. A moment before, the breath from her lips was visible: now not the faintest vapour melted into the night-air.

Was she dreaming, she wondered, when the stifling grip at her heart had mercifully relaxed?

No: there was no mistake. Blent with the gurgle and cluck and whisper of the water among the lifted bladder-wrack and in and out of the pools and crannies in the rocks, there was the piteous sound of a human sob.

All at once, everything became clear to Lora. She knew that Alastair was near: she did not even dread that he was present as a disembodied spirit. He had reached the isle after all, but in some strange sorrow had not sought her straightway.

"*Alastair!*" she cried yearningly.

No one answered; no one-stirred; nothing moved. But the muffled sobbing was hushed.

"Alastair! Alastair!"

Slowly from a sand-drift beside the ferry-rock a tall figure arose. For a few moments it stood motionless, black against the yellow shine of the moon. The face was pale; that of a man, young, with the thin lips, the shadowy eyes that in sunlight would shine sea-blue, the high oval features, the tangled, curly, yellow-tawney hair of the islesmen of the ancient Suderöer,[33] in whose veins the Celtic and the Scandinavian strains commingle.

Alastair was as visible as though he were in the noon-light.

Lora looked at him, speechless. She saw that in his strained eyes, in his wrought features, which told her he had drunken of sorrow. His dishevelled hair, his whole mien and appearance showed that he was in some dire extremity.

"Alastair!"

He heard the low, passionate appeal, but at first he did not stir. Then, and yet as though constrainedly and in weariness, he raised and stretched forth his arms.

Swift as a gliding shadow, Lora was beside him, and clasped to his heart.

For a time, neither spoke. His heart beat loud and heavily: against his breast her head lay, with her breath coming and going like a wounded bird panting in the green-gloom of the thicket.

"O Alastair, Alastair, what is it?" she murmured at last, raising her head and looking into his pale, distraught face.

"What made you come out in the dark, *Lora-mùirnean?*"

"I could not rest. I was too unhappy. I thought — I thought, — no, I do not think I dared to believe that you might come to-night after all; but something made me long to go down to the sea. Did you see me only now, dear heart?"

"No, Lora."

For a moment she was still, while she gazed fixedly at Alastair.

"Ah," she whispered at last, "then you have been here all this night, and I not knowing it! Ah, Alùinn, it was *your* heart crying to mine that made me rise and leave the cottage and come out into the dark. But why did you not come to me? When did you come to Innisròn? How did you come?"

<hr>

33 The Western Isles of Scotland were part of the Kingdom of Norway in the 11th and 12th centuries, when they were known as Sodor (Suor-eyjar, the south islands, as opposed to the north islands of Orkney and Shetland) and their inhabitants as Suderoer.

"Dear, I could not wait for the *Clansman.* I left Greenock three hours earlier by the *Foam,* James Gilchrist's tug; for he undertook to put me ashore at the haven below Craig-Sionnach. Thence I walked to Dunmore. But I was not well, Lora; and I was so long on the way that I missed the *Clansman* as well as the Dunmore herring-steamer. Before nightfall, however, I persuaded Archibald Macleod, of Tighnacraigh, to bring me here on his smack. I landed at the Rock of the Seafold. It was already dusk and my heart was against yours in longing, my beautiful gloom: yet over me came such a sorrow that I could not bear the homing, and so moved restlessly from shadow to shadow. I felt as though it would be better for me to deal with my sorrow alone and in the night, and that it was more bearable since I was so near you, and that any moment I could go to you."

"Why, why did you not come, Alastair? Oh, I longed, longed for you so!"

"Once I came close to the cottage, almost happy since I knew that you were so near to me. The red glow that warmed the dark without comforted me. I thought I would look in upon you for a moment; and if you and Mary were awake and talking, that I should let you know I had come. But I saw that you lay in sleep; and I had scarce time to withdraw ere, as I feared, Mary saw me — though see me, indeed, perhaps she did, for in a brief while she opened the door and came out, and would have discovered me but that I moved swiftly to the shadow of the birk-shaws.[34] Then, after a little, I wandered down by the shore. There was a voice in the sea — calling, calling. It was so cool and sweet: soft was the balm of the air of it, as the look of your eyes, Lora, as the touch of your hand. I was almost healed of my suffering, when suddenly the pain in my head sprang upon me, and I crouched in the hollow yonder, chill with the sweat of my agony."

"O Alastair, Alastair, then you are no better: that great doctor you went so far to see has done you no good?"

"And in the midst of my pain, Lora my Rest, I saw you standing by the sea upon the ferry-ledge. At first I took you for a vision, and my heart sank. But when the moonlight reached the isle and enfolded you, I saw that it was you indeed. And once more my pain and my sorrow overcame me!"

"Alastair, I am terrified! It was not thus for you before you went away. Great as was your pain, you had not this gloom of sorrow. Oh, what is it, what is it, dear heart? Tell me, tell me!"

Slowly Alastair held Lora back from him, and looked long and searchingly into her eyes.

She shrank, in an apprehension that, like a bird, flew bewildered from the blinding light that flashed out of the darkness — a vain bewilderment of foredoom.

Then, with a great effort, she bade him tell her what he had to say.

Too well he knew there was no time to lose: that any day, any moment, his dark hour would come upon him, and that then it would be too late. Yet he would fain have waited.

"Lora, have you heard aught said by any one concerning my illness?"

"Dear, Father Manus told me, on the day you went away, that you feared the trouble which came upon your father, and upon your father's father; and oh, Alastair my beloved, he told me what that trouble was."

"Then you know: you can understand?"

"What?"

"That which now appals me . . . now kills me."

"Alastair!"

"Yes, Lora?"

34 Birk-shaws (Sc.): birch-groves.

"Oh, Alastair, Alastair, you do not mean that . . . that . . . you too . . . *you* are . . . are . . . that you have the . . . the . . . mind-dark?"

"Dear heart of mine, this sorrow has come to us. I — "

"With a sharp cry Lora held him to her, despairingly, wildly, as though even at that moment he were to be snatched from her. Then, in a passion of sobbing, she shook in his arms as a withered aspen-leaf ere it fall to the wind.

The tears ran down his face; his mouth twitched; his long, thin fingers moved restlessly in her hair and upon her quivering shoulder.

No other sound than her convulsive sobs, than his spasmodic breathing, met in the quietude of whisper-music exhaled as an odour by the sea and by the low wind among the corries and upon the grasses of the isle.

A white moth came fluttering slowly toward them, hovering vaguely awhile overhead, and then drifting alow and almost to their feet. In the shadow it loomed grey and formless — an obscure thing that might have come out of the heart of the unguarded brain. Upward again it fluttered, idly this way and that: then suddenly alit upon the hair of Alastair, poising itself on spread wings, and now all agleam as with pale phosphorescent fire, where the moonlight filled it with sheen as of white water falling against the sun.

The gleam caught Lora's eyes as, with a weary sigh, she lifted her head.

A strange smile came into her face. Slowly she disengaged her right arm, and half raised it. Alastair was about to speak, but her eyes brought silence upon him.

"*Hush!*" she whispered at last.

He saw that her eyes looked beyond his, beyond him as it seemed. What did she see? The trouble in his brain moved anew at this touch of mystery.

"What is it, Lora?"

"Hush, hush! . . . I see a sign from heaven upon your forehead . . . the sign of the white peace that Sheumais says is upon them who are of the company of the Belovëd."

"Lora, what are you saying? What is it? What do you see?"

His voice suddenly was harsh, fretful. Lora shrank for a moment; then, as the white moth rose and fluttered away into the dark, faintly agleam with moonfire till it reached the shadow, she pitifully raised her hand to his brow.

"Come, dear, let us go in. All will be well with us, whatever happens."

"Never . . . never . . . never!"

"O Alastair, if it be God's will?"

"Ay, and if it be God's will?"

"I cannot lose you: you will always be mine: no sorrow can part us: nothing can separate us: nothing but the Passing, and that . . . . ."

"Lora!"

For answer she looked into his eyes.

"Lora, it is of that, of the Passing: . . . are you . . . are you brave enough not only to endure . . . but to . . . if we thought it well . . . if I asked you . . . ?"

A deep silence fell upon both. Hardly did either breathe. By some strange vagary of the strained mind, Lora thought the throb of her heart against her side was like the pulse of the engines of the *Clansman* to which she had listened with such intent expectation that very evening.

From the darkness to the north came the low monotone of the sea, as a muffled voice prophesying through the gates of Sleep and Death. Far to the east the tide-race tore through the Sound with a confused muttering of haste and tumult. Upon the isle the wind moved as a thing in pain, or idly weary: lifting now from cranny to corrie, and through glen and hollow, and among the birk-shaws and the rowans, with long sighs and whispers where by Uisghe-dhu[35] the valley of moonflowers sloped to the sea on the west, or among the reeds, and the gale, and the salt grasses around the clachan that lay duskily still on the little brae above the haven.

"Lora . . . would you . . . would . . . ?"

Only her caught breath at intervals gave answer. The short lisp and gurgle of the water in the sea-weed close by came nearer. The tide was on the flood, and the sand about their feet was already damp.

The immense semicircle of the sky domed sea and land with infinity. In the vast space the stars and planets fulfilled their ordered plan. Star by star, planet by planet, sun by sun, universe by universe moved jocund in the march of eternal death.

Beyond the two lonely figures, seaward, the moon swung, green-gold at the heart with circumambient flame of pearl.

Beautiful the suspended lamp of her glory: a censer swung before the Earth-Altar of the Unknown.

In their human pain the two drew closer still. The remote alien silences of the larger life around vaguely appalled them. Yet Lora knew what was in his thought: what he fore-shadowed: what he wished.

"It shall be as you will, Alastair, heart of me, life of me," she whispered. Then, with clasping arms, and dear entreaty, she urged him homeward.

"Come, come home, Alastair, *Alùinn.* Enough of sorrow to-night. Speak to me tomorrow of all that is in your mind; but to-night . . . to-night, no more! My heart will break. Come, dearest. Come, *mo mùirnean!* Hark! the wind is crying in the corrie: it is rising again on the other side of the isle; and we are already chill — oh, cold, so cold!"

Hand in hand, they moved slowly upward along the little pathway of mingled grass and shingle which led to the clachan from the ferry: he with bowed head, she with upward face.

A dog barked from a byre, another answered from a sheiling beyond. Suddenly there was a rushing sound, and Ghaoth, Alastair's dog, came leaping upon his master, whining and barking with joy. He stooped and fondled it; but in vain tried to quell its ecstasy in seeing him again.

Whether aroused by the barking of Ghaoth, or having awoke and found Lora absent from the cottage, Mrs. Maclean had risen, lit a candle, and now stood upon the threshold, looking intently at the twain as they approached.

Among the islefolk many words are not used. The over-arching majesty of the sky — the surrounding majesty of the sea, the loneliness of these little wind-swept spots of earth isled in remote waters, leave a hush upon the brain, and foster eloquent silences rather than idle words.

Mrs. Maclean knew intuitively that something of disaster was in this nocturnal return of Alastair: that he and Lora had met by chance, or through a summons unknown to her: and that now they came — to her, in their youth, so tragically piteous under the shadow of calamity — craving only for that impossible boon of the young in sorrow: peace.

When they drew near to her, she turned and placed the candle on the table. Then, facing them, she came forward, led them in by the hand, and closed the door. She saw that Alastair was hatless, and his clothes damp and travel-stained; so with quiet, home-sweet words, she persuaded him to change his things while she laid some food for him to break his long fast with.

But though wearily he did the one, he would have nothing of the other save a draught of warm milk.

---

35 Uisghe-dhu (G.): black water.

A heavy drowsiness was now upon him. He could scarce uplift the lids from his eyes. His voice, when he spoke at all, was so low that it was barely audible.

After a silence, during which he had looked long at the fire, and closed his eyes at the last, with Lora's gaze hungrily set upon him, and the dark, sweet gloom of Mrs. Maclean's, wet with the dew of unshed tears, upon both of the twain whom she loved so passing well, he murmured huskily and confusedly —

"By green pastures ... I will lay me down to sleep . . . It calleth, calleth . . ."[36]

Suddenly Mrs. Maclean arose. Taking Lora's hand, she led her to the fireside and motioned her to kneel beside Alastair. Then, blowing out the candle-flame, she too knelt. Only the fireglow now lit the room, filled with brooding shadows in the corners and with warm dusk where the two women kneeled and the man slept.

With arms lifted as if in invocation, the elder woman — her face wan under her grey hair, though touched with an unreal glow from the flaming peats — in a low, crooning voice, repeated the ancient rest-words, the ancient prayer of her people, said at the covering up of the fire against the hours of sleep:

"Smalàidh mise an teine,
Mar a smàlas Mac Moire.
Gu'm bu slan an tigh's an teine,
Gu'm bu slan do'n chiudeachd uile.
Co sid air an làr?
Peadair agus Pòl,
Co air a bhith 's an aire 'nochd?
Air Moire geal 's air a Mac.
Beul De a dh' innseas
Aingeal geal a lann'rass,
Aingeal 'an dorus gach taighe
Gu solus geal a maireach."

I will cover up the fire aright,
Even as directed by the Virgin's Son.
Safe be the house, and safe the fire,
And safe from harm be all the indwellers.
Who is that that I see on the floor?
Even Peter himself and Paul.
Upon whom shall this night's vigil rest?
Upon the blameless Virgin and her Son:
God's mouth has spoken it.
A white-robed angel shall be with us in the dark,
Till the coming of the sun at morn.

When she ceased, there was no sound save the low sobbing of Lora and the quiet breathing of the sleeper in the high-backed chair.

Having made the sign of the cross upon her breast and over the fire, she covered up the flame with ash and charred peat. Quietly, then, she placed her strong arm around Alastair, and half guided, half lifted him to the bed in the adjoining room where he and Lora were wont to sleep. The girl-wife followed, and, with deft hands, unclad Alastair and laid him gently in the bed. Swiftly disrobing herself, she lay down by his side, her dark hair mingling on the pillow with his tangle of dull gold.

36 In the first two phrases Alastair is paraphrasing Psalm 23.

The gleam still emitted between the bars from beneath the covered peats passed into the room through the open doorway and fell upon the bed.

Alastair stirred; opened his eyes; looked with wild, startled gaze at Lora, then at Mrs. Maclean, who had again knelt, and with raised arms had began her "Blessing of Peace."

With a sigh he closed his eyes, and the terror passed from his face. Once or twice he muttered parts of the lines of that ancient sleep-prayer, familiar to him since his boyhood, and before it was ended deep slumber had come upon him:

> *"Laidhidh mise 'nochd*
> *Le Moire 's le Mac,*
> *Le mathair mo Righ,*
> *'Ni mo dhion 'o dhroch-bheairt,*
> *Cha laidh mise leis an olc,*
> *'S cha laidh an t' olc leam;*
> *Ach laidhidh mì le Dia,*
> *'S laidhidh Dia ma' rium,*
> *Lamh dheas Dhe fo'm cheann,*
> *Crois nan naoi aingeal leam.*
> *'O mhullach mo chinn*
> *Gu craican mo bhonn.*
> *Guidheam Peadair, guidheam Pòl,*
> *Guidheam Moir-oigh' 'sa Mac.*
> *Guidheam an da ostal deug,*
> *Gun mise 'dhol eug le'n cead.*
> *'Dhia 'sa Mhoire na gloire.*
> *'S a Mhic na oighe cubhraidh*
> *Cumabh mise o na piantan dorcha*
> *'S Micheal geal' an cò 'ail m'anama."*

This night I will lay me down to sleep
With Virgin Mary and her Son,
Even with the mother of my King,
Who protects me from all evil;
Nor shall evil lie down to sleep with me,
But I shall sleep with God:
And with me shall God lie down.
His right arm shall be under my head:
The cross of the Nine Angels be about me,
From the top of my head
To the soles of my feet.
I supplicate Peter, I supplicate Paul,
I supplicate Mary the Virgin and her Son,
I supplicate the twelve Apostles,
That evil befall us not this night.
Mary, in thy goodness and glory,
And Thou, Son of the sweet-savoured Virgin,
Protect us this night from all the pains of darkness.
And thou, Michael, guardian of souls, abide with us, watching.

When she looked down, at the end of her prayer, Mary saw that Lora's eyes also were closed; though by the muttering of the lips she knew her dear one was not asleep.

Softly she closed the door behind her; then, passing by the fire, went into the third room of the cottage.

Soon she too was in bed, softly repeating, as the weariness of sleep came over her —

Cha laidh mise leis an olc,
'S cha laidh an t' olc leam.

Without, came the rising sound of the tide among the pebbles on the shore, the incessant chime of wave lapsing over wave on flat rocks. The sough of the wind fell from the corries of Craig-an-Iolair, and died in whispers among the fern and dew-cold grasses.

So went the hours from silence into silence. And in tune came the dawn, and an ashen-grey upon the sea, and a grey gloom upon each leaf and every dusky frond and blade. But when the black of the mainland became gold, and a trouble or light moved, swiftly-throbbing, across the eastern water, Michael the Watcher withdrew.

At the window of the room where Alastair and Lora slept, the beautiful sunflood of the new day poured in rejoicingly.

One long streamer of light fell upon his yellow hair and kissed the eyelids of a veiled, subsiding mind. Downward it moved, and filled with its gleam the dark-brown hair which lay across the white breast of Lora. Then, surely, it passed beneath the flower of her bosom and into her heart, and warmed it with joy; for with a smile she awoke, murmuring, "Pharais, Pharais."

III.

BEFORE the want of that day, the rumour went among the scant population of Innisròn that Alastair, son of Diarmid of Macleod, was mad: that, in the phrasing of the islesman, he had the mind-dark.

Men and women whispered the thing with awe. In the West, something almost of a hieratic significance is involved in the poetic phrase that God has filled with dusk the house of the brain. Not thus is spoken of the violence of insanity — the mere insurgence of delirium from the fever of hate, or from jealousy, or love, or evil of the blood, or the curse of drink. But that veil of darkness which comes down upon the mind of man or woman in the fullness of life, and puts an impermeable mist or a twilight of awful gloom about the soul, is looked upon not only with an exceeding tenderness, but with awe, and as of a bowing of the head before a divine mystery.

Yet the rumour was not true, for Alastair Macleod, though he stood within the shadow, had not yet sunk into the darkness.

As it had chanced, Mrs. Maclean was not the only person who had seen him and Lora on their return.

Late in the night Ian Maclean had come back from the western side of the isle, and was standing in the shadow of the byre when, hand in hand, Lora and Alastair approached.

The old man had been unhappy, and, after leaving his kinsman at Ardfeulan, had wandered up among the corries. In the wail of the wind along the heights, in the sough of it in the little glens and shelving uplands, he heard voices to which he would fain not have listened, for they spoke of a terror that was in the air.

The moment he saw Alastair's eyes, dark within the moonlit pallor of the face, he knew that his premonitions were no mere imaginings. On his forehead he saw the shadow of doom.

With a sigh he turned, and, having entered the byre and gone to the part of it shut off for his use, lay down upon his bed of fragrant fern. But, weary as he was, he could not sleep.

Again the vision came to him: and once more he saw Alastair move blindly in an unfamiliar place, with the mist no longer up to his waist only, but risen now to his throat, and with thin tongues reaching upward still.

The long night went drearily past. When the day was come, Ian rose and let out the kye. The sweet freshness of the air was as balm to weariness. The wind blew cool upon his brows, and a breath of the sea mingled with the myriad suspiration of the earth and gave him the intoxication of the dawn. His eyes grew brighter, his step firmer, his mien no longer that of profound dejection; and when Ghaoth came leaping towards him, and barked about the half amused, half angry cows—who stopped to plash their hooves in the thick white dew, against which the warm breaths fell revolvingly like grey whorls of steam, and to swing their great horns against their flanks, wild and shaggy as the brown hill-sides in autumn—then all the gloom of the night went from him.

"Mayhap it was but a dream," he muttered: "and who can tell the folly of the mind?"

Then, with Ghaoth's help, he got the steers from the neighbouring shed and "Righ-geal,"[37] the-great tawny-shaggy bull, whose either horn could have pierced right through and beyond the biggest drover who ever crossed the Kyles[38] at Colintraive, and urged all the kine upward to the higher pastures, where the thyme was so sweet, close-clustered as it was among the soft green hair of the isle-grass.

It seemed to him as though all the larks on Innisròn were singing at one time and just there, everywhere around and above him. In the birk-shaws, there was a mavis that was as a fount wherefrom music spilled intoxicatingly: by the burn, the merles[39] called, recalled, and called yet again, and over and over, sweet and blithe, and with loud, reckless cries of mirth and joy. On every gorse-bush, yellow with bloom, fragrant almost to pain, and filled with the murmur of the wild-bee and the high, thin hum of the wood-wasp, a yellow-hammer flitted to and fro, or sang its *tweet – tweet – tweet – o-o-oh sweet – sweet!*

The sky was almost cloudless save for an angry-flush in the north-east—a deep, living blue of infinite, though indiscernibly faint gradation. Here and there, too, were thin, almost invisible grey mare's-tails swept upward, as though they were snow-dust or sea-spray, before the flying feet of the Weaver of the Winds.

As soon as Ian had reached the last dyke, and had seen "Righ-geal" lead his impatient following toward the uplands, he stood swaying his grey head slowly to and fro, with his right hand moving automatically in rhythmic accord, while he repeated the familiar "Rann Buachailleachd," or Rune on the driving of the cattle to the pasture: —

Siubhal beinne, siubhal coille,
Siubhal gu rèidh fada, farsuinn,
Banachag Phadruig ma'n casan,
'S gu faic mise slàn a rithisd sith.

---

37 Righ geal (G.): white king.
38 Kyles (G. *caolas*): narrows.
39 Mavis: thrush; merle: blackbird (both Sc.).

An seun a chuir Moire mu 'buar,
Moch 'us anmoch 'sa tigh 'n bhuaidh',
Ga'n gleidheadh O pholl, Oeabar.
O fheithe, O adh'rcean a cheile,
O liana' na Craige-Ruaidhe,
'S o Luaths na Féinne.
Banachag Phadruig ma'n casan,
Gu'm bu slàn a thig sibh dhachaidh.

Wandering o'er uplands, wandering thro' woods,
Hence and far away wander ye still,
St. Patrick's own milkmaid attend your steps
Till safe I see you return to me again.
The charm that Mary made to her cattle,
Early and late, going and coming from pasture,
Still keep you safe from quagmire and marsh,
Form pitfalls and from each other's horns,
From the sudden swelling by the Red Rock,
And from the hound Luath of the Fingalians.
St. Patrick's milkmaid attend your feet,
Safe and scatheless come ye home again.

Then, calling Ghaoth from the already scattered kye, he turned and made his way back to the clachan.

When he entered Mrs. Maclean's cottage, where his breakfast of porridge was ready, he made and received the usual salutation of blessing: and then sat down in silence.

The room was full of sunlight—so full that Mrs. Maclean had hung a screen of bracken from an iron hook, so that it shielded the peat-fire and let the life of the flame burn unchecked.

He did not look at Alastair; and, indeed, all the morning-blitheness had gone out of the eyes of the old man. Not that any there noticed his taciturnity. Mrs. Maclean moved softly to and fro. Alastair sat broodingly in the leathern chair before the fire: Lora on a stool at his feet, with her right hand claspt in his left and her eyes fixt on his face. On the table the porridge was untouched, the new bread uncut, the warm milk grown tepid.

With a sigh, Alastair rose at last. Crossing the room, he went to the east window and stared forth unseeingly, or, at any rate, without sign of any kind. Then, restlessly, he began to pace to and fro. Repressing her tears, Lora seated herself at the table and tried to eat, hopeful that she might thus induce him to do likewise. Mrs. Maclean followed her example, but ate in silence. She had almost ended, when Lora saw that she had abruptly laid down her spoon and was looking intently at Ian.

The old man now followed every motion of the invalid with a look as of one fascinated. When, suddenly, Alastair turned, went to the door and crossed the threshold, Ian rose and followed.

A few seconds later he came back, his withered face almost as white as his hair.

Mrs. Maclean met him ere he could speak.

"Not a word before *her*," she whispered. "Meet me at the byre: I shall be there in a minute or two."

But just then Lora rose and went out.

"Ian Maclean, what is it?"

"Mary, my kinswoman, he is not alone."

"Not alone?"

"I have seen *the other*."

She knew now what he meant. He had seen the shadow-self, the phantasm of the living that, ere death, is often seen alongside the one who shall soon die. Mrs. Maclean knew well that this shadowy second-self simulated the real self, and that even all the actions of the body were reproduced with a grotesque verisimilitude. But she was also aware how, sometimes, one may learn from the mien of the phantasm what is hidden in the aspect of the doomed.

"Last night," Ian went on in a dull voice, "I had the sight again. I saw the mist of death as high about him as when a man is sunken in a peat-bog up to the eyes."

"Well? I know you have more to say."

"Aye"

"Speak, Ian!"

With a long, indrawn breath, the old man resumed in a slow, reluctant voice.

"When I came in, a little ago, I saw the sorrow there was on every face. My vision, too, came back upon me, and I had trouble. I meant to eat and go out quickly. But when Mr. Alastair began to move about, I saw that he was not alone. I knew *the other* at once. There could be no mistake. In dress, in height, in face, in movement, they were the same. But there was a difference."

Mrs. Maclean shuddered slightly, and her lips opened as though she were about to speak. With a gesture, however, she signed to Ian to continue.

"Aye there was a difference. I hoped against my eyes; but when I followed him yonder I saw what I saw, and what killed my hope."

"Speak, speak, Ian!"

"In all things the same but one, and that was in the eyes, in the expression. Those of Mr. Alastair were dull and lightless, and brooding low; those of *the other* were large and wild, and stared in terror and amaze; and on the face of the thing the Fear lay, and moved, and was alive."

"O Ian, Ian, what does it mean?"

"It means this, Mary, daughter of Donnacha, what, sure, you know well: that not only is the shadow of death near this house, but that upon Alastair Mac Diarmid is the mind-dark that lay upon his father and upon his father's father."

"The curse of Michael be upon this evil, Ian!"

"Even so, Mhoire nighean Donnacha."

"His father was the third of his race in succession, who, soon or late, fell under that shadow. And we all know, sure we all know, that after the third generation the veil is withdrawn. This thing is an evil dream of yours, Ian Maclean!"

"It is an evil doing of *some one*," muttered the old man, with sombre eyes.

"Perhaps" — . . .

But before Mrs. Maclean could say what was in her mind, Alastair and Lora entered.

With downcast eyes Ian passed out, giving a furtive, terrified look behind him ere he closed the door.

It was through the old islesman that the rumour of Alastair Macleod's madness went abroad.

Long before the stormy afternoon which followed the beautiful youth of that day, with its ominous morning-red in the north-east, had waned to gloaming, there was not a soul on Innisròn who did not know of the sorrow.

Yet no one came near out of a cruel sympathy: no one spoke heedless words either of question or solace to Mrs. Maclean; for none could be said to the two most concerned, neither Alastair nor Lora having been seen throughout the day.

Nevertheless, a deep resentment prevailed against one person upon the island. Not only had the Spring gone ill with the fishing, but the nets had been torn and trailed in a way that suggested something beyond the blind malice of wind and wave and the currents of the deep sea and the savage dog-fish. Several cows had ceased to give milk; hens had ceased to lay; and Gregor McGregor's white mare had dropped a dead foal, the first time such a thing had happened on the isle. And now that, unforeseen and in the heyday of youth and health, the worst of all troubles had come upon Alastair Macleod, many recalled how his father, Macleod of Dunvrechan, who had died on Innisròn, had not only once denounced old Ealasaid MacAodh as a woman of the evil eye, but had cursed her ere he died, and attributed his misery to a blight of her working.

As one spake to another, the same thought came into each mind: that the old widow who lived at Craig-Ruaidh, at the head of the Glen of the Dark Water, had put her malice upon Alastair Mac Diarmid.

Some one, in a group by the ferry, reminded her hearers that, by a mischance, every one on the isle save Widow MacAodh had been invited to the feast in the little mission-house, when "*Lora nighean maighstir Tormaid*" was wedded; and how it was well known that old Ealasaid had been full of anger and pain at the slight, and had since scarce spoken with any one save Mrs. Maclean, with whom no bitterness was ever long to endure.

"Ay, ay, it's her doing — it's her doing," was muttered all round; "she has put the spell of the evil eye upon him — foreigner that she is."

Many years had gone by since Duncan bàn MacAodh, a Hebridean who had settled in Innisròn, brought thither a wife out of remote St. Kilda. Long since he had gone to his rest, and lay among the few dead under the great runic cross at the extreme of Ardfeulan, on the west of the isle: yet he was still "the man from Uist," as his widow was still the "outlander."

"Ian," said Pòl Macdonald, one of the oldest of the fishermen, "you too are said to have *the thing* in you, though you always look through both eyes, and with good will to man and beast. Let you, and two others of us, go to-night to Widow Ealasaid's, and do you look upon her and find out if she is accursed: ... and then ... and then . . ."

No one spoke, though a veiled consenting glance went between Macdonald and Ian and a young islesman, Ronald Macrae, who lived over by Ardfeulan.

It was not a subject to discuss further in that hour of uncertainty. One or two members of the group had already edged away, when Kathia Macdonald suddenly drew attention to the appearance of the first three of the returning herring-boats, anxiously expected for over an hour past.

The brown-sailed wherries came in under the lee of the isle in a smother of foam. Already a snarling north-easter was racing over the sea, still smelling of the ling and bracken it had flattened as it tore over the summits of the mainland hills.

The water was of a shifting emerald near the haven; of a dark bottle-green beyond; and, out in the open, black, fretted and torn with staring white splashes and a myriad-leaping surge.

The race of the sea-horses had begun, and no one on Innisròn was at ease till the last boat had come safely round from Ardgheal, the point whence on the yestereve Lora had so eagerly watched for the coming of her husband.

A fiery sunset disclosed the immense and swirling procession of clouds high over the isle — cloud not only racing after cloud, but often leaping one upon the other as flying sheep in panic. Toward the east, the vapours were larger and darker: the cohorts more densely massed. Above the mainland stretched one vast unbroken phalanx of purple-livid gloom, out of the incessant and spasmodically convulsive travail in whose depths swept monstrous cloudbirths.

As the night fell, there was audible beyond the hills the noise of a baffled thunderstorm — a tempest which had been caught among the mountains, and could no more lift itself over the summits than a screaming and wrestling eagle could tear itself from a stag in whose hide its talons had become irremovably gript.

Above the peaks and along the flank of the mass of livid gloom, spears of lightning were swung against the wind; and with splinter and flash, there was a rain of whirled lances as against some unseen assault from below.

The tumult soared, hurled downward, and fell upon Innisròn. The isle-folk listened in the dark with awe. Roar and crash, and a frightful, terrifying howling followed every blast, as of a volcano belching forth avalanche after avalanche, and shaking to the valleys the débris of all the hills. Roar upon roar, crash upon crash, howl upon howl: with the strident raucous scream of the wind, yelling a paean of triumph as it leaped before the javelins of the lightning and tore in its ruinous might far out across the heaving, swaying, moaning sea.

It was a night for all who fare by or upon the deep waters to remember with awe: for those whose lives, and kin, and gear had gone scatheless, to recollect with thanksgiving: for those whose weal went with it, to recall with bowed heads or wet eyes.

An hour or more after nightfall, three figures moved with the wind across the isle: blurred shadows astir in the tempest-riven dark. Ronald Macrae carried a lantern; but speedily laid it down by a cairn, for the flame could not live.

He and Ian and Pòl were grimly silent, not only on the path through the wind-swept heather, but when under shelter from a bight of hillside or overhanging crag. The business that took them out in that tempest lay heavy upon them.

If, out of her own mouth, or by sign or deed of her own, Ealasaid should convict herself of the use of the evil-eye, her doom would be fixt. Even in the bitterness of superstition, however, the islesmen were not bent upon the extreme penalty, the meed of those who deal in witchcraft. The dwellers on Innisròn, as all who live among the outer isles in general, are too near the loneliness of life and death to be wanton in the taking away of that which is so great in the eyes of man and so small in the eyes of God.

The worst they intended was to make Ealasaid bring her own doom upon her: then, on the morrow, her sheiling would be burned to the ground and the ashes scattered to the four quarters, while she herself would be exiled from the island under ban of cross, mystic word, and the ancient Celtic anathema.

So wild was the wind and dark the way, that a full hour passed before they reached the Glen of the Dark Water, and heard the savage ramping and charging of the endless squadrons of the waves against the promontory of Ardfeulan.

As they drew near the little cottage, a lonely dwelling on the brae which sloped to the glen, they saw that the occupant had not yet gone to bed, for a red gleam of light stole comfortingly across the forlorn dark.

With a significant touch on the shoulder of each of his companions, Ian led them to within a yard or two of the window.

"Hush," he whispered, in a momentary lull; "make no noise as we look in. She might hear, and blast us with her evil eye. Perhaps she is even now talking with some warlock or fiend."

Trembling, the three men huddled under the wall. At last, slowly, and with hearts wildly athrob, they raised themselves and looked within.

The room was bare in its clean poverty. On the rickety wooden table was a bowl with a little unfinished porridge in it. A yard away was an open Gaelic Bible, with a pair of horn spectacles laid across the open page. At a spinning stool between the table and the peat fire was an old woman, kneeling, with her hands clasped and her face upraised. On the poor, tired, worn features was a look of pathetic yearning, straining from a white and beautiful peace.

So rapt was she that she did not see a hand move the outer latch of the window, or feel the sudden breath of the night-air.

Then those without, waiting to hearken to sorcery more appalling than the savagery of the tempest, heard old Ealasaid repeat this prayer:

Tha 'n la nis air falbh ùainn,
Tha 'n oidhche 'tighinn orm dlùth;
'S ni mise luidhe gu dion
Fo dhubhar sgiath mo rùin.
O gach cunnart 's o gach bàs,
'S o gach nàmhaid th' aig Mac Dhe,
O nàdur dhaoine borba,
'S o choirbteachd mo nàduir fèin,
Gabhaidh mis' a nis armachd Dhe,
Gun bhi reubta no brisd',
'Sge b' oil leis an t'sàtan 's le phàirt
Bi'dh mis' air mo gheàrd a nis.

The day is now gone;
Dark night gathers around,
And I will lay me safely down (to sleep)
Under the shadow of my Beloved One's wing.
Against all dangers, and death in every form,
Against each enemy of God's good Son,
Against the anger of the turbulent people,
And against the corruption of my own nature,
I will take unto me the armour of God —
That shall protect me from all assaults:
And in spite of Satan and all his following,
I shall be well and surely guarded.

When, after an interval of speechless prayer, the lonely old woman rose painfully to her feet, she noticed the open window, and heard the sough of the wind without.

With a tired sigh, she crossed the room to close the inside latch. But, at the window, she stood irresolute, held by the noise of the sea beating against the clamour of the wind. She stooped, and peered forth.

Not a thing was visible. Suddenly a broad wavering gleam of sheet-lightning lit up the whole brae. Almost, she fancied, she could have sworn she saw three human figures, with bowed heads, moving across the brow of the slope.

She could not know that three men, stricken with shame and remorse – remorse which would ere long bloom into the white flower of repentance, to be worn lovingly by all on the isle—were stealing homeward from a vain and wicked errand.

With a shudder, she crossed herself, fearing that the figures she had imagined, or had really seen, were the three dreadful Accursed who drove the spear into Christ's side and the nails into His hands and feet, and with mocking offered Him the bitter sponge.

Slowly repeating—

O gach cunnart 's o gach bàs,
'S o gach nàmhaid th' aig Mac Dhe,

she quenched with charred peat the flame of her fire, and was soon in a child-like rest "under the shadow of the wing of her Beloved One."

When midnight came upon the isle, the worst violence of the storm was over. Nevertheless, upon the sea was the awfulness of desolation, the rumour of a terrible wrath.

All slept at last: the innocent Ealasaid, the foolish seekers of evil, the islefolk one and all—except two.

Alastair and Lora lay in each other's arms as children terrified in the dark.

That afternoon his madness had come upon him for a while; and he had smiled grimly at he knew not what, and laughed while the tears streamed from the eyes of Lora and Mary; and moaned betimes; and cried out against the calling of the sea; and closed his ears against the frightful wailing of a kelpie[40] in the tarn beyond the byre; and, at the last, shook as in an ague before the fire, fearful of some informulate terror, but with such a crown of sorrow on his forehead that the two women bowed their faces in their hands, speechless with grief: with such a horror in his eyes that Gaoth shrank from him with bristling fell and upcurled, snarling lip.

But with the night came yet another merciful lifting of the veil.

While the storm raged at its worst, the three kneeled, and Mrs. Maclean read from the beautiful Gaelic Scripture. Then, with all the tenderness of her childless passion of maternity, she prayed for God's balm and peace and the healing of His hand.

When, in time, she went to her own room, Alastair and Lora talked for long in a low voice.

On the day he had first heard that the seed of life had taken root in her womb, and knew that a child was to be born of their great love, he had known a thrill of such rapture that he could scarce see Lora for the blinding of the tears of joy.

Beautiful she was to all: to him, lovely and tender as twilight and dear beyond words: but at that moment, when he learned from her own lips of her only half explicable trouble, he knew he had passed into a Holy of Holies of love and reverent passion such as he had but vaguely dreamed of as possible.

But now, on this wild night of storm without and more awful dread within, he recalled with horror what had been driven from his mind.

Bitter as was the doom he and Lora had to face, tenfold bitter was it made by the thought that they were to bring into the world yet another soul shrouded in the shadow of his own intolerable ill.

And so it was that, at the last, Alastair and Lora Macleod, knowing his madness was at hand and could be cured of no man, and that their lives were spilled out as lees from a cup, and that they were witlessly dooming the unborn child to a heritage of grief, gave solemn troth to each other that on the morrow they would go forth hand in hand,

---

40 Kelpie (Sc.): water-demon.

and, together in death as in life, lay themselves beneath that ever wandering yet ever returning wave which beats day and night, and week by week, and year by year, and without end for ever, about the sea-gathered graveyard on the remote west of Innisròn.

Then was a great peace theirs. For the last time they laid themselves down on their bed: for the last time twined their arms around each other, while on the same pillow their heads lay side by side, the hair about his forehead wet with her falling tears: for the last time they kept vigil through the terror of the dark—an awful terror now, with the wrath of the sea without, with the shadow of Death within the room, with the blackness of oblivion creeping, creeping from chamber to chamber in the darkened house of a dulled, subsiding brain.

Ere dawn, Alastair slept. Lora lay awake, trembling, longing for the day, yet praying God to withold it; sick with baffled hope, with the ache of weariness, with the sound of the moan and hollow boom of the sea. More deep and terrible in her ears grew that midnight Voice, reverberant in the room as in the whorl of a shell: a dreadful iterance of menace, a dirge that confusedly she seemed to know well, a swelling chant, a requiem.

IV.

AN hour after sunrise there was not a cloud in the sky. The first day of June came clad in the fullness of summer. Sea and land seemed as though they had been immersed in that Fount of Life which wells from the hollow of the Hand which upholdeth Tir-na-h'Oighe, the isle of eternal youth.

The low island-trees had not suffered as had those on the mainland: yet everywhere were strewn branches, and, on the uplands, boughs wrenched away, and often hurled far from the parent tree.

But upon all the isle there was now a deep quiescence. In the warm languor, even the birds sang less wildly clear, though the high, remote, falling lark-music floated spirally earthward, poignantly sweet. An indescribably delicate shimmer of haze lay on the heights and pastures, and where the corries sloped jaggedly seaward, each with a singing burn splashing or wimpling adown its heart. From the uplands came the lowing of the kine, the bleating of the ewes and lambs, the rapid whirring gurgle of the grouse among the heather. The wailing of curlews rose and fell; the sharp cries of the cliff-hawks beat against Craig-Ruaidh. High overhead, as motionlessly in motion as the snow-white disc of the moon lying immeasurably more remote within the vast blue hollow of the sky, an eagle poised on outspread wings, and then, without visible effort or movement, drifted slowly out of sight like a cloud blown by the wind.

Only upon the sea was something of the tumult of the past night still a reality.

Around the isle, and in the wide Sound between it and the mainland, the "white sheep" moved in endless procession, no longer wildly dispersed and huddled and torn by the wolves of the tempest. Oceanward the sea-horses swept onward magnificently, champing and whirling white foam about their green flanks, and tossing on high their manes of sunlit rainbow gold, dazzling white and multitudinous far as sight could reach.

Clamour of gulls, noise of waves, lisp and chime and flute-call of the shallows among the rock-holes and upon the whispering tongues of the sea-weed—what joy, and stir, and breath of life!

Hand in hand, in the hot noon, Lora and Alastair went idly along the sheep-path leading from the clachan to the promontory of Ardgheal. The smell of the brine from the sea and wrack-strewn shore, the sun-wrought fragrance of the grass and thyme, of bracken and gale, of birch and hawthorn and trailing briar, of the whole beautiful, living, warm body of the earth so lay upon the tired senses with a healing as of balm, that even the tears in Lora's eyes ceased to gather, leaving there only a softness as of twilight-dew in violets.

It was to be their last walk in the sunshine of that day — their last participance in the sunshine of life.

All the morning had been spent by Alastair in writing and brooding. Once again he had talked over with Lora that projected deed, which to them seemed the one right and fitting end to the tragedy of circumstance. She had promised that even if the darkness came down upon his mind irretrievably she would fulfil her troth with him. Great love casteth out fear; but even if this had not been so with her, she bore in mind the menace of what he had said about the child.

She, too, had spent a little of that last morning in writing, though her letter was not to go across the sea to the mainland, but to be left with old Ian to give to Mary on the morrow.

It was close upon noon when she saw that Alastair's gloom was upon him again, though he was now as quiet as a child. Taking his hand, she led him forth, heedful to avoid the clachan, and vaguely wishful to visit once more that little eastern haven of Ardgheal where, but two days ago, she had longingly awaited Alastair's return, and where, months before, he had first won her love.

He seemed to take pleasure in the sight of the sea he loved so well, and in the songs of the birds, and to be vaguely displeased because Ghaoth would not leap to his caress as usual, or else would crouch at his feet with startled eyes and low whine.

When Lora spoke, he answered seldom; but when he did, she knew that he understood. Once or twice he looked at her strangely; and once, with a thrill of awe and dread, she saw that it was unrecognisingly.

With a sob, she turned and put her arms about him. Never had he seemed so fair in her sight — tall and comely as a young pine, of a beauty beyond that of any man she had ever seen. No wonder that her father, familiar lover of the Ossianic ballads, had been wont, remembering the beauty of the second son of Usnoth, lord of Etha, to call Alastair *Ailthos*.

"Dear, my dear one, Ailthos, Alastair!" she cried, clinging close. "Look at me! Speak to me! Do you not know me?"

Slowly he turned his eyes upon her, and after a brief perplexity the shadow went out of them, and he smiled gently.

"Let us go home, my fawn," he whispered. "I am tired. It would be too sad to go down to Ardgheal."

He had already caught sight of the smoke of a steamer beyond Dunmore Point; and fearing that it might be the *Clansman* – for he thought the hour much later than it was – he hoped to spare Lora another needless pang. Moreover, his growing dread of seeing any one was stronger than ever upon him.

So they turned thus soon even in that last sunshine, and entering the cottage, sat before the smouldering peat-fire; he brooding darkly, Lora dreaming through her slow-welling tears, and both . . . waiting.

Though, at dusk, a heavy sea still ran, it was partly due to the surge of the ground-swell and to the turbulence of the tide, for there was but little wind even away from the shelter of the isle, and what there was came mostly in short, sudden puffs and wandering breaths.

In the quietude of the gloaming, it was as though the sea called all round Innisròn as a beast of prey stalks about a high sheepfold, growling, breathing heavily, ravening.

After the supper, eaten frugally and in silence, Lora and Alastair listened once again to the peat-prayer and the Blessing of Peace of Mrs. Maclean; then, not daring to say any word to her but that of a husky farewell for the night, and fearful even of meeting the glance of her quiet eyes, they went to their room, there to sit silently awhile in the darkness, hand in hand.

No one saw them leave the cottage an hour later: not a soul heard them as they passed through the clachan.

The road they chose was that sheep-path through the heather which led to Ardfeulan by the Glen of the Dark Water. Each knew the way well, otherwise their faring westward would have been difficult, for the sky was veiled by a thin mist and the moon was not visible.

They walked in silence; sometimes Lora in advance, but, whenever practicable, together, and hand in hand.

At last they reached the Glen of the Dark Water, and perceived through the gloaming the sheiling of Ealasaid MacAodh. This they skirted, and then entered a sloping hollow, at the base of which was audible the hoarse murmuring of the sea. Lora knew the place well. A week ago she had been there with Alastair, and remembered that the whole slope was a mass of moonflowers, tall, white, and so close-clustered that the green stems could hardly be seen.[41]

The wan glimmer of them was perceptible now, like the milky way on a night when a faint frost-mist prevails. Around, there was nothing else visible. Not a tree grew in that place: not a crag rose out of the sea of death-white blooms. The low-hanging mist-cloud veiled all things. It was as though the grave had been passed, and this was the gloom of the Deathsleep Land that lies beyond. Only *there* is eternal silence: here, the dull menace of the sea made a ceaseless murmur about the obscure coasts.

As they entered the valley of moonflowers, dimly seeing their way a few yards beyond them, and hearkening to the inwash and resurgence of the tide moving along the extreme frontiers of the land, a sense of unspeakable dread came over Alastair and Lora.

They stood still, hardly daring to breathe. Both vaguely remembered something: they knew not what, save that the tragic memory was linked with reminiscence of a valley of moonflowers seen in a dark twilight. Was it all a dream, coincident in their minds? Or had life once before, in some unremembered state, wrought tragic issues for them by a valley of white flowers seen in the darkness, with a deeper darkness around, a veiled sky above, and the hoarse, confused prophesying of the sea beyond?

As they stood, the moon – about an hour risen – glimmered through the veil of cloud. As with a hand, the rift was slowly made; but though the light was now clearly visible, it still gleamed through filmy shrouds of vapour. There was no shape, no central luminous spot even: only a diffused sheen which spread for a great span northward and southward, though it illumed nothing beneath save the long sloping hollow filled with moonflowers. The blooms rose almost to the knees of the two silent and trembling figures. For some inscrutable reason, the advance of light had not brought any comfort to either: rather, their vague terror increased almost unendurably.

The sea called below. Lora shuddered, and drew back a step or two.

A long, wavering, greenish light appeared high above the south-west. As the sheet-lightning fled shudderingly northward, it lapsed into ashen tremors before it was swallowed up of the darkness, as a wounded sea-bird in the deep.

---

41 A tall, cream-white merguérite, native to the Outer Isles and the Hebrides, is known to the Islanders as the Moonflower. [Sharp's note]

In that brief gleam, Alastair turned and looked into Lora's eyes.

She moved to his side again, and once more took his hand. Then, slowly, and still without word one to the other, they moved downward through the hollow.

There was not a sound about them save the susurrus of their feet going through the moonflowers. From the glen alone came any break in the inland stillness, the noise of water running swiftly from ledge to ledge. In the darkness where the sea was, there broke the fluctuating moan and boom of ocean. From far across the wave came a thin, forlorn sound that was the crying of the wind.

Minute by minute, as they waded through that death-white wilderness, the moon wove the cloud-shroud into thinner veils, till at last, as the two figures emerged upon the shore by the side of a precipitous scaur, they were of a filmy gossamer that no longer obscured the golden-yellow globe that wheeled solemnly through the appalling upper solitudes of the night.

The tide, at the last reach of the ebb for nearly an hour past, was now on the flood: though the first indeterminate babble of returning waters was scarce different from the lapsing ebb-music in aught save a gurgling swiftly-repetitive undertone.

The scaur by whose side they stood was hollow, and was known as the Cave of the Sea-Woman. It could be reached dry-shod, or nearly so, only at low water, and even then only during calm, or when the wind did not blow from the south or west. For years beyond record it had been almost unvisited, for the cavern was a place of deadly peril except just before and after the extreme ebb. But after the death of two of his sons — one in the effort to swim outward against the inrush of the tide; the other by falling, or being swept backward to the deep chasm that lay at the far end of the cave — old Macrae, of Ardfeulan Farm near by, had caused rude steps to be cut in the funnel-like hollow rising sheer up from the sloping ledge that lipped the chasm and reached the summit of the scaur.

The smell of the brine from the dripping boulders smote shrewdly upon Alastair and Lora as they stood at the weedy mouth of the cavern. Then for the first time that night they turned their backs upon the sea, and moved slowly across the long, flat slabs of rock.

It was not dark at the entrance to the Cavern of the Sea-Woman, for the moonlight moved within it as the hand of a blind man groping blankly in an unfamiliar place. The arch of the rock was clear, and even the frondage of fern and sea-plants suspended from its lower curve; also, beneath, a mass of mossed crag, just beyond the highest reach of the tides. Among this dark crag-vegetation grew strange plants; but none stranger or so rare as the sea-grape, or mermaid's-fruit of the islanders. No one on Innisròn knew its proper designation, and it had become known at all as the sea-grape only because some student of rare things discovered and wrote about it under that name, as perhaps the culminating treasure-trove of the botanist in the Scottish West. It is a plant which clings as a tendril, choosing only the summit of high rocks or boulders in some sunless place where it can breathe the ooze from dead or dying sea-weed, and can feel the salt air reach it with a chilly touch. It lies low, with its thin, moist, ash-grey stems; its round, pale-green, transparent leaves faintly spotted with livid blotches; and its infrequent clusters of small, juicy berries of a hue of dusky yellow.

The isle-folk regard it with awe. Though the fruit is poisonous, and a deadly draught can be distilled from the leaves, a few berries would not suffice to kill. To eat sparingly of the sea-grape is not to invite death necessarily, but to bring about a stupor so deep that for an hour or more no familiar sound can reach the ear, no ordinary shock vibrate along the nerves, no common pain affect the body. If the eater of the mermaid's-fruit be left undisturbed, he will not stir for twelve or even fifteen hours, though the first death-like trance does not prevail beyond an hour, or at most two: while, if forcibly aroused, he is so weak in body and so dazed in mind that he cannot long be kept awake without peril to the brain, and indeed to life itself.

It was because of this fruit of oblivion that Alastair and Lora had sought the Cave of the Sea-Woman.

They had feared not so much their own instinctive evasion of death as that, in the final struggle, they might not go down into the shadow together.

The idea that the Silence should come upon them unawares—that, arms about each other in a last embrace, the wave should encroach upon their deep unheeding slumber—had given them a strange elation. The thought was Alastair's. Though he was not a native of Innisròn, he had often visited it from Dunvrechan even before he had come to love Lora, and was familiar with each of the treacherous caves and all the desolate, boulder-strewn, uninhabited south-western side of the island, as well as with everything in animate or inanimate nature which was to be found therein. Not only had he often heard of the sea-grape which grew almost inaccessibly in some of the caverns on the western side, but he knew where in the Cave of the Sea-Woman it was to be obtained with little difficulty.

Letting Lora's hand drop gently to her side, he climbed the rough, broken ledges to the right, and swiftly returned holding in his hand a cluster of limp leaves from which hung snakily several stems of the dusky-yellow fruit.

Lora looked at the berries curiously, and yet with a strange indifference. With that awful menacing sound of the sea beyond, with that more awful murmur of dread in her heart, with that rising tide of death all about them, it mattered little to her that Alastair laid such stress on those small, poisonous things, those petty messengers of a mere oblivion of the senses.

Just beyond where they stood, and at the beginning of those long, flat, inward-sloping ledges which formed the floor of the cavern till the abrupt ending over the dark chasm at the extreme end, was a bed of soft white sand, shelving from one of the ledges past and underneath another, and then among rocks covered with bladder-wrack and adder's-tongues and other sea-weed, with tangled masses of the long, trailing dead-man's-hair.

Still without speech, here Alastair and Lora lay down, side by side.

There is an ebb in the tide of human hope that must reach a limit. When this limit is attained there is too great weariness for any further revolt, for any protest, for anything but dull acquiescence.

Slowly Alastair stripped a few of the dusky berries from the plant and held them in the hollow of his hand to Lora.

Taking them, she leaned forward, looking intently upon his face, but failing to see into his eyes, because of a deeper shadow therein than that which environed them.

"*Alastair,*" she whispered.

He made no answer; but wearily raised his hand to his mouth, and with his tongue crushed against his palate the acrid juice of the sea-grapes.

"O Alastair! speak to me! speak to me!"

He turned slowly. Then suddenly he put out his arms, and gathered her to his breast.

"My beautiful gloom—Lora—my Rest—my Joy—O you who are my Pharais—all the Pharais I care for now or dream of—if there be indeed a pitiful God, He will have mercy upon us. If we do wrong, we sin believing that we are doing the right, the sole right thing. But sweet it is—O Lora, sweet and dear at the last, after all our dark bewildered pain, to be here and know that all is over now, and that we two go into the Silence together: and if there be any waking, that together we shall wake. *Mo ghràidh, mo mùirnean,* my dear one, what peace there is for you and me that I die thus: free from that crushing, crushing pain and darkness that has filled my brain."

"Alastair! O my dear love—dearest—shall we—shall we meet again after this dreadful night? Shall there be any day for us? I cannot die—oh, I cannot die in this awful darkness . . . thus . . . We are both so young . . . and I . . ."

She ceased abruptly.

A low splashing sound, with long-drawn suffocating surge and susurrus, told that the sea had begun to creep forward with stealthy swiftness.

It was not the menace of the tide, however, that froze the words upon her lips.

Alastair had begun to croon, in a drowsy, yet strained, uncertain voice, a snatch of fisher-lore.

"Alastair! Alastair! Alastair!"

He gave a low laugh, as he turned on his side, and with wandering fingers played idly with the sand.

"Alastair! . . . my husband! . . . Beloved . . . Alastair! . . . Oh, say farewell to me at the least . . . Do not turn from me!"

"It called—called—called: and she cried to me, Come, my Belovèd: and then I knew Lora was dead. Why do you laugh at me? She is dead, I tell you: *dead, dead, dead!* She, my beautiful Lora—my dream—my joy—she who to me was Pharais itself: she is *dead!*"

In the grip of supreme woe, a woman has a heroism of abnegation beyond all words to tell of it.

Her grief rose within Lora as a phantom, and chilled her to the very heart and to the very brain. But with a great effort she stirred, leaned over and pluckt some of the fatal fruit, and swallowed it: for she had crushed in her hand the berries he had given her.

Then, having risen, with deft hands she pulled toward her some long strings of dead-man's hair and rope-weed; and, with those which were firmly affixed to rocks or heavy stones, she wove a girdle about the waist of Alastair, and so round her own.

She could scarce see to finish her task, for the moon had passed upward into the denser cloud, and the faintly luminous veils of vapour beneath it were now scarce distinguishable from the obscurity all around.

The insistent wash of the tide was coming steadily nearer. She could feel the cold breath of its moving lip.

Absolute darkness prevailed; while, with shaking hands, having unloosed her long, black hair, she tied it firmly in two places with the curly tangle of him whom she loved so passing well in death as in life.

No gleam fell from the veiled moon. Not a thing was visible save a faint phosphorescent line that moved slowly inward. Lora could not see Alastair's face, not even his body, not even the two shaking hands she held over him while she prayed inaudibly, and with a suffocating, bewildering pain at her heart, at her lungs, in her head.

No sound came from the isle. The noise of the falling stream in the glen was merged in the confused clamour of the tide-race. Shoreward, there was that awful tidal whisper. Seaward, the march of wave after wave, of billow after billow, in vast processional array; squadron after squadron, battalion after battalion, of the innumerable army of the deep: and among them all, over them all, beneath them all, a Voice, loud, reverberant, menacing, awful as brooding thunder, terrible as the quaking of the dry land when the hills o'er-topple the cities of the plain: a Voice as of the majesty of Death, swelling through the night with all the eternal pain, the forlorn travail, the incommunicable ache of all the weary, weary World.

Then, ere all remembrance died for her, Lora knew that Alastair slept and was at peace.

She stole her arm round his neck and held him close, but was too weak now to lean over and kiss those white lips, parted as a child's in dreamless slumber.

It was her last pain: the last unavailing bitterness of woman's woe.

Thereafter she lay still, vaguely hearkening the tide run up the deep channel beyond the little isle of sand, already damp with the under-ooze.

She listened to the slipping of the water along the ledges. A wave came out of the darkness and stalked through the gloom as a wild beast to its lair. Ledge over ledge she heard it swiftly move: then suddenly there was a blank . . . a hoarse muffled noise . . . the hollow reverberation of the billow as it fell heavily into the black unfathomed gulf wherein at the flood was swept all that drifted into the cave.

A windy sigh arose in the cavern. The tide moved upward, feeling along the walls with stealthy, groping hands. A faint phosphorescence appeared momently, now here, now there.

The second channel, to the left, suddenly brimmed. The water spilled over upon the sandy track beyond. Then a long rolling wave raced inward, leaped along one of its ledges, poised a moment, and, breaking into a seething foam in its fall, tore this way and that the weedy bonds which bound the sleepers.

Beyond, in the darkness, the loud moan, the deep, monotonous boom of the sea filled the whole vast void of the night.

V.

THE loud and terrifying violence of the sea throughout that day; the oppressive gloom of that night; the weight of undischarged electricity which everywhere brooded; all made sleep impossible for Ealasaid MacAodh.

So ill was she when evening set in, that she had moved her things from the bed in the second of the two rooms of which the sheiling consisted, so as to sleep in the box-bed in the larger, within sight and feel of the fire-glow.

She had not slept there since her husband died. Perhaps this was because that, even after the lapse of years, she could not endure the solitudes of memory. They had been lovers in their youth, she and her Hebridean: they had been lovers during their brief married life, ere he, after the too frequent wont of the islesmen, found death in the wave wherein he sought the means of life: and when his drifted body had been recovered, and laid in the island soil, she had remained his lover still. Doubtless, she thought of him even yet with his yellow hair and laughing eyes; perhaps of herself, too, as lithe of limb and with soft, fair skin as unwrinkled and hair as brown and supple as when he had first caused the trouble of a new and strange tide in the calm waters of her girl's heart.

To sleep in the bed where she had lain by his side, where a child had been born to her and had died just as with glad pain she had recognised in the little one the eyes of its father, may have seemed to her a cross of suffering which she was unable to take up and bear.

Or, it may be, there lurked darkly in her mind the ancient secret Celtic dread of sleeping in the bed where any of one's own blood-kin has died: the dread of the whisper that is on the pillow in the dark hours, of the hand that gropes along the coverlet, of the chill breath that comes without cause and stirs the hair as it falls suddenly upon the cheek of the awakened sleeper.

On this night, however, she dreaded not only her own weakness, but the dark. Vaguely, she wondered how she had for so long a time slept away from the comforting light and warmth of her peat-fire.

She was so old, so weary, she thought pitifully. Would Duncan be sure to know her again? Why was she kept so long there, waiting for the summons that never came? Had God forgotten her? No kin had she: not one to claim her body for the place of sleep when her dark hour came. Useless were her days to all: to herself, each day a rising sorrow; each night a setting grief.

Yet that infinite patience of the poor was hers, that poignant pathos of womanhood in childless and husbandless old age, which to the very end endures — till the last thread has been used in the weaving of the Crown of Sorrow.

Beautiful this austere Diadem worn by aged and lonely women: sweet-eyed bearers of crowns among the myriad procession of the weary poor of all the world, all going gloriously apparelled and wreathed with green garlands which fade not in the sight of Him who leadeth His feeble folk to kingship and honour.

For a brief while she lay brooding, with dull old eyes fixt upon the red heart of the peats. Then the gaze withdrew slowly, and the lids closed; as though a bird, flying softly through the twilight, had passed beneath the low-hung leaves over its nest.

She could not have been long asleep, for the glow was still ruddy upon the floor, when she was startled by a sudden barking and whining. She sat up, listening intently. She could hear no step, no voice. The whining terrified her. If the noise were that of a dog at all, and not of Luath or some other phantom hound, whose dog was it, and why its sudden appearance at her door at that hour of night, — its eager, unceasing clamour?

But when, with louder and louder barks and an impatient scraping, the unwelcome visitor showed he was not to be denied, she rose, put on her things, and then, having wrapped a shawl about her head and lit a lantern which she lifted from a hook, opened the door.

For a moment, she thought that nothing was there. Then her ears caught the sound of panting breath, and something wet and warm touched her suspended left hand.

With timid, yet caressing voice, she lured the dog across the threshold. The moment she could see clearly, she recognised him as Ghaoth, the white-breasted, tawny-haired, amber-eyed collie that belonged to Alastair Macleod.

The dog would not bide. His whining never ceased, save when it was interrupted by loud, eager barks. To and fro he ran, and at last sprang out into the night again, only to return a few minutes later in a state of excitement bordering on frenzy.

"Some evil must have happened to Alastair Macleod," Ealasaid muttered, as after a brief hesitation she took the lantern and followed Ghaoth.

To her dismay, the dog tried to lead her towards the hollow of the moonflowers. Could Alastair possibly be there, or on the shore beyond? Why, if he were down there, lying helpless, the tide would be upon him shortly, and then his doom would be certain. Again, of what avail was she, so old and frail, and now with some new weakness upon her? She feared she had not the strength to move downward in the dark through that dense jungle of white blooms: still less to climb homeward again.

But while she pondered, she saw that Ghaoth leaped no more in the direction of the valley, but along the grassy ridge which led to the summit of Craig-Geal, so perilous by night because of the sloping, precipitous hole which gave entrance to the funnel-like passage issuing from the Cave of the Sea-Woman.

"Ah!" she cried, as it flashed upon her that Alastair had fallen, or been hemmed-in in the cavern by the tide, "God help him if he is *there!*"

With panting breath she hurried along the ridge, heedless now of Ghàoth, who had suddenly darted off to the left and disappeared among the moonflowers. She had not gone far, however, before she stopped. What use to hurry onward, if all she could do was to shout down into the darkness — a cry that would likely never be heard, and if heard would be of no avail to the hearer?

No sooner did she realise the uselessness of her errand than she turned, and, with shaking limbs and labouring breath, made her way along a sheep-path which led to the opposite brae of Craig-Ruaidh, where Angus Macrae and his son Ranald lived. So exhausted was the old woman by the time she had reached the farm and aroused the inmates, that two or three minutes passed before she could explain.

Ranald Macrae saw at once that one of two things had happened: either that Alastair had wandered to the cave in his madness, and there, ignorant or oblivious of the steps cut in the hollow columnar passage at the far end, been cut off by the sea; or else that he had wittingly made his way there, with intent to drown himself in the Kelpie's Pool — an abyss that never give back what it swallowed.

It was during this hurried explanation to his father that Ealasaid learned for the first time the truth of what had reached her as a vague rumour in the mouth of a herd-boy. Eager as she was to be of help, she was now too weak to accompany the men, even if it were possible for her to keep pace with them, which it was not, as they had started off at a run.

She knew that old Macrae's advice was right: that she could best help by going home at once, and making preparation to receive Alastair if he were still alive. There was no room for him at the farm, where Ranald's wife had given birth to a child two days before. So with tittle Pòl, the herd-boy, she set out once more, leaning often upon the lad's shoulder and wondering if, after all, God were going to let her be of some service before he led her through the blind way till her hand should slip into that of her husband.

Before they left the farmstead, the Macraes had provided themselves with lanterns, a long rope, and a pine torch dipped in tar.

As they neared the summit of Craig-Geal, they could hear the frenzied barking of Ghaoth in the darkness down by the sea — loud when caught on an eddy of wind and borne upward, scarce audible when overborne by the moan and boom and ever recurrent breaking surge of the advancing tide.

At the dark circular exit of the cavern, they waved lanterns and shouted themselves hoarse: but without seeing aught, or winning response.

Angus Macrae silently drew back, rose, and lit the pine torch. Flaring abruptly into the dark before a gust of wind, it was like a blood-red wound in the flank of some vast black creature of night.

Having fastened the torch to the rope, he swung it far down the narrow funnel, up which came the smell of wrack and sea-damp and an obscure, muffled sound.

Still there was nothing visible. No shout followed the sudden glare.

The old man stood silent, craning forward with brooding eyes; for now he was thinking of the two sons he had lost. With a shudder, he moved slowly back and turned to Ranald.

"Will you go down?"

"Aye, father, that I will: if you will breathe the holy word before me and after me. The kelpie . . . the Sea-Woman . . . won't catch *me*, for I am sure of hand and foot."

"So your brother Sheumais thought."

Ranald hesitated, looked at the cave-mouth, then at his father.

"Is it true Sheumais died in *that* way?"

"It is true. The tide hemmed him in, and a heavy sea foamed at the mouth of the cavern. There was no chance but to gain some ledge high above the Sea-Woman's Pool. He did gain a hold on a ledge, for long afterward we found his knife on it. Then the accursed kelpie rose out of her lair and took him by the legs, and pulled him down, and tore him, and broke the bones of him, — my son, my son, my beautiful Sheumais!"

As the old man spoke, his voice had grown louder, his tone more intense; and at the last the memory of his loss so wrought upon him that, with a sudden cry, he dashed forward and whirled one of the lanterns into the dark, echoing chasm.

"Let me go, let me go," he cried, as his son tried to withhold him. "If she must have one of us again, let it be me! Let go, boy! You have your wife and child: and I am old, and have lost Sheumais and Andras and the mother who bore them!"

Without a word, Ranald desisted. The old man went on his knees, crawled forward, and pulled up the flaming torch. Then, having fastened the rope round his waist and secured a lantern in his belt, he slipped over the edge and began the descent, cautiously feeling his way with his feet as he went.

As he reached further and further into the darkness, he wondered why he heard no more the barking of Ghoath. A grim thought came into his mind: the dog had been caught by the Sea-Woman, and was even now drifting round and round in her pool, strangled, with glazed, protruding eyes.

At last, both sight and sound told him that he was nearly over the abyss — sight and sound, and his careful counting of the steps in his descent.

The tidal wash, the heavy lapse and then heavier resurge, with the rush and cataract-roar of the seas as they fell far down into the chasm, assailed his ears continuously. Peering down, he could see the foam upon the flood, as it swept ravening round the cave and then fell headlong into the abyss, above which was a misty pulsating whiteness, the send and spray of tons of whirled water.

There was almost no need to descend further, he thought. The strongest swimmer, if caught in that inrush, would be swept irresistibly into the horrible cauldron where the Sea-Woman brewed her spells of storm and disaster.

There was but one chance for Alastair; if, in truth, he were in the cave at all and still alive. A little way below where the islesman stood, there were three or four broad ledges of which even the lowest would still be unswept by the sea. He dreaded to descend; for it was on the first of those ledges that his son, Sheumais, had been dragged, screaming, into the abyss. With a muttered prayer, however — a prayer that was half an incantation — he once more slowly crawled downward.

When he came to the third ledge, he stopped, crouched, and peered downward and forward.

For a moment his brain swung.

What was it that he saw? What fantasy was this? What horrible caprice of his eyes? Had Ghaoth slain the kelpie, and was he now perishing there with his teeth fixed in the neck of the Sea-Woman?

For Ghaoth, and no other, was the dog that crouched on the lowest ledge; and a woman it was who lay beside him, upheld at the neck by his strong teeth.

He saw the gleam in the dog's eyes, fixed upon him unwaveringly. He understood their appeal. Slowly he unfastened and raised his lantern.

When he recognised Lora, he knew intuitively what had happened. With uplifted arm, he let the light fall all around — above weedy, sea-swept boulders, and the dark, inward-moving flood, broken here and there into a seethe of foam that shone ghastly white in the lantern-glow.

There was no sign of Alastair.

It was clear he was either already swept into the chasm, or had been sucked seaward in the undertow.

With utmost care, Macrae stepped on to the lowest ledge.

Stooping, he looked intently in Lora's white face. Then be put his hand to her heart. He fancied he felt it beat, but could not be sure. Drawing a flask from his pocket, he poured some of the contents down her throat, then upon her temples and breast, with rough hand laving the spirit across the bosom which, cold as it was, had not the unmistakable chill of death. A new strength came to the old man. He had lost all fear now, and had no other thought but to save this poor creature who had already looked on the face of Death, and nigh perished with the horror of it.

Taking her in his arms, he was swiftly securing her to his body by the rope, when he was startled to see Ghaoth, who had at once let go his hold, leap into the surge and swim seaward.

The dog went to its doom, he knew, in a vain quest for Alastair. With a moment's sigh, he turned to what he had to do.

An arduous and perilous climb it was ere the old islesman at last neared the summit, and felt Ranald grasp him by the shoulder and help him and his burden over the edge.

He would have swooned from the long strain upon him, had not his son hastily put the flask of whiskey to his mouth and imperatively bid him drink.

As soon as he could breathe freely once more, he recounted what had happened. The young man wanted to go down at once into the cave and seek for Alastair, in the hope that he might still be swimming in the open or be somewhere afloat, and that Ghaoth might reach him and bring him to the spot where the dog had guarded Lora — almost from the moment, though of course neither Macrae nor his son knew aught of this, when the first ledge-sweeping wave broke upon the sleepers and reft asunder their impotent weedy bonds.

But of this project Angus Macrae would hear nothing further. Was his son mad, he asked him, to believe that Alastair could still be alive, since he was visible nowhere?

"No," he added, "he is in the deep sea by now, or lies gript by the Woman in her hole. But, Ranald, if to search for his body you are so fain, you can go down later. Maybe you will find the dog, though I think neither you, nor I, nor any one else will ever see dog or man again. Meanwhile, take up this poor soul and carry her to Widow Ealasaid's."

"She is big with child," whispered the young man, as awe-struck he wrapped Lora in his warm plaid and raised her in his arms.

"Aye: God have pity on this lost ewe and her poor, wee lammie. Be careful, Ranald, be tender — aye, as tender as if she were your own Cairistine, and the babe that is now moving within her were blood of your blood and bone of your bone."

In silence, and as swiftly as possible, the two men, with their still more silent burden, crossed the slopes of the ridge and ascended the grassy, boulder-strewn brae. In due time, they were met at the door by Ealasaid.

With a low, crooning wail, the old woman helped to lay Lora on the bed in the inner room. She had already warmed the clothes, and had poured boiling water in a tub, with hot flannels for swathing. All island-women act thus on any hint of accident, for the hunger of the sea is the cause of nearly every disaster for them and their loved ones. Besides — had not Duncan Ban once been brought home, and all this and more done for him, though the chill upon him was not that of the sea only?

Suddenly she saw there was no time to lose.

"Quick, quick, Pòl," she cried: "take a lantern and run like the wind across to the clachan, and tell Mrs. Mary Maclean that she is to come here at once, for Alastair

Macleod is dead and his wife is lying here in labour, and that the last pains may come upon her speedily."

The boy hesitated a moment, glanced at his grandfather, and then fled into the night, heedless of any lantern, and sure-footed as a goat.

Finding that he could be of no use, and that Mrs. MacAodh wished only his father to remain, Ranald Macrae slipped quietly away: and in a brief while had reached the cave entrance, descended, and searched vainly for any trace of either Alastair or the dog.

To Ealasaid's unceasing care Lora owed her life. The old woman seemed to have grown years younger. A new strength was in her arm, a new light in her worn eyes, a new spirit in her frail body. With deft hands, she rubbed the skin aglow, wrapped warm flannels about the limbs, breathed into breast and back, soothed the convulsive strainings of the sides and heavy womb, fed the unconscious sufferer with sips of broth and warmed spirit, and often the while kissed the poor faintly quivering lips. It seemed to her as if her heart swam in tears; but with the unnoticed heroism of women, she let no grief overmaster her, no flagging of mind or body usurp her will.

In the outer room Angus Macrae sat, intent at first upon the keeping up of the fire and the fulfilment of Ealasaid's divers commands. Then, nigh an hour later, when through the open doorway he heard a strange moaning from the inner room, he sat down by the low, rude table, and, taking the Gaelic Bible which lay there, began in a slow, monotonous voice to read from the page which caught his eye as he opened the book:—

"I returned, and saw under the sun, that the race is not to the swift, nor the battle to the strong, neither yet bread to the wise, nor yet riches to men of understanding, nor yet favour to men of skill; but time and chance happeneth to them all. For man also knoweth not his time: as the fishes that are taken in an evil net, and as the birds that are caught in the snare, even so are the sons of men snared in an evil time, when it falleth suddenly upon them."[42]

As he read steadfastly onward through this moving last chapter of *Ecclesiastes*, his voice rose, and took a rhythmic chant, and filled the room, as a rising wind fills a valley set among the hills.

But when he read:

"As thou knowest not what is the way of the wind, nor how the bones do grow in the womb of her that is with child; even so thou knowest not the work of God who doeth all—"

he stopped abruptly, for he heard a sound at the outer door, and guessed, even before he saw her, that the comer was Mrs. Maclean.

Angus rose, and took her hand. Then, seeing the speechless sorrow in her eyes, he let go his hold of her, and, bowing his head, did not lift up his eyes again till Mary had entered the inner room.

He knew that, with these two women there, all would go well with Lora, if it were ordained that she was to live. But he feared that death was already entered in at the door; and he knew not what passionate sorrow might come upon and undo those who ministered to the woman who even now was in those pains of labour that ere morn should end in the birth of a child. Long he sat brooding. Then, weary of his vigil, once more he began to read, resuming with the verse where he had been interrupted:—

---

42 Angus is reading Ecclesiastes 9.11–12; we are given the text from the (English) King James version of the Bible. The following passages are verses 5–7 from the same chapter (though 'doeth all' has been changed from 'maketh all' in KJV).

"Even so, thou knowest not the work of God who doeth all.

"In the morning sow thy seed, and in the evening withhold not thine hand: for thou knowest not which shall prosper, whether this or that, or whether they both shall be alike good."

Looking up, he saw Ealasaid standing at the door, a wonderful light on her old face.

"It lives," she said simply. "Mary said that the child would certainly be born dead; but it lives. She says now it has the shadow upon it, and must die ere long; but they told me that my own little blossom was strong, and would live: . . . and even as they were wrong, wrong also may Mary Maclean be."

Hearing a call, she turned, and went within.

The old islesman muttered for a while, with bent head and closed eyes. Then he began to read again: —

"Truly the light is sweet, and a pleasant thing it is for the eyes to behold the sun."

"Hush!"

It was Mary who spoke. She had that in her face which made him rise.

"Hush, Angus Macrae. Truly, the eyes are the delight of the body, but this is not the time for the bitterness of that saying. Never for this child, that is born in the shadow of death, and can itself live but a brief while, shall there be the sweet light of which you speak, nor the pleasantness of beholding the sun, nor the way of the day betwixt rise and set."

"Is the child blind?"

"Ay . . . blind . . . blind."

"And weakling?"

"Ay."

"And she?"

"God hath given her strength to endure."

"Does she know all that has happened?"

"If she did, she would be with Alastair. Her mind is dazed. She is as one distraught. My friend, read no more to-night. Go home now, and God be with you. Bring on the morrow what tidings you have."

Soon after the departure of the old man, a great stillness fell upon the house. Lora slept in a stupor like unto death. The child lay upon her breast, as a frail flower drifted there by a chance wind. Ealasaid sat by the bed watching. Mary knelt against it, crying silently.

Toward dawn, Mrs. Maclean rose, and looked out upon the chill dusk. When she came back, she kneeled again; and, in a low voice, repeated a strange Celtic "Prayer of Women": —

O Spirit, that broods upon the hills
And moves upon the face of the deep,
And is heard in the wind,
Save us from the desire of men's eyes,
And the cruel lust of them,
And the springing of the cruel seed
In that narrow house which is as the grave

146

For darkness and loneliness . . .
That women carry with them with shame, and weariness, and long pain,
Only for the laughter of man's heart,
And the joy that triumphs therein,
And the sport that is in his heart,
Wherewith he mocketh us,
Wherewith he playeth with us,
Wherewith he trampleth upon us . . .
Us, who conceive and bear him;
Us, who bring him forth;
Who feed him in the womb, and at the breast and at the knee:
Whom he calleth Mother,
And Mother again of his wife and children:
When he looks at our hair, and sees it is white;
And at our eyes, and sees they are dim;
And at our lips, straitened out with long pain;
And at our breasts, fallen and seared as a barren hill;
And at our hands, worn with toil;
And, seeing, seeth all the bitter ruin and wreck of us —
All save the violated womb that curses him —
All save the heart that forbeareth . . . for pity —
All save the living brain that condemneth him —
All save the spirit that shall not mate with him —
All save the soul he shall never see
Till he be one with it, and equal;
He who hath the bridle, but guideth not;
He who hath the whip, yet is driven;
He who as a shepherd calleth upon us,
But is himself a lost sheep, crying among the hills!
O Spirit, and the Nine Angels who watch us,
And Thy Son, and Mary Virgin,
Heal us of the Wrong of Man:
We, whose breasts are weary with milk,
Cry, cry to Thee, O Compassionate!

Ealasaid trembled. She had never heard words such as these before, and was afraid; yet even more of the strange intensity in the voice of Mrs. Maclean, in the shine of her usually quiet eyes.

"God be with you, Mary Maclean."

"And with you, Ealasaid MacAodh."

Therewith Mrs. Maclean arose, looked at Lora to see if she still slept, and then went into the adjoining room, where she seated herself before the hot glow of the peats; and, as the day broke, read below her breath in the third chapter of the Book of Job.[43]

Weeks passed, and there was no word of Alastair. For twenty days after the coming of the child, Lora lay distraught, knowing no one about her, though oftentimes looking long and lovingly in the eyes of Mary, whose face had won again an exceeding peace, and who went, as of yore, girt about with a beautiful silence as with a garment.

---

43 In this chapter, having been visited with terrible suffering, Job begins to 'curse his day' (Job 3 1)

But on the last day of the third week, Lora awoke in her right mind. Mary had given the frail, blind babe to young Cairistine Macrae to suckle. This was well; for had Lora looked upon it that day, she would have died.

Nevertheless, in a brief while thereafter she knew all. It seemed strange, both to Mary and Ealasaid, that she did not appear greatly to care. She had that in her heart which would have enlightened them; but grief, as well as madness or evil, has its cunning, and so she veiled her purpose in absolute secrecy.

Not a sign of Alastair! This was what she could not accept. Till his body, or some trace of it, were found, she said she would not return with Mary to her home. Nothing, however, repaid the most scrupulous search: no clue was gained — unless the discovery of the body of Ghaoth, caught in a trawling net one night a mile seaward, could be called a clue.

On that day of agony when she had at last looked on the face of her child, and knew it stricken with frailty and blind for all its days, and heritor perhaps of that curse which had caused her to sin and incur this punishment, she had made a covenant with herself to go down as soon as she could to the shore, at low tide, and with her child follow Alastair into that abyss in the cavern where she felt assured he had been swept by the sea.

Two weary weeks passed before an opportunity came. One afternoon, Mary went across Innisròn, so as to reach the clachan and meet the *Clansman* for somewhat she expected: and as she was to come back with Ranald Macrae, and he was not to return till after dark, Lora felt secure.

Early in the evening, she sent Ealasaid on a message to Parlan Macalister's wife, who lived in a cottage about a mile along the shore beyond the promontory of Ardfeulan.

It was a lovely evening in mid-July. The moon was at the full, and made a golden dust upon the isle and a glory of pale gold upon the sea.

As she went once more down the hollow of the moonflowers — not so dense now as then, and many withered by the heat of the sun and the month-long drought — she stopped again and again, overcome by the heat even of the dusk.

In her ears was the bewildered, plaintive cry of the lapwings: and, as an undertone, the low, soft chime — the long, sweet ululation of the myriad-swung bell of the sea.

She was weary when she reached the shore. An unspeakable horror of the cavern came upon her, and she turned and went slowly towards the long sandy tract that stretched beyond the base of the hollow. There she laid the child gently down in the soft sand at her feet, and seated herself on a low rock.

After all, was it worth while to seek Death, when Death had already whispered that the little one was to be his own so soon, and had stealthily removed all but the last barriers that guarded her own poor life?

Would God not be even more wroth with her — punish her even more heavily; though this, indeed, seemed impossible?

How lovely that vast ocean veiled in violet dusk, save where lit gloriously with moonlight: how full of alluring peace, she thought, that wave-whisper all around her.

Surely the music was woven into a song that was dear and familiar in her ears?

She turned her head away from the sea, and looked idly along the sand: though, as she did so, the vague strain ceased.

Then Lora stood, trembling in a great awe, and with a passionate hope in her eyes, in her heart, at the very springs of life.

In the moonshine, she saw a tall figure moving slowly towards her, naked-white, and walking with a proud mien. The erect body, the flashing eyes, the grace and beauty, were those of a king — of a king among men: and as a king the naked figure was crowned, with moonflowers and yellow sea-poppies woven into his gold-sheen hair.

Suddenly he saw her. He stood as though wrought in impassioned stone. The moonshine fell full upon his white skin, upon the beauty of his face, upon the flower-tangle wherewith he had crowned himself.

Then, without a sound, he turned and fled like the wind, and vanished into the gloom that lay beyond the dusk.

And Lora, lifting the child and staggering homeward, knew that she had seen Alastair.

VI.

IT was not till many weeks later that the way of Alastair's escape from death became known.

On that dark night when he had lain down to die, the wave which fell across Lora and himself, and tore asunder the bonds she had woven, was followed by no other for a time: otherwise, the end of both would have been attained. But so great was the shock, that his apathy of mind and body was rudely broken. The tired blood stung in his veins; the instinct of life was as a flame of fire that consumed all the stupor due to the sea-fruit he had eaten — an instinct that wrought him to a passion of effort.

Shaken and trembling, he staggered to his feet. Nothing but a profound darkness beyond, behind, above: a darkness filled with the voices of the wind, the seething tide, wave falling over wave, billow leaping after billow and tearing it into a yeast of foam — itself to stagger the next moment, and struggle and strangle furiously in a cloud of spray ere flung a dead mass upon the shore.

He had no remembrance of Lora, of what had brought them here, of the grave that was ready where the Sea-Woman watched.

But fear was left to him: and when he was aware of something moving across the ledges to his left, and heard it splash through the tide-wash in its effort to reach him, he gave a terrified cry, and dashed seaward to escape the grip of the kelpie.

Stumbling, he fell heavily forward. But it was into deep water; and, powerful swimmer as he was, he fought the surge, and so was not thrown back upon the rocks till, unwittingly, he was caught in a cross-current and swept southward on the backs of the reeling sea-horses.

A horrible tumult was in his ears. The darkness was upon him as a heavy hand. As idle flotsam, the waves swung him backward and forward.

A deathly cold beset his limbs; then utter weariness. His hands ceased to propel, and only automatically and instinctively kept him afloat.

Yet even now, at the last extremity, when memory was no more, terror remained.

There was something swimming near, something moving toward him through the dark.

The next moment he threw up his hands, overcome by the sickness of fear and a fatigue that he could no longer withstand. As he sank, he was conscious of a body surging up against his: of a hot breath against his face; of a gasping whine against his ear. Then in a flash he recognised, or by instinct divined, that it was Ghaoth who had followed into the darkness, and was there to save him.

The dog had indeed followed, having but an hour ago escaped from the byre where Ian Maclean had risen from his sleep to let him out because of his ceaseless whining. He had raced across the island, and along Alastair's and Lora's track, till he found them where they lay. Thence, after seeing the two whom he loved lying silent and motionless in a way that made him whine with fear, and knowing, as faithful dogs do know, that he must win help without delay, he had sped back to the nearest cottage. Once convinced that old Ealasaid was following to succour those whom he had left, he had sprung away again through the moonflowers, and had reached the entrance to the cave after fierce baffling with the tide-race. Just as Alastair had risen and was staggering towards the sea, Ghaoth had caught sight of him, and had plunged without hesitation into the black bewilderment of waters which had swallowed up the friend whom he loved with his life.

Fortunately, the spent swimmer was still near the shore — nearer, even, than when he had first fallen; for he was now close to the headland of Craig-Geal, and was already in shallow water, which swung on to a long shelf of sand lying against the entrance to another of the innumerable caverns of that side of the island. But here the sea, though at full-flood it covered the sand and moved its hungry lip for a few feet within, did not enter, as a beast of prey halting unassuaged at the entrance to its lair.

Ghaoth had gripped him by the hair of his neck, and was now struggling to reach the shore. Man and dog were still flung to and fro by the waves; but the living sport of the sea was no longer separate. With Ghaoth's help, Alastair made renewed, if despairing, efforts.

Suddenly his feet touched the ground for a moment. Then, with a staggering rush, having shaken himself free of the dog, he gained the shore, stumbled blindly up the low shelve of the sound, and fell unconscious among the soft, powdery grit, midway in the wide half-roofless hollow known as the Cave of the Sùlaire, from the solan geese which often congregated there in the blinding snow-storms of winter.[44]

Ghaoth stood panting beside him awhile. At last, with a low whine, the dog pressed his muzzle against the white face in the white sand; turned aside, whined again, and came back with lolling tongue. Then, suddenly, he sprang away into the darkness, and back into the drowning surge, with all his loyal, loving heart — beautiful love of the dumb animal-soul that God heedeth and cherisheth no less than that other wandering fire He hath placed in the human — eager to baffle with drift and billow till he reached the cavern once more, in time to save Lora, of whose body he had caught a glimpse as he dashed after Alastair.

In time, and no more. He had not long rescued Lora, who, also, had been partially roused by the shock of the breaking wave. She had been half-standing, half-leaning against the higher ledge, to which, with difficulty and in blind instinct, she had clung; but, as Ghaoth reached her, she sank wearily and lay back against the dog, dreaming she had waked in terror, but was now safe in Alastair's arms.

It was thus that Angus Macrae discovered them. Long afterwards, the islesman recalled how he had seen the dog leap back into the darkness. Whether Ghaoth failed to reach the Cave of the Sùlaire, and was carried seaward by a current; or whether his strength failed him in his last effort, and he was swung lifelessly from wave to wave; whatever the first word of his fate was, the last was the finding of his sea-mangled body in the trawl-net of a fisherman more than a mile oceanward from Innisròn.

When Alastair woke, an hour or more after dawn, he remembered nothing of what had happened. His memory, though not killed, was clouded by his madness; and, doubtless, the shock of what he had gone through, with the action of the mermaid's fruit, had further weakened it.

---

44 Solan geese (Sc.): gannets.

He rose and looked about him wonderingly. Around, were the precipitous rocks; beyond, the sea stretched far into the morning mists, calm, with a silver sparkle in the south-east, and turquoise-blue elsewhere, except in green straits under the shadow of the isle, till it faded into opal and dove-grey where the veils of mist slowly dispersed, re-wove, lifted, in-wove, and sank to the wave again, or sailed indefinitely away.

Though he could still recall nothing of the past night, he recognised, as soon as he stepped from the cave and went down by the sea-marge, the head-land of Craig-Ruaidh and that of Craig-Geal just behind him. His one wish was to hide, so that none should see him. His fantasy led him to seek remote places, and to fear the face of his fellows.

Turning towards the sun, he looked scrutinisingly along the coast. Somewhere beyond Craig-Geal, he remembered vaguely, there was another hollow which led to a series of intricate and unexplored caves, perilous places of evil repute among the islanders.

If he were to go there . . . but at that moment his wandering gaze lighted upon an object moving black in the shine of the sea.

Was it a whale sunning itself, or a pollack moving idly after the liath?[45] Then he saw that it was a boat—one of many torn from moorings or swept from the beach by the recent gale.

So methodical were his actions, that none seeing him would believe his mind was so darkly veiled, that his reason was only partially in exercise.

Having taken off his coat, he wrapt it round a heavy stone and threw the bundle far into the sea. Then he thrust his boots into a cranny in a fissured boulder that at full flood was covered.

A few seconds later he was in the water, swimming swiftly toward the derelict.

While he neared the boat, amid a sheen of sparkling foam as he urged his way through the sun-dazzle which lay upon that part of the sea, he broke intermittently into a mournful Gaelic chant, but with words so incoherent, and with interjections so wild and strange, that the fishermen on a coble, hid in the mist a few fathoms away, believed they listened to a sea-kelpie, or to that vague object of their profoundest dread known as "the thing that hides beneath the boat." They were southward bound; but at that forlorn wailing they hauled down their flapping sail, and, with their oars, made all haste northerly to their island or mainland haven. Not a man among them would have persevered in that voyage on that day.

Alastair heard the sound of the oar-wash, and ceased his fitful chant. It must, he thought, be dead seamen rowing to and fro, looking for the newly drowned to take their places as warders of the treasures and keepers of the secrets which lie among the weed-tangle and sunless caverns of the deep. At the thought, he laughed loud, but mirthlessly; and the echo of his laughter, falling against the ears of the fishermen, added to their horror and consternation.

With his hands gripping the gunwale, he swayed for some time to and fro, fascinated by the lustrous green beneath the keel—green in the sunlit spaces as leaves of the lime in April, and in the lower as emerald lapsing into jade, and then as jade passing into the gloom of pines at dusk.

At last he raised himself on the water, bending the gunwale low, and half fell, half crawled into the boat. Indifferently, he noticed that it was named *Fionnaghal*. Clearly it had drifted away from moorings; for not only were oars and sail-enveloped mast lying taut under the thwarts, but a rope trailed from the bow far down the water.

---

45   This is confused. That there's only one of them, and that it is visible on the surface of the sea, suggests Sharp means *pellock*, the Scots name for a porpoise; by liath he must mean lythe, a white fish (known in England as the pollack).

He rowed for some time. At last, becoming weary, or perhaps puzzled by the mists which crept behind and all around him, he desisted. A flurry of air struck his right cheek. Instinctively he put up the palm of his hand to feel if the wind were coming from the south-east or the south-west. Then, adjusting the mast and setting the sail, he seated himself at the tiller.

Eddy followed eddy, and soon a breeze blew freshly from the southeast. By the time the *Fionnaghal* was three or four miles to the north-west of Innisròn, there was not a mist upon the sea. Immeasurably vast it stretched; blue, or glittering in a diamond-sparkle sheen, or wimpling over in violet hollows, with the white lambs beginning to collect and leap merrily onward in the pathway of the sun.

Alastair became drowsy with the warmth of the glow upon his back and the chime of the sea-music. Long before noon he slept. For hours the boat went idly adrift.

When he woke, he saw an island less than half-a-mile to starboard. Looking northward, he could descry nothing but sea; to the westward, nothing but sea; nothing but sea to the southward. Far eastward, a dim blue line of hills rose above the horizon: here and there — lying apparently against it, and scarce bigger to his eye than the gannets and sea-mews which flew overhead — two or three patches of amethyst. These were the isles he had left, though he did not recognise them: Ithona, most westerly; Innisròn, remote in the south-east; I-na-Trilleachan-tràhad, lost in its northerly purple-greys.

Though the words brought no meaning to him, or awakened nothing beyond mere visual reminiscence, his lips, as he looked at the island he was now approaching, framed its name, "I-Mònair."

Heedless of the fact that he was running straight upon a shore set with reefs like gigantic teeth, he tautened the sail and let the boat rush forward, and was almost havened when, with a grinding rip, the *Fionnaghal* stopped, filled, leaned over, and hung upon a jagged reef, as a dead body suspended on the horn that has gored it.

Alastair was thrown forward by the shock. Bruised and stunned, he lay motionless for a few seconds while the water poured over him. Then, rising, and casting a keen glance around, he stepped on to the reef, sprang thence to a rock nearer the shore, and thence to the shore itself.

As he left the boat, it split. The larger half went drifting on the tide.

He sat down to watch idly for the disappearance of the few planks which remained. Suddenly, without cause, he rose, stared wildly at the sea and along the shore on either hand, and then moved rapidly inland — often casting furtive glances behind him, now on the one side, now on the other.

No other lived on I-Mònair than a shepherd and his wife, and they only through the summer months. Sometimes weeks passed by without their seeing another soul: without other sign of the world of men than the smoke of a steamer far upon the horizon, or the brown patches in the distance when the herring-trawlers ventured oceanward.

No wonder, then, that Fearghas McIan gave a cry of astonishment, that was partly fear, when he saw a man walking swiftly towards him . . . a man who appeared to have dropped from the clouds; for, looking beyond the stranger, the shepherd could see no sign of trawler, wherry, or boat of any kind.

"Diònaid, Diònaid," he cried to his wife, who had come to the door of the cottage to see if he were at hand for his porridge; "Trothad so . . . bi ealamh, bi ealamh: quick, quick, come here."

They stood together as Alastair slowly drew near. When he was close, he stopped, looking at them curiously, and with an air as if he wondered who they were and why they were there.

"What is your name?" he asked quietly, looking at the shepherd.

"C'ainm' tha ort?" he repeated, as the man stared at him in surprise and something of alarm.

"Fearghas McIan."

"And yours?" he asked of the woman.

"Diònaid McIan."

"Cò tha sin?" he added abruptly, pointing to the cottage: "who is there?"

"No one."

"I thought I saw some one come out, look at us, and go in again."

Fearghas and Diònaid glanced at each other with eyes of dread.

"C'ainm' tha ort?" asked the former, in turn.

Alastair looked at him, as if uncomprehendingly; and then, in a low, dull voice, said that he was tired; that he was hungry, and thirsty, and wet.

"Tha mi glé sgìth; tha an t' acras orm; tha am pathadh orm; tha mi flìuch."

"How did you come here?"

"Tha mi glé sgìth."

"Did you come in a boat? Where is the boat you came in?"

"Tha mi glé sgìth."

"What is your name? Are you of the isles?"

"Tha mi glé sgìth."

"What do you want with us here, on I-Mònair, where we do no wrong, O stranger who carrieth your sorrow in your eyes?"

"Tha mi glé sgìth. Tha mi flìuch. Tha an t'acras orm. Tha mi glé sgìth — tha mi glé sgìth — tha mi glé sgìth."

Alastair spoke in a strange, dull voice. It would have terrified Fearghas and Diònaid more, but that the stranger was so gentle in his manner, and had a look upon his face that awed while it reassured them.

"God has sent him," said Diònaid, simply. The poor lad has not waked — he is in a dream. God do unto us as we do unto this waif from the sea. In His good time He will whisper in the closed ears, and the man will wake, and tell us who he is, and whence he came, and whither he would fain go."

"So be it, Diònaid. You have said the word, and a good word it is. When this man's hour has come, God will deliver him. Meanwhile, let us call him Donncha, after the boy we lost nigh upon six-and-twenty years ago, who might have been as tall and comely as this stranger that is now a stranger no more, but of us and one with us."

And so it was that, from that day, Alastair Macleod, unsought by any, and unrecognised because no one came near who might have known or guessed who he was, abode on I-Monair with Fearghas the shepherd and his wife Diònaid.

He dwelt in peace. Through the long days he wandered about the shores. Often, in the gloaming, he sat on a rock and stared longingly across the waters for he knew not what, for some nameless boon he craved witlessly; stared yearningly through the dusk for something that lay beyond, that, though unseen, brought a mist into his eyes, so that when he reached the peat-fire again, where Diònaid McIan awaited him, he often could not see to eat for awhile for the blur of his slow-falling tears.

Week succeeded changeless week. The sheep ceased to look up as he passed. The yellowhammers in the gorse sang even when he stopped brooding by the bush whereon they flitted from branch to branch, looking at him with quiet eyes.

It was in the sixth week, after a time of storm which had lapsed into another long spell of exquisite summer, that the dream came to its end.

Late one afternoon, a herring-trawler lay off I-Mònair. The skipper, a kinsman of Fearghas, came ashore to give and learn what news there was.

Alastair had come back about the usual time from one of his daylong rambles, and, as he approached the door, his quick ear had caught the sound of an alien voice.

Whether he overheard the shepherd tell his friend, in turn for the strange and moving tale of Alastair MacDiarmid Macleod, of Innisròn, of the strange visitor he and his wife nourished, with the surmise that he, Donncha, might be no other than the missing man; or whether some other suggestion concerning his removal or identification alarmed him, no one ever knew.

But, in the cloudy dark of that night, when Rory McIan and his two mates, Dùghall and Eòghann, were drinking the crude spirit from Fearghas' illicit still, Alastair slipped into the small boat in which they had come ashore, and rowed softly away into the obscure and lonely wilderness of the sea.

Truly, as Diònaid said, God must have whispered in the closed ears, and told him whither to guide the boat, and when to rest while he let it drift, and when to take up the oars again. For, betwixt dawn and sunrise, the fugitive, oaring slowly out of a pearly haze, came abruptly upon the south-west of Innisròn.

With a cry of gladness, he leaned forward, shading with his right hand his eager eyes. He had recognised familiar features of shore and headlands. The whim took him to capsize the boat and swim ashore. In sudden excitement, he sprang to his feet. The little craft rocked wildly. The next moment Alastair had left the upturned keel to drift in the grey sea like a water-snake, and was swimming swiftly across the two or three hundred yards which lay between the island and the place where he had fallen.

When he reached the shore, he wandered slowly to and fro, his new-born energy having lapsed into a vague unrest. Aimlessly he leaned now against one boulder, now against another. At last, the chill of his dripping clothes gave him active discomfort. He looked doubtfully on the slopes, then at the sea, then again at the slopes. With the strange impulsiveness of his disease, he turned abruptly; with swift, stumbling steps, crossed the shore; passed the ridges covered with sea-grass, and entered the shaws beyond. Thence he walked quickly up the corrie behind Craig-Geal. When he gained the upper end, the sunrise shone full upon him. Flinging first one wet garment from him, and then another, he was speedily naked — beautiful in his fair youth, with his white skin and tangle of yellow hair, which, as the sun-rays blent with it, seemed to spill pale gold.

He laughed with pleasure; then raced to and fro for warmth. When tired, he stooped to pluck the thyme or tufts of gale. For awhile, he wandered thus circlewise, aimlessly happy.

The day came with heat, and hourly grew hotter. Alastair was glad to lie down in a shady place by a burn, and drowse through the long, warm hours. As the afternoon waned into gloaming, he rose, and, forgetful of or unheeding his discarded clothes, wandered idly northward by one of the many sheep-paths. It was late when, having woven for himself a crown of moonflowers into which he inserted afterward a few yellow sea-poppies, he made his way down to the sea, and hungrily ate of what shell-fish he could gather — briny cockles from the sand, and whelks and mussels from the rocks.

At the coming of the moonlight across the water, he laughed low with joy. It was only in the darkness he heard the Voice in the sea which called, called, called, and terrified him so even while it allured him. The waves, dancing and leaping in the yellow shine and breaking into a myriad little cups and fleeting hollows, sang a song that filled him with joy.

Then it was that, with erect head, flushing eyes, and proud mien, crowned with moonflowers and sea-poppies, and beautiful in the comeliness of his youth, Alastair appeared before the startled eyes of Lora, who, for the second time, had come down to that shore to woo and win Death.

When, late that night, Mary Maclean returned, she found Lora in Ealasaid's arms, sobbing and moaning hysterically.

It was long ere she was able to learn the exact truth, and at first she doubted if Lora were not suffering from a hallucination. But as the young mother grew calm, and took up her frail babe and kissed it with tears, Mary was won to believe in at least the possibility that the vision was, if not of Alastair in the body, at any rate the wraith of him, allowed to be seen of Lora out of God's pity of her despair.

The night was too far gone for anything to be done straightway; but she promised to go forth with Lora at sunrise and see if that white, flower-crowned phantom walked abroad in the day, and was no mere fantasy of the moonshine.

She had fallen asleep when, at dawn, Lora aroused her.

Without a word, she rose from the chair, wrapped a shawl about her, and then, kissing Lora gently, looked at her with quiet, questioning eyes.

"What is it, Mary?"

"You still believe that you saw Alastair . . . Alastair in the body?"

"Yes."

"Then had you not better take the child with you? I will carry the little one. If he should see it—perhaps he would . . ."

"You are right, dear friend. God has put that thought into your mind."

A few minutes later, the women passed out into the cold, fresh morning; Mary going first with the child, and keeping, wherever practicable, to the sheep-paths or to the barren ledges that ran out every here and there from the heather and bracken, and this because of the dews which lay heavily, giving a moon-white sheen to the grass, and sheathing every frond and leaf and twig as with crystal, glistening rainbow-hued.

They took a path that trailed above the hollow of the moonflowers, and led deviously shoreward by the side of Craig-Geal.

When they reached the summit of the grassy brae, where the path diverged, they looked long in every direction. Nowhere could they discern sign of any human being. Not a soul moved upon the upland moors; not a soul moved upon the boulder-strewn, rowan-studded slopes; not a soul moved by the margin of that dead-calm sea, so still that even the whisper of its lip was inaudible, though the faint aerial echo of the crooning of its primeval slumber-song slipped hushfully into the ear.

They were half-way down toward the shore when Mrs. Maclean, holding up a warning hand, stopped.

"What is it, Mary?" Lora whispered. "Do you see anything? Do you see him?"

"Look!" and, as she spoke, Mary pointed to a dip in the little glen.

Under it rowan, heavy with clusters of fruit, as yet of a ruddy brown touched here and there with crimson, a white figure stooped, leaning over one of the pools wherein the falling burn slept and dreamed awhile ere it leaped again from ledge to ledge, or slipt laughing and whispering through time-worn channels.

He was like some beautiful creature of an antique tale. Even as a wild deer, he stooped and drank; looked questioningly through the rowans and birches, and then across the bracken where the sunrays slid intricately in a golden tangle; then, stooping again, again drank.

The sunlight was warm about him. His shoulders and back gleamed ivory-white, dusked flickering here and there with leaf-shadows. A shadowy green-gloom lay upon his curved breast and against his thighs, from the sheen of the water passing upward through the dense fern that overhung the stream.

"It is the young god," thought Mary; "the young god who, Sheumais the Seer says, was born of human hope, weaned with human tears, taught by dreams and memories, and therewith given for his body, Beauty . . . and for his soul, Immortal Joy."

But aloud she murmured only, "It is he — the Beautiful One — of the *Domhain Tòir!*"

Lora, did not look at her; but below her breath whispered, *"It is Alastair."*

Swiftly and silently, they moved forward.

So intent was Alastair, after he had quenched his thirst, upon what he saw or imagined in the pool beneath him, that he did not hear their steps till they were but a few yards away.

"Alastair!"

He lifted his head and listened.

"Alastair!"

The sudden fear passed from his eyes. A smile came into them, and his lips parted:

"Lora . . . Lora bhàn . . . Lora, my beautiful gloom . . . my fawn . . . my little one . . ."

As he spoke, with low, caressing, yearning voice, he looked into the heart of the pool again, and stretched forward his arms longingly.

A sob behind him fell upon his ears. Startled, he sprang back.

For more than a minute, he looked intently at Lora and Mrs. Maclean. Then, slowly, some reminiscence worked in his brain. Slowly, too, the dark veil began to lift from his mind; slightly, and for a brief while at most.

"Mary!"

Mrs. Maclean made a step toward him, but stopped. The peace that was about her at all times breathed from her, and lay upon him. The benediction of her eyes upheld him.

Quietly she spoke, with her right hand pointing to the sobbing woman at her side.

"Alastair . . . this is Lora, who has sought you far, and now has found you."

"Lora? Lora is dead! She is a beautiful spirit, and sleeps in that pool under the rowan. She walked with me last night in the moonshine. She has a beautiful child that is our child. It is now a song, singing in the sunshine. I heard it at dawn, when I was listening to the stars calling one to another. It is a song of joy about the doorway of Pharais. I saw the golden doors open a brief while ago — the doors of Pharais. Our little child danced in the glory as a mote in a sunbeam. But Lora is dead."

"Hush! Lora is not dead, but liveth. Lora is here. See, her tears run for you — her bosom heaves for you — her arms reach for you!"

Slowly the dreamer advanced. He would not come quite close at first, but there was a wonderful new light in his eyes.

"Alastair! Alastair! It is I, Lora! Come to me! Come to me!"

"If, indeed . . . if, indeed, you are Lora . . . Lora, my joy . . . where is our child whose soul I heard singing in the sunshine over against Tigh-na-Pharais?"

Without a word, and swiftly, Lora took her poor blind blossom from Mary, and held the child toward him.

"It is God's gift to us, Alastair," she added at last, seeing that he came no nearer, and looked at the child wonderingly.

He advanced slowly, till his breath fell upon Lora's hands, and made her heart strain with its passion. Stopping, he stretched forth his right hand and gently touched the sleeping face. A sunray fell upon it. Then a smile grew upon the little parted lips, as the spirit of a flower might grow and bloom bodiless in dreamland.

Alastair smiled. With soft, caressing hand, he smoothed the child's face and little, uplifted arm. Then he took it gently from its mother, kissed it, handed it to Mary.

And having done this, he opened his arms and said one word: "Lora!"

None saw their return. Mrs. Maclean went before them with the child, and at once sent Ealasaid out to keep watch and ward against the coming of any one. Thereafter she swiftly made all ready for those whom God had lifted out of the grave.

But so weary was Alastair — so far spent by hunger, and fatigue, and exposure — that he could not put on the clothes laid ready for him. So Lora led him gently to bed; and there, after he had swallowed a little broth and warm milk, he fell into a profound sleep which lasted till dark, and then, after a brief interval wherein he ate ravenously, till late on the morrow.

From that time forth, Alastair's madness took a new form. All of dark gloom, of dread or vague fear, went from him. His reason seemed to be a living energy again, though still bewilderingly distraught at times, and ever veiled.

Nevertheless, that day of his awakening after his long, life-saving slumber was the last wherein the things of his past and the affairs of the present were realities to him. Concerning these, he could listen to little and speak less; and, again and again, his struggling thought became confused and his words incoherent.

Yet Lora learned enough to know what his one passionate wish was. Full well he knew that the end was not far from him; but before he entered into the silence he might live many months; and he longed to leave Innisròn. Beyond words, he longed to die in that little lonely isle of Ithona which was his sole heritage from his mother, and where he had been born; for his father had brought his fair Eilidh there from his old gloomy castle at Dunvrechan for the travail that was her doom.

Upon Ithona no one dwelt other than an old islander whose fathers had been there before him for generations.

Sheumais Macleod was at once shepherd and fisherman, and caretaker of the long, low farmhouse: alone now, since the death of his wife at midsummer of that year. There was room and to spare for Alastair and Lora and the little one; for Mary also — for Mrs. Maclean never dreamed of parting from these her children.

And thus it was arranged, ere dusk came and filled with violet shadows all the hollows that lay-betwixt the cottage and the sea.

Three days thence, late on a hot afternoon scarce cooled by the breeze that moved soundlessly though steadily over the upland crags of Innisròn, a company of islanders was met at the little western haven betwixt Ardfeulan and Craig-Ruaidh. Every one on the isle was there, indeed, except the one or two who were weakly or in extreme old age.

On the water, moored to a ledge, a herring-trawler, the *Ellù*, lay with her brown sail flapping idly. In the stern sat Lora, with her child at her breast, and beside her Mrs. Maclean. In the waist, with a leg on either side of the seat, Angus Macrae, who owned the boat, leaned against the mast.

The islanders made a semi-circular group. In the middle were six or seven old men: on either side were the younger men, women old and young, and the children. Behind were the collie dogs, squatted on their haunches or moving restlessly to and fro.

Some mischance had made it impossible for Mr. Macdonald, the old minister of these outer isles, to be present. Father Manus, a young priest of Iona, took his place, and had already blessed the sea, and the *Ellù* that was to voyage across it, and those who were going away for ever from Innisròn, and the weary hearts they carried with them, and the sad hearts of those who were gathered to see them go.

Alastair, tall, frail, with wild eyes strangely at variance with the quiet pallor of his face—and to many there scarce recognisable, so greatly had he altered—was bidding farewell to the elders one by one.

Not a word else was spoken by any than the familiar good-bye—*Beannachd leibh*. The hearts of all were too full.

At the last, Alastair came to where Ealasaid MacAodh stood, crying silently. He took her in his arms, and kissed her on the brow and then upon both eyes.

She watched him as he moved slowly down to the *Ellù*. He stepped on board, followed by Ranald Macrae, and sat down beside Lora, whose hand he took in his, and with the other stroked it gently.

As old Angus Macrae shook out the sail, Ealasaid suddenly fell on her knees, and, swaying to and fro, began a wailing lament:

"*Tha mo latha goirid,*
Tha mo feasgar fada,
O, oi, oi, tha cèo air a' bheinn,
O, oi, oi, tha drùchd air an fheur!"

My day is short,
Long is my night—
O, alas, alas, the mist upon the hill,
O, alas, alas, the dew upon the grass!

Slowly the *Ellù* moved out from the haven.

Lora and Mary sat with bowed heads. Alastair had turned and was staring seaward, where a glory of gold and scarlet was gathered against the going down of the sun.

"*O, oi, oi, tha cèo air a' bheinn,*
O, oi, oi, tha drùchd air an fheur!"

sang the islanders in a long, wailing chant.

Suddenly the sail filled, became taut. The boat moved swiftly before the wind.

A deep silence fell upon all. Then Griogair Fionnladh, the oldest of the islesmen, raised the pipes from his shoulder and began to play.

But the wild, mournful, plaintive air was not the expected Lament of Farewell. It was the ancient Coronach for the Dead.

One by one, every man doffed his bonnet; the white-haired elders bowing their heads, and, with downcast eyes, muttering inaudibly. Sobs where heard and tears fell; but no word was spoken.

When the sun set, the *Ellù* was far on her way—a black speck in the golden light. With the coming of the gloaming, the islanders slowly dispersed. Soon there was none left, save Fionnladh and Ealasaid.

For a long while thereafter upon the twilight-water rose and fell, mingling with the solemn, rhythmic chant of the waves, the plaintive, mournful wail of the Coronach for those who have passed into the silence.

When that, too, had ceased, there was no sound that the sea heard not nightly, save the sobbing of the woman Ealasaid.

VII.

WEEK after week, month after month, until nigh the end of the fourth, passed by on Ithona: and they who dwelt there took no heed of the passage of the days.

There are no hours for those who are beyond the rumour of that "time or chance" of which the Preacher speaks. Day grows out of night, and in night fulfilleth itself again: the stars succeed the diurnal march of the sun, and hardly are they lost in his glory ere they come again. Scarce distinguishable are the twilight of the dawn and the twilight of the eve: and even as the coming and going of these similar shadows are the appearance and evanishing of the shadows whom we know for our fellow-men, so little differing one from the other, individual from individual, people from people, race from race.

And even as a shadow, to those who abode on Ithona, was that world they had seen so little of, but of which they had yet known enough.

In that remote island, solitary even among the outer isles of which it was one of the most far-set in ocean, there was little to break the monotony of the hours. No steamer drew near, save at long intervals. The coastguard cutter arrived intermittently, but sometimes not for months, coming like an alien sea-bird, and as a strange bird of the seas going upon its unknown way again. Few even of the herring-trawlers sailed nigh, except in the late summer, when the mackerel came eastward in vast shoals.

Morning and noon, afternoon and evening, night and the passing of night, dawn and sunrise: these were the veils that seemed to curtain off this spot of earth. Storm followed calm; calm succeeded storm: the winds came and went: the tides rose and fell. In summer, the rains from the south; in autumn, the rains from the west; in winter, the rains from the north. Change followed change, but orderly as in processional array. The poppies reddened the scanty fields of rye; the swallows and martins haunted the island-ways; the wild rose bloomed, as with white and pink sea-shells made soft and fragrant. Then a little while, and the ling grew purple at the passing of the roses; the hawks swung in the wind when the swallows had vanished; the campions waved where the poppies had fallen; the grey thistle usurped the reaped grain. In summer, the Weaver of Sunshine rested there; there, during the equinox, the Weaver of the Winds abode; in winter, the Weaver of the Snow made a white shroud for the isle and wove a shimmering veil for the dusking of the sea. And as one spring was like another spring, and one autumn like another autumn, so was one year like another year, in the coming and in the going.

Save for the encroaching shadow of death, there was nothing to mark the time for the dwellers on Ithona. Mary was aware that not Alastair only, but Lora, was becoming frailer week by week. Lora, as well as Mary, knew that the child's face grew more wan and thin almost day by day. Old Sheumais Macleod was weary at heart with the pity of all that he saw. Only Alastair was happy, for he dreamed; and his dream was of the loveliness of earth and sea and sky, of the pathway that came down from heaven at sunrise and led back at nightfall through the avenue of the stars to the very gates of Pharais. More happy, too, grew the others as the autumn waned, and the golden peace of St. Martin's aftermath lay upon sea and land; for their eyes saw more and more through the dreaming eyes of Alastair, more and more clearly they heard strains of the music that haunted his rapt ears.

Daily he went about clad with dream: a strange sweetness in his voice, a mystery upon his face. His eyes no longer brooded darkly; there was in them a bright light as of a cloudless morning.

If, months ago, God had filled with dusk the house of the brain, it was now not the dusk of coming night, but of the advancing day. Fantasies beset him often, as of yore, but never with terror or dismay. The moorland tarn held no watching kelpie: instead, he heard the laughter of the fairies as they swung in the bells of the foxglove; the singing of an angel where the wind wandered among the high corries; whispers and sighs of fair spirits in the murmur of leaves, or falling water, or chime of the waves.

Sometimes Lora walked or lay beside him for hours, listening to his strange speech about the things that he saw — things too lovely for mortal vision, but ultimately as real to her as to him. Hope came back to her; and then Peace; and, at the last, Joy.

When not with Lora, he loved well to be with Mary or with Sheumais.

In the eyes of the former he would sometimes look for a long time, seeing there the secret home of peace, and perhaps, deeper, the unveiled beauty of the serene and lovely soul.

Sheumais he had loved from childhood. The old islesman had never once been on the mainland; though in his youth he had sailed along its endless coasts. Tall and strong he was, despite his great age; and his eyes were the eyes of a young man who hears his first-born laughing and crooning against its mother's breast. Ignorant as he was of the foreign tongue of the mainland, ignorant of books, and unable to read even a verse in the Gaelic Scriptures of which he knew so many chapters by heart, he was yet strong in knowledge and wise in the way of it beyond most men. For he knew all that is to be known concerning the island and the surrounding sea, and what moved thereon and lived therein; and, in his humbleness and simplicity, he saw so deep into the human heart and into the mystery of the soul, that he was not ashamed to know he was man, nor to pray to God to guide him through the shadows.

It was from Sheumais that Alastair, in boyhood and youth, had learned much, not only of his store of legends and ancient runes and old Celtic poetry, but also of that living poetry which makes the heart of the Gael more tender than that of other men, and his brain more wrought with vision. From him he had first heard how that for one to have died is to have "gone into the silence;" that for an old man or woman to pass away in extreme age is to "have the white sleep;" that for a fisherman to drown is for him to have "the peace of the quiet wave."

Sheumais had filled his brain with lovely words — lovely in themselves and their meaning; but he had made his clansman a poet by one thing that he did and said.

For once, after Alastair had returned to the West from the University in St. Andrew's, he went to Ithona to stay for some weeks. At sunrise on the morrow of his arrival, on his coming out upon the grass which sloped to the shore a few yards away, he saw Sheumais standing, with his wide, blue bonnet in his hand, and the sun shining full upon his mass of white hair — not praying, as at first Alastair thought, but with a rapt look on his face, and with glad, still-youthful eyes gazing lovingly upon the sea.

"What is it, Sheumais?" he had asked; and the old islesman, turning to him with a grave smile, had answered:

"Morning after morning, fair weather or foul, after I have risen from my prayers and ere I have broken my fast, I come here and remove my hat and bow my head, with joy and thanksgiving, before the Beauty of the World."

From that day, the world became a new world for Alastair.

In the quietude of dusk—and day by day the dusk came sooner and the dawn later—Mary would sometimes sing, or Sheumais repeat some favourite Ossianic *duan*,[46] or chant a fugitive song of the isles. But, towards the close of November, a silence fell more and more upon all. Each had grown a little weary with the burden of life: all knew Who it was that was coming stealthily across the waters, and for whom first.

It was on the dawn of December that the child died. It seemed to lapse from life as an ebbing wavelet from a pool.

The evening before, Alastair had carried the little one to the shore. He had never understood that the child's eyes were sealed, and often thought that it slept when it was really awake. When he came to a favourite pool of his, that at low tide was wont to flush with any red light spilled across the wave, he held his tiny burden up, laughing and crooning to it.

"Look, my pretty one," he would murmur; "that red light is the blood of your elder brother. Fair is He, the white Christ. He has put that there to show that He loves you." Or, again, he would kneel, and with one hand warily move aside the bladder-wrack and other sea-weeds; and then, pointing into the translucent water, would tell the blind sleeper to look into the heart of the pool and he would see, far down beyond a vast vista of white columns, flight after flight of shining golden stairs, which led at last to a great gate flashing like the sea in a noon-dazzle. And at the gate was a little child like unto himself, singing a sweet song; and just within the gate was a beautiful spirit, whose face was that of Lora, and who could not sing as the little child did, because, though she was clad with joy as with a robe, in her eyes there was still a last lingering mist of human tears.

"And in Pharais, my bonnie," he would add whisperingly in the child's unheeding ear, "in Pharais there are no tears shed, though in the remotest part of it there is a grey pool, the weeping of all the world, fed everlastingly by the myriad eyes that every moment are somewhere wet with sorrow, or agony, or vain regret, or vain desire. And those who go there stoop, and touch their eyelids with that grey water, and it is as balm to them, and they go healed of their too great joy: and their songs thereafter are the sweetest that are sung in the ways of Pharais."

Often Lora or Mary would be with him when he was thus speaking; for each was fearful lest some day he should discover that his little *uan* was blind, and could never even open the sealed lids.

But on that last twilight of November Alastair seemed to have been impressed by the passive stillness of the child, and to be troubled when he looked at it. He had kissed the eyes again and again, but they had not opened; he had whispered loving words in the tiny ears, but they had not hearkened.

All that night he was restless, and rose often to look at the two sleepers in the bed opposite his own. Just before dawn, he looked for the last time. He was satisfied now. The little one smiled . . . but it was because that in the soundless, breathless passage from one darkness to another, it had heard a sweet voice at last, and at last had, with suddenly illumined eyes, beheld a new glory.

So white and still was it that, when the cold of the tiny hands against her bosom awoke Lora, she lay looking upon it for a while, rapt in a new and strange awe. Then, having aroused Mary, she went to Sheumais, and brought him in to the room. Mary had already waked Alastair, and he sat holding the small white body on his knees, stroking it gently.

---

46   'Duan' is the term James Macpherson (1736–96) used for the divisions of his long prose-poems, published in the 1760s, which claimed to be based on the compositions of an ancient Gaelic poet called Ossian, preserved over centuries in the oral lore of the Highlands. They were mostly fabrications, but they were translated 'back' into Gaelic to become a (problematic) part of its literature. Sharp probably imagines Sheumais as a carrier of the original tradition.

When Lora told him that their baby was dead, and asked him if he knew what she said, he did not reply; but a tear rolled down his cheek, and he put his hand to his heart as though to still the ache of his inarticulate pain.

But after Mary had read from the Book of Psalms, and prayed in a low voice, all rose and passed out into the sunshine; and Alastair, already oblivious of his loss, went down by the shore, and smiled with pleasure at the leap and fall, and chime and whisper, and sweet, low laughter of the sunny waters.

About a hundred yards inland from the cottage, a gigantic pointed stone rises from out of the heather. It is known among the isles as Fingal's Bolt, though neither Fionn nor his son, Ossian, ever threw that huge, flat-sided, fang-like rock. A few rude lines and even letters are still discernible on the side next the sun; but there is probably none who could decipher that old-world rune, carved in bygone ages by the hand of a Druid.

Of all places in the island, except the rocky headlands whose flanks were laved by the sea, this Stone of the Past, as Sheumais called it, was that most frequented by Alastair. At its base he had listened, as a boy, to the tales of the old islander; beneath it, his fantasy now persuaded him, was one of the hidden ways that led to that House of Paradise of which he so often dreamed.

There the four silent mourners met that afternoon to fulfil the wish of one among them, who loved to think that his little *uan* would come back some moonshine night or in a still dawn, and, taking their hands, lead his father and mother by that secret pathway through *Domhan Tòir* to *Tir-na-h'Oigh,* whence, in good time, they would arise and go up into Pharais.

Lora had already been on the spot with Sheumais. While the latter had dug the place of sleep, she, with white chalk picked from the shore, had printed in large, heavy letters these words upon the seaward side of the stone:

"Take unto Thy compassion this little one, and us who follow."

There were no words spoken as Mary, kneeling, took the child from Lora's arms, and laid it, wrapped in a white sheet filled with fragrant gale, in the wood-shored grave that had been reverently prepared.

The afternoon had grown chill. Seaward, a gray mass had risen as if out of the waste of waters.

All were still kneeling — while Sheumais laid turf and heather above the small wooden lid covering the narrow house that would give the body sanctuary for a time — when the snow began to come down.

There was no wind, so the flakes fell light as feathers, grey in the gathering dusk as the down that falls from the wind-swept breasts of wild swans in their flight to or from the Polar seas.

Denser and denser it came; soundless at first, but after a while with a faint rustling and whirling, as though the flakes were wings of invisible birds of silence.

The grey gloom thickened. Already the sea was obscured. Its voice was audible the more loudly. . . a calling voice; but dull, listless, melancholy with ancient, unforgotten pain and all its burthen of immemorial lore.

The four mourners rose. The two women, with bowed heads, murmured words of prayer and farewell. Sheumais, crossing himself, muttered: "Deireadh gach comuinn, sgaoileadh; deireadh gach cogaidh, sìth" — "the end of all meetings, parting; the end of all striving, peace." Alastair looked eagerly through the snow-dusk lest the child should come again at once and go by them unseen.

By the time they reached home, there was a thick twilight all about them. A little later, looking out into the night, they saw the flakes drift over and past them like a myriad of winged things hurrying before a wind that pursued, devouring. The island lay in a white shroud. At the extreme margin, a black, pulsating line seemed to move sinuously from left to right.

Suddenly a deeper sound boomed from the sea, though no wind ruffled the drifts which already lay thick in the hollows. Till midnight, and for an hour beyond, this voice of the sea was as the baying of a monstrous hound.

None in the homestead slept. The silence, broken only by that strange, menacing baying of the waves as they roamed through the solitudes environing the isle, was so intense that sometimes the ears echoed as with the noise of a rush of wings, or as with the sonorous suspensions between the striking of bell and bell in monotonously swung chimes.

Then again, suddenly, and still without the coming of wind, the sea ceased its hoarse, angry baying, and, after lapse within lapse till its chime was almost inaudible, gave forth in a solemn dirge the majestic music of its inmost heart.

At last, after long vigils, all slept, though none so deeply, so unawakeningly as Lora.

Three hours before dawn the snow ceased to fall. An icy sparkle glittered league after league oceanward, as the star-rays pierced the heaving flanks and bowed heads of the sea-horses which had abruptly sprung up before the advancing ground-swell.

The cold was the cold of the Black Frost — bitter, sharp as a sword, nigh unendurable.

Shortly after dawn, Alastair awoke, shivering. He rose, threw some more peats on the fire; and then, having dressed and wrapped his plaid about him, and softly opened and closed the door, stepped out into the snow.

His breath caught with the cold, and a greater weakness even than that customary of late made him reel, then lean against the wall for a few minutes.

Soon his faintness passed. The exceeding beauty of sunrise over that vast stretch of waters, over the isle in its stainless white shroud, filled him with an exalted joy. Thereafter, for a time, he walked to and fro; sometimes staring absently seaward, again glancing curiously at his shadow — scarce more insubstantial than he himself had grown within the last month, and particularly within the last few days — as it lay upon or moved bluely athwart the snow.

After a brief space, a rapt look came into his face. He turned, and gazed expectantly at the door.

No one coming forth, he entered, and, with a loving smile, crossed to Lora's bed.

"Sweetheart . . . my white flower . . . come. It is so beautiful. Pharais has opened to us at last. I can see the steps gleaming gold within the yellow shine of the sun. Beyond, I saw a mist of waving wings. Come, Lora . . . Come!"

Cold and white was she as the snow. Alastair bent, kissed her lips, but was so wrought by his vision that he did not notice the chill of them, nor see the blue shadow in the pallor of the face.

"Ah, *mùirnean, mo mùirnean,* see, I will carry you," he murmured suddenly.

He stooped, lifted the beautiful dead body he had loved so well, and, staggering beneath the weight, half carried, half dragged it to the snow-slope beyond the door. Gently he placed Lora down. Then, going for and returning with a deer-skin, laid her upon it, and sat down beside her.

For a brief while, he waited patiently for her awakening. Then his eyes wandered again, now fixed upon the majesty of the sea, reaching intolerably grand from endless horizons to horizons without end; now upon the immense dome of the sky, where, amid the deepest blue, high in the north-west the moon turned a disc of pale gold out of an almost imperceptible flush, and confronted the flashing, blazing sunfire that, in the south-east, moved swiftly upward.

Suddenly he leaned forward; his lips parted; his eyes agleam with the inner flame that consumed him.

"Lora . . . Lora, my fawn," he whispered. "Look! The gates are opening! Dear, all is well at the last. God has given me back to you. My trouble is healed. Speak to me, dear; too great is my happiness!" No sound: no movement of the hands: no stir of the closed eyelids.

"Lora!"

It was strange. But he would be patient.

Idly he watched a small, grey snow-cloud passing low above the island.

A warm breath reached the heart of it, and set the myriad wings astir. Down, straight down above the isle and for a few fathoms beyond it, they fluttered waveringly.

The fall was like a veil suspended over Ithona: a veil so thin, so transparent, that the sky was visible through it as an azure dusk; and beneath it, the sea as a blue-flowing lawn wherever its skirts trailed; while behind it, the rising sunfire was a shimmer of amber-yellow that made every falling flake glisten like burnished gold. The wind was utterly still; the sky cloudless, but for that thin, evanishing veil of dropping gold.

The sea lay breathing in a deep calm all around the isle. But, from its heart that never slumbers, rose as of yore, and for ever, a rumour as of muffled prophesyings, a Voice of Awe, a Voice of Dread.

Ian Maclaren, 'Domsie'.
From *Beside the Bonnie Briar Bush* (1894)[1]

I

A Lad o' Pairts

The Revolution reached our parish years ago, and Drumtochty has a School Board, with a chairman and a clerk, besides a treasurer and an officer.[2] Young Hillocks, who had two years in a lawyer's office, is clerk, and summons meetings by post, although he sees every member at the market or the kirk. Minutes are read with much solemnity, and motions to expend ten shillings upon a coal-cellar door passed, on the motion of Hillocks, seconded by Drumsheugh, who are both severely prompted for the occasion, and move uneasily before speaking.

Drumsheugh was at first greatly exalted by his poll, and referred freely on market days to his "plumpers,"[3] but as time went on the irony of the situation laid hold upon him.

"Think o' you and me, Hillocks, veesitin' the schule and sittin' wi' bukes in oor hands watchin' the Inspector. Keep's a', its eneuch to mak' the auld Dominie turn in his grave.[4] Twa meenisters cam' in his time, and Domsie put Geordie Hoo or some ither gleg laddie, that was makin' for college, thro' his facin's,[5] and maybe some bit lassie brocht her copy-buke. Syne they had their dinner, and Domsie tae, wi' the Doctor.[6] Man, a've often thocht it was the prospeck o' the Schule Board and its weary bit rules that feenished Domsie. He wasna maybe sae shairp at the elements as this pirjinct body we hae noo, but a'body kent he was a terrible scholar and a credit ta the parish.[7] Drumtochty was a name in thae days wi' the lads he sent tae college. It was maybe juist as weel he slippit awa' when he did, for he wud hae taen ill with thae new fikes,[8] and nae college lad to warm his hert."

The present school-house stands in an open place beside the main road to Muirtown, treeless and comfortless, built of red, staring stone, with a playground for the boys and another for the girls, and a trim, snug-looking teacher's house, all very

---

1 Ian Maclaren was the pseudonym of Rev. Ian Watson (1850–1907), who began his career in the Free Church of Scotland (see note 20 below) but from 1880 ministered to a Presbyterian congregation in Liverpool.

2 The 'Revolution' referred to is the effect of the Education (Scotland) Act of 1872, which took the administration of schools out of the hands of the Church of Scotland and gave it to locally-elected School Boards, with a national inspectorate to check on standards. It also made schooling compulsory for all children from 5 to 13, which necessitated a widespread programme of school-building.

3 Plumper: 'a vote cast at an election for a single candidate when the voter has the right to vote for two or more' (*OED*). Drumsheugh and Hillocks are marked as wealthy farmers by being referred to by the names of their farms: the class of men who can be expected to take up such local responsibilities.

4 Keep's a': [God] keep us all (an exclamation); Dominie: schoolmaster (both Sc.).

5 Gleg (Sc.): ken, smart, alert; put [...] thro' his facin's: put through his drill (see *OED* 'facing' 4a).

6 Syne (Sc.): then. As in clear later, the 'Doctor' is the parish minister (a Doctor of Divinity).

7 Perjinct: precise, scrupulous, fussy; a'body kent: everyone knew (all Sc.); terrible: here, awesome.

8 Fikes (Sc.): troubles, petty cares, annoyances.

neat and symmetrical, and well regulated. The local paper had a paragraph headed "Drumtochty," written by the Muirtown architect, describing the whole premises in technical language that seemed to compensate the ratepayers for the cost, mentioning the contractor's name, and concluding that "this handsome building of the Scoto-Grecian style was one of the finest works that had ever come from the accomplished architect's hands." It has pitch-pine benches and map-cases, and a thermometer to be kept at not less than 58° and not more than 63°, and ventilators which the Inspector is careful to examine. When I stumbled in last week the teacher was drilling the children in Tonic Sol-fa with a little harmonium, and I left on tiptoe.

It is difficult to live up to this kind of thing, and my thoughts drift to the auld schule-house and Domsie. Someone with the love of God in his heart had built it long ago, and chose a site for the bairns in the sweet pine-woods at the foot of the cart road to Whinnie Knowe and the upland farms. It stood in a clearing with the tall Scotch firs round three sides, and on the fourth a brake of gorse and bramble bushes, through which there was an opening to the road. The clearing was the playground, and in summer the bairns annexed as much wood as they liked, playing tig among the trees, or sitting down at dinner-time on the soft, dry spines that made an elastic carpet everywhere. Domsie used to say there were two pleasant sights for his old eyes every day. One was to stand in the open at dinner-time and see the flitting forms of the healthy, rosy sonsie bairns in the wood, and from the door in the afternoon to watch the schule skail,[9] till each group was lost in the kindly shadow, and the merry shouts died away in this quiet place. Then the Dominie took a pinch of snuff and locked the door, and went to his house beside the school. One evening I came on him listening bare-headed to the voices, and he showed so kindly that I shall take him as he stands. A man of middle height, but stooping below it, with sandy hair turning grey, and bushy eye-brows covering keen, shrewd grey eyes. You will notice that his linen is coarse but spotless, and that, though his clothes are worn almost threadbare, they are well brushed and orderly. But you will be chiefly arrested by the Dominie's coat, for the like of it was not in the parish. It was a black dress coat, and no man knew when it had begun its history; in its origin and its continuance it resembled Melchisedek.[10] Many were the myths that gathered round that coat, but on this all were agreed, that without it we could not have realised the Dominie, and it became to us the sign and trappings of learning. He had taken a high place at the University, and won a good degree, and I've heard the Doctor say that he had a career before him. But something happened in his life, and Domsie buried himself among the woods with the bairns of Drumtochty. No one knew the story, but after he died I found a locket on his breast, with a proud, beautiful face within, and I have fancied it was a tragedy. It may have been in substitution that he gave all his love to the children, and nearly all his money too, helping lads to college, and affording an inexhaustible store of peppermints for the little ones.

Perhaps one ought to have been ashamed of that school-house, but yet it had its own distinction, for scholars were born there, and now and then to this day some famous man will come and stand in the deserted playground for a space. The door was at one end, and stood open in summer, so that the boys saw the rabbits come out from their holes on the edge of the wood, and birds sometimes flew in unheeded. The fireplace was at the other end, and was fed in winter with the sticks and peats brought by the scholars. On one side Domsie sat with the half-dozen lads he hoped to send to

---

9 Sonsie bairns: sturdy, thriving children (SND 'sonsie' 3[2]); skail: scatter (both Sc.).

10   Alluding to Psalms 110.4, 'The Lord hath sworn, and will not repent, Thou art a priest for ever after the order of Melchizedek'.

college, to whom he grudged no labour, and on the other gathered the very little ones, who used to warm their bare feet at the fire, while down the sides of the room the other scholars sat at their rough old desks, working sums and copying. Now and then a class came up and did some task, and at times a boy got the tawse for his negligence,[11] but never a girl. He kept the girls in as their punishment, with a brother to take them home, and both had tea in Domsie's house, with a bit of his best honey, departing much torn between an honest wish to please Domsie and a pardonable longing for another tea.

"Domsie," as we called the schoolmaster, behind his back in Drumtochty, because we loved him, was true to the tradition of his kind, and had an unerring scent for "pairts" in his laddies.[12] He could detect a scholar in the egg, and prophesied Latinity from a boy that seemed fit only to be a cowherd. It was believed that he had never made a mistake in judgment, and it was not his blame if the embryo scholar did not come to birth. "Five and thirty years have I been minister at Drumtochty," the Doctor used to say at school examinations, "and we have never wanted a student at the University, and while Dominie Jamieson lives we never shall." Whereupon Domsie took snuff, and assigned his share of credit to the Doctor, "who gave the finish in Greek to every lad of them, without money and without price, to make no mention of the higher mathematics." Seven ministers, four schoolmasters, four doctors, one professor, and three civil service men had been sent out by the auld schule in Domsie's time, besides many that "had given themselves to mercantile pursuits."

He had a leaning to classics and the professions, but Domsie was catholic in his recognition of "pairts," and when the son of Hillocks' foreman made a collection of the insects of Drumtochty, there was a council at the manse. "Bumbee Willie," as he had been pleasantly called by his companions, was rescued from ridicule and encouraged to fulfil his bent. Once a year a long letter came to Mr Patrick Jamieson, M.A., Schoolmaster, Drumtochty, N.B.,[13] and the address within was the British Museum. When Domsie read this letter to the school, he was always careful to explain that "Dr Graham is the greatest living authority on beetles," and, generally speaking, if any clever lad did not care for Latin, he had the alternative of beetles.

But it was Latin Domsie hunted for as for fine gold, and when he found the smack of it in a lad he rejoiced openly. He counted it a day in his life when he knew certainly that he had hit on another scholar, and the whole school saw the identification of George Howe. For a winter Domsie had been "at point,"[14] racing George through Caesar, stalking him behind irregular verbs, baiting traps with tit-bits of Virgil.[15] During these exercises Domsie surveyed George from above his spectacles with a hope that grew every day in assurance, and came to its height over a bit of Latin prose. Domsie tasted it visibly, and read it again in the shadow of the firs at mealtimes, slapping his leg twice.

"He'll dae! he'll dae!" cried Domsie aloud, ladling in the snuff. "George, ma mannie, tell yir father that I am comin' up to Whinnie Knowe the nicht on a bit o' business."

Then the "schule" knew that Geordie Hoo was marked for college, and pelted him with fir cones in great gladness of heart.

"Whinnie" was full of curiosity over the Dominie's visit, and vexed Marget sorely,

---

11 Tawse: a heavy leather belt with which children were struck across the hand as a punishment in Scottish schools.
12 Pairts (Sc.): talents.
13 N.B.: 'North Britain', an occasionally-used official designation for Scotland in the eighteenth and nineteenth centuries.
14 The hunting metaphors that follow suggest the narrator has in mind the alertness of a pointer dog to game, but this usage is not listed in *OED*.
15 Publius Vergilius Maro (70 –19 BC), the pre-eminent poet of classical Rome.

to whom Geordie had told wondrous things in the milk-house. "It canna be coals 'at he's wantin' frae the station, for there's a fell puckle left."[16]

"And it'll no' be seed taties," she said, pursuing the principle of exhaustion, "for he hes some Perthshire reds himsel'. I doot it's somethin' wrang with Geordie," and Whinnie started on a new track.

"He's been playin' truant maybe. A' mind gettin' ma paiks for birdnestin' masel.[17] I'll wager that's the verra thing."

"Weel, yir wrang, Weelum," broke in Marget, Whinnie's wife, a tall, silent woman, with a speaking face; "its naither the ae thing nor the ither,[18] but something I've been prayin' for since Geordie was a wee bairn. Clean yirsel and meet Domsie on the road, for nae man deserves more honour in Drumtochty, naither laird nor farmer."

Conversation with us was a leisurely game, with slow movements and many pauses, and it was our custom to handle all the pawns before we brought the queen into action.

Domsie and Whinnie discussed the weather with much detail before they came in sight of George, but it was clear that Domsie was charged with something weighty, and even Whinnie felt that his own treatment of the turnip crop was wanting in repose.

At last Domsie cleared his throat and looked at Marget, who had been in and out, but ever within hearing.

"George is a fine laddie, Mrs Howe."

An ordinary Drumtochty mother, although bursting with pride, would have responded, "He's weel eneuch, if he had grace in his heart," in a tone that implied it was extremely unlikely, and that her laddie led the reprobates of the parish. As it was, Marget's face lightened, and she waited.

"What do you think of making him?" and the Dominie dropped the words slowly, for this was a moment in Drumtochty.

There was just a single ambition in those humble homes, to have one of its members at college, and if Domsie approved a lad, then his brothers and sisters would give their wages, and the family would live on skim milk and oat cake, to let him have his chance.

Whinnie glanced at his wife and turned to Domsie.

"Marget's set on seein' Geordie a minister, Dominie."

'If he's worthy o't, no' otherwise. We haena the means though; the farm is highly rented, and there's barely a penny over at the end o' the year."

"But you are willing George should go and see what he can do. If he disappoint you, then I dinna know a lad o' pairts when I see him, and the Doctor is with me."

"Maister Jamieson," said Marget, with great solemnity, "ma hert's desire is to see George a minister, and if the Almichty spared me to hear ma only bairn open his mooth in the Evangel, I wud hae naething mair to ask ... but I doot sair it canna be managed."

Domsie had got all he asked, and he rose in his strength.

"If George Howe disna get to college, then he's the first scholar I've lost in Drumtochty ... ye 'ill manage his keep and sic like?"[19]

"Nae fear o' that," for Whinnie was warming, "tho' I haena a steek (stitch) o' new claithes for four years. But what about his fees and ither outgaeins?"

"There's ae man in the parish can pay George's fees without missing a penny, and I'll warrant he 'ill dae it."

"Are ye meanin' Drumsheugh," said Whinnie, "for ye 'ill never get a penny piece

---

16 Fell puckle (Sc.): considerable amount.
17 Mind: remember; paiks: beating (both Sc.).
18 Naither the ae thing nor the ither (Sc.): neither the one thing nor the other.
19 Sic (Sc.): such.

oot o' him. Did ye no' hear hoo the Frees wiled him intae their kirk,[20] Sabbath past a week, when Netherton's sister's son frae Edinboro' wes preaching the missionary sermon, expectin' a note,[21] and if he didna change a shillin' at the public-hoose and pit in a penny. Sall, he's a lad, Drumsheugh; a'm thinking ye may save yir journey, Dominie."

But Marget looked away from her into the past, and her eyes had a tender light. "He hed the best hert in the pairish aince."[22]

Domsie found Drumsheugh inclined for company, and assisted at an exhaustive and caustic treatment of local affairs. When the conduct of Piggie Walker, who bought Drumsheugh's potatoes and went into bankruptcy without paying for a single tuber, had been characterised in language that left nothing to be desired, Drumsheugh began to soften and show signs of reciprocity.

"Hoo's yir laddies, Dominie?" whom the farmers regarded as a risky turnip crop in a stiff clay that Domsie had "to fecht awa in." "Are ony o' them shaping weel?"

Drumsheugh had given himself away, and Domsie laid his first parallel with a glowing account of George Howe's Latinity, which was well received.

"Weel, I'm gled tae hear sic accoonts o' Marget Hoo's son, there naething in Whinnie but what the spune puts in."

But at the next move Drumsheugh scented danger and stood at guard. "Na, na, Dominie, I see what yir aifter fine; yet mind hoo ye got three notes oot o' me at Perth market Martinmas a year past for ane o' yir college laddies. Five punds for four years; my word, yir no' blate (modest). And what for sud I educat Marget Hoo's bairn? If ye kent a' ye wudna ask me; it's no' reasonable, Dominie. So there's an end o't."

Domsie was only a pedantic old parish schoolmaster, and he knew little beyond his craft, but the spirit of the Humanists awoke within him, and he smote with all his might, bidding goodbye to his English as one flings away the scabbard of a sword.

"Ye think that a'm asking a great thing when I plead for a pickle notes to give a puir laddie a college education. I tell ye, man, a'm honourin' ye and givin' ye the fairest chance ye'll ever hae o' winning wealth. Gin ye store the money ye hae scrapit by mony a hard bargain, some heir ye never saw 'ill gar it flee in chambering and wantonness.[23] Gin ye hed the heart to spend it on a lad o' pairts like Geordie Hoo, ye wud hae twa rewards nae man could tak frae ye. Ane wud be the honest gratitude o' a laddie whose desire for knowledge ye hed sateesfied, and the second wud be this—anither scholar in the land; and a'm thinking with auld John Knox that ilka scholar is something added to the riches of the commonwealth.[24] And what 'ill it cost ye? Little mair than the price o' a cattle beast. Man, Drumsheugh, ye poverty-stricken cratur, I've naethin' in this world but a handfu' o' books and a ten-pund note for my funeral, and yet, if it wasna I have all my brither's bairns tae keep, I wud pay every penny mysel'. But I'll no see Geordie sent to the plough, tho' I gang frae door to door. Na, na, the grass 'ill no' grow

20 The Church of Scotland split in 1843, with a new 'Free Church of Scotland' rejecting the right of landowners to impose ministers on congregations on their estates. This 'patronage' was finally abolished in 1874, but the split had been a bitter one, and Presbyterian congregations remained divided between the two churches even in very small communities until the vast majority of Free Churches rejoined the Church of Scotland in 1929.

21 That is, expected a banknote (for one pound or above) from Drumsheugh in the collection-plate.

22 Aince (Sc.): once.

23 Gin: if; gar: make (both Sc.); chambering: sexual promiscuity.

24 John Knox (c.1510–1572), preacher, theologian and historian, and leader of the Scottish Reformation. Ilka (Sc.): each

on the road atween the college and the schule-hoose o' Drumtochty till they lay me in the auld kirkyard."

"Sall, Domsie was roosed," Drumsheugh explained in the Muirtown inn next market. "'Miserly wratch' was the ceevilest word on his tongue. He wud naither sit nor taste, and was half way doon the yaird afore I cud quiet him. An' a'm no' sayin' he hed na reason if I'd been meanin' a' I said. It wud be a scan'al to the pairish if a likely lad cudna win tae college for the want o' siller. Na, na, neeburs, we hae oor faults, but we're no' sae dune mean as that in Drumtochty."

As it was, when Domsie did depart he could only grip Drumsheugh's hand, and say Maecenas,[25] and was so intoxicated, but not with strong drink, that he explained to Hillocks on the way home that Drumsheugh would be a credit to Drumtochty, and that his Latin style reminded him of Cicero.[26] He added as an afterthought that Whinnie Knowe had promised to pay Drumsheugh's fees for four years at the University of Edinburgh.

II

How We Carried the News to Whinnie Knowe

Domsie was an artist, and prepared the way for George's University achievement with much cunning. Once every Sabbath in the kirk-yard, where he laid down the law beneath an old elm tree, and twice between Sabbaths, at the post-office and by the wayside, he adjured us not to expect beyond measure, and gave us reasons.

"Ye see, he has a natural talent for learning, and took to Latin like a duck to water. What could be done in Drumtochty was done for him, and he's working night and day, but he'll have a sore fight with the lads from the town schools.[27] Na, na, neighbours," said the Dominie, lapsing into dialect, "we daurna luik for a prize. No' the first year, at ony rate."

"Man, Dominie. A'm clean astonished at ye," Drumsheugh used to break in, who, since he had given to George's support, outran us all in his faith, and had no patience with Domsie's devices, "a' tell ye if Geordie disna get a first in every class he's entered for, the judges 'ill be a puir lot," with a fine confusion of circumstances.

"Losh, Drumsheugh, be quiet, or ye'll dae the laddie an injury," said Domsie, with genuine alarm. "We maunna mention prizes, and first is fair madness.[28] A certificate of honour now, that will be aboot it, may be next to the prizemen."

Coming home from market he might open his heart. "George 'ill be amang the first sax, or my name is no' Jamieson,"[29] but generally he prophesied a moderate success.

There were times when he affected indifference, and talked cattle. We then regarded him with awe, because this was more than mortal.

It was my luck to carry the bulletin to Domsie, and I learned what he had been enduring. It was good manners in Drumtochty to feign amazement at the sight of a

---

25 Gaius Cilnius Maecenas (70–8 BC) was a Roman aristocrat who was the patron of many poets including Virgil.

26 Marcus Tullius Cicero (106–43 BC), the lawyer, statesman and philosopher on whose Latin style students were taught to model their own.

27 The town schools: that is, the grammar schools which specialised in preparing boys for university.

28 Maunna (Sc.): must not.

29 Sax (Sc.): six.

letter, and to insist that it must be intended for some other person. When it was finally forced upon one, you examined the handwriting at various angles and speculated about the writer. Some felt emboldened, after these precautions, to open the letter, but this haste was considered indecent. When Posty handed Drumsheugh the factor's letter, with the answer to his offer for the farm, he only remarked, "It'll be frae the factor," and harked back to a polled Angus bull he had seen at the show. "Sall," said Posty in the kirkyard with keen relish, "ye'll never flurry Drumsheugh." Ordinary letters were read in leisurely retirement, and, in case of urgency, answered within the week.

Domsie clutched the letter, and would have torn off the envelope. But he could not; his hand was shaking like an aspen. He could only look, and I read :

"DEAR MR JAMIESON, — The class honour lists are just out, and you will be pleased to know that I have got the medal both in the Humanity[30] and the Greek."

There was something about telling his mother, and his gratitude to his schoolmaster, but Domsie heard no more. He tried to speak and could not, for a rain of tears was on his hard old face. Domsie was far more a pagan than saint, but somehow he seemed to me that day as Simeon, who had at last seen his heart's desire, and was satisfied.[31]

When the school had dispersed with a joyful shout, and disappeared in the pine woods, he said, "Ye'll come too," and I knew he was going to Whinnie Knowe. He did not speak one word upon the way, but twice he stood and read the letter which he held fast in his hand. His face was set as he climbed the cart track. I saw it set again as we came down that road one day, but it was well that we could not pierce beyond the present.

Whinnie left his plough in the furrow, and came to meet us, taking two drills at a stride, and shouting remarks on the weather yards off..

Domsie only lifted the letter. "Frae George."

"Ay, ay, and what's he gotten noo?"

Domsie solemnly unfolded the letter, and brought down his spectacles. "Edinburgh, April 7th." Then he looked at Whinnie, and closed his mouth.

"We'll tell it first to his mither."

"Yer richt, Dominie. She weel deserves it. A'm thinking she's seen us by this time." So we fell into a procession, Dominie leading by two yards; and then a strange thing happened. For the first and last time in his life Domsie whistled, and the tune was "A hundred pipers and a' and a'," and as he whistled he seemed to dilate before our eyes, and he struck down thistles with his stick — a thistle at every stroke.

"Domsie's fair carried," whispered Whinnie, "it cowes a'."[32]

Marget met us at the end of the house beside the brier bush, where George was to sit on summer afternoons before he died, and a flash passed between Domsie and the lad's mother. Then she knew that it was well, and fixed her eyes on the letter, but Whinnie, his thumbs in his armholes, watched the wife.

Domsie now essayed to read the news, but between the shaking of his hands and his voice he could not.

"It's nae use," he cried, "he's first in the Humanity oot o' a hunderd and seeventy

---

30 Humanity: the name in Scottish universities for the study of Latin language and literature.

31 In the New Testament, Simeon is the devout Jew who has been promised that he will not die until he has seen the saviour; when he encounters the infant Jesus, he recognises him, and says 'Lord, now lettest thou thy servant depart in peace, according to thy word: / For my eyes have seen thy salvation' (Luke 2.29–30).

32 Cowes a' (Sc.): surpasses everything.

lads, first o' them a', and he's first in the Greek too; the like o' this is hardly known, and it has na been seen in Drumtochty since there was a schule. That's the word he's sent, and he bade me tell his mother without delay, and I am here as fast as my old feet could carry me."

I glanced round, although I did not myself see very clearly.

Marget was silent for the space of five seconds; she was a good woman, and I knew that better afterwards. She took the Dominie's hand, and said to him, "Under God this was your doing, Maister Jamieson, and for your reward ye'ill get naither silver nor gold, but ye hae a mithers gratitude."

Whinnie gave a hoarse chuckle and said to his wife, "It was frae you, Marget, he got it a'."

When we settled in the parlour Domsie's tongue was loosed, and he lifted up his voice and sang the victory of Geordie Hoo.

"It's ten years ago at the brak up o' the winter ye brought him down to me, Mrs Hoo, and ye said at the schule-hoose door, 'Dinna be hard on him, Maister Jamieson, he's my only bairn, and a wee thingie quiet.' Div ye mind what I said, 'There's something ahint that face,' and my heart warmed to George that hour.[33] Two years after the Doctor examined the schule, and he looks at George. 'That's a likely lad, Dominie. What think ye?' And he was only eight years auld, and no big for his size. 'Doctor, I daurna prophesy till we turn him into the Latin, but a've my thoughts.'[34] So I had a' the time, but I never boasted, na, na, that's dangerous. Didna I say, 'Ye hev a promisin' laddie, Whinnie,' ae day in the market?"

"It's a fac'," said Whinnie, "it was the day I bocht the white coo." But Domsie swept on.

"The first year o' Latin was enough for me. He juist nippet up his verbs. Caesar could na keep him goin'; he wes into Virgil afore he was eleven, and the Latin prose, man, as sure as a'm living, it tasted o' Cicero frae the beginning."

Whinnie wagged his head in amazement.

"It was the verra nicht o' the Latin prose I cam up to speak aboot the college, and ye thocht Geordie had been playing truant."

Winnie laughed uproariously, but Domsie heeded not.

"It was awfu' work the next twa years, but the Doctor stood in weel wi' the Greek. Ye mind hoo Geordie tramped ower the muir to the manse thro' the weet an' the snaw, and there wes aye dry stockings for him in the kitchen afore he had his Greek in the Doctor's study."

"And a warm drink tae," put in Maiget, "and that's the window I pit the licht in to guide him hame in the dark winter nichts, and mony a time when the sleet played swish on the glass I wes near wishin' —" Domsie waved his hand.

"But that's dune wi' noo, and he was wirth a' the toil and trouble. First in the Humanity and first in the Greek, sweepit the field, Lord preserve us. A' can hardly believe it. Eh, I was feared o' thae High School lads. They had terrible advantages. Maisters frae England, and tutors, and whatna', but Drumtochty carried aff the croon. It'll be fine reading in the papers—

Humanity—First Prize (and Medal), George Howe, Drumtochty, Perthshire.
Greek—First Prize (and Medal), George Howe, Drumtochty, Perthshire."

---

33   Div: do; ahint: behind (both Sc.).
34   Daurna (Sc.): dare not.

"It'll be michty," cried Whinnie, now fairly on fire.

"And Philosophy and Mathematics to come. Geordie's no bad at Euclid. I'll wager he'll be first there too. When he gets his hand in there's naething he's no fit for wi' time. My ain laddie — and the Doctor's — we maunna forget him — it's his classics he hes, every book o' them. The Doctor 'ill be lifted when he comes back on Saturday.[35] A'm thinkin' we'll hear o't on Sabbath. And Drumsheugh, he'll be naither to haud nor bind in the kirk-yard.[36] As for me, I wad na change places wi' the Duke o' Atholl," and Domsie shook the table to its foundation.

Then he awoke, as from a dream, and the shame of boasting that shuts the mouths of self-respecting Scots descended upon him.

"But this is fair nonsense. Ye'll no mind the havers o' an auld dominie."[37]

He fell back on a recent roup,[38] and would not again break away, although sorely tempted by certain of Whinnie's speculations.

When I saw him last, his coat-tails were waving victoriously as he leaped a dyke on his way to tell our Drumtochty Maecenas that the judges knew their business.

III

In Marget's Garden

The cart track to Whinnie Knowe was commanded by a gable window, and Whinnie boasted that Marget had never been taken unawares. Tramps, finding every door locked, and no sign of life anywhere, used to express their mind in the "close,"[39] and return by the way they came, while ladies from Kildrummie, fearful lest they should put Mrs Howe out, were met at the garden gate by Marget in her Sabbath dress, and brought in to a set tea as if they had been invited weeks before.

Whinnie gloried most in the discomfiture of the Tory agent, who had vainly hoped to coerce him in the stack yard without Marget's presence, as her intellectual contempt for the Conservative party knew no bounds.[40]

"Sall, she saw him slip aff the road afore the last stile, and wheep roond the fit o' the gairden wa' like a tod (fox) aifter the chickens.[41]

"'It's a het day, Maister Anderson,' says Marget frae the gairden, lookin' doon on him as calm as ye like. 'Yir surely no' gaein' to pass oor hoose without a gless o' milk?'

"Wud ye believe it, he wes that upset he left withoot sayin' 'vote,' and Drumsheugh telt me next market that his langidge aifterwards cudna be printed."

When George came home for the last time, Marget went back and forward all afternoon from his bedroom to the window, and hid herself beneath the laburnum to see his face as the cart stood before the stile. It told her plain what she had feared, and Marget passed through her Gethsemane with the gold blossoms falling on her face. When their eyes met, and before she helped him down, mother and son understood.

---

35 Lifted (Sc.): cheered, elated.
36 Neither to haud not bind (Sc.): beyond restraint.
37 Havers (Sc.): nonsense, rambling.
38 Roup (Sc.): public auction, usually of household and farming gear when a family leaves a farm.
39 Close (Sc.): here, courtyard.
40 Stack yard: where sheaves were stored prior to threshing. Northern Scotland, and especially Highland areas, were a stronghold of the Liberal Party throughout the nineteenth century.
41 Afore: before; wheep: whip; fit: foot (all Sc.)

"Ye mind what I told ye, o' the Greek mothers, the day I left. Weel, I wud hae liked to have carried my shield, but it wasna to be, so I've come home on it."[42] As they went slowly up the garden walk, "I've got my degree, a double first, mathematics and classics."

"Ye've been a gude soldier, George, and faithfu'."

"Unto death, a'm dootin, mother."

"Na," said Marget, "unto life."

Drumtochty was not a heartening place in sickness, and Marget, who did not think our thoughts, endured much consolation at her neighbours' hands. It is said that in cities visitors congratulate a patient on his good looks, and deluge his family with instances of recovery. This would have seemed to us shallow and unfeeling, besides being a "temptin' o' Providence," which might not have intended to go to extremities, but on a challenge of this kind had no alternative. Sickness was regarded as a distinction tempered with judgment, and favoured people found it difficult to be humble. I always thought more of Peter Macintosh when the mysterious "tribble" that needed the Perth doctor made no difference in his manner, and he passed his snuff box across the seat before the long prayer as usual, but in this indifference to privileges Peter was exceptional.

You could never meet Kirsty Stewart on equal terms, although she was quite affable to anyone who knew his place.

"Ay," she said, on my respectful allusion to her experience, "a've seen mair than most. It doesna become me to boast, but tho' I say it as sudna, I hae buried a' my ain fouk."[43]

Kirsty had a "way" in sick visiting, consisting in a certain cadence of the voice and arrangement of the face, which was felt to be soothing and complimentary.

"Yir aboot again, a'm glad to see," to me after my accident, "but yir no' dune wi' that leg; na, na, Jeems, that was ma second son, scrapit his shin aince, tho' no' so bad as ye've dune a'm hearing (for I had denied Kirsty the courtesy of an inspection). It's sax year syne noo, and he got up and wes traivellin' fell hearty like yersel'. But he begood to dwine (sicken) in the end of the year, and soughed awa' in the spring.[44] Ay, ay, when tribble comes ye never ken hoo it 'ill end. A' thocht I wud come up and speir for ye.[45] A body needs comfort gin he's sober (ill)."

When I found George wrapped in his plaid beside the brier bush whose roses were no whiter than his cheeks, Kirsty was already installed as comforter in the parlour, and her drone came through the open window.

"Ay, ay, Marget, sae it's come to this. Weel, we daurna complain, ye ken. Be thankfu' ye haena lost your man and five sons, besides twa sisters and a brither, no' to mention cousins. That wud be something to speak aboot, and Losh keep's,[46] there's nae saying but he micht hang on a whilie. Ay, ay, it's a sair blow aifter a' that wes in the papers. I wes feared when I heard o' the papers; 'Lat weel alane,' says I to the Dominie; 'ye 'ill bring a judgment on the laddie wi' yir blawing.' But ye micht as weel hae spoken to the hills. Domsie's a thraun body at the best,[47] and he was clean infatuat' wi' George. Ay, ay, it's an awfu' lesson, Marget, no to mak' idols o' our bairns, for that's naethin' else than provokin' the Almichty."

---

42 According to the first-century AD Greek historian Plutarch, Spartan mothers would send their sons to battle with the words: 'Return with your shield, or upon it'. Fleeing the field meant jettisoning the heavy Hoplite shield, so this means: return victorious, or dead.

43 Sudna: should not; fouk: folk (both Sc.).

44 Begood: began; soughed awa': breathed his last (both Sc.).

45 Speir (Sc.): ask.

46 Losh keep's: Lord keep us.

47 Thraun, usually thrawn (Sc.): stubborn.

It was at this point that Marget gave way and scandalized Drumtochty, which held that obtrusive prosperity was an irresistible provocation to the higher powers, and that a skilful depreciation of our children was a policy of safety.

"Did ye say the Almichty? I'm thinkin' that's ower grand a name for your God, Kirsty. What wud ye think o' a faither that brocht hame some bonnie thing frae the fair for ane o' his bairns, and when the puir bairn wes pleased wi' it tore it oot o' his hand and flung it into the fire? Eh, woman, he wud be a meeserable cankered jealous body. Kirsty, wumman, when the Almichty sees a mither bound up in her laddie, I tell ye He is sair pleased in His heaven, for mind ye hoo He loved His ain Son. Besides, a'm judgin' that nane o' us can love anither withoot lovin' Him, or hurt anither withoot hurtin' Him.

"Oh, I ken weel that George is gaein' to leave us; but it's no because the Almichty is jealous o' him or me, no' likely. It cam' to me last nicht that He needs my laddie for some grand wark in the ither world, and that's hoo George has his bukes brocht oot tae the garden and studies a' the day. He wants to be ready for his kingdom, just as he trachled in the bit schule o' Drumtochty for Edinboro'.[48] I hoped he wud hae been a minister o' Christ's Gospel here, but he 'ill be judge over many cities yonder. A'm no' denyin', Kirsty, that it's a trial, but I hae licht on it, and naethin' but gude thochts o' the Almichty."

Drumtochty understood that Kirsty had dealt faithfully with Marget for pride and presumption, but all we heard was, "Losh keep us a'."

When Marget came out and sat down beside her son, her face was shining. Then she saw the open window.

"I didna ken."

"Never mind, mither, there's nae secrets atween us, and it gar'd my heart leap to hear ye speak up like yon for God, and to know yir content. Div ye mind the nicht I called for ye, mother, and ye gave me the Gospel aboot God?"

Marget slipped her hand into George's, and he let his head rest on her shoulder. The likeness flashed upon me in that moment, the earnest deepset grey eyes, the clean-cut firm jaw, and the tender mobile lips, that blend of apparent austerity and underlying romance that make the pathos of a Scottish face.

"There had been a Revival man, here," George explained to me, "and he was preaching on hell. As it grew dark a candle was lighted, and I can still see his face as in a picture, a hard-visaged man. He looked down at us laddies in the front, and asked us if we knew what like hell was. By this time we were that terrified none of us could speak, but I whispered "No.'

"Then he rolled up a piece of paper and held it in the flame, and we saw it burn and glow and shrivel up and fall in black dust.

"'Think,' said he, and he leaned over the desk, and spoke in a gruesome whisper which made the cold run down our backs, 'that yon paper was your finger, one finger only of your hand, and it burned like that for ever and ever, and think of your hand and your arm and your whole body all on fire, never to go out.' We shuddered that you might have heard the form creak.[49] 'That is hell, and that is where ony laddie will go who does not repent and believe.'

"It was like Dante's Inferno, and I dared not take my eyes off his face. He blew out the candle, and we crept to the door trembling, not able to say one word.

"That night I could not sleep, for I thought I might be in the fire before morning. It was harvest time, and the moon was filling the room with cold clear light. From my

---

48 Trachled (Sc.): struggled.
49 Form: bench.

bed I could see the stooks standing in rows upon the field,[50] and it seemed like the judgment day.

"I was only a wee laddie, and I did what we all do in trouble, I cried for my mother.

"Ye hae na forgotten, mither, the fricht that was on me that nicht."

"Never," said Marget, "and never can; it's hard wark for me to keep frae hating that man, dead or alive. Geordie gripped me wi' baith his wee airms round my neck, and he cries over and over again, 'Is yon God?'"

"Ay, and ye kissed me, mither, and ye said (it's like yesterday), 'Yir safe with me,' and ye telt me that God micht punish me to mak me better if I was bad, but that he wud never torture ony puir soul, for that cud dae nae guid, and was the Devil's wark. Ye asked me:

"'Am I a guid mother tae ye?' and when I could dae naethin' but hold, ye said, 'Be sure God maun be a hantle kinder.'[51]

"The truth came to me as with a flicker, and I cuddled down into my bed, and fell asleep in His love as in my mother's arms.

"Mither," and George lifted up his head, "that was my conversion, and, mither dear, I hae longed a' thro' thae college studies for the day when ma mooth wud be opened wi' this evangel."

Marget's was an old-fashioned garden, with pinks and daisies and forget-me-nots, with sweet-scented wall-flower and thyme and moss roses, where nature had her way, and gracious thoughts could visit one without any jarring note. As George's voice softened to the close, I caught her saying, "His servants shall see His face," and the peace of Paradise fell upon us in the shadow of death.

The night before the end George was carried out to his corner, and Domsie, whose heart was nigh unto the breaking, sat with him the afternoon. They used to fight the College battles over again, with their favourite classics beside them, but this time none of them spoke of books. Marget was moving about the garden, and she told me that George looked at Domsie wistfully, as if he had something to say and knew not how to do it.

After a while he took a book from below his pillow, and began, like one thinking over his words:

"Maister Jamieson, ye hae been a gude freend tae me, the best I ever hed aifter my mither and faither. Wull ye tak this buik for a keepsake o' yir grateful scholar? It's a Latin Imitation, Dominie, and it's bonnie printin'.[52] Ye mind hoo ye gave me yir ain Virgil, and said he was a kind o' Pagan sanct.[53] Noo here is my sanct, and div ye ken I've often thocht Virgil saw His day afar off, and was glad. Wull ye read it, Dominie, for my sake, and maybe ye 'ill come to see—" and George could not find words for more.

But Domsie understood. "Ma laddie, ma laddie, that I luve better than onythin' on earth, I'll read it till I die, and, George, I'll tell ye what livin' man does na ken. When I was your verra age I had a cruel trial, and ma heart was turned frae faith. The classics hae been my bible, though I said naethin' to ony man against Christ. He aye seemed beyond man, and noo the veesion o' Him has come to me in this gairden. Laddie, ye hae dune far mair for me than I ever did for you. Wull ye mak a prayer for yir auld dominie afore we pairt?"

There was a thrush singing in the birches and a sound of bees in the air, when George prayed in a low, soft voice, with a little break in it.

---

50 Stooks (Sc.): hay-cocks.

51 Hantle (Sc.): a great deal.

52 *De imitatione Christi* (The Imitation of Christ) by Thomas à Kempis, a classic of medieval Catholic piety, first published around 1418.

53 Sanct (Sc.): saint.

"Lord Jesus, remember my dear maister, for he's been a kind freend to me and mony a puir laddie in Drumtochty. Bind up his sair heart and give him licht at eventide, and may the maister and his scholars meet some mornin' where the schule never skails, in the kingdom o' oor Father.'

Twice Domsie said Amen, and it seemed as the voice of another man, and then he kissed George upon the forehead; but what they said Marget did not wish to hear.

When he passed out at the garden gate, the westering sun was shining golden, and the face of Domsie was like unto that of a little child.

IV

A Scholar's Funeral

Drumtochty never acquitted itself with credit at a marriage, having no natural aptitude for gaiety, and being haunted with anxiety lest any "hicht" should end in a "howe,"[54] but the parish had a genius for funerals. It was long mentioned with a just sense of merit that an English undertaker, chancing on a "beerial" with us, had no limits to his admiration. He had been disheartened to despair all his life by the ghastly efforts of chirpy little Southerners to look solemn on occasion, but his dreams were satisfied at the sight of men like Drumsheugh and Hillocks in their Sabbath blacks. Nature lent an initial advantage in face, but it was an instinct in the blood that brought our manner to perfection and nothing could be more awful than a group of those austere figures, each man gazing into vacancy without a trace of expression, and refusing to recognise his nearest neighbour by word or look. Drumtochty gave itself to a "beerial" with chastened satisfaction, partly because it lay near to the sorrow of things, and partly because there was nothing of speculation in it. "Ye can hae little rael pleesure in a merrige," explained our gravedigger, in whom the serious side had been perhaps abnormally developed, "for ye never ken hoo it will end; but there's nae risk about a 'beerial.'"

It came with a shock upon townsmen that the ceremony began with a "service o' speerits," and that an attempt of the Free Kirk minister to replace this by the reading of Scripture was resisted as an "innovation." Yet every one admitted that the seriousness of Drumtochty pervaded and sanctified this function. A tray of glasses was placed on a table with great solemnity by the "wricht," who made no sign and invited none.[55] You might have supposed that the circumstance had escaped the notice of the company, so abstracted and unconscious was their manner, had it not been that two graven images a minute later are standing at the table.

"Ye 'ill taste, Tammas," with settled melancholy.

"Na, na; I've nae incleenation the day; it's an awfu' dispensation this, Jeems. She wud be barely saxty."

"Ay, ay, but we maun keep up the body sae lang as we're here, Tammas."

"Weel, puttin' it that way, a'm no' sayin' but yir richt," yielding unwillingly to the force of circumstance.

"We're here the day and there the morn, Tammas. She wes a fine wumman— Mistress Stirton—a weel-livin' wumman; this 'ill be a blend, a'm thinkin'."[56]

"She slippit aff sudden in the end; a'm judgin' it's frae the Muirtown grocer; but a body canna discreeminate on a day like this."

---

54 Hichts and howes (Sc.): literally, heights and hollows; figuratively, ups and downs.
55 Wricht (Sc.): presumably, the carpenter who has made the coffin.
56 That is, a blended, rather than a single malt, whisky.

Before the glasses are empty all idea of drinking is dissipated, and one has a vague impression that he is at church.

It was George Howe's funeral that broke the custom and closed the "service." When I came into the garden where the neighbours were gathered, the "wricht" was removing his tray, and not a glass had been touched. Then I knew that Drumtochty had a sense of the fitness of things, and was stirred to its depths.

"Ye saw the wricht carry in his tray," said Drumsheugh, as we went home from the kirk-yard. "Weel, yon's the last sicht o't ye 'ill get, or a'm no Drumsheugh. I've nae objection ma'sel to a nee'bur tastin' at a funeral, a' the mair if he's come frae the upper end o' the pairish, and ye ken I dinna hold wi' thae teetotal fouk. A'm ower auld in the horn to change noo. But there's times and seasons, as the gude Buik says,[57] and it wud hae been an awfu' like business tae luik at a gless in Marget's gairden, and puir Domsie standing in ahint the brier bush as if he cud never lift his heid again. Ye may get shairper fouk in the uptak', but ye 'ill no' get a pairish with better feelin's. It 'ill be a kind o' sateesfaction tae Marget when she hears o't. She was aye against tastin', and a'm judgin' her tribble has ended it at beerials."

"Man, it was hard on some o' yon lads the day, but there wesna ane o' them made a mudge. I keepit my eye on Posty, but he never lookit the way it wes. He's a drouthy body,[58] but he hes his feelin's, hes Posty."

Before the Doctor began the prayer, Whinnie took me up to the room.

"There's twa o' Geordie's College freends with Marget, grand scholars a'm telt, and there's anither I canna weel mak oot. He's terrible cast doon, and Marget speaks as if she kent him."

It was a low-roofed room, with a box bed and some pieces of humble furniture, fit only for a labouring man. But the choice treasures of Greece and Rome lay on the table, and on a shelf beside the bed College prizes and medals, while everywhere were the roses he loved. His peasant mother stood beside the body of her scholar son, whose hopes and thoughts she had shared, and through the window came the bleating of distant sheep. It was the idyll of Scottish University life.

George's friends were characteristic men, each of his own type, and could only have met in the commonwealth of letters. One was of an ancient Scottish house which had fought for Mary against the Lords of the Congregation, followed Prince Charlie to Culloden, and were High Church and Tory to the last drop of their blood.[59] Ludovic Gordon left Harrow with the reputation of a classic, and had expected to be first at Edinboro'. It was Gordon, in fact, that Domsie feared in the great war, but he proved second to Marget's son, and being of the breed of Prince Jonathan, which is the same the world over, he came to love our David as his own soul.[60] The other, a dark little man, with a quick, fiery eye, was a Western Celt, who had worried his way from a fishing croft in Barra to be an easy first in Philosophy at Edinboro', and George and Ronald Maclean were as brothers because there is nothing so different as Scottish and

---

57 'To every thing there is a season, and a time to every purpose under the heaven: / A time to be born, and a time to die [...]' (Ecclesiastes 3.1–2).

58 Mudge: movement; drouthy: thirsty (both Sc.).

59 Referring to the Catholic Mary Queen of Scots and the Protestant nobles who opposed her in the Scottish Reformation; and to the Catholic Charles Edward Stuart's attempt to restore his family to the British throne, finally defeated at the battle of Culloden in April 1746. But 'High Church' means Episcopalian rather than Catholic: that is, the Scottish branch of the Anglican communion. Harrow, mentioned in the next sentence, is a famous English private school.

60 Jonathan is the son of King Saul; after the shepherd David slays Goliath, 'the soul of Jonathan was knit with the soul of David, and Jonathan loved him as his own soul' (1 Samuel 18.1).

Highland blood.

"Maister Gordon," said Marget, "this is George's Homer, and he bade me tell you that he coonted yir freendship ain o' the gifts o' God."

For a brief space Gordon was silent, and, when he spoke, his voice sounded strange in that room.

"Your son was the finest scholar of my time, and a very perfect gentleman. He was also my true friend, and I pray God to console his mother." And Ludovic Gordon bowed low over Marget's worn hand as if she had been a queen.

Marget lifted Plato, and it seemed to me that day as if the dignity of our Lady of Sorrows had fallen upon her.

"This is the buik George chose for you, Maister Maclean, for he aye said to me ye hed been a prophet and shown him mony deep things."

The tears sprang to the Celt's eyes.

"It was like him to make all other men better than himself," with the soft, sad Highland accent; "and a proud woman you are to hef been his mother."

The third man waited at the window till the scholars left, and then I saw he was none of that kind, but one who had been a slave of sin and now was free.

"Andra Chaumers, George wished ye tae hev his Bible, and he expecks ye tae keep the tryst."

"God helping me, I will," said Chalmers, hoarsely; and from the garden ascended a voice, "O God, who art a very present help in trouble."

The Doctor's funeral prayer was one of the glories of the parish, compelling even the Free Kirk to reluctant admiration, although they hinted that its excellence was rather of the letter than the spirit, and regarded its indiscriminate charity with suspicion. It opened with a series of extracts from the Psalms, relieved by two excursions into the minor prophets, and led up to a sonorous recitation of the problem of immortality from Job, with its triumphant solution in the peroration of the fifteenth chapter of 1 Corinthians. Drumtochty men held their breath till the Doctor reached the crest of the hill (Hillocks disgraced himself once by dropping his staff at the very moment when the Doctor was passing from Job to Paul), and then we relaxed while the Doctor descended to local detail. It was understood that it took twenty years to bring the body of this prayer to perfection, and any change would have been detected and resented.

The Doctor made a good start, and had already sighted Job, when he was carried out of his course by a sudden current, and began to speak to God about Marget and her son, after a very simple fashion that brought a lump to the throat, till at last, as I imagine, the sight of the laddie working at his Greek in the study of a winter night came up before him, and the remnants of the great prayer melted like an iceberg in the Gulf Stream.

"Lord, hae peety upon us, for we a' luved him, and we were a' prood o' him."

After the Doctor said "Amen" with majesty, one used to look at his neighbour, and the other would shut his eyes and shake his head, meaning, "There's no use asking me, for it simply can't be better done by living man." This time no one remembered his neighbour, because every eye was fixed on the Doctor. Drumtochty was identifying its new minister.

"It may be that I hef judged him hardly," said Lachlan Campbell, one of the Free Kirk Highlanders, and our St. Dominic. "I shall never again deny that the root of the matter is in the man, although much choked with the tares of worldliness and

Arminianism."[61]

"He is a goot man, Lachlan," replied Donald Menzies, another Celt, and he was our St Francis, for "every one that loveth is born of God."[62]

There was no hearse in Drumtochty, and we carried our dead by relays of four, who waded every stream unless more than knee deep, the rest following in straggling, picturesque procession over the moor and across the stepping stones. Before we started, Marget came out and arranged George's white silken hood upon the coffin with roses in its folds.

She swept us into one brief flush of gratitude, from Domsie to Posty.

"Neeburs, ye were a' his freends, and he wanted ye tae ken hoo yir trust wes mickle help tae him in his battle."[63]

There was a stir within us, and it came to birth in Drumsheugh of all men:

"Marget Hoo, this is no' the day for many words, but there's juist ae heart in Drumtochty, and it's sair."

No one spoke to Domsie as we went down the cart track, with the ripe corn standing on either side, but he beckoned Chalmers to walk with him.

"Ye hae heard him speak o' me, then, Maister Jamieson?"

"Ay, oftentimes, and he said once that ye were hard driven, but that ye had trampled Satan under yir feet."

"He didna tell ye all, for if it hadna been for George Howe I wudna been worth callin' a man this day. One night when he was workin' hard for his honours examination and his disease was heavy upon him, puir fellow, he sought me oot where I was, and wouldna leave till I cam' wi' him.

"'Go home,' I said, 'Howe; it's death for ye to be oot in this sleet and cold. Why not leave me to lie in the bed I hae made ?'

"He took me by the arm into a passage. I see the gaslicht on his white face, and the shining o' his eyes.

"'Because I have a mother …'

"Dominie, he pulled me oot o' hell."

"Me tae, Andra, but no your hell. Ye mind the Roman Triumph, when a general cam' hame wi' his spoils. Laddie, we're the captives that go with his chariot up the Capitol."

Donald Menzies was a man of moods, and the Doctor's prayer had loosed his imagination so that he saw visions.

"Look," said he, as we stood on a ridge, "I hef seen it before in the book of Joshua."

Below the bearers had crossed a burn on foot, and were ascending the slope where an open space of deep green was fringed with purple heather.

"The ark hass gone over Jordan, and George will have come into the Land of Promise."[64]

The September sunshine glinted on the white silk George won with his blood,[65] and fell like a benediction on the two figures that climbed the hard ascent close after the man they loved.

Strangers do not touch our dead in Drumtochty, but the eight of nearest blood lower

---

61 The Free Church was especially strong in the Highlands. St Dominic was founder of an order of friars noted for their preaching and doctrinal rigour. Arminianism is an alternative version of reformed theology to that of the orthodox Calvinism of the Scottish churches.

62 St Francis here representing Christian charity (in contrast to the heretic-hunting St Dominic).

63 Mickle (Sc.): much.

64 Donald refers to the Israelites' crossing of the Jordan, carrying the Ark of the Covenant, to take possession of the Promised Land in Joshua 3.

65 Referring to the white lining of the academic gown worn by an Scottish M.A..

the body into the grave. The order of precedence is keenly calculated, and the loss of a merited cord can never be forgiven. Marget had arranged everything with Whinnie, and all saw the fitness. His father took the head, and the feet (next in honour) he gave to Domsie.

"Ye maun dae it. Marget said ye were o' his ain bluid."

On the right side the cords were handed to the Doctor, Gordon, and myself; and on the left to Drumsheugh, Maclean, and Chalmers. Domsie lifted the hood for Marget, but the roses he gently placed on George's name. Then with bent, uncovered heads, and in unbroken silence, we buried all that remained of our scholar.

We always waited till the grave was filled and the turf laid down, a trying quarter of an hour. Ah me! the thud of the spade on your mother's grave! None gave any sign of what he felt save Drumsheugh, whose sordid slough had slipped off from a tender heart,[66] and Chalmers, who went behind a tombstone and sobbed aloud. Not even Posty asked the reason so much as by a look, and Drumtochty, as it passed, made as though it did not see. But I marked that the Dominie took Chalmers home, and walked all the way with him to Kildrummie station next morning. His friends erected a granite cross over George's grave, and it was left to Domsie to choose the inscription. There was a day when it would have been, "Whom the gods love die young."[67] Since then Domsie had seen the kingdom of God, and this is graven where the roses bloomed fresh every summer for twenty years till Marget was laid with her son:

GEORGE HOWE, M.A.,
Died September 22nd, 1869,
Aged 21.
"They shall bring the glory and honour of the nations into it."[68]

It was a late November day when I went to see George's memorial, and the immortal hope was burning low in my heart; but as I stood before that cross, the sun struggled from behind a black watery bank of cloud, and picked out every letter of the Apocalypse in gold.

---

66 Slough: outer covering, husk.
67 This is from the *Fragments* of the Greek playwright Menander (c.342–291 BC).
68 Revelations 21.26 (this book of the Bible is known as the Apocalypse of St. John)

Poems by John Davidson (1857–1909)

The Rev. Habakkuk McGruther of Cape Wrath, in 1879 [1]

God save old Scotland! Such a cry
    Comes raving north from Edinburgh.[2]
It shakes the earth, and rends the sky,
    It thrills and fills true hearts with sorrow.
'There's no such place, by God's good grace,
    As smoky hell's dusk-flaming cavern?'
Ye fools, beware, or ye may share
    The hottest brew of Satan's tavern.

Ye surely know that Scotland's fate
    Controls the whole wide world's well-being;   10
And well ye know her godly state
    Depends on faith in sin's hell-feeing.[3]
And would ye then, false-hearted men,
    From Scotland rape her dear damnation?
Take from her hell, then take as well
    From space the law of gravitation.

A battle-cry for every session
    In these wild-whirling, heaving last days:
'Discard for ever the Confession;[4]
    Abolish, if you choose, the Fast-days;   20
Let Bible knowledge in school and college
    No more be taught – we'll say, "All's well."
'Twill scarely grieve us, if you but leave us
    For Scotland's use, in Heaven's name, Hell.'

---

1 From *In a Music-Hall and Other Poems* (London, 1891). That speaker of this poem is ascribed a 'parish' which does not exist. Cape Wrath, the extreme north-west tip of the Scottish mainland, was inhabited, even in the nineteenth century, by only a few shepherds and the lighthouse-keepers; hardly enough for a congregation.

2 The immediate occasion of this poem was the trial of William Robertson Smith, Professor of Oriental Languages and Old Testament Exegesis at the Free Church College in Aberdeen, by the Free Church Assembly in 1878. The charge was heresy, for applying historical methods in the analysis of biblical texts, thus calling into question their literal truth. Smith was cleared, but subsequently (and after this poem was written) removed from his post. Strictly orthodox Highland ministers were particularly outraged at Smith's assault (as they saw it) on their religion: such a one is being satirised here. On the origins of the Free Church of Scotland see note to 'The Rev. E. Kirk, B.D.' below.

3 Feeing: wages.

4 That is, the Westminster Confession of Faith: the 1646 statement of Calvinist orthodoxy taken as foundational by the Church of Scotland and other Presbyterian denominations; not the Catholic sacrament. The 'session' of the first line of this stanza is the body of elders governing an individual Presbyterian church.

The Rev. E. Kirk, B.D.[5]

So here I have by happy chance
    A rambling tower of Babel
A crow-stepped, roof-bent, rough-cast manse
    With fruit on every gable.

My glebe is fifty acres round,[6]
    And there my corn is growing;
My poultry cluck with cosy sound;
    I hear my cattle lowing.

Above my plane-trees, gray and high
    My solid steeple rises;   10
It looms between me and the sky
    Like other earthly prizes.

But I have clear and without fail,
    Or trust in harvest's ripe end
For fiars' prices, on the nail,[7]
    Five hundred pounds of stipend:

And naught to do, the truth to speak,
    Save sit and sip my toddy,
And write a sermon once a week,
    And bury anybody.   20

Some half-dozen marriages
    Come in the pairing season;
I visit sick folk if they please –
    Or anything in reason.

The world is here some ages late,
    And stagnant as a marish:
I thank my stars it is my fate
    To have a country parish;

For wearing done with constant use
    For me has no inducement,   30
And city charges play the deuce
    With all a man's amusement.

The sheep are few: somehow to God
    I'll answer how I fed mine…
And there's my gallant salmon-rod,
    And there my famous red-line.

---

5 From *In a Music-Hall and Other Poems* (London, 1891).

6 The 'glebe' is the agricultural land attached to a church, the rent from which supplies the minister's income.

7 Grain prices were fixed every year at the Fiars' Court in order to regulate the level of agricultural rents.

With these last autumn on the Earn[8]
    I killed a thirty-pounder
That seemed amid the lapping fern
    No glossier, nor rounder,   40

Than cased in glass it looks there: see,
    Beneath my gun and pipe-rack –
The gun the earl presented me,[9]
    My seasoned pipes, a ripe stack.

My single life contents me yet;
    I have some oats to scatter:
A barmaid or a ballet-pet
    Is no such deadly matter,

When one is on the sunny side
    Of thirty and an athlete: 50
At thirty-five I'll take a bride,
    And make the narrow path meet,

As many a man has done before,
    The broad one: it will lead me
To live in health and see fourscore,
    And have my son succeed me.

In Romney Marsh [10]

As I went down to Dymchurch Wall,
    I hear the South sing o'er the land;
I saw the yellow sunlight fall
    On knolls where Norman churches stand.[11]

And ringing shrilly, taut and lithe,
    Within the wind a core of sound,

---

8 A salmon river in Perthshire.

9 The relation between the established Church of Scotland with landowners in rural areas was a cause of great contention in nineteenth-century Scotland. Until 1874, rural landowners had the right to impose a minister of their choice on congregations on their estates, despite the nominally self-governing constitution of Presbyterian congregations. The speaker's closeness to an earl aligns his personal moral complacency with this recently-abolished arrangement. Discontent with the subordination of religion to secular power had caused evangelical ministers to split from the official church to form the Free Church of Scotland in the 'Disruption' of 1843.

10 First published in *The Speaker* for 17 March, 1894, p.308.

11 Romney, with Hythe, Hastings, Dover and Sandwich, are the 'Cinque Ports' on the S.E. coast of England, militarily important since the eleventh-century Norman conquest. Dymchurch Wall is the barrier, first built by the Romans but renewed many times since, that protects low-lying Romney from the sea.

The wire from Romney town to Hythe
    Alone its airy journey wound.

A veil of purple vapour flowed
    And trailed its fringe along the Straits;   10
The upper air like sapphire glowed;
    And roses filled Heaven's central gates.

Masts in the offing wagged their tops;
    The swinging waves pealed on the shore;
The saffron beach, all diamond drops
    And beads of surge, prolonged the roar.

As I came up from Dymchurch Wall,
    I saw above the Downs' low crest
The crimson brands of sunset fall,
    Flicker and fade from out the west.   20

Night sank: like flakes of silver fire
    The stars in one great shower came down;
Shrill blew the wind; and shrill the wire
    Rang out from Hythe to Romney town.

The darkly shining salt sea drops
    Streamed as the waves clashed on the shore;
The beach, with all its organ stops
    Pealing again, prolonged the roar.

Song of a Train [12]

A monster taught
To come to hand
Amain,
As swift as thought
Across the land
The train.

The song it sings
Has iron sound;
Its iron wings
Like wheels go round.   10

Crash under bridges,
Flash over ridges,
And vault the downs;
The road is straight –
Nor stile, not gate;
For milestones – towns!

---

12 First published in *The Speaker* for 2 June, 1894, p.614.

Voluminous, vanishing, white,
The steam plume trails;
Parallel streaks of light,
The polished rails.   20

Oh, who can follow?
The little swallow,
The trout of the sky:
But the sun
Is outrun,
And Time passed by.

O'er bosky dens,
By marsh and mead,
Forest and fens
Embodied speed   30
Is clanked and hurled;
O'er rivers and runnels;
And into the earth
And out again
In death and birth
That know no pain,
For the whole round world
Is a warren of railway tunnels.

Hark! hark! hark!
It screams and cleaves the dark;   40
And the subterranean night
Is gilt with smoky light.
Then out again apace
It runs its thundering race,
The monster taught
To come to hand
Amain,
That swift as thought
Speeds through the land
The train.   50

Thirty Bob a Week [13]

I couldn't touch a stop and turn a screw
    And set the blooming world a-work for me,
Like such as cut their teeth – I hope, like you –
    On the handle of a skeleton gold key;
I cut mine on a leek, which I eat it every week:
    I'm a clerk at thirty bob as you can see.

---

13 First published in *The Yellow Book* for July 1894, pp.99–102.

But I don't allow it's luck and all a toss;
 There's no such thing as being starred and crossed;
It's just the power of some to be a boss,
 And the bally power of others to be bossed: 10
I face the music, sir; you bet I ain't a cur;
 Strike me lucky if I don't believe I'm lost!

For like a mole I journey in the dark,
 A-travelling along the underground
From my Pillar'd Halls and broad Suburban Park,
 To come the daily dull official round;
And home again at night with my pipe all alight,
 A-scheming how to count ten bob a pound.

And it's often very cold and very wet,
 And my missis stitches towels for a hunks;[14]   20
And the Pillar'd Halls is half of it to let –
 Three rooms about the size of travelling trunks.
And we cough, my wife and I, to dislocate a sigh,
 When the noisy little kids are in their bunks.

But you never hear her do a growl or whine,
 For she's made of flint and roses, very odd;
And I've got to cut my meaning rather fine,
 Or I'd blubber, for I'm made of greens and sod:
So p'r'aps we are in Hell for all that I can tell,
 And lost and damn'd and served up hot to God. 30

I ain't blaspheming, Mr. Silver-tongue;
 I'm saying things a bit beyond your art:
Of all the rummy starts you ever sprung,[15]
 Thirty bob a week's the rummiest start!
With your science and your books and your the'ries about spooks,[16]
 Did you ever hear of looking in your heart?

I didn't mean your pocket, Mr., no:
 I mean that having children and a wife,
With thirty bob on which to come and go,
 Isn't dancing to the tabor and the fife: 40
When it doesn't make you drink, by Heaven! it makes you think,
 And notice curious items about life.

I step into my heart and there I meet
 A god-almighty devil singing small,

---

14 Hunks: a miser.

15 I.e., 'of all the strange goings-on you ever discovered'. For this usage, see Little Swills at the
  inquest in Dickens's *Bleak House* chapter 11: 'Being asked what he thinks of the proceedings,
  characterizes them (his strength lying in a slangular direction) as "a rummy start"'.

16 Spiritualism was much in vogue in certain intellectual circles in the last decade of the
  nineteenth century, attracting (for example) W.B. Yeats and Arthur Conan Doyle.

Who would like to shout and whistle in the street,
      And squelch the passers flat against the wall;
If the whole world was a cake he had the power to take,
      He would take it, ask for more, and eat them all.

And I meet a sort of simpleton beside,
      The kind that life is always giving beans;   50
With thirty bob a week to keep a bride
      He fell in love and married in his teens:
At thirty bob he stuck; but he knows it isn't luck:
      He knows the seas are deeper than tureens.

And the god-almighty devil and the fool
      That meet me in the High Street on the strike,
When I walk about my heart a-gathering wool,
      Are my good and evil angels if you like.
And both of them together in every kind of weather
      Ride me like a double-seated bike.   60

That's rough a bit and needs its meaning curled.
      But I have a high old hot un in my mind –
A most engrungious[17] notion of the world,
      That leaves behind your lightning 'rithmetic behind:
I give it at a glance when I say 'There ain't no chance,
      Nor nothing of the lucky-lottery kind.'

And it's this way that I make it out to be:
      No fathers, mothers, countries, climates – none;
No Adam was responsible for me,
      Nor society, nor systems, nary one: 70
A little sleeping seed, I woke – I did, indeed –
      A million years before the blooming sun.

I woke because I thought the time had come;
      Beyond my will there was no other cause;
And everywhere I found myself at home,
      Because I chose to be the thing I was;
And in whatever shape of mollusc or of ape
      I always went according to the laws.

I was the love that chose my mother out;
      I joined two lives and from the union burst;   80
My weakness and my strength without a doubt
      Are mine alone for ever from the first:
It's just the very same with a difference in the name
      As 'Thy will be done.' You say it if you durst!

---

17 The speaker's mistake for 'egregious', or his neologism for something like it.

They say it daily up and down the land
    As easy as you take a drink, it's true;
But the difficultest go to understand,
    And the difficultest job a man can do,
Is to come it brave and meek with thirty bob a week,
    And feel that that's the proper thing for you.   90

It's a naked child against a hungry wolf;
    It's playing bowls upon a splitting wreck;
It's walking on a string across a gulf
    With millstones fore-and-aft about your neck;
But the thing is daily done by many and many a one;
    And we fall, face forward, fighting, on the deck.

A Loafer [18]

I hang about the streets all day
    All night I hang about;
I sleep a little when I may,
    But rise betimes the morning's scout;
For through the year I always hear
    Afar, aloft, a ghostly shout.

My clothes are worn to threads and loops;
    My skin shows here and there;
About my face like seaweed droops
    My tangled beard, my tangled hair;   10
From cavernous and shaggy brows
    My stony eyes untroubled stare.

I move from eastern wretchedness
    Through Fleet Street and the Strand;
And as the pleasant people press
    I touch them softly with my hand,
Perhaps to know that still I go
    Alive about a living land.

For, far in front the clouds are riven;
    I hear the ghostly cry,   20
As if a still voice fell from heaven
    To where sea-whelmed the drowned folks lie
In sepulchres no tempest stirs
    And only eyeless things pass by.

In Piccadilly spirits pass:
    Oh, eyes and cheeks that glow!
Oh, strength and comeliness! Alas,

---

18 From *Ballads and Songs* (London, 1894).

The lustrous health is earth I know
From shrinking eyes that recognise
          No brother in my rags and woe.   30

I know no handicraft, no art,
          But I have conquered fate;
For I have chosen the better part,
          And neither hope, nor fear, nor hate.
With placid breath on pain of death,
          My certain alms, alone I wait.

And daily, nightly comes the call,
          The pale, unechoing note,
The faint 'Aha!' sent from the wall
          Of heaven, but from no ruddy throat   40
Of human breed or seraph's seed,
          A phantom voice that cries by rote.

A Ballad in Blank Verse [19]

His father's house looked out across a firth
Broad-bosomed like a mere,[20] beside a town
Far in the North, where Time could take his ease,
And Change hold holiday; where Old and New
Weltered upon the border of the world.

'Oh now,' he thought – a youth whose sultry eyes,
Bold brow and wanton mouth were not all lust,
But haunted from within and from without
By memories, visions, hopes, divine desires –
'Now may my life beat out upon this shore   10
A prouder music than the winds and waves
Can compass in their haughtiest moods. I need
No world more spacious than the region here:
The foam-embroidered firth, a purple path
For argosies that still on pinions speed,
Or fiery-hearted cleave with iron limbs
And bows precipitous the pliant sea;
The sloping shores that fringe the velvet tides
With heavy bullion and with golden lace
Of restless pebble woven and fine spun sand;   20
The villages that sleep the winter through,
And, wakening with the spring, keep festival
All summer and all autumn: this grey town

---

19 First published in *Ballads and Songs* (London, 1894), under the title 'A Ballad in Blank Verse
    of the Making of a Poet'; under this title in later collections of Davidson's work.

20 Davidson was brought up from the age of nine in Greenock, where his father was a minister
    for the Evangelical Union; so the firth evoked here is that of the Clyde.

That pipes the morning up before the lark
With shrieking steam, and from a hundred stalks
Lacquers the sooty sky; where hammers clang
On iron hulls, and cranes in harbours creak
Rattle and swing, whole cargoes on their necks;
Where men sweat gold that others hoard or spend,
And lurk like vermin in their narrow streets: 30
This old grey town, this firth, the further strand
Spangled with hamlets, and the wooded steeps,
Whose rocky tops behind each other press,
Fantastically carved like antique helms
High-hung in heaven's cloudy armoury,
Is world enough for me. Here daily dawn
Burns through the smoky east; with fire-shod feet
The sun treads heaven, and steps from hill to hill
Downward before the night that still pursues
His crimson wake; here winter plies his craft,   40
Soldering the years with ice; here spring appears
Caught in a leafless brake, her garland torn,
Breathless with wonder, and the tears half-dried
Upon her rosy cheek; here summer comes
And wastes his passion like a prodigal
Right royally; and here her golden gains
Free-handed as a harlot autumn spends;
And here are men to know, women to love.'
His father, woman-hearted, great of soul,
Wilful and proud, save for one little shrine   50
That held a pinch-beck cross, had closed and barred
The many mansions of his intellect.[21]

'My son,' he said – to him, fresh from his firth
And dreams at evening; while his mother sat,
She also with her dingy crucifix,
And feeble rushlight, praying for her boy –
'My son, have you decided for the Lord?
Your mother's heart and mine are exercised
For your salvation. Will you turn to Christ?
Now, young and strong, you hanker for the world;   60
But think: the longest life must end at last,
And then come Death and Judgment. Are you fit
To meet your God before the great white throne?
If on the instant Death should summon you,
What doom would the Eternal Judge pronounce –
'Depart from me' or 'Sit on My right hand'?
In life it is your privilege to choose,
But after death you have no choice at all.
Die unbelieving, and in endless woe

---

21 John 14.2: 'In my Father's house are many mansions…I go to prepare a place for you' (King James Bible).

You must believe throughout eternity.   70
My son, reject not Christ; he pleads through me;
The Holy Spirit uses my poor words.
How would it fill your mother's heart and mine,
And God's great heart with joy unspeakable,
Were you, a helpless sinner, now to cry,
'Lord I believe: help Thou mine unbelief'.'[22]
He clenched his teeth; his blood, fulfilled of brine,
Of sunset, and his dreams, boomed in his ears.
A vision rose before him; and the sound
Husky and plaintive of his father's voice   80
Seemed unintelligible and afar.
He saw Apollo on the Dardan beach:
The waves lay still; the winds hung motionless,
And held their breath to hear the rebel god,
Conquered and doomed, with stormy sobbing song,
And crashing discords of his golden lyre,
Reluctantly compel the walls of Troy,
Unquarried and unhewn, in supple lines
And massive strength to rise about the town.[23]

A quavering voice shattered his fantasy: 90
His father's pleading done, his mother cried,
With twitching forehead, scalding tears that broke
The seal of wrinkled eyelids, mortised hands
Where knuckles jutted white: 'Almighty God!
Almighty God! – Oh save my foolish boy.'
He glanced about the dreary parlour, clenched
His teeth, and once again his blood, fulfilled
Of brine, of sunset, and of dreams, exhaled
A vision. While his parents clutched their hearts,
Expecting his conversion instantly,   100
And listened if perchance they might o'erhear
The silent heavens burst into applause
Over one lost repentant, he beheld
The Cyprian Aphrodite,[24] all one blush
And glance of passion, from the violet sea
Step inland, fastening as she went her zone.
She reached a gulf that opened in the ground
Deep in a leafless wood and waited there,
Battling the darkness with her wistful eyes.
Then suddenly she blanched and blushed again,   110

22 Mark 9.24: 'And straightway the father of the child cried out, and said with tears, Lord, I
    believe; help thou mine unbelief' (King James Bible).
23 Zeus punished Apollo and Poseidon for a failed rebellion by making them servants to King
    Laomedon, for whom they built the city of Troy, on the Dardanelles Strait in Asia Minor:
    hence 'Dardan beach' in line 82. Apollo was the god of music, poetry, and the arts generally,
    among other things.
24 Aphrodite, the Greek goddess of love, was born in the sea and came ashore on Cyprus. The
    'zone' mentioned in line 106 is the girdle or belt that made her irresistible to men.

And her divinely pulsing body bowed
With outstretched arms over the yawning earth.
Straightway Adonis,[25] wonderstruck and pale,
Stole from the sepulchre, a moonbeam wraith.
But Aphrodite with a golden cry
That echoed round the world and shook the stars,
Caught him and thawed him in her warm embrace,
And murmuring kisses bore him to her bower.
Then all the trees were lit with budding flames
Of emerald, and all the meads and leas,   120
Coverts and shady places, glades and dells,
Odoured and dimly stained with opening flowers,
And loud with love-songs of impassioned birds,
Became the shrine and hostel of the spring.

His wanton face grew sweet and wonderful,
Beholding Aphrodite. But they thought –
His father and his mother, sick with hope –
It was the Holy Ghost's effectual call.[26]
Entranced he rose and glided from the room;
They, undeceived, like little children sobbed.   130

Slowly he broke his mother's tender heart,
Until she died in anguish for his sins.
His father then besought him on his knees,
With tears and broken speech and pleading hands.

'My son,' he said, 'you open all the wounds
Daily and nightly of the Lord of Heaven:
You killed your mother, you are killing me:
Is it not sin enough, poor foolish boy?'

For this was in the North, where Time stands still
And Change holds holiday, where Old and New   140
Welter upon the border of the world,
And savage faith works woe.

---

25 Aphrodite rescues Adonis as a baby when his mother is turned into a Myrrh tree (don't
   ask); leaves him in the care of Persephone in the underworld; then returns for him once he
   has grown into a handsome youth, whence a struggle ensures with Persephone, who doesn't
   want to give him up; this is resolved when Zeus judges that he should spend half the year
   with Persephone in Hades and half with Aphrodite in the over-world. Hence the seasons,
   winter and summer: the return of Adonis causing Spring is dramatised in the following
   lines. That something very like this myth, with its attendant fertility rituals, also appears
   in Egyptian and many other ancient religions, had been established in 1890 by the Scottish
   classical scholar James Frazer in the first two volumes of *The Golden Bough*. Implicit, though
   never stated, in *The Golden Bough* is that the story of Christ's death and resurrection is other
   version of the same myth. This may inform Davidson's use of Adonis and Aphrodite as a
   source of his hero's mental resistance to the claims of orthodox Christianity in this poem.
26 'Effectual calling' is the moment in the Calvinist's spiritual life where he or she becomes
   convinced (though God's agency) of his or her state of sin and embraces Christ as his or her
   salvation from it.

                              'Oh, let it be!'
The dreamer cried, and rushing from the house
He sought the outcast Aphrodite, dull,
Tawdry, unbeautiful, but still divine
Even in the dark streets of a noisome port.[27]

At times he wrote his dreams, rebellious still
That he should be constrained to please himself
As one is eased by roaring on the rack.
Desperate he grew, and wandering by his firth,   150
Exclaimed against the literature he loved.
'Lies, lies!' he muttered. 'And the noblest, lies!
Why should we lie? what penalty is this –
To write, and sing, and think, and speculate,
Hag-ridden by ideas, or 'twixt the shafts
Like broken horses, blinded, bitted, reined,
And whipped about the world by steel-tagged creeds!'

Wasted and sad with wantonness, and wan
With fantasy – a furnace seven times hot,
Wherein he tried all things; and wrung with woe   160
To see his father dying for his sake,
And by the memory of his mother's death,
He yielded tamely and professed himself
Convinced of sin but confident in Christ.

Then to the table of the Lord he went,[28]
Ghastly, with haunted eyes that shone, and limbs
That scarcely bore him, like a heretic
Led to the chamber where tormentors stood
Muffled and silent, earnest to explore,
With cunning flames and cords and engines dire,   170
The sunken wells of pain, the gloomy gulfs
Obscurely wallowing in the souls of men.

In solemn tones the grey-haired presbyter –
'This is My body which is given for you,
This do in memory of Me.'

                              The boy,
Whose blood within him clamoured like a storm,
Uttered a smothered cry and rose, but lo!
The happy triumph on his father's face!
'Why do I not die now? like husks of corn,
The bread, like vitriol the sip of wine!   180

----

27 The cult of Aphrodite in ancient times involved ritual prostitution in her temples. The ritual
    element was presumably missing in Victorian Greenock.
28 I.e., to communion.

I eat and drink damnation to myself[29]
To give my father's troubled spirit peace.'
The stealthy elders creaked about the floor,
Guiding the cup and platter; looking down,
The children in the gallery smirked and watched
Who took the deepest draught; and ancient dames
Crumpled their folded handkerchiefs, and pressed
With knuckly fingers sprays of southernwood.

Ah! down no silver beam the Holy Grail
Glided from Heaven, a crimson cup that throbbed   190
As throbs the heart divine; no aching sounds
Of scarce-heard music stole into the aisle,
Like disembodied pulses beating love.

But in the evening by the purple firth
He walked, and saw brown locks upon the brine,
And pale hands beckon him to come away,
Where mermaids, with their harps and golden combs,
Sit throned upon the carven antique poops
Of treasure-ships, and soft sea-dirges sing
Over the green-gilt bones of mariners.   200
He saw vast forms and dreadful draw aside
The floating crimson curtains of the west
With far-off thunderous rustle, and threaten him
From heaven's porch; beneath his feet the earth
Quaked like a flame-sapped bridge that spans the wave
Of fiery Phlegethon; and in the wind
An icy voice was borne from some waste place,
Piercing him to the marrow. Night came down,
And still he wandered helpless by the firth,
That under clouded skies gleamed black and smooth 210
Like cooling pitch. But when the moon broke out
And poured athwart the glittering ebony
Torrents of molten silver, hurtling thoughts
Trooped forth disorderly.

                                  'I'll have no creed,'
He said. 'Though I be weakest of my kind,
I'll have no creed. Lo! there is but one creed,
The vulture-pheonix that for ever tears
The soul of man in chains of flesh and blood
Rivetted to the earth; the clime, the time,
Change but its plumage. Gluttonous bird of prey,   220
More fatal than all famines, plagues and wars,

---

29   In I Corinthians 11.27–9, Paul spells out this penalty for those who take communion in an
'unworthy' spiritual state: 'For he that eateth and drinketh unworthily, eateth and drinketh
damnation to himself, not discerning the Lord's body' (i.e. as represented by the bread and
wine of the service).

I wrench you off, although my soul go too!
With bloody claws and dripping beak unfleshed,
Spread out your crackling vans that darken heaven;
Rabid and curst, fly yelping where you list!
Henceforth I shall be God; for consciousness
Is God: I suffer; I am God: this Self,
That all the universe combines to quell,
Is greater than the universe; and *I*
Am that I am.[30] To think and not be God? –   230
It cannot be! Lo! I shall spread this news,
And gather to myself a band of Gods –
An army, and go forth against the world,
Conquering and to conquer. Snowy steppes
Of Muscovy, frost-bound Siberian plains,
And scalding sands of Ethiopia,
Where groans oppress the bosom of the wind,
And men in gangs are driven to icy graves,
Or lashed to brutish slavery under suns
Whose sheer beams scorch and flay like burning blades,   240
Shall ring, enfranchised, with divine delight.
At home, where millions mope, in labyrinths
Of hideous streets astray without a clue,
Unfed, unsexed, unsoulled, unhelped, I bring
Life, with the gospel, 'Up, quit you like Gods!'

Possessed with this, upon his father's hour
Of new-found happiness he burst, and cried,
'Father, my father, I have news to tell!
I know the word that shall uproot the thrones
Of oldest monarchs, and for ever lay   250
The doting phantom with the triple crown:[31]
A word dynamic with the power of doom
To blast conventicles and parliaments,
Unsolder federations, crumble states,
And in the fining pot cast continents.
A word that shall a new beginning be,
And out of chaos make a world again.
Behold, my father! We, who heretofore,
Fearful and weak, deep-dyed in Stygian creeds
Against the shafts of pain and woe, have walked   260
The throbbing earth, most vulnerable still
In every pore and nerve; we, trembling things,
Who but an hour ago in frantic dread
Burned palsied women, and with awe beheld
A shaven pate mutter a latin spell
Over a biscuit: we, even we are Gods!

---

30 Exodus 3.14: 'And God said unto Moses, I AM THAT I AM...'
31 I.e. the Papacy. It is significant that the hero expresses his rejection of conventional religion
    as a *continuation* of the protestant project rather than its negation.

Nothing beneath, about us, or above
Is higher than ourselves. Henceforth degree,
Authority, religion, government,
Employer and employed are obsolete   270
As penal torture or astrology.
The mighty spirit of the universe,
Conscious in us, shall'...

                              Suddenly aware
Of gaping horror on his father's face,
He paused; and he, the old man, white as death,
With eyes like stars upon the crack of doom,
Rose quaking; and 'The unpardonable sin! –
The unpardonable sin!' he whispered hoarse.
'This was the sin of Lucifer – to make
Himself God's equal. If I may, my son –   280
If it be God's will, I shall go to hell
To be beside you. I shall be there first:
I have not many hours to live. I thought –
Here as I sat beside your mother's chair –
I – my boy! – I wander somewhat. Let me –
I'll sit again. – Let me remember now
How happy I have been to-day, my son
A member of the Church of Christ, and I
Beside him at Communion, seeing him
And seeing at the window of heaven the face   290
Of her who bore him, sweet and glorified.
At home I sit and think that, as he lived
Most absolute in sin, he shall, like Paul
Be as insatiable in doing well.
I think how, when my time comes, I shall go
And tell his mother of his holy life
Of labour for the Lord; and then I see
My boy at last appear before the Throne.
'By what right com'st thou here?' the Judge demands.
He hangs his head; but round about him throng   300
A crowd of souls, who cry 'He was our staff;
He led us here.' 'Sit thou on My right hand,'
The sentence falls; and we, my wife and I,
Awaiting you. ... There came a devil in
Wearing the likeness of my boy, and said
He was predestined for a reprobate,
A special vessel of the wrath of God.
Holy he was begotten; holy born;
With tearful prayers attended all his life;
Cherished with scrupulous love, and shown the path 310
To heaven by her who ne'er shall see him there;
For out of this there comes but blasphemy
And everlasting Hell. ... Ah! who are these?

My soul is hustled by a multitude
Of wild-eyed prodigals and wrenched about.
Boy, help me to blaspheme. I cannot face
Without you her that nursed you at her breast.
Let us curse God together and going forth
Plunge headlong in the waves, and be at rest
In hell for evermore. Some end to this! –   320
This awful gnawing pain in every part!
Or certainty that this will never end!
This, now, is Hell! ... There was a paltry way
Of fooling God some casuists hit upon.
How went it? Yes, that God did fore-ordain
And so foreknew that those who should believe
Should enter glory of their own free-will.
Ah! pink of blasphemies that makes of God
An impotent spectator! Let us two
Believe in this, and that shall damn us best! ...   330
I dare, but cannot; for the Lord of Hosts,
The God of my salvation, is my God:
He, ere the world began, predestined me
To life eternal:[32] to the bitter end
Against my will I persevere, a saint;
And find my will at length the will of God.
What is my son, and what the hopes and fears
Of my dead wife and me before the flame
Of God's pure purpose, His, from whose dread eyes
The earth and heaven fled and found no place!   340
Beside the crystal river I shall walk
For ever with the Lord. The city of gold,
The jasper walls thereof, the gates of pearl,
The bright foundation-stones of emerald,
Of sapphire, chrysoprase, of every gem,[33]
And the high triumph of unending day
Shall be but wildfire on a summer eve
Beside the exceeding glory of delight,
That shall entrance me with the constant thought
Of how in Hell through all eternity   350
My son performs the perfect will of God.[34]
Amen. I come, Lord Jesus. If his sin
Be not to death ... Heaven open!'...

---

32   The doctrine that God has already chosen, at the start of time, those who will be saved
     ('predestination'), is central to Augustinian versions of Christianity including Calvinism. It
     seems not to have been a doctrine subscribed to by Davidson's own father, however.
33   This is St. John's description of the New Jerusalem in Revelation 21.19: 'And the foundations
     of the wall of the city were garnished with all manner of precious stones. The first foundation
     was jasper; the second, sapphire; the third, a chalcedony; the fourth, an emerald...';
     'chrysoprase' is a type of chalcedony, another precious stone.
34   A consequence of predestination is that the sinner, without intending to, is fulfilling God's
     plan for humankind just as much as the saint.

Thus he died;
For this was in the North where Time stands still,
And Change holds holiday; where Old and New
Welter upon the borders of the world,
And savage creeds can kill.

           The trembling boy
Knelt down, but dared to think, 'A dreadful death!
To die believing in so dull a God,
A useless Hell, a jewel-huckster's Heaven!'   360
Forthwith it flashed like light across his mind,
'If it be terrible into the hands
Of the living God to fall, how much more dire
To sicken face to face, like our sad age,
Chained to an icy corpse of deity,
Decked though it be and painted and embalmed!'

He took his father's hand and kissed his brow
And, weeping like a woman, watched him long;
Then softly rose and stepped into the night.
He stood beside the house a little space,   370
Hearing the wind speak low in whispers quaint,
An irresponsible and wandering voice.
But soon he hastened to the water's edge;
For from the shore there came sea-minstrelsy
Of waves that broke upon the hollow beach,
With liquid sound of pearling surges blent,
Cymbals, and muffled drums and dulcimers.

Sparse diamonds in the dead-black dome of night,
A few stars lit the moon-deserted air
And swarthy heaving of the firth obscure.   380
He, knowing every rock and sandy reach,
All night unfalteringly walked the shore,
While tempest after tempest rose and fell
Within his soul, that like an o'er-wrought sea
Laboured to burst its continent and hang
Some glittering trophy high among the stars.
At last the fugal music of the tide,
With cymbals, muffled drums, and dulcimers,
Into his blood a rhythmic measure beat,
And gave his passion scope and way with words.   390

'How unintelligent, how blind am I,
How vain!' he cried. 'A God? a mole, a worm!
An engine frail, of brittle bones conjoined;
With tissue packed; with nerves, transmitting force;
And driven by water, thick and coloured red:
That may for some few pence a day be hired

In thousands to be shot at! Oh, a God,
That lies and steals and murders! Such a God
Passionate, dissolute, incontinent!
A God that starves in thousands, and ashamed,   400
Or shameless in the workhouse lurks; that sweats
In mines and foundries! An enchanted God,
Whose nostrils in a palace breathe perfume,
Whose cracking shoulders hold the palace up,
Whose shoeless feet are rotting in the mire!
A God who said a little while ago,
"I'll have no creed;" and of his Godhood straight
Patched up a creed unwittingly – with which
He went and killed his father. Subtle lie
That tempts our weakness always; magical,   410
And magically changed to suit the time!
"Lo, ye shall be as Gods!" – the serpent's cry –
Rose up again, "Ye shall be sons of God;"
And now the glosing word is in the air,
"Thou shalt be God by simply taking thought."
And if one could, believing this, convert
A million to be upright, chaste and strong,
Gentle and tolerant, it were but to found
A new religion, bringing new offence,
Setting the child against the father still.   420
Some thought imprisons us; we set about
To bring the world within the woven spell:
Our ruthless creeds that bathe the earth in blood
Are moods by alchemy made dogmas of –
The petrifaction of a metaphor.
No creed for me! I am a man apart:
A mouthpiece for the creeds of all the world;
A soulless life that angels may possess
Or demons haunt, wherein the foulest things
May loll at ease beside the loveliest;   430
A martyr for all mundane moods to tear;
The slave of every passion, and the slave
Of heat and cold, of darkness and of light;
A trembling lyre for every wind to sound.[35]
I am a man set by to overhear
The inner harmony, the very tune
Of Nature's heart; to be a thoroughfare
For all the pageantry of Time; to catch
The mutterings of the Spirit of the Hour
And make them known; and of the lowliest   440
To be the minister, and therefore reign
Prince of the powers of the air, lord of the world
And master of the sea. Within my heart

---

35 The Aeolian lyre, a stringed instrument hung up outside and 'played' by the wind, had been an image of the poet since the romantics.

I'll gather all the universe, and sing
As sweetly as the spheres; and I shall be
The first of men to understand himself ...
And lo! to give me courage comes the dawn,
Crimsoning the smoky east; and still the sun
With fire-shod feet shall step from hill to hill
Downward before the night; winter shall ply   450
His ancient craft, soldering the years with ice;
And spring appear, caught in a leafless brake,
Breathless with wonder and the tears half-dried
Upon her rosy cheek; summer shall come
And waste his passion like a prodigal
Right royally; and autumn spend her gold
Free-handed as a harlot; men to know,
Women to love are waiting everywhere.'

Waiting[36]

Within unfriendly walls
    We starve – or starve by stealth.
Oxen fatten in their stalls;
    You guard the harrier's health:
They never can be criminals,
    And can't compete for wealth.
        From the mansion and the palace
           Is there any help or hail
        For the tenants of the alleys,
           Of the workhouse and the jail?[37]   10

Though lands await our toil,
    And earth half-empty rolls,
Cumberers of English soil,
    We cringe for orts and doles –
Prosperity's accustomed foil,
    Millions of useless souls.
        In the gutters and the ditches
           Human vermin festering lurk –
        We, the rust upon your riches;
           We, the flaw in all your work.   20

---

36 First published in *The Chap-Book* for 15 January, 1897. The idea that urban poverty and unemployment could be solved by facilitating emigration to the 'half-empty' colonies was a recurrent one from the 1830s through to the early 20th Century. Campaigns to put this into practice never translated into government policy, however, and emigrants to the colonies from mainland Britain tended to be from the skilled working class who could pay their own fares, rather than the unskilled urban destitute described in this poem.

37 In place of financial relief from parish funds, Victorian Britain made support for the unemployed conditional on labour performed in 'workhouses', where conditions were made deliberately unpleasant to deter people from claiming their 'support' in the first place.

Come down from where you sit;
    We look to you for aid.
Take us from the miry pit,
    And lead us out undismayed:
Say, 'Even you, outcast, unfit,
      Forward with sword and spade!'
        And myriads of us idle
            Would thank you through our tears,
        Though you drove us with a bridle,
           And a whip about our ears!   30

From cloudy cape to cape
    The teaming waters seethe;
Golden grain and purple grape
    The regions overwreathe.
Will no one help us to escape?
    We scarce have room to breathe.
      You might try to understand us:
        We are waiting night and day
      For a captain to command us,
        And the word we must obey.   40

The Testament of an Empire Builder [38]

Parable.

And still he must go
Through depths profound,
O'er heights of snow,
On virgin ground
To find a grave
To find a grave.

For he knows very well
He must trample out
Through Heaven and Hell,
With never a doubt,
A way of his own
The world about.[39]

A protagonist came into the market-place, and began to sing songs that had not been sung before. As soon as they perceived that the songs were new, the people asked him why he did not sing the old songs.

The Protagonist answered, 'I am dissatisfied with the old songs and wish to sing new ones.'

With that they held their peace and listened attentively, and often with approval, because the new songs, like the old, contained many expressions of delight and hope.

---

38 Published in book form, introduced by the 'Parable' included here, in London, 1902.
39 This epigraph consists of the last lines of an earlier poem, 'The Pioneer', first published in *The Saturday Review* for 12 February, 1898.

Besides it was exactly the superficial complexion of things that this people, like most peoples, loved to contemplate. Wherefore when pain and terror, which are the blood and nerve, the entrails and inmost complexion of the world, began more fully to inform the Protagonist's songs, the people bade him cease.

'We want the old songs,' they cried, 'The old lullabies, the old flatteries; our hearts ache for these; we never tire of these.'

It was indeed the case that the poetical imagination of this people dwelt fondly in the Library, in the Cathedral, and in the Museum of Antiquities, haunts of pallid legends, barren ideals, and dead gods: pallid, barren and dead at least to this people, because the racial desire of comfort, even more than centuries of wistful loving-kindness, ineffectual enough against the facts of life, had leached out of legend, ideal and god all anguish and terror, the actual base of such.

'I should like to sing my new songs,' the Protagonist said. 'It is true I come from homes and palaces and beautiful lands, with happiness and mirth, pleasure and enchantment; but I have also been in the wilderness, the prison-house, the torture-chamber, and the dark places with solitude, travial and pain, bitter laughter and despair. I have told you The Testaments of the Vivisector and of The Man Forbid.[40] I am now about to tell you THE TESTAMENT OF THE EMPIRE-BUILDER. Afterwards I wish to tell you the Testaments of the Harlot, the Artist, the Christian, the Mendicant, the Criminal, the Millionaire, the Proletarian, the Convertite, the Evolutionist, the Deliverer, and others that are eager to be told. I understand that these Testaments are likely to displease religious and irreligious minds, the pessimist and the optimist alike. I therefore invite the attention of the free intelligences, and, it may be, of intelligences, which, although not free, are yet able to elude the vigilance of whatever creed, system or theory has them in charge.'

A huge moiety of the crowd drew off, and thought no more of him. Of those who remained, the majority, whether they approved or not, honoured themselves and him by their attention; but some began to stone him with right goodwill.

'I was broken on the wheel in Thule twelve years ago,' he told them cheerfully. 'The executioner, knowing his business and loving it well, proceeded in a leisurely manner that I might realise and savour the torture, and be maddened with anticipation of each ensuing stroke. But when he had smitten me on the breast, and left me for dead, there came one who unbound the chains which bound me to the wheel. Whereupon, although my limbs were broken and my bosom staved in, having within me that Material power formerly fabled of the gods, I arose and came down here into the market-place and began to sing again. A man who has been broken on the wheel no longer feels pain. Your stones hurt me not; but the lapidation incommodes me much. Desist, I pray you.'

However, his reflective auditors with placid austerity counselled him against petulance: and those who stoned him insisted with great good-humour that they were not stoning him.

'We are only trying to make out your meaning,' they said.

And so it seemed to them, for they were very honest people. But in the world where this happened it is in the Nature of Things that the apparent deed is often entirely different from the actual one; so that men constantly kill each other without knowing it.

---

40   These two poems were each published in book form the previous year, 1901. These proclaimed themselves 'the first of a series of poems [...] in this form'. None of those mentioned here as forthcoming represent actual works by Davidson, but *Testament of an Empire-Builder* was followed by *The Testament of a Prime Minister* (1904), 'The Testament of Sir Simon Simplex Concerning Automobilism' (in the journal *The New Age* for 28 March 1908) and *The Testament of John Davidson* (1908).

The Protagonist, reassured, reassumed his Testaments; and his audience, the reflective portion having now withdrawn, continued to make out his meaning by stoning him.

When they had killed the Protagonist they were struck with astonishment, and exclaimed to each other. 'Why, the Protagonist is dead! Who can have done this?'

'It is the Nature of Things that killed him,' declared an ancient, which had been the first to throw a stone at him.

'I wish he had finished his Testaments,' said he who had given him the death-blow. 'What were they about? I suppose we shall never know.'

'I know,' said the ancient. 'They were parts of one great song.'

'What is the name of this great song?'

'Men of judgment who know its name never tell it; because to hear or to speak the name of this song is to be filled with desire to sing it, and no Protagonist or man will ever be allowed to do so.'

'What hinders the singing of this song?'

'The Nature of Things.'

But the truth of this parable has not been established yet.

*****

'We are the mightiest,
The heirs of Rome; and with the power there lies
A ruthless obligation on our souls
To be despotic for the world's behoof.
Ruthless I say, because the destinies
Admit no compromise: we must be first,
Though everlasting war cement each course
Of empire with our blood …

To break with all the ragged past, and be
The demiurge of order and a time
Stamped in my image — is to chafe
Mankind, and mark my power and daring, carved
In deep amazement and a world-wide frown,
Is to read triumph in a storm of hate.'[41]

You must not let me lie so long … Three score
And ten! … Self-knowledge ends in self-contempt:
Man can be too familiar with himself …
Let me not lie so long: recumbent nerve
Evolves sublime designs, quintessences
Of wit, and strokes of power, when the veins swell
And tightened muscles twang; but in my head
The turbid lees of blood settle and fume
And harass me with dreams. Last night I saw
The Universe in visions more intense   10
Than any scene my memory can recall

---

41 These lines, serving as the epigraph to the poem itself, are from Davidson's 1901 play *Self's the Man: a Tragi-Comedy.*

Of things beheld and done; while voices quaint
Or awful in my sleeping ears conversed.
I seemed to pace beside an olive brook
That slumbered in a wood: the water bore
A wandering arabesque of harvest leaves,
Crimson and saffron, ebony, burnished gold,
And in its bosom, coyly stowed away,
Fantastic shadows, odds and ends of cloud,
Sunbeams and purple patches of the sky.   20
Under a chestnut-tree whose candles all
Were out, and sconces broad from green to bronze
Transmuted, Nennook, frosty-furred,[42] addressed
A group of beasts: my lord, the Elephant,
The Lion, grave and watchful as a man;
Aboma, umber-coloured, ringed and pied
With sable stains and silver, worshipped once,
A dreaded deity, in Anahuac;[43]
The Vulture-King, with wings as innocent
In dye as fleurs-de-lis, yet guilt-adorned,   30
With rose and violet and daffodil
Engrailed upon his head and sinewy neck:
Splendour and beauty are the flower and scent,
The crown and sign of epicures in blood.
Beside these humbly knelt the Groundling Ape;
The rusty Hackney, truant from his cab;
The patient Mastiff; and the placid Skunk
In stalwart odour strong against the world.
Said frosty Nennook, swaying plantigrade[44]
Upon his fur-shod soles, "The rumour runs   40
That as the rational, unbestial skill
Of Man develops energies profound
In Matter latent, all the Earth must pass
Beneath His feeble heel; and all the tribes
Of noble beasts in native strength superb
Be rooted out by Him, whether they range
Malarial marshes; brilliant deserts laced
With ivory skeletons; precipitous
Ascents; remote ravines; fens, valleys, coasts
Inclement; steaming jungles, spicy hot,   50
Inwove with gorgeous flowers, with lustrous wings;
The frozen sea, the silent waste of snow,
Iceberg and red volcano north and south:
Regions inhibited to Him unarmed,
By Him untenantable were they His,
As even the envied quarters of the world

42 'Candles' referring to the upright flower-heads of the chestnut; 'Sconces' are candlesticks
    with a screen to shelter the light. 'Nennook' is the Inuit name for the polar bear.
43 *Boa Aboma* is a large South American snake; Anahuac is the Aztec name for the Valley of
    Mexico, the heart of the Aztec empire.
44 Plantigrade: of an animal, one that walks on the soles of its feet (as bears do).

For ever are to miscreated Man
Of mean inventions stripped: the fangless wretch!
Unhappy, clawless, hoofless, tailless, polled[45]
Betrayer of the beasts; infirm, malign   60
Usurper, only strong in artifice!
How think you? Is it true?"

                                        The Mastiff bayed,
'Indubitably Man will oust you all.
I know Him — selfish as the jealous god
His orient outcasts made:[46] no perch of Earth
Will in the end escape His ruthless tools.'
'Alas,' cried Nennook., 'Shall the Heavenly Dance[47]
Illumine swarthy skies with sheaves of light,
Masses of splendid fire in diverse hues,
Impurpled carmine, ruby splashed with gold,   70
Deep violet, sapphire, emerald, orange, red,
Enarched or pulsing crystalline athwart
The darksome firmament; and none of us,
Huge-footed, serpent-headed Polar Bears
To revel in the Arctic glory, feast
On blubbered seals that slumber on the floes,
Outspeed the salmon in his element,
And for the Kingdom of the icy strand
Defeat in battle swift the sullen Morse?'[48]

A Flea, ensconced behind the Mastiff's ear,   80
Chirruped aloud, 'Nennook, my friend, take heart!
I, for example, must be soundly squelched;
But the Idea of the Flea remains,
For race continues always: permanence
Of species is established theory.'

'Established nonsense, neighbour! Hold your tongue,'
Snorted the domineering Elephant.
'Few are the species that endure beyond
Their geologic period. Answer this.
Where are the giant beasts of ancient fame,   90
The Labyrinthodon, the Plesiosaur,
Dinornis, Mammoth, Megatherium?'[49]

'Ay, and the Great Auk and the Dodo,[50] both

---

45 Polled: that is, lacking horns.
46 Orient outcasts: i.e., the Israelites, creators of the Old Testament.
47 Heavenly dance: i.e., the *aurora borealis*, the Northern Lights.
48 Morse: walrus.
49 The Labyrinthodon and Plesiosaur were both amphibious dinosaurs, and the Dinornis a
    giant moa (a bird like an ostrich), all identified from the fossil record in the 1830s and '40s;
    Megatherium was a giant ground sloth, identified from fossils in 1796.
50 Both extinct flightless birds. The Dodo, of Mauritius, was wiped out in the seventeenth
    century by the pigs, monkeys and other animals introduced by Europeans. The Greak Auk,

Extant within the memory of the Swan,
The Tortoise and the Raven,' lisped the Skunk.

'Allow the wind, good brother beast! Stand off!'
Said then the Groundling Ape, the Troglodyte.[51]
'Existence by itself abolishes
The ill-equipped of every time and style;
Or if archaic specimens impede   100
The fantasy of Matter thronged with shapes,
In cataclysms, catastrophes of fire,
Subversions aqueous and glacial drifts
Those stubborn prodigies are swallowed up
To clear the way for fresh experiment.
But this be sure of: every horn and hoof,
And every insect, feather, fur, and fin
Of use to Man survives while Man survives.
One gallant race besides, the Simian stock,
To which I have the honour to belong,   110
Of no utility for draught or food,
The science and the vanity of Man
Will foster to the end; because by it
He swears when he propounds his progress vast
From sarcoid origins and new-beloved
Hypothesis of Evolution.'[52]

                       'Shame!'
The Skunk rejoined with simulated zeal
And brandished tail. 'If Man were worth his salt
There would not now be left a single ape,
Macaque or lemur, lori or callithrix,[53]   120
Baboon or gibbon to twit him with descent
From lewd abominable quadrumanes,[54]
Mimics of Men, whose pitiful burlesque
Has helped creation's Lord to theorise
Ignobly of Himself! Base Troglodyte,
I spurn the theory, and I hold your tribe
The foulest zoological debauch,
The misbegotten brood of some insane
Unholy prehistoric Human race,
In loathsome commerce with pernicious beasts.   130
Catastrophes and cataclysms indeed!

---

an Atlantic species, was slaughtered first for food by sailors, then commercially for its down,
then finished off by egg- and specimen-collectors in the mid-nineteenth century.
51 Troglodyte: cave-dweller.
52 Sarcoid: the sponge-particle, the single-celled organism that collectively form sponges.
Charles Darwin's *On the Origin of Species by Means of Natural Selection* (1859) had implied that
humans had evolved from other life-forms; his *The Descent of Man* (1871) had been explicit.
53 Callithrix is the family that includes the marmoset, like the loris a small, cute, primate.
54 Quadrumanes: animals having opposable thumbs on both hands and feet (i.e. primates,
excluding humans).

I tell you, Troglodyte, Mankind will rise—
A natural convulsion more devout
Than pilgrimage, hegira, or crusade,[55]
More general, for the monkeys, than the Flood—[56]
And in a panic of aesthetic ire
Obliterate the libel on Himself.'

'May I be there to see!' the Vulture yapped.
'As well I wot I will be! Very sure
The Vultures and their kindred must outlive   140
All other things in order to devour
The putrid carcass of the world at last.'

'Nay,' hissed Aboma in his silken tones,
Uncoiling sumptuous wreaths of serpent; 'Man
Will see the Vultures out. My ancestors
Were gods in Anahuac: I prophesy
The final overthrow of bestial power.'

'Gods! gods?' cried frosty Nennook. 'What are gods?'

Aboma answered, 'Stock or stone, beast, bird,
Insect, or flame, or star, shadow of Man   150
Or fancied spirit, whom the Humans hold
Responsible, on whom they lightly lay
The intolerable burden of their sins.'

'Their sins!' went Nennook. 'Mystery! What are sins?'

Aboma then: 'The quaint abortion, Man,
Possesses conscience. Hearing, feeling, taste,
Sight, scent are shared alike by Him and us,
But what this conscience is no beast can tell—
Unless it be some special cowardice
In honour held by Man's perverted heart.   160
Certain it is that necessary deeds,
The lustful propagation of His kind
Or happy slaughter of His enemies,
This mouldering conscience turns to mortal sin.
Even in His war on us sin palsied Him,
Until He made His affable deity
Appoint Him regent to subdue the earth,
With perfect power over all fish, flesh, fowl,
And over all the earth and everything

---

55 Hegira: Anglicisation of *hijra*, Arabic for migration, used to refer to Mohammed's emigration
    from Mecca to Medina in 622; Davidson may be confusing this with *hajj*, the pilgrimage to
    Mecca enjoined on Muslims.
56 Referring of course to God's destruction of all living things on land, except Noah's family
    and a pair from every other species, in a great flood in Genesis 6–8.

That moves upon the earth.[57] No mortal beast   170
Can fathom the fatuity of Man!'

'We can!' the dusty Hackney neighed. 'We know
What conscience is: it is the lash; the lash,
And the corroding memory of the lash.
How out of horses to contrive machines
That shall excel machinery as an art
Excels the rule of thumb, Man's problem rose.'

'You put the cart before yourself, my friend:
Wheels were an afterthought,' Aboma hissed.

'It may be so, but let me speak my mind;   180
Give me my head, for once,' the Hackney neighed.
'How might enduring memory be evoked
In free forgetful stallions, thunderhoofed
In prairie, pampas, heath and Tartar steppe;
Exempt as winds that round the vagrant world
Pursue their idle fancies, or, in dreams,
Enamoured roam the starry wilderness?
How might an ignominious sense of shame
Invade the treasure-laden loins surcharged
With proud posterity? Those valiant hearts,   190
Triumphant in the combat for the mares
When the great miracle of grass begins
And simple emerald blades elaborate
The soul of earth, the virtue of the sun,
Replenishing the sexes! — how might they,
Those hearts of stallions eager for a heaven
Of fragrant manes, wild glances, quivering flanks,
Wherein to root their admirable race—
How might they lose their courage, how admit
The treacherous fear that undermines the will?   200
Mnemonics and a discipline adept
In conscience-rearing, Man, the traitor, wrought
With grisly human craft upon Himself.
The thing that never ceases to corrode—
That makes a memory: anguish is the soil,
The root, the stem of conscience and the flower:
The lattice scourged upon the shoulder blades,
The slit snout, eyeless sockets, lettered cheeks,
Cropped ears, maimed members, mouthless, tongueless maws!
In baths of agony and seas of blood,   210
Impalements, flayings, faggots, caldrons, wheels,
Man thrust and branded, seethed and carved in Man
A memory and a conscience.[58] So in us:

---

57 In Genesis 1.28.
58 'Wherever man has thought it necessary to create a memory for himself, his effort has been

A scalpel to the pride of life — the chief
Utilitarian sin that Man commits;
A rim of iron for the narrow way
Nailed to the dull blunt foot that might have trod
The yielding turf, in fenceless deserts free
For all time, with spreading talons armed,
Had Matter dreamed us in her warrior mood;   220
A curb of iron in the helpless mouth;
A captive's meagre fare; and all day long
Between the shafts, before the wheels, beneath
The conscientious, the memorial lash,
The torture of the intermittent rack
With super-subtle cunning self-applied.
Out of the stallion thus they carve the nag,
And crown him with a conscience. Terrible
Solicitude in labyrinthine streets
And stifling throngs of noxious Men usurps   230
The shrouded glance that matched the morning once;
A menace and a sombre mystery haunt
The sunlight and the shadow; everywhere
Impalpable, remorseless duty kills.'

With that the watchful Lion, grave and still,
In level tones began: 'He overcomes.
Within His brittle frame and tender flesh
Resides a shameful power that bids Him veil
His nature from Himself. Wherefore He swathes
His genial gifts, and muffles trunk and limbs   240
In lying garments, while His thoughts and deeds
(And all the thoughts and deeds of Man and beast
Are purely evil, Matter knows!) indued
With moral liveries, masks, disguises, names,
Parade His world of old hypocrisy
As like themselves as Men are like baboons.
This shameful power — to us unthinkable —
That sees things other than they are, inflicts
A sanction, as our wise Aboma told,
On sheer necessities, the evil use   250
Whereof delights us to the marrow. Soul,
The virtuous title for this poison-gland —
Armament, pestilence, I know not what! —
That conquers and with loathsome sanction taints
The noble evil of the Universe,

---

attended with torture, blood, sacrifice. [...] The ghastliest sacrifices and pledges [...] have their origin in that instinct which divined pain to be the strongest aid to mnemonics. [...] [B]reaking on the wheel [...]; piercing with stakes, drawing and quartering, [...] the popular flaying alive, [...] By such methods the individual was finally taught to remember five or six "I won'ts" which entitled him to participate in the benefits of society. [...] How much blood and horror lies behind all "good things"! Friedrich Nietzsche, *On the Genealogy of Morals* (1887), Second Essay: '"Guilt," "Bad Conscience," and Related Matters', III.

210

Assembles speed and strength, your mass and weight
My lord, Aboma's coiling subtlety,
The Skunk's mephitic odour,[59] Nennook's grip
And hardihood, the sorry Hackney's sense
Of duty, Troglodyte's presumptuous ease,   260
The Mastiff's courage bland, with swifter flight
And keener scent than yours, brother and king
Of vultures, into one essential force,
Whose dire enchantment felt in every nerve
Is all we know of that strange sorcery.'

'Because,' the undaunted Flea exclaimed, 'the Soul
Partakes agility phenomenal,
Outstripping me.'

                  'Well said, illustrious peer!'
The Lion laughed. 'Did I forget you, friend?
Not least in genius! Give the Elephant   270
Your saltatory power[60] — behold the Soul
As near as bestial fancy may conceive!'

But now the Lion rose and lifted up
A stormy mournful voice: 'Man overcomes!
No hope, no help for us, and no escape;
For Soul invades the furthest nook of earth;
And out of earth, not Soul itself discerns
An airy path to some uncursed abode.
How long the race of Lions shall endure
Aboma cannot tell; but this we know: 280
The desert, darkness, and the quaking things
That leave their dens aghast, when the stunned veldt
And shattered air transmit through circling leagues
The heavy summons leonine that bids
Reluctant flesh to supper, once again
Shall hear that bodeful utterance as the last
Uncaptured lion falls; then, nevermore.
Behind the bars the remnant — Oh, how long
Behind unyielding bars penned in, and starved
On morsels savourless, a gazing-stock   290
Of majesty made impotent, of old
Incarnate dread diurnally abused
By human eyes like pigmies' arrows stuck
In every pore; or scourged and branded, tamed
And disciplined ... tame Lions, caged and lashed,
Attempting human tricks! ... How long, sad earth!
And afterwards? — No lions anywhere.
But this — this strangles thought and speech: the Soul,

---

59 Mephitic: foul-smelling.
60 Saltatory: adapted for dancing or jumping.

That cannot but prevail, no scruple knows
Of self-imputed magnanimity;   300
But like a savage conquerer destroys
All record of the foe. The subtle means
Of our oblivion began, before
The Soul grew conscious of profound design,
If any consciousness to Soul belongs,
When in the zodiac His art impaled
A constellation of perfervid stars[61]
Naming it Leo; and with the forgery
Of monstrous Sphinx, a lion's limbs and trunk
With eagle's pinions, and the vacant face   310
And insolent bosom of His womankind.
These treacherous images, significant
With centuries of thought, adorned with dreams
And studied fancy of the nations, steeped
In infinite emotion as in a sea
That crusts with jewels sunken derelicts,
Shall be devoutly cherished as the Soul's
Belovëd offspring, when the splendid name
Of Lion, standing once for actual might
Of Matter's own great origin, has ceased   320
To signify. That breaks my heart.'

                            'My liege,"
Aboma hissed, sauve courtier lowly coiled,
'The Soul of Man, incontinent in art,
Protean as Amoeba, capable
Of self-division as the Annelids,[62]
Hives off in form and legend manifold,
Alike in every guise yet always new.
Most true it is that Tritons, flaming Drakes,
Mermaidens, Satyrs, Harpies, Hippogriffs,
Chimera, Cheiron, Sirius, Minotaur[63]   330
Shall in imagination overlive
The beasts they libel; but the punishment
Of that incontinence of Soul pursues
With like defeat the victor-victim, Man.
His Cæsar, Christ, Mohammed, Tamerlane[64]
Are featureless to Him; because the Soul,

---

61 Perfervid: ardent, impassioned.
62 Annelids: segmented worms.
63 Triton: a sea-god in classical mythology with human features but a fish-like tail and gills;
Drake: dragon; Satyr: the Roman version was half-man half-goat; Harpy: a bird with the
head and breasts of a woman; Hippogriff: a horse with an eagle's head and wings; Chimera:
lioness with a snake for a tail and the head of a goat growing out of her back; Cheiron: a
centaur, a horse with a man from the waist up where the head should be; Sirius is Orion's
hunting dog, and in no way hybrid as far I know.
64 Tamerlane: Timur, the 14th century Mongol emperor who conquered much of west and
central Asia.

Embarrassed by their memory, fearing yet
Or impotent to cast them out, invests
Their proper figure and significance
With increments of fond Humanity,   340
For all the world as China mussels, tricked
By pious fraud, with automatic slime
Their incommodious images veneer.
Moreover, sire, his best-beloved are these:
Hamlet the Dane, and the ingenious Knight,
Don Quixote de la Mancha, shapes unreal
As Sphinx, or Centaur, Boyg or Laidly Worm.[65]
And thus is Soul betrayed, condemned and lost,
Yet nothing knows of all its wantonness,
Abortive fantasy, and life-in-death.'   350

'Ay,' said the Lion, grave and still once more:
'It breaks my heart to think my race must pine
In infamy, and wither out at last,
To irreprievable oblivion doomed.'

Darkness, and then a road wherein I walked,
An old known road in England near the sea.
Between its bevelled slopes a silence went,
Like a full river gliding unperturbed;
And moored upon the silence or adrift,
The woodland noises floated: carnival   360
Rehearsings of that savage epicure
The throstle, who delights to tune his throat[66]
With tortured snails from battered houses torn;
Dramatic interludes of gluttonous
Starlings who gobble shell and all, with drums
And cymbals of some stubborn hammering
Nuthatch or fallow-chat, busy among[67]
The woodmites and the weevils beak and claw.
But soon sad human tones and leaden steps,
Discordant wheels and thudding hoofs broke up   370
The tuneful silence. One strong voice I heard
That uttered eager sayings by the way:
My voice it seemed, and yet my lips were still;
Myself I seemed, and yet both young and old;
And thus the voice transmuted into speech
The music of the murderous singing-birds:
'With ordure nourished, penetrating roots
Of cleanly flowers and scrupulous select
Essential virtue to enthral mankind

---

65 The Boyg is a shapeless monster in the Norwegian story of Peer Gynt; the Laidly Worm is an
    evil serpent in English folklore.
66 Throstle: song-thrush.
67 Fallow-chat: wheatear.

With passionate hue and scent, by alchemy   380
Innate sublimed, as love sublimes a blush
In faces virginal, distilled, as love
Distils a wondering sigh from innocence.
But would I daub a rose with noisome filth
In celebration of its birth and state,
Or for a badge in beauty's stomacher[68]
Impale a skull and crossbones to portend
That love and death are one? I would; and plunge,
Up to the shoulder, fingers, hands, and arms
In the world's entrails, a psychometer[69]   390
Who knows what spirit is! Let songsters kill
And banquet sumptuously as nature bids;
The pangs of molluscs if they suffer pangs
Are well endured that pliant throats may gem
The air at random, rubies, emeralds
In squandered largesse pour, and richly pave
The woodland paths with chrysolite and pearl.[70]
Since knowledge kills or cures, untie the scarf
From love's weak sight and bid him then be strong,
Beholding grossly origins uncouth,   400
The havoc of his triumph, and the vat
Of blood he steeps the world in ... Ancient news!
The world's aware! Is it so short a while
Since Cain killed Abel, since Bathsheba's son
Deciphered in a thousand ladies' eyes
The rubric of the preacher?[71] Or so long
Since Gallia slashed like fabled Behemoth
Her bluest veins in fierce self-surgery?[72]
The hardy world derides its growing pains
Even as the hardy soul. Despise, desert   410
The cities where nonchalant steeplejacks
Miraculously keep the clocks behind
A century or so. Desert the roads,
The highways laid with broken hearts of men,
And country lanes with tear-slaked ashes strewn;

---

68 Stomacher: 'ornamental covering for the chest (often covered with jewels) worn by women under the lacing of the bodice' (*OED*).
69 Psychometer: person or instrument measuring someone's spiritual or psychological state.
70 Chrysolite: a green gemstone.
71 Cain and Abel are Adam and Eve's sons: Cain commits the world's first murder when he kills his brother (Genesis 4.8). Bathsheba's son is Solomon, who had 'seven hundred wives [...] and three hundred concubines', many of them 'strange women', non-Israelites whom he allowed to set up temples to their own gods: God split up the tribes in Israel after Solomon's death as punishment for this crime (1Kings 11.1–3 and ff.), but 'the rubric of the preacher' is obscure.
72 Gallia is France; Behemoth is a biblical monster, the equivalent on land of Leviathan in the sea, but is herbivorous, and thus not given to slashing anything's veins. The political philosopher Thomas Hobbes called the parliament of the English Revolution 'Behemoth', and the intended reference here may be to the French Revolution of 1789–99, or the more recent Paris Commune of 1871, both of which resulted in atrocities.

The latticed hedges, chosen cage of birds
And rustic lyre Æolian;[73] graven ruts;
The liveried lightning's conduit manifold;
Luxuriant banks by traffic well-manured,
Where yellow dandelions all ablaze   420
And cuckoo-buds of saffron light enrich
A violet-studded ground with ivy scrolled.
Dull labour trudges here; ill-favoured wives
Whose bodies know no respite, breast or womb
Abused with offspring while their season lasts
On errands shamble; foolish couples creep
From shadow into shadow when the moon
Dapples the hedgerow path, or in the ditch
On starless nights uneasily forestall
A licensed more convenient bridal-bed,   430
And blame the eglantine's alluring scent
As potent as a philtre in the blood.[74]
Here woeful children, odds and ends of life,
Grotesquely play; and here my Lady Bung
Rolls in her landau—she who joined her strain,
Matured of old on plundered abbey-lands,
With modern stock fattened to peerage point
By drunkards witting not their final cause.[75]
Here huntsmen, gipsies, funerals, picnics, bands
Between the hedges taint the virgin air   440
With human effluence, hateful to a mind
In travail and alone. Out of it all!'

At once my dream achieved a lonely hill
Wherefrom I saw the ocean welter wide,
Like silver founded in a hollow mould
Whose confines were the jangling seaboard strung
With chords of pebble and the magical
Horizon's glittering brink. A vapour, twirled
Upon the potter's wheel, the earth, that shapes
For pity or applause the very clouds,   450
Rose like a fragile urn enveloping
The spacious air: above its rounded mouth
The firmament, a disc of amethyst,
Received and echoed back in golden showers
The lark's continual fugue. This vaporous urn,

---

73 The Aeolian harp was an instrument hung up so that the wind played its strings.
74 Philtre: a love-drug.
75   Lines 434–8 offer a sardonic potted history of the English aristocracy: descended from
    Henry VIII's sidekicks whom he rewarded with the lands of monasteries dissolved in the
    Reformation, then financially bolstered by intermarriage with wealthy capitalists until the
    family's senior male can be made a Lord. The 'final cause' of a thing is the purpose for which
    it exists or is done. 'Bung' was a term for a brewer: the 'drunkards' have been unwittingly
    contributing to the elevation of this family into the aristrocracy. 'A bung' was also slang for
    'a lie'. A landau is a type of carriage.

Wherein I stood coping its hill-crowned base[76]
Diverse of silver sea and emerald land,
Like glass annealed in water, suddenly
Upon some flaw of wind or scratch of light
Crumbled together and became a cloud   460
That wrapped me round. Aloft a tempest bore
The cloud and me; then whirled the cloud away,
And left me standing on the verge of Heaven.

The native air thereof flattered my cheek
With velvet wings, more sweet and delicate
Than newblown zephyrs when the barley bends
Its aigrettes[77] to the ocean-tempered breath
Of mundane summers; or touched me and grew still
Like scented eyelids of an odalisque[78]
Profoundly learned in love, subdued and dumb   470
With passion in the honied orient night.
I watched the figures of the blessed dead
Who wandered in the forests, or reposed
Beside the brooks in glens of amaranth,[79]
That shamed the rainbow and in fragrance bore
The bell from valley-lilies and the rose.

There were the great who triumphed easily,
In thought and glance, in word and deed supreme;
Also the agonists who kept their arms,[80]
Hatred and envy, burnished bright with use,   480
Who in their bosoms drove intolerance home,
And let it rust, making a cankered wound
To wring their hearts with rage and wind them up,
As Eastern lovers, lest their valiant love
Should slumber but a moment, in their flesh
Ingraft a poniard for a talisman,[81]
And so transcending wake and bleed to death.
There were the warriors, they who knew that war
Can deify disgrace, project and change
Ignoble causes into golden grounds,   490
Who sought their foes instinctively, as bees
With fervid song in search of honey roam,
Whose daily business was the battlefield,
Their hour of rest, the tedious interval
Between two victories, who upset the world
And deluged earth with blood; and there were those
Whose craft was silence mainly and magpie speech,

---

76 Coping: i.e., on top of.
77 Aigrettes: the 'beard' on the head of barley.
78 Odalisque: 'female slave or concubine in a harem' (*OED*).
79 Amaranth: 'an imaginary flower reputed never to fade' (*OED*).
80 Agonist: 'A person engaged in a contest or struggle' (*OED*).
81 Poniard: a small dagger.

Whose apparatus of innuendo, nod,
And supercilious lightning, cabinet
Chicanery and documental gloze[82]   500
Did and undid and never could get done,
But kept *them* still on top; and those whose prey
Was honesty and scruple, foolish greed
And sore necessity, who paved with souls
Of friend and foe their desolate path to wealth:
Kings, statesmen, emperors, proconsuls, popes,
Dishonest brokers, robbers, millionaires.
There, too, were those who fought the conquerors
And would not yield at all; and those who died,
Contemned and poor, but straining to the last   510
For power and wealth, or at their proper hands,
Refusing life because they failed to break
The world's hard heart, and for a travelling rug
Strip off its glossy hide: the fallen, the slain,
The captives, madmen, bankrupts, suicides.
Kings' mistresses in separate arbours sat,
Sedately happy to be left alone;
And harlots of the street in joyful herds
Haunted the brakes and purlieus wild of heaven.
Bevies of mothers beautiful as dawn   520
Went up the shadowy aisles: Queens of the earth
Who yielded willing harvest of their wombs
For dynasties Time garners proudly yet,
With simple wives who loved their spouses well
And bore their chubby brats while nature would.
I saw, besides, women renowned of old,
Devout adorers of their own delight,
Who treasured health, and trained their sensual powers
With that innate prerogative of lust
Desirous of a world of virile deed,   530
Which made their chamber-doors the porch of death,
Their tumbled beds to bloody biers transformed,
Implacably renewing eager youth
By slaughter of successive paramours.

All these I saw at home in Heaven. All these!
And all who challenged fate and staked their lives
To win or lose the prize they coveted,
Who took their stand upon the earth and drew
Deep virtue from the centre, helped themselves,
Desired the world and willed what Matter would.   540

A while I slaked my thirsty sight with draughts
Of heavenly vision till harmonious news
Assailed my ears with music, deeply stained

---

82 Gloze: i.e. gloss, commentary.

And sweeter than the scent of asphodel:[83]
It seemed inherent in the empyreal air,[84]
Attuned my pitch to Heaven's, transpierced by soul
With rapture at the thought of agony,
And made me search the depths for Tartarus[85]
Where those stupendous pangs of wind-driven wheels,   550
Recoiling stones, of water borne in sieves,
Of famished mouths with ghostly delicates
Deluded momently, were wont to wring
Ixion, Sisyphus, the impious host,
And those sweet fifty, all save one, who slew
Their virgin bridegrooms in their wedding-beds.[86]
Nowhere beholding these antiquer sights,
My eyes began to ransack space for Hell,
And Christian torments of the damned. I looked,
And looked again to see the City of Dis[87]
Where heretics their heresies regret,   560
Or scorn eternal pain, regretting nought,
Entombed in sepulchres of fire, unpaved
Till judgment, to be sealed for ever then;
Or the deep-sighing forest ominous
Where suicides like thorns and briars grow,
Uncouth and barren wildings, rookery
Obscene of mongrel birds; or to o'erhear
That storm instinct with lamentation shrill,
Where souls of tender lovers whirled about
In utter darkness on the unstable air,   570
Uplift unhallowed voices loud against
The withering blast and terror of their flight.
Like a swift pang of Hell it stung my mind,
'There is no Hell! All these courageous ones—
Ixion, lover of the Queen of Heaven,
The Phrygian humorist who cooked strange flesh
To test immortal palates, Corinth's lord

---

83 Asphodel: a beautiful S. European flower, in poetry imagined as immortal.
84 In the pre-Copernican cosmology, the Empyrean was the highest sphere of those surrounding the Earth, and made of fire and inhabited by angels.
85 Tartarus: the lowest part of the underworld in Greek and Roman myth.
86 In Greek myth, Ixion was condemned to turn for ever on a wheel of fire in the underworld, for attempting to seduce Hera, Zeus's wife; Sisyphus, King of Corinth, to endlessly pushing a great stone up a slope down which it always rolled back from the top, for repeatedly tricking his way out of the underworld. The 'impious host' is Tantalus, a Phrygian, who served a feast to the gods that included his own son Pelops (suitably cooked): his punishment was to thirst and starve in a lake whose waters always retreated from his lips, hung with fruits that did likewise. 'The sweet fifty' were the daughters of Danaus, King of Argos, who, on the terms of a peace-treaty with Danaus's brother Aegyptus, were obliged to marry the latter's fifty sons. Knowing that Aegyptus had ordered his sons to then kill their wives, Danaus orders the girls to kill their husbands first. Only one refuses; the other 49 'Danaids' were condemned in the underworld to perpetually carry water in sieves.
87 The City of Dis is the Sixth Circle of Hell in Dante's *The Divine Comedy* (1308–21): what follows is taken from its description in book V of the *Inferno*.

Who mocked at Death and laid him by the heels,
The nuptial homicides of Argos, strong
To keep their maidenheads for whom they chose,   590
Arrogant Farinata, the Capuan, blind,
Betrayed, but master of his fate,[88] and all
Who paired unwed, their seedtime having come,
Are here with me in everlasting joy!'

But that sweet music, in my heart of hearts
As vibrant as an octave bell that hums
Harmonic mirth to hear his neighbour chime,
Betokened agony, as certainly
As braided strains of mundane sound denote
A pitiful ambition-broken gang   590
Of drilled executants, an orchestra;
Announced a Hell, however peopled, ruled
And wrought to such delight. Assured, I scanned
The wide domain of Heaven, and in the midst
Beheld a seated figure, richly clad
In purple. Golden-haired, with luminous eyes
And deep, he played upon a dazzling range
Of adamantine notes; chromatic mail
Of chrysoberyl, ruby, sardonyx,
Topaz and emerald, and many a gem   600
Unknown, plated the intermediate keys.
A loom of strings or grove of tuneful pipes
I nowhere saw; only in Heaven's midst
The jewelled keyboard on a jasper plinth,
And that celestial one who played thereon.

At random glancing, by the music held
In ecstasy, I marked, far off and faint
As from the earth the galaxy appears,
A glimmering colour diaper the light[89]
Wherein the ethereal bowers of Heaven were hung.   610
Thrusting my whetted eyes athwart the abyss —
For on the instant I foreboded Hell —
Importunate, my vision first defined
A nebula that girt the firmament;
Then like a tapestry seemed the thickening haze,
An arras-cloth with human eyes embossed,
With glaring eyes; thereafter as a cliff,
Precipitous it hung, a bastioned steep,
Encompassing afar the golden clime,
And vigilant with a million million eyes.   620

---

88 Farinata degli Uberti (1212–64), a Florentine nobleman whom Dante places in the fourth
   circle for heresy, but he remains unrepentant (*Inferno* X). Farinata's heresies may have
   included disbelief in life after death.
89 Diaper: 'To adorn with diversely coloured details; to variegate' (*OED*).

At last, my gaze dynamic grown, I saw
That this remote environment of Heaven,
Tier upon tier of flesh from base to crown,
This human amphitheatre was Hell
Itself, constructed of its denizens.
My knitted brows and roofed hand swept the vast
Eternal cirque of heinous agony[90]
Still as an icy frontier in the moon,
Except that groups and terraces of folk
Distended myriad mouths for every key   630
The gracious player struck: like drifts and flaws
Of wandering air that ripple summer tides,
The transient multitudinous gape and cry
Flickered about the pallid wall. I knew
As though myself had been the artificer,
The whole design; in every bone and nerve,
In every sinew and pulse of those that built
Perdition up, the faculty of Hell,
More vehement than flame, intensely wrought
Perpetual and intolerable woe;   640
And, subtler than the torturer's poison used
To palsy action and invigorate sense
In bloody gropings at the roots of life,
Mortised each body-and-soul in ordered rank,
Inhibiting spontaneous deed or sound.
The gracious player on the jewelled keys
By power celestial loosed with every touch
Imprisoned horror in a massive cry
Tuned to the fingered note, while winnowing space
Mellowed the shriek of women and the roar   650
Of men into immortal harmony,
The ineluctable beatitude
That moulded the demeanour of the blest,
And lit their faces with eternal looks
Subtle and sweet of malice gratified,
The salt of beauty and the exquisite
Original of all felicity.

Materials of Hell? The altruists;
Agnostics; dreamers; idiots, cripples, dwarfs;
All kinds of cowards who eluded fact;   660
Dwellers in legend, burrowers in myth;
The merciful, the meek and mild, the poor
In spirit; Christians who in very deed
Were Christians; pessimistic celibates;
The feeble minds; the souls called beautiful;
The slaves, the labourers, the mendicants;
Survivors of defeat; the little clans

---

90 Cirque: amphitheatre.

That posed and fussed, in ignominy left
By apathetic powers; the greater part
Of all the swarthy all the tawny tribes;   670
Degenerates; the desultory folk
In pleasure, art, vocation, commerce, craft;
And all deniers of the will to live,
And all who shunned the strife for wealth and power:
For every soul that had been damned on earth
Was damned in Hell — set there, replete with pangs,
To watch eternally the infinite
Delight of Heaven, extorted from himself
And those beside him in the rampire built.[91]
Eternal justice, it was good to see   680
Dives in Heaven and Lazarus in Hell
Maugre two thousand years of Christendom![92]
A dream of blasphemous inspiration? No;
If Justice is, then there is Justice now;
What is, will always be, if Justice is.

Do I believe in Heaven and Hell? I do;
We have them here; the world is nothing else.
Beauty and power and splendour and delight
Of chosen ones, elect ere Time began,
In loathsomeness, debility, disgrace,   690
Humiliation, travail, terror, woe,
Of multitudes, of myrmidons,[93] of all
The labourers, soldiers, servants, rooted deep:
He is a slave: a prisoner: damned: in Hell,
Whose daily bread depends on toil approved.
For me, I clambered into Heaven at once
And stayed there; joined the warfare of the times
In corner, trust, and syndicate: upheaved
A furrow, hissing through the angry world,
A redhot ploughshare in a frozen glebe,   700
And reaped my millions long before my prime.
Then, being English, one of the elect
Above all folks, within me fate grew strong.
The authentic mandate of imperial doom
Silenced the drowsy lullaby of love,
(Though now my turbid blood and nerves disused
Complain of mystery unrevealed, and haunt
Imagination day and night with looks —
With beckoning looks, soft arms and fragrant breath;
For even in Heaven each ransomed soul frequents   710
A private, an inevitable Hell!)
Undid my simple, immature design,

---

91   Rampire: archaic version of 'rampart'.
92   In Luke 16.19–31, Lazarus is the poor man who suffers in this life to be rewarded in Heaven,
     Dives the rich man who goes to Hell.
93   The Myrmidons are a people in Greek myth who have come to represent unquestioning
     followers of their leaders.

And made me—What! tenfold a criminal?
No other name for Hastings, Clive, and me![94]
I broke your slothful dream of folded wings,
Of work achieved and empire circumscribed,
Dispelled the treacherous flatteries of peace,
And thrust upon you in your dull despite
The one thing needful, half a continent
Of habitable land! The English Hell   720
For ever crowds upon the English Heaven.
Secure your birthright; set the world at naught;
Confront your fate; regard the naked deed;
Enlarge your Hell; preserve it in repair;
Only a splendid Hell keeps Heaven fair.

The Crystal Palace [95]

Contraption, - that's the bizarre, proper slang,
Eclectic word, for this portentous toy,
The flying-machine, that gyrates stiffly, arms
A-kimbo, so to say, and baskets slung
From every elbow, skating in the air.[96]
Irreverent, we; but Tartars from Thibet
May deem Sir Hiram the Grandest Lama, deem
His volatile machinery best, and most
Magnific, rotatory engine, meant
For penitence and prayer combined, whereby   10
Petitioner as well as orison
Are spun about in space: a solemn rite
Before the portal of that fane unique,
Victorian temple of commercialism,
Our very own eighth wonder of the world,
The Crystal Palace.

---

94   Referring to the two men most influential in establishing Britain's power in India in the eighteenth century: Warren Hastings (1732 –1818), first Governor General of India for the East India Company in 1773–84, later impeached for corruption; Robert Clive, (1725 –74), general whose victories in India, especially at Plassey, (1757), gave the Company its dominance of Bengal.

95   First published in two parts in the *Westminster Gazette* for 29 November 1908 (ll.1–145, 282–309) and 3 January 1909 (ll. 146–281); then as a single work in *Fleet Street and other Poems* (London, 1909). The Crystal Palace, a wonder of Victorian engineering when it was built in Hyde Park to house the Great Exhibition of 1851, had been moved to the South London suburb of Sydenham Hill in 1854. To remain financially viable it had to remain open on Sundays, the only day most working-class people had off work, to the outrage of fundamentalist Christians. Its huge building contained the wide range of attractions, from the 'educational' to the tawdry, described by the poem.

96   Sir Hiram Maxim (1840 –1916), inventor of the machine gun, was less successful in his attempt to build a steam-powered aircraft; the prototype on show at the Crystal Palace of course never got off the ground. The lines that follow compare this machine to the prayer-wheels of Tibetan Bhuddists: the juxtaposition representative of the medley of items exhibited.

222

                              So sublime! Like some
Immense crustacean's gannoid skeleton,
Unearthed, and cleansed, and polished! Were it so
Our paleontological respect
Would shield it from derision; but when a shed,   20
Intended for a palace, looks as like
The fossil of a giant myriapod! ...
'Twas Isabey[97] – sarcastic wretch! – who told
A young aspirant, studying modern art
And medicine, that he certainly was born
To be a surgeon: 'When you try,' he said,
'To paint a boat you paint a tumour.'

                                             No
Idea of its purpose, and no mood
Can make your glass and iron beautiful.
Colossal ugliness may fascinate   30
If something be expressed; and time adopts
Ungainliest stone and brick and ruins them
To beauty; but a building lacking life,
A house that must not mellow or decay? –
'Tis nature's outcast. Moss and lichen? Stains
Of weather? From the first Nature said 'No!
Shine there unblessed, a witness of my scorn!
I love the ashlar and the well-baked clay;
My seasons can adorn them sumptuously:
But you shall stand rebuked till men ashamed,   40
Abhor you, and destroy you and repent!'

But come: here's crowd; here's mob; a gala day!
The walks are black with people: no one hastes;
They all pursue their purpose business-like –
The polo-ground, the cycle-track; but most
Invade the palace glumly once again.
It is 'again'; you feel it in the air –
Resigned habitués on every hand:
And yet agog: abandoned, yet concerned!
They can't tell why they come; they only know   50
They must shove through the holiday somehow.

In the main floor the fretful multitude
Circulates from the north nave to the south
Across the central transept – swish and tread
And murmer, like a seaboard's mingled sound.
About the sideshows eddies swirl and swing:
Distorting mirrors; waltzing-tops – wherein
Couples are wildly spun contrariwise
To your revolving platform; biographs,
Or rifle-ranges; panoramas: choose!   60

---

97   Jean Baptiste Isabey (1767–1855), French painter.

As stupid as it was last holiday?
They think so, — every whit! Outside, perhaps?
A spice of danger in the flying-machine?
A few who passed that whirligig, their hopes
On higher things, return disconsolate
To try the Tartar's violent oratory.
Others again, no more anticipant
Of any active business in their own
Diversion, joining stalwart folk who sought
At once the polo-ground, the cycle-track,   70
Accept the ineluctable; while some
(Insidious anti-climax here) frequent
The water-entertainments – shallops, chutes
And rivers subterrene: – thus, passive, all,
Like savages bewitched, submit at last
To be the dupes of pleasure, sadly gay –
Victims, and not companions, of delight.

Not all! The garden-terrace: – hark, behold,
Music and dancing! People by themselves
Attempting happiness! A box of reeds –   80
Accordian, concertina, seraphine –
And practiced fingers charm the advertent feet!
The girls can dance; but, O their heavy-shod,
Unwieldy swains! – No matter: – hatless heads,
With hair undone, eyes shut and cheeks aglow
On blissful shoulders lie: – such solemn youths
Sustaining ravished donahs! Round they swing,
In time or out, but unashamed and all
Enchanted with the glory of the world.
And look! – Among the laurels on the lawns   90
Torn coats and ragged skirts, starved faces flushed
With passion and with wonder! – hid away
Avowedly; but seen – and yet not seen!
None laugh; none point; none notice: multitude
Remembers and forgives; unwisest love
Is sacrosanct upon a holiday.
Out of the slums, into the open air
Let loose for once, their scant economies
Already spent, what was there left to do?
O sweetly, tenderly, devoutly think,   100
Shepherds and shepherdess in Arcady!

A heavy shower; the Palace fills; begins
The business and the office of the day,
The eating and the drinking – only real
Enjoyment to be had, they tell you straight
Now that the shifty weather fails them too.

But what's the pother here, the blank dismay?
Money has lost its value at the bars:
Like tavern-tokens when the Boar's Head rang
With laughter and the Mermaid swam in wine,   110
Tickets are now the only currency.
Before the buffets, metal tables packed
As closely as mosaic, with peopled chairs
Cementing them, where damsels in and out
Attend with food, like disembodied things
That traverse rocks as easily as air –
These are the havens, these the happy isles!
A dozen people fight for every seat –
Without a quarrel, unturbulently: O,
A peaceable, a tame, a timorous crowd!   120
And yet relentless: this they know they need;
Here have they money's worth – some food, some drink;
And so alone, in couples, families, groups,
Consuming and consumed – for as they munch
Their victuals all their vitals ennui gnaws –
They sit and sit, and fain would sit it out
In tedious gormandize till firework-time.
But business beats them: those who sit must eat.
Tickets are purchased at besieged Kiosks,
And when their values spent – with such a grudge! – 130
They rise to buy again, and lose their seats;
For this is Mob, unhappy locust-swarm,
Instinctive, apathetic, ravenous.

Beyond a doubt a most unhappy crowd!
Some scores of thousands searching up and down
The north nave and the south nave hungrily
For space to sit and rest to eat and drink:
Or captives in a labyrinth, or herds
Imprisoned in a vast arena; here
A moment clustered; there entangled; now   140
In reaches sped and now in whirlpools spun
With noises like the wind and like the sea,
But silent vocally; they hate to speak:
Crowd; Mob; a blur of faces featureless,
Of forms inane; a stranded shoal of folk.

Astounding in the midst of this to meet
Voltaire, the man who worshipped first, who made
Indeed, the only god men reverence now,
Public Opinion. There he sits alert –
A cast of Houdon's smiling philosophe.[98]   150
Old lion-fox, old tiger-ape – what names
They gave him! – better charactered by one

98 This is a copy of Jean Antoine Houdon (1741–1828)'s statue of the great French sceptic
    Voltaire (François-Marie Arouet, 1694–1778).

Who was his heir: 'The amiable and gay.'
So said the pessimist who called life sour
And drank it to the dregs.[99] Enough: Voltaire –
About to speak: hands of a mummy clutch
The fauteuil's arms; he listens to the last
Before reply; one foot advanced; a new
Idea radiant in his wrinkled face.

Lunch in the grill-room for the well-to-do,   160
The spendthrifts and the connoisseurs of food –
Gourmet, gourmand, bezonian, epicure.
Reserved seats at the window? – Surely; you
And I must have the best place everywhere.
A deluge smudges out the landscape. Watch
The waiters since the scenery's not on view.
A harvest-day with them, our Switzers – knights
Of the napkin! How they balance loaded trays
And though they push each other spill no drop!
And how they glare at lazy lunchers, snatch   170
Unfinished plates sans 'by your leave', and fling
The next dish down, before the dazzled lout
(The Switzer knows his man) has time to con
The menu, every tip precisely gauged,
Precisely earned, no service thrown away.
Sign of an extra douceur, reprimand
Is welcomed, and the valetudinous
Voluptuary served devoutly: he
With cauteries on his cranium; dyed moustache;
Teeth like a sea-wolf's each a work of art   180
Numbered and valued singly; copper skin;
And nether eyelids pouched: – why, he alone
Is worth a half-day's wage! Waiters for him
Are pensioners of indigestion, paid
As secret criminals disburse blackmail,
As Attic gluttons sacrificed a cock
To Esculapius to propitiate
Hygeia[100] – if the classic flourish serves!

'Grilled soles?' – for us: – Kidneys to follow. – Now,
Your sole, sir; eat it with profound respect.   190
A little salt with one side; scarce a pinch!
The other side with lemon; tenderly!
Don't crush the starred bisection: count the drops!
Those who begin with lemon miss the true
Aroma: quicken sense with salt, and then
The subtle, poignant, citric savour tunes

---

99 I have been unable to trace this reference: 'pessimism' as a philosophical position is usually
    linked to Arthur Schopenhauer (1788–1860), though the quote is untraced and the personal
    description does not fit.
100 Æsculalpius was the Roman god of healing, Hygeia his daughter.

The delicate texture of the foam-white fish,
Evolving palatable harmony
That music might by happy chance express.
A crust of bread – (eat slowly: thirty chews,   200
Gladstonian rumination) – to change the key.
And now the wine – a well-decanted, choice
Chateau, *bon per*; a decade old; not more;
A velvet claret, piously unchilled.
A boiled potato with the kidney ... No!
Barbarian! Vandal! Sauce? 'Twould ruin all!
The kidney's the potato's sauce. Perpend:
You taste the esoteric attribute
In food; and know that all necessity
Is beauty's essence. Fill your glass: salute   210
The memory of the happy neolith
Who had the luck to hit on roast and boiled.
Finish the claret. – Now the rain has gone
The clouds are winnowed by the sighing south,
And hidden sunbeams through a silver woof
A warp of pallid bronze in secret ply.

Cigars and coffee in the billiard-room.
No soul here save the marker, eating chops;
The waiter and the damsel at the bar,
In listless talk. A most uncanny thing,   220
To enter suddenly a desolate cave
Upon the margent of the sounding Mob!
A hundred thousand people, class and mass,
In and about the palace, and not a pair
To play a hundred up! The billiard-room's
The smoking-room; and spacious too, like all
The apartments of the Palace: – why
Unused on holidays? The marker: aged;
Short, broad, but of a presence; reticent
And self-respecting; not at all the type: –   230
'O well,' says he; 'the business of the room
Fluctuates very little, year in, year out.
My customers are seasons mostly.' One
On the instant enters: a curate, very much
At ease in Zion – and in Sydenham.
He tells two funny stories – not of the room;
And talks about the stage. 'In London now,'
He thinks, 'the play's the thing. He undertakes
To entertain and not to preach: you see,
It's with the theatre and the music-hall,   240
Actor and artiste, the parson must compete.
Every bank-holiday and special day
The Crystal Palace sees him. Yes; he feels
His hand's upon the public pulse on such
Occasions.' O, a sanguine clergyman!

Heard in the billiard-room the sound of Mob,
Occult and ominous, besets the mind:
Something gigantic, something terrible
Passes without; repasses; lingers; goes;
Returns and on the threshold pants in doubt   250
Whether to knock or enter, or burst the door,
In hope of treasure and a living prey.
The vainest fantasy! Rejoin the crowd:
At once the sound depreciates. Up and down
The north nave and the south nave hastily
Some tens of thousands walk, silent and sad,
A most unhappy people. – Hereabout
Cellini's Perseus ought to be. Not that;
That's stucco – and Canova's:[101] a stupid thing;
The face and posture of a governess –   260
A nursery governess who's had the nerve
To pick a dead mouse up. It used to stand
Beside the billiard-room, against the wall,
A cast of Benvenuto's masterpiece –
That came out lame, as he foretold, despite
His dinner dishes in the foundry flung.
They shift their sculpture here haphazard. – That?
King Francis – by Clesiger;[102] on a horse.
Absurd: most mounted statues are. – And this?
Verrochio's Coleone.[103] Not absurd: 270
Grotesque and strong, the battle-harlot rides
A stallion; fore and aft, his saddle, peaked
Like a mitre, grips him as in a vice.
In heavy armour mailed; his lifted helm
Reveals his dreadful look; his brows are drawn;
Four wrinkles deeply trench his muscular face;
His left arm half-extended, and the reins
Held carelessly, although the gesture's tense;
His right hand wields a sword invisible;
Remorseless pressure of his lips protrudes   280
His mouth; he would decapitate the world.

The light is artificial now; the place
Phantasmal like a beach in hell where souls
Are ground together by an unseen sea.
A dense throng in the central transept, wedged
So tightly they can neither clap nor stamp,

---

101 Benvenuto Cellini (1500–71), Italian Renaissance sculptor: 'Perseus with the Head of Medusa'
   is one of his most famous works. Antonio Canova (1757–1822) produced a later statue with
   a same name. These, and all the other works mentioned, were present in the Crystal Palace
   only as copies.
102 A statue of Francis I by the French sculptor Jean-Baptiste Clesinger (1814–83).
103 Andrea del Verrochio (1435–88), Florentine sculptor of the statue of Venetian general
   Bartolommeo Colleoni.

Shouting applause at something, goad themselves
In sheer despair to think it rather fine:
'We came here to enjoy ourselves. Bravo,
Then! Are we not?' Courageous folk beneath   290
The brows of Michael Angelo's Moses dance
A cakewalk in the dim Renascence Court.
Three people in the silent Reading-room
Regard us darkly as we enter: three
Come in with us, stare vacantly about,
Look from the window and withdraw at once.
A drama; a balloon; a Beauty Show: –
People have seen them doubtless; but none of these
Deluded myriads walking up and down
The north nave and the south nave anxiously –   300
And aimlessly, so silent and so sad.

The day wears; twilight ends; the night comes down.
A ruddy targelike moon in a purple sky,
And the crowd waiting on the fireworks. Come:
Enough of Mob for one while. This way out –
Past Linacre and Chatham, the second Charles,
Venus and Victory – and Sir William Jones[104]
In placid contemplation of a State! –
Down the long corridor to the district train.

---

104 The final verse-paragraph registers statues or paintings of Thomas Linacre (1460–1524), founder of the Royal College of Physicians; William Pitt, Earl of Chatham (1708–78), empire-building English statesman; and William Jones (1746–94), jurist and orientalist.

Jane Helen Findlater, 'The Pictures'.[1]

The shores of Olnig on a summer night were like the shores of Heaven as weary mortals think of these: the long white beaches were just kissed by the scarcely moving tide, and on the horizon floated dim purple outlines that might have been the Isles of the Blessed.[2]

There was no stirring of the atmosphere on such a windless night as this, but sometimes a great freshness would breathe in gently from the ocean and as suddenly die away — it carried with it the scent of leagues of sea. Then the sun would go down in a spectacular manner, lighting up the sky to a blazing scarlet behind the purple islands, ... it was all unbelievably exquisite.[3] Yet "wee Katie" (as she was always called) when released from her toil in the byre would stand and gaze out at this wonder of beauty without a single exclamation of surprise or pleasure.

Katie was one of the humblest creatures God ever made; she seemed scarcely to have a life of her own at all, just to have appeared on this planet to work for other people, toiling on, day after day, at her obscure tasks, without joy and almost without remuneration. She was thirteen on the day that she first arrived at the Farm, fresh from the tender mercies of an unloved aunt who had brought her up somehow on a pittance wrung from a very reluctant father. Such pittances are always joyfully discontinued at the earliest opportunity permitted by the law, so when Katie became a financial burden she had to go out to work at once. Her figure was stumpy and ill-proportioned, and she had a lamentable habit of never managing to hook her frock rightly, which did not add to her charms. Though Katie's hair was supposed to be "up," it was much more often half "down" her back in a tumbled, untidy plait, and wisps of it fell across her eyes and had to be brushed or tossed back when she looked up to speak to anyone: a doleful figure wee Katie, as ever stepped. Her day was no sinecure: cows are milked three times a day on well regulated farms, and Katie had the milking of five to attend to. Between times, there were pails to wash, and churns to scald, and shelves to scrub, and basins to cleanse — an endless, fatiguing, unchanging round of work. And here was all the child's diversion when the long day was done — to wander down to the white shore, and look out to sea: a poor amusement Katie found it. What to her were the long white beaches, the lisping waves, or even the scarlet banners of sunset? The heart of man is unsearchable, and one never gets to the end of the surprises that are to be found in character; to look at Katie one would have thought her almost too dull to have any aspirations or longings — but this was far from being the case; in her heart there burned a wild thirst for amusement. How this had been stifled all the long, long winter months at Olnig, Heaven alone could tell! If little Johnnie Ross, the farmer's son, extracted a few screeching notes from his concertina, Katie would execute a clumsy caper on the stone floor of the dairy, and down her hair would tumble about her ears, and Mrs. Ross would reprove her sharply, telling her to "mind her work and niver heed Johnnie and the concertina." Then sometimes Ran Reid, the lately demobilised tinker,[4] would appear with his pipes at the door of the Farm. And at the first sound of the thin, gay, skirling notes, Katie flung down whatever she was doing and rushed to the door to listen.

Ran was quite a personage in the country-side since his return from Mesopotamia: he still, by virtue of his late adventures, wore a ragged khaki coat, and it was only the

---

1   First published in *A Green-Grass Widow and Other Stories* (London: John Murray, 1921).
2   In Greek mythology, the paradisal islands to which heroes went when they died.
3   All ellipses, as here, are in the original.
4   Demobilised: i.e., discharged from the army at the end of the First World War. Ran has served in Mesopotamia (Iraq), in the British campaign against the (Turkish) Ottoman Empire. A 'tinker' is a travelling craftsman: a gypsy, more or less.

outward sign of the profound inward awakening that the man had gone through.

Ran had seen the world, and though he preferred like the sow that was washed to return to wallowing in the mire, he wallowed, so to speak, with his eyes open. As he stalked alongside of his donkey-cart, his pipes under his arm, Ran had quite the air of a man of the world. Ross, the farmer, often came to the door to speak to him on a winter afternoon when there was little doing out of doors, and Katie would always manage to edge herself behind the door to listen, for his sanguinary tales of Mesopotamia delighted her fancy, and she pondered them as she went about her work in the byre.

Olnig in winter was indeed no foretaste of Heaven. Katie was often so buffeted by the gale that she almost failed to make her way between the house and the byre. Wrapped in an old oilskin coat, her hands blue with cold, she had to face the flying sleet that drove in pitilessly from the Atlantic. There were no purple islands and lisping waves then, only a hoarse, roaring waste of billows, desolate and terrible beyond description. Katie's one preoccupation was to get under cover as quickly as might be; but she had always a moment of acute struggle with the bolt of the byre door which refused to open at once to the touch of her benumbed fingers; then, dripping, blown about, exasperated by this fight with the elements, she gained the shelter of the byre. There at least the cows were warm, and Katie would lean against their hot, rough sides with a sigh of relief as their kindly breath thawed her frozen cheek ... .

Then the snowstorms came, smothering and white, with sometimes, to follow, an awful frost that seemed as if it would nip life at its very sources. Grand pictures were to be seen in these winter storms by anyone with seeing eyes: but Katie's eyes were holden.[5] On nights of intense frost, the great indigo vault of the sky, strewn with myriads of stars, was a sight to awe and terrify the beholder, making him turn back, with longings for the homely earth, from these pathless wastes of space. But no distressing thoughts of the terrors of space or the insignificance of man's place in it visited Katie's brain when she looked out of the skylight window of her freezing little attic bedroom. Her shudders, poor child, were of a much less subtle kind, as she drew the heavy homespun blankets round her, and wondered if she would ever feel warm again. But snowstorms did not last for ever, even at Olnig, and the long, despairing Highland spring began, with ceaseless rain and tireless wind, soaking and battering the farm for weeks on end, till it seemed as if summer must be only a fable that could never come true; yet there were signs of life — calves in the byre, and lambs — shivering little lambs — on the hillside, and frogs arriving in the pools of the old peat cuttings. Katie was constantly in the byre feeding the calves now, with her head tied up in a little tartan shawl, and her person wrapped in every additional garment she possessed.

She was young enough to find it rather fun, and would sometimes laugh outright at the gambols the creatures gave as they ran towards her, to guzzle up the milk from the pail. It was at this spring season that her feud with Flora Reid, the eldest of Ran Reid's six olive-branches, first began. Flora was what the expressive phrase "a limb" indicates.[6] With her mop of fiery red hair, and her slanting blue eyes she was an incarnation of lawlessness and mischief.

The most importunate beggar of all the begging tinker clan, Flora had, as it were, acquired fresh powers in her trade during the troubled years of the war. For though she, her three brothers, her sister and her mother lived in affluence they had never dreamt of before, they would have been the last to acknowledge this fact. Instead of doing so, Flora added a new, long and very effective clause to her usual begging whine:

---

5   Holden: constrained, bound (*OED*).
6   That is, 'a limb of Satan': 'a young imp or rascal' (*OED*).

"Will ye no' gie me a puckle tea, Mistress? for faither's awa' fechtin' the Germans, an' mither's four weans, an' mysel', an' maybe faither 'll no' come hame ... could ye no' gie's an auld coat or a bit shawl for it's gey cauld the day? ... faither's awa' fechtin' the Germans an' mither's a' her lane an' maybe faither 'll no' come back ... have ye ony auld castin' wad keep the baby frae the cauld the nicht?[7] he's no' verra weel, an' noo that faither's awa' fechtin' the Germans ... etc., etc ... ."

So her endless tale of requests had gone on during the two war winters when Ran was away; but now that her father was safely home again, Flora had to change her tune. The sympathies of the country-side had been almost drained, so she invented what she called Mesoptamy Fever to revive sympathy afresh:

"Will ye gie's a puckle tea, if *you* please, faither's back from fechtin' the Germans an' he's bad wi' Mesoptamy fever ... if ye'd an auld blanket by ye, mistress could ye no' gie it for faither? He's come back wi' Mesoptamy fever on him, ye ken, aye, it gaes an' comes awful" (this to account for Ran's appearance of rude health); "whiles he'll be near deid wi't.[8] ... Gie's a drop broth, if *you* please, Mistress...."

Mrs. Ross was much too liberal to the tinkers, and Flora never asked in vain; but one spring evening it happened that Mrs. Ross had gone with her husband in the cart to Achinbeg, leaving Katie in sole charge of the house. Katie was very busy and *affairée*,[9] with everything to do. She had swept out the kitchen, put fresh peats on the fire, and laid the table for tea to be ready for Mrs. Ross on her return. Then in marched Flora, just about her own age, and incredibly importunate. First, she wanted tea, of course; Katie refused; then a scone from the pile on the table; a second refusal; then a "drop milk"; refusal number three; then an old skirt—but at this Katie became impatient and told her to go away in no bated language:

"Awa' wi' ye, or I'll send Rover at ye!" she threatened, pointing to the collie on the hearth.

"I'll no' gang—the Mistress aye gie's me a puckle tea."[10]

"Gang aff, ye're a fair torment!" cried the exasperated Katie, brandishing a broom, and advancing across the kitchen at Flora. Rover jumped up with a growl to join in the fray, and at sight of his bared white teeth, Flora ran out through the open door without further delay. But from that hour, war was declared between the two children—a war in which the stupid Katie was always the loser.

One of Flora's tricks was to make her way into the dairy and torment Katie to fill her "tinny" with milk. When Katie refused to do this, the little beggar ran off to the farmhouse and wheedled Mrs. Ross into saying that she might get what she wanted; then Katie had the humiliation of having to fill the "tinny," and Flora carried it away in triumph. It was extraordinary in how many ways she managed to annoy Katie—she seemed to be endowed with an uncanny knowledge of how to do it. Mrs. Ross might leave her whole family-washing on the hillside to bleach, and none of it would be touched; but if Katie left any of her poor little garments out at night, some of them would be sure to have disappeared before morning. Katie used to sit on an old log of wood near the door in her few spare moments, knitting herself a pair of black worsted stockings; if Mrs. Ross called to her from the kitchen, she would lay down her knitting on the log, and perhaps not return for ten minutes or so. Twice, however, she had returned to find her needles pulled out and half the stocking pulled down.

---

7   Puckle: small quantity; fechtin': fighting; weans: children; gie's: give us; gey cauld: pretty cold; her lane: on her own; castin': cast-off (all Sc.).
8   Whiles (Sc.): at times.
9   *Affairée*: 'busy, involved' (*OED*).
10 Gang: go; aye: always (both Sc.).

Katie began to think her work was bewitched, for it was impossible to see how the needles could have come out by themselves. Mrs. Ross said it must have been the kitten: Katie did not believe her ... . One day all the milk pans had been scoured and put out in the sun to dry. An hour afterwards they were found face downwards in the mud, and had all to be scoured over again ... . Another day the dairy floor, newly scrubbed out, was covered with filth—the hens had been driven in from the yard across it, while Katie was having her dinner ... . Yet this guerilla warfare was carried out with such cleverness that it would have been impossible to lay the blame on Flora—no one had seen her anywhere near the farm; but Katie knew that her little enemy was the cause of every trouble.

Remote as Olnig Farm was, some modern ideas had penetrated to it; so Katie suddenly demanded an "afternoon out," with as great determination as any town young woman; she had read about "afternoons out" in the *Weekly Scotsman*, and decided to have one. Her demand was granted, and then the question was, what to do with these long vacant afternoons?

It was all very well for Katie to put on her Sunday gown, and even to cram her empurpled hands into a pair of cotton gloves; but when this was done, the poor child had nothing more amusing to do than to walk in solitary (albeit gloved) splendour, along the wind-swept moor road to Achinbeg. If she persisted in her determination to reach the village, the four long miles had to be walked all over again on the way home. And the village—what did it afford in the way of amusement? There was little to see there. The Hotel, closed for nine months of the year; the Post Office, presided over by old Mrs. McIvor; the Shop where it was possible to buy sandy chocolate and liquorice lozenges—this was all the village had to offer as entertainment for Katie's young mind, unless you include the Station, where two or three trains came crawling in almost at a foot pace!

Still Katie persisted in her weekly pilgrimages to Achinbeg. It is difficult for those who have always lived in towns to understand the craving for variety that young people in the country feel so deeply. But the fact is, that what the human being wants to make him or herself happy is often the opposite of what he or she already has. The country-dweller hungers for stir and amusement; the town-dweller for quiet and repose; it is hard to say which craving is the stronger. Poor "wee Katie," trailing along the desolate hill road to Achinbeg in search of amusement, had a sick longing for variety that was pitiful to behold. Oh, for something—*anything* to happen! But week followed week, and month followed month, yet no excitement came poor Katie's way. And here she was on this beautiful midsummer evening, as dull as ever.

Her starved fancy projected itself into the week ahead, striving to see any hope of change in the monotonous round of her days. No: she could see no possible source from which help could come.

To-morrow morning she knew she would have to rise at six, as she had done every day that summer, to light the kitchen fire, and sweep the floor, and put on the big black kettle to boil. Then the cows had to be milked, and the pails and pans had to be scalded, and there was the dairy floor to scrub, and the churn to work, and then the cows to be milked again, and more pails to scald, and so on, and so on ... .

Katie shook her head, and repeated aloud to herself in a dismal little rhyme, "*Aye, aye, there's aye the kye*"—the cows seemed to fill the whole foreground of her life, there was no getting away from them, and the milk pails, and the churn, and the butter ... .

"I wonder, will James the herring-man be here the nicht?" she thought. James was one of the few links that connected Olnig Farm with the outer world—didn't he drive all the way from Mallaig, and sometimes had a paper on him that he would leave with

Ross?[11] Not that Katie took any interest in the larger happenings of the world; but sometimes there was a thrilling murder case reported in the paper, and she liked to read it by daylight, though after dark the memory of its thrills had an unpleasant way of coming back into her mind.

To-night she longed for some such unpleasant excitement. "Yon one aboot the corp found in the cellar was awfae interestin'," she meditated ... . Beside her at that moment the sheep were nibbling the short green sward that grew close to the shore, all embroidered with thyme; and the tide was coming in, running up the long white shore with a gentle sound like millions of kisses — and Katie sat deaf and blind to it all, longing for a rag of a newspaper that might tell her more about a corpse found in a cellar.

Then, as if in answer to her longing, Katie saw the herring-cart come in sight round the curve of the bay. Maggie, the starved old black pony that drew the cart, always quickened her slow pace as the Farm came in sight, because she was allowed to graze for a few minutes on the turf beside the door, while her master sold his herrings to Mrs. Ross.

"Ech! I wonder will James hae a paper wi' him the nicht?" Katie said to herself, making all haste across the shore towards the farm.

Mrs. Ross had come out to the door with a dish, and stood waiting while James piled the herrings on to it.

"There ye are, mistress, there's the dissen for ye, bonnie fish, an' real cheap,"[12] he said, and then, turning to Katie, he added:

"Here's for ye, m' lassie—ye'll no' verra offen get the chance o' the likes o' this." He took from his pocket a bright pink bill, printed in startling black type, and handed it to Katie as he spoke. Her heart almost stood still for a moment as she read the announcement:

FOR ONE NIGHT ONLY

EAST LYNNE: (The World's most famous novel, filmed for the first time by Ford's Cinema at Achinbeg).[13]

Tickets 2s., 1s., 6d., and standing room 1d.

Katie read on, scarcely taking in the fulness of delight that it might mean to her if she could really see a Cinema at last! Often she had read of this delight, but she had never hoped to enjoy it. She looked up into Mrs. Ross's face, and there was a world of pleading in her voice as she asked humbly:

"Will I get tae gang, mistress? I'd like *awfae* tae gang."

"What aboot the kye, lassie?" Mrs. Ross replied; but there was a smile lurking round her mouth as she spoke. Katie fingered the pink bill and looked down, making no answer; the cows were a solid obstacle not to be lightly put aside, she knew. There were ten of them, and five of these were her charge. Mrs. Ross could never milk the

11 Mallaig is a fishing-port on the west coast: this detail confirms the setting of the story as the area around the village of Arisaig ('Achinbeg') to its south, already suggested by the combination of white sand beaches, a view of islands, and the railway.

12 Dissen (Sc.): dozen.

13 *East Lynne* was a hugely successful 'sensation novel' of 1861 by Ellen Wood. Its melodrama lent itself to theatrical adaptation and then to the new form of (silent) film. Findlater probably has in mind the 1916 film starring Theda Bara, but a new version was released in the same year as *A Green-Grass Widow* was published.

whole ten. As she stood there in silence a blind fury of indignation surged up in Katie's heart. Could it be possible that the cows were going to deprive her of this wonderful treat? She was far too unsophisticated to question the justice of the universe; but this choking feeling of resentment overcame her, she had not a word to say, could not even plead her cause, could not raise her eyes from the ground, in case she should read final refusal in the face of her mistress. She stood there trembling, awaiting her fate.

Mrs. Ross and the herring-man exchanged a wink of great amusement, then Mrs. Ross spoke again:

"I might maybe get auld Annie from the Croft to help wi' the kye," she said, thoughtfully. "Johnnie'll be wantin' tae get tae see it, Katie, an' he's sic a laddie for playin' himsel' on the road, ye'd need tae look after him." Katie drew a long, slow breath of delight, and looked up. Mrs. Ross and the herring-man were both laughing, and he added to her bliss by suggesting that Johnnie and she might drive the four miles to Achinbeg in the herring-cart if they chose. Here was a delightful suggestion, indeed! Katie had never driven to an entertainment in her life, and the prospect of this herring-scented drive filled her with ecstasy — she could wear her new blue merino,[14] and her white cotton gloves, even if the night was wet!

"Ye see, I'm aye on the road on Fridays," James reminded them. "An' the cairt can hold the twa o' them fine."

What would many *blasé* persons give to have wee Katie's keen appetite for enjoyment? All the week that followed was to her a blissful dream of anticipation. She looked forward to every moment of the evening's programme, from the one when she would mount the cart in her blue merino, to that of her return at night. It seemed to her that she would be a new creature then — she would have seen a Cinema at last. Though Katie appeared to be plodding in and out of the byre on her broken shoes just as usual, she really trod on air all that week. She began to count the days off one by one — six, five, four, three, two — at last she was able to say "to-morrow" would be the great day, and to-morrow would soon be here. She stood by the door that evening, and looked up into the clear amber-coloured sky. Ross was winding up his fishing reel beside her, and examining his fly-hook. Katie, who was rather in awe of her master, never addressed him in general; but to-night anxiety conquered her shyness.

"Will it be fine the morn?" she asked timidly. Ross wound away at his reel with a practised hand, and looked up into the sky for a moment.

"Aye, that it will — a grand day," he pronounced, little guessing the delight his words gave.

Katie went to bed even earlier than usual that night. She wished to prepare for the great evening by a wonderful effort of the toilet. She had seen one of the maids at the Lodge crimp her hair by means of plaiting it into a great many tiny plaits and damping them. Katie resolved to follow her example. With extraordinary patience she damped and plaited till her head was a mass of hard little knobs all over. Pride often feels a great deal of pain, in spite of the proverb which tells the opposite, and certainly Katie felt a good deal that night. She could not rest her head for any time on the pillow, without feeling one of the knobby plaits drive into her skull, till she writhed with discomfort. Far be it from her, however, to undo the plaits — they must remain as they were at whatever cost to personal ease. So Katie tossed to and fro until the breaking of the day. She heard the lisping tide run up the sands, the cries of the sea birds, the bleating of the lambs and the answer of the sheep; she even got up and looked out of the little window, across to the blue Skye hills rising through the morning mists — but she saw

---

14 Merino is a type of fine wool: by extension, a dress or shawl made from it.

them with unseeing eyes — she was thinking of nothing but the Cinema. At last, tired out with her vigil of vanity, Katie fell sound asleep. She wakened, startled, to find Mrs. Ross speaking loudly in her ear:

"Rise, Katie! Rise, an' come doon the stair as quick 's ye can — the bairn's got convulsions, an' the Master's awa' tae Achinbeg for the doctor!"[15]

The poor woman was so distraught with anxiety that she never noticed Katie's most comical appearance, with the armour of plaits all over her head. She ran downstairs again to attend to the child, and Katie still half dazed with sleep, jumped out of bed, rubbing her eyes as she struggled into her clothes.

Everything was in disorder downstairs — the fireside still choked with the ashes of last night's fire, the cupboard doors standing open after a frantic search for medicines had been made there. Katie could see into the bedroom beyond, where Mrs. Ross stooped over the cradle of the sick child.

"Pit on the fire, lassie," she called through to Katie, who was standing in the middle of the kitchen, bewildered by this sudden summons. "Pit on the fire, an' boil the kettle, tak' the bellows tae it, an' a' the dry sticks ye can find, an' dinna stand glowerin' there."

Katie knelt down and scrabbled out the cinders on to the hearth with her hands; she was an untidy, badly trained worker, and this method of going to work sent clouds of dust and wood ashes out into the room. Then she seized the big black kettle and ran out to fill it at the spout by the door. When full, it was far too heavy for her to lift easily, and she had to heave it on to the hook above the fire by a tremendous effort of all her strength. This done, she went into the bedroom to look at the baby with great curiosity. She had never seen a child in convulsions, and all was fish that came to Katie's net.

"Ech! he's twitchin' awfae!" she cried, almost enjoying the excitement if the truth be told. But she was not allowed to sate her curiosity for long. As Mrs. Ross bent over the cradle, she issued a long string of commands to Katie which might have dismayed even a practised worker:

"Get on the parritch for the men's breakfast, an' pit oot the plates an' the bannocks on the table,[16] an' get a bit butter from the dairy, an' rin oot bye an' bring in the wee tub that's under the spout — I'm wantin' it for a bath for the bairn — an' bring ben the kettle when it's come through the boil, an' when yer through wi' a' that, gang up tae the Croft an' ask auld Annie will she come doon an' help ye wi' the kye, for I canna leave the bairn a meenit."

At this last command, Katie stood stock still in the midst of all her work, for a dreadful fear had flashed across her mind; what if the bairn wasn't better by the evening? Old Annie couldn't milk all the ten cows, and there was no other woman anywhere near who could be got to help her. Could Fortune be going to play this cruel trick upon her? But Katie might have been a student of New Thought to judge by the swiftness and vigour with which she "repelled" this unwelcome suggestion;[17] she refused to admit it for a moment, and, as it were, banged the door in its face. Then that protective instinct which comes to the help of us all in times of anxiety, taught Katie that work was the best antidote she could find. She went plunging about the disordered kitchen, attacking one task after another, never giving herself time to think quietly in case this dreadful fear should steal into her mind again. To and fro she went, opening and shutting drawers, banging down plates and cups upon the table in a sort

---

15 Bairn (Sc.): child.

16 Parritch: porridge; bannocks: oatcakes (both Sc.).

17 'New Thought' was a metaphysical or deist version of the Victorian creed of 'self-help', originating the U.S. in the late nineteenth century: it emphasised the healing effects of 'positive thinking'.

of maze of misery. Then the sound of the cows lowing in the byre, sent her running up to the Croft to fetch old Annie and begin the milking.

As she gained the crest of the hill, Katie paused to take breath. Stretched far below her was the sea, blue and sparkling, and across the strait, clear against the cloudless heaven, the astonishing outline of the hills of Skye ... it did not astonish Katie in the least; she was so entirely preoccupied with the thought of how she could get to the Pictures, that she might have been blind, for any effect the beauties of the outer world had upon her.

She panted on up the steep little path that led to the Croft, the only cottage within miles of the farm.

Old Annie came to the door in response to Katie's knock, and eyed the child sourly. She was a most unpleasing old woman to look at, as she stood in the doorway, her hands rolled in her apron, her deep set, hard old eyes peering out from a little wrinkled face as brown as leather.

"Weel?" she asked laconically.

"Mistress Ross says," panted Katie, "will ye kindly come doon an' gie a hand wi' the kye, for the bairn's taen the convulsions an' she daurna leave him?"[18]

Annie pushed out her under lip in an ugly grimace, and uttered a grunt that sounded like "Oo."

"Will ye come?" Katie asked again.

"She'll be payin' me for't?" Annie queried.

"She didna say," Katie had to confess; but in her eagerness to secure Annie's help she decided to encourage the idea that remuneration would be on an ample scale: "She'll be that grateful, ye ken," she said. Annie had always meant to come, her hesitation had only been assumed for the sake of being disagreeable; so she flung her little "shawlie" over her head and set off down the hill with Katie. Here was Katie's opportunity; she grasped it.

"Hoo mony kye can ye mulk by yersel', Annie?" she asked.

"I've seen the day I could mulk eicht—I wouldna' care tae try mair nor five noo—I'm auld, ye ken, lassie," the old woman said. Katie was dismayed.[19]

"Five! but there's ten o' them!" she cried. "Ech! could ye no' manage them a', Annie?"

The old woman shook her head.

"Na, na, I'm ower auld for that—but ye're a stoot lass yersel', ye can mulk the five o' them fine."

"I'll no' be here the nicht—I'm tae gang tae the Picters," Katie blurted out.

The old woman stood still in the roadway, and gazed at Katie. "In a' the warl what'll that be?" she asked. As "The Movies" had not yet passed across her mental horizon, she might well be bewildered.

Katie burst into a fervent description of what she supposed the Pictures to be like, and the old woman listened with attention to all that she said, then as Katie paused for a moment, she gave her opinion on the whole matter.

"Sic a daft-like thing I niver heard tell o' in a' my days. Bide at hame, lassie, an' dinna gang stravagin' tae the likes o' that."[20]

"Ech! I *canna* bide at hame—I maun get tae see the Picters![21] Will ye no' mulk a' the

---

18 Daurna (Sc.): dare not.
19 Mair nor (Sc.): more than.
20 Bide: stay; stravaig: wander (both Sc.).
21 Maun (Sc.): must.

kye for me, Annie, an' let me gang?" Katie cried.

But she had come up against a heart as hard as flint. Her cry for help did not move Annie one whit; the deep disapproval of one generation for the amusements of another was expressed in every tone of her voice as she refused to countenance Katie's longings after pleasure.

"The lasses are a' daft for pleesuring noo," she said severely, "It's no' wurk ava, jist pleesuring."[22]

"It's no' muckle pleesuring I get!" Katie cried, "I'm wurkin' a' the week through in the byre, exceptin' the aifternoon on Thursdays. I'm up at six in the mornin' an' I'm no' beddit till nine — is that no' wurk?"

But Annie would not admit that it was. Her ideas on work had been formed in the stern times when afternoons out were unknown, and four o'clock in the morning was thought none too early for a young woman to rise from bed and attack an eighteen hours' day of work.

She had just imparted these stern views to Katie when they reached the farm, and there was no more leisure for discussion.

. . . . .

The doctor's hard-worked little car — as hard-worked as the doctor — did not pant up to the farm till the afternoon. It was then announced that the baby's gums must be lanced, an exciting operation which, another time, would have interested Katie mightily — to-day she was too much pre-occupied with her own affairs to pay much attention to the sufferings of the baby. Her rather inept hands were indeed full, for as Mrs. Ross could not leave the child for a minute, all the work of the house devolved upon Katie.

She was deep in very unscientific preparations for dinner, when, through the open door of the kitchen, her sworn foe Flora Reid effected an entrance. Never had Flora been more importunate; but her begging this morning was for a very definite object, and did not degenerate into the usual whine for "a puckle tea" that was generally on her lips.

"Gie's twa bawbees, mistress, if *you* please,"[23] she whined, calling through to Mrs. Ross, whom she had unhappily caught sight of for a moment. Then, as Mrs. Ross paid no attention to her plea, Flora went into detail about why she required the two bawbees. Ran, it appeared, had had a worse than usual attack of Mesoptamy fever last night, and hadn't the doctor in the Army told him that sulphur was the only cure; and wasn't Flora herself on the way to Achinbeg to buy the sulphur? "Jist twa bawbees, if *you* please," she chanted again and again, till Mrs. Ross, exasperated and over-easily persuaded, called to Katie to find the sum that was required. Katie sought in an old jug where pennies were kept, and produced two battered halfpennies because she thought these insignificant coins were less gratifying to Flora than the one more important one would be.

"There's for ye — there's yer twa bawbees, awa' wi' ye, I'm ower thrang the day to have ye standin' there," she told her. And Flora, grinning with the pride of success in her trade, grabbed the bawbees into her little skinny yellow hands (which were tanned to the colour of finnan haddocks by the smoke of the camp fires)[24] and skipped out of

---

22 Ava (Sc.): at all.
23 A bawbee is a ha'penny.
24 'Finnon haddies' are smoked haddocks from the village of Findon, south of Aberdeen.

the kitchen. Relieved of Flora's presence, Katie went on with her cooking. It is to be hoped that Ross the farmer was no epicure, for Katie's preparation of the meal left much to be desired. If you had looked into the farm kitchen that morning, you would only have seen a very untidy, plain- looking girl hard at work, and you would never have guessed at the turmoil of feeling that was raging in her heart as she gashed away at the potatoes and tore the heads off the herrings with hasty, unskilful fingers. So separated are our souls from each other, that it never occurred to Mrs. Ross that Katie was unhappy—her own anxiety had swallowed up any sympathy she might have had with the poor child at another time. As Mrs. Ross knelt beside the cradle or paced up and down with the baby in her arms, she would call out directions to Katie of one sort or another; but she had completely forgotten all about the Cinema.

Long afterwards this August day would be remembered by the mother as the one on which her child had nearly died, while to Katie it would always just be "The Picture Day," when she had suffered such unbearable suspense.

For, as the hours dragged past, her suspense grew more and more acute. She longed to end it, by asking Mrs. Ross plainly whether she might go to the Pictures in the evening or not; but whenever she tried to ask the question, she found it impossible to speak. The jangling old kitchen clock struck five, then it struck half-past five, and Katie knew that her fate must be sealed speedily: the pictures began at half-past six, and how were the cows to be milked, she asked herself, in time to allow her to dress and drive the four long miles to Achinbeg?

At this moment little Johnnie Ross ran noiselessly in on his bare feet, and came up to where Katie stood washing the teacups in a basin of greasy water.

"Are ye no' gettin' ready, Katie?" he whispered, glancing through the half-open door that led into the bedroom, with a child's dim perception of something he didn't understand going on there.

"Weesht!" Katie warned him, "I'm no' through wi' the tea things yet."

"James is comin' along in the cairt, d'ye no' mind he's tae tak' us?" the boy whispered.

"I mind fine—but I'm no' ready. Ye maun pit on yer buits, Johnnie, an' yer Sunday claes, a' the folk in Achinbeg 'll be at the Picters the nicht," Katie admonished him. She was yearning to begin her own toilet, especially to see the effect when these most uncomfortable plaits should at last be undone and her hair might be combed out. It struck her that Johnnie's Sunday clothes would introduce the subject of the Pictures as well as anything. With this design in her mind she went across to the bedroom door.

Mrs. Ross, with that almost awful maternal patience that seems as if it could never tire, was still pacing up and down, up and down, as she had paced the livelong afternoon, and at each step she gave a tender little touch, as regular as the beating of her own heart, to the baby's suffering body—it seemed to keep him quiet ... .

Katie advanced into the doorway.

"Johnnie's seekin' his Sunday claes an' his buits, please," she said. "It's the Picters the nicht, ye mind ..." she added. Her words died away into silence and she stood there dumb, awaiting her fate.

"The Picters—eh, I didna' mind—weel, get oot the laddie's claes for him, Katie, I canna lay doon the bairn for a meenit—ye'll find them in the drawer there." Mrs. Ross spoke abstractedly, and without pausing for a moment in her slow pacing up and down the room.

Katie opened the drawer, gathered up the suit in her arms, and walked to the door; there she faced round and got the fatal question out at last.

"Will I get tae go, mistress?"

Mrs. Ross stood still and looked at her. She took in, perhaps, something of the yearning there was in Katie's face, but at that moment the baby sent up a thin trembling cry, and gave a horrible jerk in her arms.

"Ech! puir wee mannie!" she said, all her attention turned to the baby and away from Katie.

"Ye see I canna stand still a meenit," she said, then a moment later she added:

"Ye canna get tae the Picters the nicht, lassie, there's the kye tae mulk an' a' thing tae sort forbye – ye'll maybe get anither time."[25]

"*There's no' anither time!*" poor Katie blurted out; but Mrs. Ross scarcely heeded the anguish there was in the cry. To her, fighting for the life of her child, this petty disappointment of Katie's seemed beneath contempt. She resumed her pacing again, and only repeated, as she passed Katie:

"Ye canna go, lassie, there's ower muckle tae dae."[26]

Blind and choking with disappointment, Katie turned away without another word. As if to make things worse, she saw James the herring-man draw up his cart at the door, and heard his hearty voice call out to know if they were ready? She went to tell him the bad news; but the words stuck in her throat, and she stood there, a grotesque, sad little figure. Even to the old man's uncritical eye, Katie's appearance suggested that she was not quite ready to start for the evening's entertainment. Her whole head was covered with a sort of helmet of plaits, she wore an old faded frock, and had tied a dirty sack round her instead of an apron. The shoes she wore were large, and broken across the uppers, and had seen service in the byre all winter.

Surely, James thought, the lassie wasn't going to Achinbeg like that? He put the question in a more polite form.

"Ye'll no' be quite ready yet maybe – but there's no great hurry – I'm glad o' a rest mysel' and Maggie here's glad of a bite," he said, indicating the old black pony who was already hard at work snatching her usual mouthfuls with famished haste.

Many children of Katie's age would have begun to cry at such a crisis of misery as this was to her. But though Katie's voice was tense with the effort she had to make to keep back her sobs, she did not cry as she explained to James that she could not come with him. James was much more concerned about the baby's illness than about Katie's disappointment; to his elderly mind there was simply no comparison at all between the two distresses, and he stood there exclaiming, "Eh! I'm real sorry aboot the bairn, jist real sorry," and never bestowed a thought upon poor wee Katie's grief.

Then Johnnie, hastily stuffed into his Sunday clothes and a pair of loudly creaking boots, rushed out of the house and jumped into the cart, his little sunburnt face shining with soap and anticipation – never a thought did he give either to Katie's desolation. James got more slowly to his place in the cart and tugged up Maggie's reluctant head from the grass: a moment later and off they all went along the sunny road to Achinbeg.

Katie stood in the doorway and watched until the cart disappeared round the bend of the road. She felt as if her heart would burst with pent-up tears.

But there was no escape yet from the inexorable wheel of Duty – her grief could not be indulged in at present. For the cows came streeling down from the field in a long, slow procession on their way to the byre for the evening milking.[27] Donald, the herd boy, appeared behind them, flourishing his stick, shouting to Rover, and trying to urge the cows beyond their usual slow pace. Fatally, Katie suspected the reason of

---

25 Forbye (Sc.): as well.
26 Owre muckle (Sc.): too much.
27 Streeling (Sc.): trickling.

his haste—he, even he—was going to the Pictures! He would only have time to "clean himsel" (as Katie phrased it) and be off to join the jubilant crowd at Achinbeg.

She had guessed truly. As Donald drove the cows past the door, he shouted to her in huge excitement:

"I'm awa' tae the Picters, Katie! Are ye no' comin'?"

But he was in too great haste to wait for her reply. Then, the last cow driven in, Donald went off at a tremendous pace to clean up for the entertainment, and once more Katie was left alone. Her bitter cup was not drained to the dregs yet, however. With a rattle over the stony road, the Reids' donkey cart drew near, Ran stalking beside it, Flora seated in the cart. Katie felt in no mood to cope with her enemy at that moment; but no tinker's cart ever was known to pass the door of a farm without stopping at it, so there was little hope of escape from Flora. Sure enough, Ran called to the cuddy to halt, in a stentorian military voice acquired in Mesopotamia, and then, too fine (like all tinker men) to beg himself, he affected to arrange the harness while Flora slipped out of the cart and tried to dart into the kitchen as usual. But Katie barred the way.

"No' the nicht—ye'll no' get onything: the mistress has a bairn ill—awa' wi' ye!" she said roughly.

Flora persisted, and even pushed at Katie in her effort to get in through the doorway. The struggle became almost a fight, and Ran stood by and laughed delightedly. Then what did poor Katie hear? Did her ears deceive her, or did Ran address his daughter in these words:

"*Bing Avree* (come away), Flora," he cried, in the ancient lingo of his race, and then, with a sudden descent into modernity, "*We'll no' be in time for the Picters, lassie!*"

It was too much for Katie altogether. "They'll no' let tinklers in," she cried, hot with indignation and none too polite in consequence; but Flora had the best of the situation in a moment.

"I'm a sojer's bairn, an' that's mair than ye'll ever be,"[28] she assured poor Katie. "My faither's been awa' fechtin' the Germans, sae I'll get in!"

And then she began to caper about, executing a triumphant sort of jig upon the doorstone, both her skinny little hands held high above her head, while she chanted out these words:

"*Standin' room for twa bawbees, Standin' room for twa bawbees!*" and Katie saw that between the finger and thumb of each hand Flora was displaying the ha'pennies she had begged from Mrs. Ross in the morning. Truly the wicked flourish like the green bay tree:[29] Katie, who had toiled late and early, must now continue to toil with never a ray of amusement to brighten her days, and Flora, who habitually ate the bread of idleness, was off to the Pictures on the money she had begged on false pretences. Is it any wonder that Katie's fortitude broke down as she watched the up-to-date tinkers rattle off along the road to Achinbeg? She turned away from the house and rushed into the warm darkness of the byre. There, among the cows, she was alone at last, and might weep out her bitter tears.

. . . . .

Two hours later, when the cows had been milked, and old Annie had gone home, Katie still sat in the byre and refused to come in to the farm for supper. Her face was

---

28 Sojer: soldier.
29 Psalms 37.35: 'I have seen the wicked in great power, and spreading himself like a green bay tree.'

swollen with much weeping, and a sob would still, at long intervals, rise in her throat, though she had now dried her tears. Everything was quiet round the house; the hens gone to roost, Rover asleep on the doorstone. Then Katie heard Ross come out, and knew that he was probably looking for her.

"Katie! Are ye there, Katie!" he called. She made no reply. Again he called:

"Come out an' ye'll see something ye'll no' see the likes of twice in a lifetime."

Katie's curiosity was faintly roused.

"What is't?" she called back in a husky voice.

"Come you an' see," Ross persisted.

Reluctantly Katie emerged from the gloom of the byre and came out to where the farmer stood.

He pointed to the horizon. "Look West, Katie—as far's ye can see—d'ye ken that's the Island of Barra ye're seeing there—like a wee boat it's that far away? D'ye see it?"

Katie raised her swollen eyelids and gazed out towards the blazing West. The whole arch of the sky was scarlet, the sea ran in scarlet waves, and the mountains of Skye were purple against the glow. But as far as the eye could venture—so far that it seemed more like a delusion of the senses than a reality—away on the utmost horizon, another Island had become visible.

"D'ye see it! Yon's Barra![30] I've no' seen it for years," the farmer repeated.

But Katie did not see anything to be excited about.

She turned away without a second glance at the land that was very far off.

"I'm no' carin'," was all she said.

---

30 Yon's (Sc.): that's.

Violet Jacob, 'Thievie'.[1]

The side street of the Angus town was as grey a thing as could be seen even on this grey dripping day. The houses, thick-walled, small-windowed, sturdily uniform and old-fashioned, contemplated the soaking cobble-stones and the 'causeys' which ran like rivers on either side;[2] the complacent eyes of their dark panes, made yet darker by the potted geraniums whose smouldering red gave no liveliness to a reeking world, stared out, endlessly aloof, upon the discomfort of the occasional passer-by. Under their breath they seemed to be chorusing unanimously the words of St. Paul and saying, "None of these things move me."[3] The dried haddocks, which usually hung on their wooden 'hakes' nailed to the walls, had been brought in, as had the small children whose natural playground was the pavement; chalk-marks made by schoolboys in their various evening games had been obliterated from the flags. Newbiggin Street was a featureless place given over to the sulky elements.

All night it had rained steadily, for with evening the fitful drizzle of the day before had settled down to business. The woman who stood framed in the only open doorway of the street looked up and down, frowning. She was a thickset, bony woman, one of those who, unremarkable in feature, are yet remarkable in presence, and though in daily life she made no bid for attractiveness, it was because she did not happen to know where, or in what, attraction lay. Her eyes were steady, and full, at times, of a purposeful though not alluring light. Her hair was dark and thick, her skin sallow, and her head well carried. She was dressed tidily, in stout, ill-fitting clothes, in strong contrast to which she wore a cheap, new hat with a crude blue flower; this was a recognition of the occasion, for she had walked yesterday from her home, five miles away, with her bundle in her hand, to see an aunt whose voice could now be heard in conversation behind her. She was not paying the smallest attention to the old woman's talk; her return journey was before her and the prospect did not please her.

A lad came up the street with his hands in his pockets and his head ducked into his collar under the downpour.

"Bad weather," she observed, as he passed the doorstep.

"Bad weather!" he exclaimed, with a half-contemptuous laugh; "wumman, hae ye seen the river?"

Her face changed. She stood hesitating, staring; then, without a word to the unseen aunt within, she gathered up her bundle and stepped out.

Soon she was in the movement of the main street which declined in a steep hill to the lower levels; there were many others making in the same direction and as she went along she could hear, above the noise of wheels and footsteps, a steady roaring. Not a breath of wind was stirring to make the sound fluctuate, and the even relentlessness of it awed her a little. She crossed the way that lay at right angles to the bottom of the street and stood looking down over the iron-railed wall which held up the road at the riverside. The grey, moving mass that slipped by was almost up to the railings.

Beyond her and all along the row of houses, the people were gathered to watch the rising water. The doors of the one-storied dwellings were choked with furniture that was being lugged out and carried away. Chairs, tubs, tables, birds in cages appeared and disappeared up the hill; women screamed angrily to venturesome children whose

---

1   From *Tales of My Own Country* (London: John Murray, 1922).

2   Causeys are normally cobblestones, but Jacob here clearly means gutters.

3   Contemplating the dangers of a journey to Jerusalem, Paul tells the elders of the church, 'But none of these things move me, neither count I my life dear unto myself' (Acts 20.24).

curiosity had lured them from the maternal skirts, frightened infants cried, men pushed about laden with cooking-pots and bedding; boys shouted to each other, running about in the crowd, the thud of their bare feet lost in the changeless, covetous voice that rose from between the banks. A blind man was being led towards the rise of the hill; he too was playing his part, for he carried a 'wag-at-the-wa'' clock with a gaudily-painted face clasped in his arms.[4] She paused a few minutes to look up and down the torrent and then struck away from the crowd, seeking through the outlying streets for her straightest line home.

Janet Robb's life had been much concerned with the elements. The house for which she was making at her steady, uncompromising tramp was a waterside cottage just above the spot where the river wound into a lake-like estuary on its way to the North Sea.[5] Here she was born, here she had lived out her thirty-four years, for her father had been ferryman until the building of a new bridge a short distance up-stream had shovelled his trade into the limbo of outworn necessities. She had kept house in it almost ever since she could remember; for her mother, who had been an invalid, died when her girl was thirteen, and the ferryman, in spite of the prophecies of his neighbours, did not marry again. Women had no attraction for him, and the need of a housekeeper, which, more than any other cause, drives middle-aged working men into matrimony, did not exist while he had a daughter like Janet, so well able and so well accustomed to grapple with domestic needs. She was a hardy woman now, close-fisted and shrewd. She had been an invaluable help, both in the house and out of it; the two had worked the ferry between them, for the river was not wide and the traffic was small. Carts and horses had to go round to a point about a mile westward, and only foot-passengers on their way to the town troubled that part of the shore; when her father was out she could leave her house-work to put them across to the farther bank without much interruption to it.

The ferryman was not an inspiring acquaintance. Though he belonged, in company with publicans, barbers, and blacksmiths, to a trade eminently social in its opportunities, he cared nothing for that part of it. He could put over a boatful of people without addressing a word to any of them and with scarcely an answer to any man enterprising enough to attack his silence. He was not popular, and, as those who give nothing of their mind to the world must perforce submit to have the gaps they create filled up according to the taste of their neighbours, a whole crop of tales sprang up at the water-side like so much duckweed. He was a secret drinker; he was worth ten thousand pounds; he kept a woman in the town whom he ill-treated — had she not been seen with her head bandaged, crying ill names after him on the public road? — he starved his daughter; she starved him — all these whisperings surrounded his unconscious head. He was a spare man, smaller in build than Janet, lined and clean-shaven. Besides his recognised business he had a cart and an old horse by means of which he did a little carrying, going townwards three times a week, whilst she took charge of the boat; and though nobody outside the cottage knew anything about it, he received substantial help from a son who had left home early and was making a good income in Canada. While the neighbours went wide of the mark in most of the rumours they set afloat about him, one of these had a fragile foundation of truth. Davie Robb kept no woman and cared as little for drink as he did for company; there was only one thing that he cared about at all, and that lay in a box under his bed. The contents of this box did not

---

4   The clock is a wall-mounted one with an unencased pendulum.
5   This is the Montrose Basin; the river is thus the South Esk, and the 'country town' Brechin, five miles upstream from the Basin.

amount to ten thousand pounds, but they went into several hundreds. They were his soul, his life. Waking, he thought of them; and sleeping, they were not far from his dreams. When he opened the lid to add to the hoard he counted and re-counted them, running up the figures on paper. It mattered not to him that he knew them by heart; he would roll them about in his brain as a child rolls a sweet about in its mouth.

Not even Janet knew the amount of these savings, though she made many guesses and was, perhaps, near enough to the truth. The box was never spoken of between father and daughter. It was the ferryman's god, and in one sense it had the same place in their household as God has in most others: it was never mentioned, even when taken for granted. In another sense, its place was different: for it was continually in the mind of both.

Janet thrust along the road, leaving the country town quickly behind her, urged on by strong necessity. Her father was now permanently disabled, for some years almost crippled by rheumatism. He was an old man, shrunken and very helpless. The cottage was two-storied, and its upper floor was approached by an outside staircase running up at the gable end. There was a stair inside, too, which had been added later because of the occasional spates in the river, to allow the inmates to move to the upper room without opening the door when water surrounded the walls. Old Robb slept upstairs and was just able to get down by himself, though he could never manage to get up again without assistance; and yesterday, before leaving home, Janet had arranged with a boy who lived up-stream near the new bridge that he should come in the evening to convey the old man to his bedroom. The lad had consented reluctantly, for, to the young, there was something uncanny about 'Auld Thievie.' Scottish people are addicted, perhaps more than any others, to nicknames, and the ferryman's surname, combined with his late extortions as a carrier, had earned him the title by which he was known for some miles round. Nobody liked Thievie.

Not even Janet. It was scarcely affection that was hastening her. Perhaps it was duty, perhaps custom. Something was menaced for which she was responsible. That, with capable people, is generally all that is wanted in the way of a key to wind them up and set them going. The rain had stopped and she put down her dripping umbrella. The blue flower in her unsuitable hat had lost its backbone and flagged, a limp, large thing; there was a fine powdering of wet on her thick eyebrows and the harsh twist of hair at the back of her head. Mist was pouring in from the sea, the wind having sat in the south-east — the wet quarter on the east coast — for three days; and though it had dropped like lead with last night's tide, the 'haar' was coming miles inland as though some huge, unseen engine out seaward were puffing its damp breath across the fields. The cultivated slopes of the Sidlaws, a mile on her right, diminishing in height as they neared the estuary, were hidden. The Grampians, ten miles away on her left, were hidden too; that quarter of the horizon where, on ordinary days, they raised their blue and purple wall, being a mere blank. The river whose infancy they cradled had burst from them angrily, like a disobedient child from its parents, and was tearing along, mad with lust of destruction, to the sea.

When she was some way out of the town a figure emerged from the vapour ahead, growing familiar as the two wayfarers approached each other. Her expression lightened a little as she recognised the advancing man. He was smiling too.

"Hey, Janet!" he cried, "I was wond'rin' what like daft wife was oot on sic a day."[6]
His face was red and moist with the mist.

"I've been at Newbiggin Street. I'm just awa' hame," said she.

---

6   Sic (Sc.): such.

He was a connection of the Robb family, so her words conveyed something to him. "An' foo's auntie?" he inquired.[7]

"Weel eneuch – but I maun awa' back. There's an awfae spate, ye ken."

"Tuts, bide you a minute. I haena seen ye this twa weeks syne."[8]

She made no move to go on. Willie Black had a different place in her mind from anyone else. It was not easy to deflect Janet Robb from her way, but she would do more for this man, a little younger than herself and infinitely her inferior in will, than for any other person. He was the only male living being who approached her from the more easy and lighter standpoint from which such men as she knew approached girls, and their quasi-relationship had brought them into a familiarity which she enjoyed. He was one of those who looked upon women in a general way with a kind of jocose patronage, always implied and often expressed. He meant no harm by this manner; it was natural to him, and he was not nearly so bold a character as his attitude would suggest. Janet was so much unlike the other women he knew that he would have thought it right to assume superiority even had he, in her case, not felt it. She attracted him, not through his heart and certainly not through his senses, but as a curiosity to be explored in a mildly comic spirit. He knew, too, that Thievie was well off; for once, in a moment of confidence, Janet had hinted at her father's savings, and Black felt vaguely, but insistently, that in the fullness of time he would be wise in proposing to her. The day was distant yet, but meanwhile he sought opportunities of considering her and discovering how far she would be endurable as a wife.

Janet fidgeted from one foot to the other. By one half of herself she was urged to continue her way; the other half being impelled to stay by the invitation in his eyes. She did not know for how much this counted, so great was her ignorance of the amenities of men. Black was the only man who had ever come nearer to her life than the baker's cartman from whom she took the bread at her door or the cadger from whom she bought the fish. She had a great longing to be like other women, a factor in the male world. She was too busy to brood over the subject, and had inherited too much of her father's love of money-making to be deeply affected by any other idea. But when she was with Black she was conscious of all she lacked and was lured beyond measure by her perception of his attitude. It suggested that she took rank with the rest of her sex.

"I'll need awa'," she began, "feyther's himsel' i' the hoose. There's an awfae water comin' doon an' he canna win up the stair his lane.[9] I maun hae tae gang on."

"I didna ken ye thocht sic a deal o' Thievie. Ye micht think o' me a bittie," he added, with knowing reproachfulness.

She looked away from him into the blankness of the mist.

"Houch! you?" she exclaimed.

"He's an auld, dune crater. Ye could dae weel, wantin' him."

"Haud yer tongue!" she cried, actuated purely by a sense of what was fitting.[10]

"Weel, what's the advantage o' him sittin' yonder, an' a' that siller just nae use ava' till him – an' nae use tae ony ither body?"[11]

She made no reply. There is something silencing in hearing another person voice an idea one believes to be one's own private property.

"Ye'd be a real fine lass wi' yon at yer back," he continued; "it's a fair shame ye should be dancin' after the like o' yon auld deil when ye micht be daein' sae muckle better."[12]

---

7   Foo (Sc.): how (a specifically North-East form).

8   Weel eneuch: well enough; maun: must; bide: stay; syne: since (all Sc.)

9   Win: get; his lane: alone (both Sc.).

10   Cratur: creature; wantin' him: without him; haud: hold (all Sc.).

11   Siller: silver, i.e. money; ava: at all (both Sc.).

12   Yon: that; muckle: much (both Sc.).

She withdrew her gaze from the mist and met his eyes.

"What would I be daein' better?" she inquired, rather fiercely.

He gave a sort of crowing laugh.

"What wad ye be daein'? Gie's a kiss, Janet, an' maybe I'll tell ye."

Before she had time to think he had flung his arm about her and the roughness of his dripping moustache was on her lips.

She thrust him from her with all her very considerable strength. He laughed again.

It was the first time that a man had ever attempted such a thing and her heart almost stopped. She was torn between wrath and a thrilling, overmastering sense of something achieved. She stood panting, her bundle fallen into the mud. Then she snatched it and dashed into the greyness. It took but a moment to swallow up her figure, but he stayed where he was, staring, his coarse shoulders shaking with laughter. She could hear his jesting voice calling after her as she went. When she had gone a little distance she paused, listening to discover whether he was following; but there was no sound of footsteps.

She hurried on though she had ceased to think of her goal. Her thoughts drove her, rushing and tumbling like birds with beating wings, crowding and jostling and crying in her ears. Black's words had let them loose, stirring her as much as his action. Yes, it was quite true. She was tied, as she had been all her life, to her father and his box. She drudged for him, year in, year out, and got nothing by it, while he clung like an old dog in the manger to the thing he would neither use nor share. She would be a wife worth having for any man with the contents of that box to start housekeeping on! Willie Black would realise that. She remembered her years at the ferry in fair weather and foul, the picking and scraping she had done and suffered in the house, that the hoarding might go on that was no good to anyone. There had never been any love lost between herself and Thievie, and though he was her father she had long known that she hated him. Yes, she hated him. She had no fear of work and had taken it as a normal condition, but it had come between her and all that was worth having; the toil that had been a man's toil, not a woman's, had built a barrier round her to cut her off from a woman's life. All this had lurked, unrecognised, in her mind, but now it had leaped up, aroused by a man's careless, familiar horseplay.

Her breath came quick as she thought of her own meagre stake in the world. She knew herself for some kind of a power, and that was awaking the dormant realisation of her slavery, all the more bitter for its long sleep. She pushed back her hat and the drops came tumbling to her shoulder from the draggled blue flower, now a flower in name only, a sodden streak of blackened colour. She found herself shaking all over and she longed to sit down, but the milestone, which had often served her for a seat on her walks to and from the town, was a good way on.

The roadside landmarks were growing a little clearer. It was almost noon, and the flash of false brightness which that hour will often bring hovered somewhere in the veiled sky. She heard the ring of a hammer coming muffled from the smithy ahead, and pushed on, thinking to sit a little in some corner behind the ploughs and harrows. She was unnerved by the tumult in her; anger and self-pity were undermining her self-control; she was a self-controlled woman, and the agony of disorganised feeling was, in consequence, all the worse. It seemed that she had never been aware of the large injustices of life till now. Her difficulties had been small, physical ones and she had known how to scatter them with a high hand; but these new ones pressed round her like a troop of sturdy, truculent beggars, clamouring and menacing. Another woman might have wept but she only suffered.

She reached the smithy door and looked in. The smith was at his anvil, holding a red-hot horseshoe with the tongs. The blowing had ceased and in the dimness of the shed a pair of huge, patient Clydesdales were in process of being shod. A young 'horseman' was standing by, his hands in his pockets, watching the sputter of flaming sparks that rose with each blow and fell here and there. The hot scent of horses and leather and scorching hoof seemed one with the rich browns and warm shadows that hang about smithy fires. Behind the mysterious limbs of the bellows the elf-like face of the smith's 'prentice-lad peered at Janet, though both the men's interest in the matter in hand made them unaware of the woman who slipped noiselessly in.

She laid her bundle down behind a cart that stood jacked up with a wheel off, amid a medley of implements, and sat down, concealed by the litter, in a cobwebby corner of the long building. The hammering stopped and one of the carthorses shifted its feet and blew a shattering sigh into the rafters; the horseman gave one of those sudden expostulatory cries that his profession addresses to its charges, and all was still again. The smith threw down his hammer and left the shoe to cool a little.

"They'll be haein' a bad time doon at the hooses yonder," said he, nodding his head backwards in the direction of the low ground.

"Aye, coorse," said the horseman.

"I wad believe that," continued the smith, whose noisy trade gave him less opportunity of hearing his own voice than he liked. "I mind weel eneuch when we got a terrible-like spate — saxteen year syne, come Martinmas. I was doon aboot Pairthshire way then, an' I wasna lang merriet, an' the wife was that ta'en up aboot it. She was frae the toon, ye understan', an' she didna like tae see the swine an' the sheep jist rowin' past i' the water.[13] Ah weel, ye see, we'll jist hae tae dae oor best."

"Aye," said the horseman.

"There'll be big losses. Aye, weel, weel, we canna control the weather, ye see."

"Na," said the horseman.

"An' I doot auld Thievie doon at the ferry'll be swampit. Aye, ye see, ye canna tell when yer time's tae come."

"The auld scabbit craw," said the horseman.[14]

The smith took up his tools, and approaching one of the horses, laid hold of an enormous hind foot and began, strenuously, to pare the hoof. The beast looked round with an all-embracing toleration. The horseman spat.

Janet sat still, trying to quell the storm within her and to think connectedly. There had been no need for the blacksmith's words to bring her father's plight before her. In all likelihood the riverside cottage was already surrounded, and the fact that the few neighbours were well aware that none knew better than she how to handle oars might easily make them slow to bestir themselves on Thievie's behalf. The old ferry-boat, still seaworthy, lay in its shed some way up the bank, ready for the occasional use to which it was put; and no one but the little boy who had been in to help the old man on the preceding night knew that Janet was absent; and the boy was probably at school.

Even now her freedom might be coming to her on the rising spate! She shivered, chilled after her excitement and her transit from hot heartburning to the cold horror upon which, with the inward eye, she looked. Thievie could not get up the ladder-like stair — not even with the gurgling water behind him — without a helping hand. It was years since he had even been willing to try. Perhaps she had only to stay where she was and to take what gift this day might bring! Her hands were shaking, though she

13   Row (Sc.): move smoothly in water (*SND*).
14   Scabbit craw: scabby crow.

had clasped them tightly on her lap, and she set her teeth, almost fearing that their chattering would betray her to the smith and his taciturn companion. Of what use was that old withering life by the riverside to itself or to any other living thing? It was as dead, already, as the dead money in the box below the bed. But the money would be dead no longer. Willie Black would not think it dead. She would wait where she was; the smith might go to his dinner when the shoeing was done, but the smithy door stood always open and she would sit, unmolested, till such time as she judged. ...[15]

Her thoughts stopped there and she closed her eyes, leaning her head against the wall.

She could not hang about the road in such weather, waiting. She had not the courage to do that, for fear of drawing attention and making her neighbours ask inconvenient questions ... afterwards. Though she assured herself that no one would guess, or be sufficiently interested to try to guess, what was causing her to loiter, her nerves would not allow her to face so much as an innocent stranger. She wished the lad behind the bellows had not peered at her in that way. Suppose he should tell the smith — but anything was better than the public road! She tried to force herself into composure.

All at once a loud voice sounded at the door. She opened her eyes and recognised a local carrier through her screen of lumber. He took off the sack which enveloped him and shook it till the drops flew.

"No muckle daein' the day," he began. "Dod aye, the water that's oot! Whiles I couldna get forrit."[16]

The smith looked up from the hairy foot gripped between his knees.

"Queer times, queer times," he said. "Weel, we canna change it, ye see."

"How's a' wi' you, Ake?" said the carrier, turning to the horseman.

"Whoa. S-ss-ss!" cried the latter, for the horse, feeling the smith's movement, tried to release its foot.

"I was thinkin' Thievie wad be drooned," continued the carrier, grinning from ear to ear and remembering the days when they had been rivals on the road.

"And is he no?" inquired the horseman, roused to interest at last.

"No him. I'm tae hae a word wi' some o' they folk by the brig. I saw the river-watcher's boat gaein' oot nae lang aifter it was licht, an' I cried on him, whaur was he gaein'? Dod, when he tell't me he was awa tae seek Thievie, I was fair angert. 'Let him be,' I says, 'wad ye cast awa' the Lord's maircies yon way?' But there's the auld thrawn stock safe an' soond,[17] and folk lossin' their guid cocks an' hens. Fie!"

The horseman gave a loud shout of laughter and relapsed immediately into gravity.

"Aye, the ways o' Providence," observed the smith.

"Weel, I maun be movin'," said the carrier. "Thievie'll be on the pairish yet. There's mair water tae come doon frae the hills afore it's finished. There'll be naething left o' the sma' hoosies on the bank. A'thing 'll just gang traivellin' tae the sea.[18] There was naebody believed it wad be sae bad the morn, airly, when I was doon by the auld ferry, but lord! they tellt me an hour syne that there's no been onything like it this aichty year past. An' the tide's comin' in, ye ken."

He called the last sentence over his shoulder as he turned from the door.

---

15 This and all ellipses are in the original.
16 Dod: a euphemism for God; forrit: forward (both Sc.).
17 Thrawn (Sc.): stubborn.
18 A'thing (Sc.): everything.

Janet had all but cried out aloud during the carrier's speech. Her father was gone—sitting safe now under some sheltering roof above the reach of the insurgent river!

But it was not the thought of this which overwhelmed her. She knew from long experience that there was hardly anything he would not do to prevent anyone, even herself, from seeing his precious box, and she could swear that he would never consent to expose it to a strange human eye while there was the smallest possibility of keeping it hidden. At that hour, soon after daybreak, when the carrier had seen the boat go for him, the torrential rain which was to follow had not yet turned the ordinary spate into something unknown for half a century. That being so, it was plain to her that, sooner than disclose the box to his rescuer, Thievie would leave it in what had been, at other spate-times, the perfect security of the upper story. So completely was she convinced of this that she would have staked everything she had on it. But she had nothing; and all that she had a prospect of having was surely lying in the rickety upper room waiting for the abnormal torrent to wreck the little house and carry its precious contents to the fathomless recesses of the sea.

She sprang up, the frantic idea banishing all else; and she had dashed boldly out of the smithy under the astonished gaze of the two men before it struck her with measureless relief that she had now nothing to fear from the most suspicious eye. Her father was safe; her secret design thwarted by the river-watcher; the reason for anything she did was of interest to no one. She saw now how futile her fears had been; the outcome of disorganised nerves. Conscience had almost made her believe that she carried her thoughts outside her body like her clothes.

At last, breathless, the perspiration on her face mingled with the wet, she reached the diverging road that led to the river, and as she turned into it the mist began to lift. It grew brighter behind the cloud-wrappings that veiled the world. She stopped, listening for the river's voice. The noonday gleam had strengthened and she came out suddenly from a belt of vapour into comparative clearness and saw the submerged levels lying some little way before her. The broken water above them was all that told her where the banks were, and here and there she could recognise certain tall clumps of alder above the swirl. She redoubled her pace till, at the place in the road from which Thievie's cottage could be seen, she noted with rising hope that the flood had not yet reached the tops of the ground-floor windows. The outside stair was still practicable.

At the water's edge, at the nearest spot to the little house, she stood still. She had hung her bundle and her umbrella on a stout thorn-tree growing on a knoll by the wayside. She would need both hands for what she was going to do. The boat-shed was safe, but she would have to wade almost to the knees to reach it. She drew up her skirts and walked into the chilly water.

She felt its steady push against her legs, and her riverside knowledge told her that the tide at the estuary's mouth had turned and was coming in. It was thrusting the overflow out from the banks on either side and the area of dry fields was diminishing. She looked up apprehensively, for the gleam of brightness had paled in the last few minutes and she dreaded lest the mist should close in again before her task was done.

At last she reached the shed. The oars were afloat inside, kept from sailing away by the pressure of the incoming tide on the flood-water. She waded through the doorway and mounted, hampered by the weight of her soaking boots, on a projecting wooden ledge; then as she clung to an iron hook in the wall, she stretched out her foot and drawing the old craft towards her, stepped in. When she had secured the oars, she loosed the painter from its ring and guided herself out between the narrow walls.

It was easy work rowing, in spite of the slight current against her. The boat was not a heavy one, and only built to carry a few people at a time across fifty yards of water. She rowed as fast as she could, for the damp vapour was drifting in again, and the sun's face, which had looked like a new shilling above her, had now withdrawn itself, leaving a blurred, nebulous spot in its place. Pulling across the shallows on the skirts of the spate, she refused to picture what might happen should she find, on emerging from the cottage with the box, that all landmarks were lost in the mist. Her only guide would then be the sound of that menacing rush from which it would take all the strength of her arms to keep clear.

When the boat's nose bumped against the outside stair she made the painter fast to the railings and stood up, wringing the water from her petticoats. As she clambered out and ascended to the stairhead, small streams trickled down the stone steps from her boots. The door of the upper room was locked inside, but she was not much perturbed by this, having expected it, and moreover she knew the old crazy wood could not stand much ill-usage. Its thin boards were gaping inside and had been pasted up with brown paper by her own hands. She drew back to the outer edge of the stairhead and flung her whole weight against them. The door cracked loudly, and though the lock held, she saw that another couple of blows would split it at one of its many weak places. Again and again she barged into it, and at last the wood parted in a long, vertical break. She was down the steps in a moment and dragging one of the short, stout oars from the boat. She stood on the stairhead, looking round. She could still see the boathouse, a dark blur, no more, but from the south-east there came a splash of rain. She struck the door with the butt end of the oar, once, twice. It gave suddenly, almost precipitating her into the room. She recovered her balance, and then, with that boatman's prudence which never left her, carried her weapon down and threw it into its place.

In another minute she had thrust her way in and was face to face with her father.

Thievie was sitting crouched under the tiny window with his box in his arms. His nostrils were dilated, his eyes looked as though he would strike, though his hand was still. He had sat listening to the bumping of the boat below and to the blows that burst in the rotten door; humanity seemed to have gone from him, leaving in its place the fierce, agonised watchfulness of some helpless, murderous thing, some broken-backed viper. His eyes fixed Janet, unrecognising. Not a word came from his lips.

"What are ye daein' there?" cried Janet hoarsely.

Her knees were shaking, but not from her exertions at the door.

His tongue passed over his lips. He looked as though he would bite. She sickened, she knew not why, but revulsion passed shuddering through her.

"Foo is't ye're no awa'?" she exclaimed, mastering herself.

"I wadna gang."

He smiled as he said this and held the box tighter. As she looked at it in his grasp, some inherited instinct rose in her, and though it had been mainly valuable to her for what it would bring, should it pass from his drowned hands into her living ones, it became, at that moment, a thing desired and desirable for itself. She did not know what sum was in it, but the rage for possession of it came to her.

He laughed quietly, his toothless mouth drawn into a long line. She pounced on him, shaking his arm.

"Weel, awa' ye come noo—the boat's waitin' on ye!"

He shook his head.

She had never laid rough hands on him before, but she gripped him now. She was strong and he was helpless; and he knew, in his helplessness, that she had come for the box. He had feared the river-watcher, and he now feared her. He did not know what she meant to do to him; his mind was obsessed by the box and the fear of its loss, and unhinged by the flood. He would have liked to resist her, but he could not, should he dare try. His concentrated hate shot at her like a serpent's tongue.

"I ken what's wrang wi' ye!" she shouted. "Ye're feared for yer box! Ye're feared yon man gets a sicht o' it! Aye, but he'll be here syne—he's aifter ye! I saw his boat i' the noo, an' him in it—ye'd best come."

His face changed. On the dusty window-pane the drops beat smartly.

"Ach, ye auld fule!" she cried savagely, "wad ye loss it a'? Div ye no see the rain? Div ye no ken the water's creepin' up? Muckle guid yer box'll dae ye when the spate's owre yer heid an' you tapsalterie amang the gear the water's washin' doon![19] Haste ye noo. We'll need awa' frae this."

She dragged him to his feet and he leaned on her, clutching his burden and unable to resist her violence.

They struggled across the floor and through the broken-down door. It was raining pitilessly. Thievie took no notice of it. He, who had known the river in every phase of drought or flood, should have had small doubt of the danger in which they stood. The roaring of its voice was increasing and there were fewer stone steps to be seen than when Janet made her entrance. It was pouring in the hills and the tide had yet a few hours to rise before it turned. Thievie looked this way and that. What he feared most was to see the river-watcher slide out of the mist in his boat; for the elements, the world and all the men and women in it were, to his disordered imagination, intent on one thing—the box. He would never sleep peacefully again should a strange eye see it. He would be robbed. He had long since been the slave of this one thought, and now it overwhelmed his dim, senile mind, even as the resistless water was overwhelming the land about them.

It took all her force and resolution to get him into the boat; he was so crippled and his arms so much hampered by the burden he carried. Though he cursed her as they went down the stair, his thoughts were of the river-watcher. In the middle of their descent he laughed his mirthless laugh.

"God-aye, but he'll be comin'!" he said, "but it'll no be there—he'll no get a sicht o't!"

At last she got him safely afloat, and having loosed the boat, rowed away from the stairs. The surrounding floods were peppered by the onslaught of heavy drops from the low sky, and then, as though a sluice-gate had been pulled up in the firmament, a very deluge was upon them. The little they could see was washed out and they were isolated from everything in a universe without form and void,[20] at the inmost heart of the hissing downpour. The river's noise was lost in it and all sense of direction left Janet. She pulled blindly, believing that she was heading for the boathouse. Soon they bumped and scraped against some projection and the stern swung round. She felt the boat move under her, as though drawn by a rope. She tried to straighten it, but the blinding descent of the rain bewildered her; a branch of an alder suddenly loomed out of it, the lower twigs sweeping her face. Thievie cried out and crouched, clinging with frenzy to his box, and she guessed they had drifted above the deep, wide drain whose mouth was in the river. Her blood ran cold, for its swollen waters must inevitably carry them into the very midst of the tumult.

The drain was running hard under the floodwater and she despaired of being able to struggle against it. They were broadside on; besides which she dreaded to be swept

---

19 Tapsalterie (Sc.): topsy-turvie.
20 Echoes Genesis 1.2: 'And the earth was without form, and void; and darkness was upon the face of the deep'.

out of her seat by another branch, for there were several alder trees by the edge of the channel. The rain began to slacken.

As its fall abated, the river grew louder and the sky lifted a little and she could see the large alders, gaunt and threatening as spectres, blurred and towering over them. With that strange observance of detail, often so sharp in moments of desperate peril, she noticed a turnip, washed out of the ground and carried by the torrent, sticking in a cleft between two straggling branches, just below water-level. She made a tremendous effort and slewed the boat straight; and working with might and main at her oars, got it out of the under-tow that urged it riverwards.

All at once the river-watcher's voice rang out from the direction of the boathouse, calling the old man's name. She answered with all the breath she had left.

"Yon's him! Yon's the river-watcher!" shrieked Thievie, from where he still crouched in the bottom of the boat.

She ignored him, tugging at her oars and pulling with renewed strength towards the sound.

He raised himself, and clinging to one of them, tried to drag it from her. She wasted no breath but set her teeth, thrusting out at him with her foot. He clung with all his weight, the very helplessness of his legs adding to it. She dared not let go an oar to strike at him. She could not have believed him able to hamper her so – but then, neither had she believed he could get himself up the inside stair of the cottage unaided; and yet he had done it. It was as though the senseless god of his worship, lying in the box, gave him the unhallowed tenacity by which he was delivering them over to the roaring enemy they could not see, but could hear, plain and yet plainer.

She was growing weary and Thievie's weight seemed to increase. Could she spare a hand to stun him she would have done so for dear life. She had heard of the many-armed octopus of the southern seas, and she remembered it now in this struggle that was no active struggle because one would not, and one dared not, lose grip.

The boat, with one oar rendered useless, swung round and drifted anew into the channel between the trees. Again the river-watcher was heard calling and again Janet tried to answer, but her breath was gone and her strength spent. The current had got them.

Thievie relaxed his grip as he felt the distance increase between himself and the voice. A branch stayed their progress for a moment, whipping the sodden hat from Janet's head; her clothes were clinging to her limbs, her hair had fallen from its ungainly twist and hung about her neck. They went faster as they neared the racing river. Then the swirl caught them and they spun in its grip and were carried headlong through the mist. Janet shut her eyes and waited for the end.

Time seemed to be lost in the noise, like everything else. They sped on. At last they were not far from the estuary and the river had widened. Once they were all but turned over by a couple of sheaves, the spoil of the late harvest, which came driving alongside; once they passed within a foot of a tree which rode the torrent, plunging, its roots sticking up like gaunt arms supplicating mercy from the shrouded sky.

Finally they found themselves drifting in the comparative quiet of the broad sheet of tidal water, among the bits of seaweed carried inland above the deeps of the river-bed. The terrors of death had blinded Janet as they were swept along, and she now awoke as from a nightmare. An oar had been reft from her grasp in the stress of their anguished journey. Thievie was staring at her like an animal; his sufferings, as they were battered between one death and another on the boiling river, were nothing compared to hers. His god had upheld him. He had crawled back to his seat in the stern.

"Aye, he micht cry on us," he said. "We're far awa' frae him noo – he'll no ken what I've got here!"

He began to rock about, laughing as he thought of the river-watcher's fruitless attempt to find him.

"Haud still," said Janet sternly. "God, hae ye no done eneuch mischieve the day? Gin yon mist doesna lift an' let them see us frae the shore we'll be oot tae sea when the tide gangs back."[21]

"Naebody'll see us, naebody'll see us!" he exclaimed, hugging the box and rocking himself again.

Janet rose to her feet, fury in her eyes; she could no longer keep her hands off him.

As he saw her movement, he snatched the box from where it lay at his feet.

"Stand still, or I'll tak' it frae ye!" she cried loudly, making towards him.

He gave one cry of horror and, with the box in his arms, hurled himself sideways into the waters that closed over him and his god.

The tide was on the turn and the rain had ceased. A wind had sprung up in the west, driving the 'haar' before it back to the sea whence it came. Some men from the fishing village near the lighthouse were rowing smartly out into the tideway where a boat drifted carrying a solitary human being, a woman who sat dazed and frozen and who had not so much as turned her head as they hailed her.

As they brought her ashore one of them took off his coat and wrapped it round her. She seemed oblivious of his action.

"Hae," said he, with clumsy kindness, "pit it on, lass. What'll yer lad say gin ye stairve?"[22]

Janet thrust the coat from her.

---

21 Gin (Sc.): if.
22 Stairve, sterve (Sc.): freeze (nothing to do with hunger).

Joe Corrie
IN TIME O' STRIFE (1927)

CHARACTERS

JOCK SMITH	A Miner
JEAN SMITH	His Wife
JENNY SMITH	Their Daughter (22)
LIZZIE SMITH	Their Daughter (13)
BOB SMITH	Their Son (17)
TAM PETTIGREW	A Miner
AGNES PETTIGREW	His Wife
KATE PETTIGREW	Their Daughter (22)
TAM ANDERSON	A Young Miner
WULL BAXTER	A Young Miner

ACT ONE

The kitchen of the Smiths' home in the mining village of Carhill in Scotland.
A bed, heavily curtained, occupies almost the whole of the left side of the room (Spectators). A dresser, covered with nick-nacks, stands at the back. To the right of the dresser is a four-paned window through which can be seen the colliery in the distance.
The table stands in the centre of the floor.
Between dresser and window is a stool, on which stands the pail and a tinnie.
The door leading to the outside is at left back.
The door to room at right is at right back.
The time is night, and the lamp has been lit and window curtains drawn.
The period of the play is the mining crisis of 1926.[1]
At rise of curtain LIZZIE, pencil in her mouth, is on her knees on a chair at the table-side, poring over her home-lessons.
JENNY sits at fireside, converting an old hat into a new one with a piece of blue ribbon.
The sound of marching people can be heard singing:

> We'll hang every blackleg to the sour apple tree,[2]
> We'll hang every blackleg to the sour apple tree,
> We'll hang every blackleg to the sour apple tree,
> As we go marching on.

The tune is 'John Brown's Body.'
When they have faded away in the distance,

LIZZIE: *(Sings)*
> We'll hang every blackleg to the sour apple tree,
> We'll hang every blackleg to the sour apple tree,

---

1   For these circumstances see 'Introduction'.
2   Blackleg: strike-breaker.

We'll hang every blackleg to the sour apple tree,
As we go marching ...

JENNY: Here! you get thae sums done.[3]

LIZZIE: (Shortly) I canna dae them, you better ha'e a shot at them, Jenny.

JENNY: What kind are they, thae kind wi' the dots?

LIZZIE: Ay.

JENNY: Weel, you'll need to try Bob.

LIZZIE: Bob! He canna dae decimals ... I'll get the strap the morn if I dinna ha'e them done.[4]

JENNY: Let him try and gi'e you the strap, and there'll be some fun.

LIZZIE: He's done it before.

JENNY: Ay, but there's a strike on noo, and we're lookin' for blood. But does he no' let you see hoo to dae your sums?

LIZZIE: Ay, but he thinks we're a' as clever as him. I wish I was awa' frae the schule, Jenny, I dinna like it.

JENNY: We a' wish we were awa' frae the schule,[5] but we're no' lang till we wish we were back to it.

(Singing of crowd can be heard faintly in distance.)

LIZZIE: Is the strike aboot finished, Jenny?

JENNY: God knows. It was as like finishin' six weeks ago as it is the day.[6]

LIZZIE: Will we ha'e ony tea the nicht before we go to bed?

JENNY: I'll be able to tell you that at bed-time. Get your lessons done.

LIZZIE: It's no' easy daein' lessons when you're hungry. (Sings)
We'll hang every blackleg to the sour apple tree,
We'll hang every blackleg to the sour apple tree,
We'll hang every ...

JENNY: Shut it! D'ye want to wauken him?

(JENNY nods her head in direction of room. The door opens, and AGNES PETTIGREW enters. She is rather shabby and there is the look of illness on her face. She walks wearily, and is troubled with a little, harsh cough.)

AGNES: Is your mither in, Jenny?

JENNY: No, she's awa' doon the street, auntie ... Sit doon.

(AGNES sits at left side of table.)

JENNY: What's a' the noise aboot the nicht?

AGNES: I dinna ken.[7] There's been a meetin' in the hall aboot something. Oor Tam'll no' go to the meetin's to let us ken what's gaun on.

LIZZIE: Can you dae sums, auntie?

JENNY: Here! shut that book till Bob comes in.

LIZZIE: Bob canna dae them.

JENNY: Weel, awa' to the schoolmaister and get him to do them, that's what he's gettin' payed for.

(AGNES coughs.)

JENNY: That cauld's no' leavin' you in a hurry, auntie.

AGNES: No ... It's no' sae bad in the daytime, but it keeps me off my sleep at nicht.

---

3   Thae (Sc.): those.

4   The strap: a heavy leather belt with which children were struck across the hand as a punishment in Scottish schools. The morn (Sc.): tomorrow.

5   We a' ... awa' frae the schule (Sc.): we all ... away from the school.

6   The day (Sc.): today.

7   Dinna ken (Sc.): don't know.

256

JENNY: Ha'e ye seen the doctor yet?

AGNES: What guid would he dae? He'd just order me to my bed, and gi'e me a line for medicine.[8] And what guid is that when there's no' a penny in the house?

JENNY: It's true, auntie.

LIZZIE: I wish the strike was finished till I get my new frock.

JENNY: Where is Kate the nicht, auntie?

AGNES: She's sittin' mendin' wee Wullie's troosers. I think she's gaun to the soup-kitchen dance the nicht.

JENNY: She's lucky. A nicht's dancin' noo and I'd ha'e nae shoon left.[9] Anither month o' this strike and we'll be gaun aboot as naked as savages.

AGNES: It canna last much langer noo, Jenny, it canna, or the half o' us'll gang mad.[10]

JENNY: This is the worst week we have had; it'll be the same wi' you, I suppose?

AGNES: I dinna ken hoo to turn, Jenny; we're clean knocked oot. We'll need to hunger noo till we get the Pairish relief the morn[11] ... I'm gettin' tired, Jenny.

JENNY: The strike canna last lang noo, auntie, and twa week's work'll put us on oor feet again.

AGNES: We've been sayin' that for the last twa months, but the end doesna seem to be ony nearer.

(She takes a fit of coughing. JENNY goes to her, and gives her a drink of water.)

JENNY: You'll need to see the doctor, auntie, that cough's gettin' worse.

AGNES: Ay, I'll need to see him, Jenny. But I'll wait a day or twa ... If he puts me to my bed I'll never rise again, I doot.

JENNY: That's nonsense: he'll gi'e ye a bottle that'll stop that cough in a nicht ... You should ha'e mair claes on tae.[12]

AGNES: Mair claes! *(She laughs hysterically.)* Mair claes! ... I wonder if I'll get a sleep the nicht? ... When the cough does stop I canna sleep for thinkin' o' the bairns.

JENNY: You'll need to stop thinkin' o' the bairns.

AGNES: That's no' easy, Jenny, when you're a mither you'll see that ... Puir wee things, they seem to ken, for they just sit and look like wee lambs and never say a word when I've to put them to bed to sleep the hunger off them. *(She holds her brow with her hand.)* Jenny, I'm no' weel.

JENNY: I ken you're no' weel, it's your bed you should be in. Kate can look after the bairns weel enough.

AGNES: I'm feart to go to bed.[13] I ha'e the feelin' that if I lie doon ... *(Rises)* Ach: God kens what we have been broucht on the face o' this earth for.

JENNY: You get awa' doon hame, and ha'e a rest for a while. A guid nicht's sleep, and you'll be like anither woman in the mornin'.

AGNES: *(Going off)* Peace! ... peace! ... I wonder when we'll ever get peace?

(She goes out coughing. JENNY goes with her.)

LIZZIE: *(Singing):*
>   We'll hang every blackleg to the sour apple tree,
>   We'll hang every blackleg to the sour apple tree,
>   We'll hang every blackleg to the sour —

---

8   Line (Sc.): written authorization; here, prescription.

9   Gaun: going; shoon: shoes (both Sc.).

10   Gang (Sc.): go.

11   Until the Local Government Act of 1929 handed all their responsibilities to the counties, financial assistance for the destitute was the responsibility of individual Parish Councils.

12   Claes on tae (Sc.): clothes on too.

13   Feart (Sc.): afraid.

JOCK: *(Loudly from room)* Shut up, in there!
(LIZZIE shuts up suddenly, and puts her finger in her mouth. JENNY re-enters.)
JENNY: Was that him shoutin'?
LIZZIE: No.
JENNY: It's a wonder he hasna been cryin' for water.
(Enter BOB, a reckless kind of youth, light of foot as an Irish ragman.)
BOB: What about some chuck?[14]
JENNY: What aboot it?
BOB: Weel, what aboot it?
JENNY: You'll need to rin and play hide and seek till my mither comes hame — and
        mebbe efter she comes hame tae.
LIZZIE: Can you dae decimals, Bob?
BOB: Can I dae what?
LIZZIE: Decimals?
BOB: What's decimals?
LIZZIE: Sums, fatheid.
BOB: What are you askin' that for?
LIZZIE: I have to dae them for my hame lessons, and I canna dae them.
BOB: Decimals! Och, ay, they're easy.
LIZZIE: Dae them for me, Bob.
BOB: You surely think it. I'm on strike, and I'm no' gaun to blackleg noo ... By gee!
        I'm hungry.
JENNY: *(To BOB)* What's a' the noise aboot the nicht?
BOB: D'ye mean to tell me you dinna ken that there's likely to be a break-awa' the
        morn?
JENNY: Is there?
BOB: Ay, and that sweethe'rt o' yours is yin that would like to start[15] ... By gee! If
        he tries to go to the pit ...
JENNY: Wha tellt you that?
BOB: Never you mind, but it's true. Some man, him! My uncle Tam is anither yin.
        (A shout is heard in the distance.) Listen! ... that's anither meetin' in the fitba
        park. *(He goes to fire and puts the poker up his sleeve.)*
JENNY: Where are you gaun wi' that poker?
BOB: I'll be yin o' the pickets.
JENNY: Put that poker doon and no' be daft. *(She struggles with him and takes the poker
        from him.)* If the polis catch you wi' that you'd get penal servitude.[16] You stay
        here and leave the picketin' to the men.
BOB: Am I no' a man?
LIZZIE: Some man.
BOB: I don't want ony o' your auld buck, see![17]
JENNY: And I don't want ony o' yours. Awa' doon and meet my mither.
BOB: I'm on strike.
(Enter KATE, a dark, handsome lass, with a proud air.)
LIZZIE: Can you dae decimals, Kate?
JENNY: No, she canna dae decimals.

---

14 Chuck: food (not a specifically Scottish usage, but in Scotland apparently specific to Fife and
    the Lothians, and to miners more generally: see *SND*).
15 Yin (Sc.): one.
16 Polis (Sc.; stress on the first syllable): police.
17 Old buck: insolence.

KATE: I used to could dae them, Lizzie, I'll ha'e a try before I go oot ... I'm up to see if you're gaun to the dance, Jenny?

JENNY: Your mither was sayin' you were gaun.

KATE: Too true I am.

JENNY: Where did you get the money?

KATE: Threepence for some auld jam jars ... I think you should come, Jenny; it'll be a good dance.

JENNY: My shoon wouldna stand it, Kate ... Are you in a hurry?

KATE: I'm finished hurryin', it's a mug's game.

JENNY: Tak' off your coat then, and sit doon.

(She takes off her coat and hangs it over a chair. She sees BOB, who is trying to light a stump of cigarette with a lighted paper.)

KATE: You're there, Bob? ... No' thinkin' aboot startin' to your work?

BOB: D'ye see ony green in my eye?[18]
(Holds down his eyelash.)

KATE: There's some thinkin' aboot startin', I hear.

BOB: Ay, and your faither's yin o' them.

KATE: Wha said that?

BOB: He said it himsel' at the street corner.

KATE: And did naebody bump him?

BOB: Tam Anderson tellt him that if he tried it he would knock his bloody heid off.

JENNY: Here! keep that kind o' language for the street corner.

KATE: I'll knock his bloody heid off mysel' if he tries it.

BOB: And the worm that rins efter Jenny here is talkin' aboot gaun to his work tae. By gee! let him try it. I don't know where I'll be if he gets there without gettin' his skull cracked.

KATE: Wull Baxter! ... Surely he's no' gaun to try and break awa', Jenny?

JENNY: He'll no' blackleg, Kate.

BOB: He was ay a gaffer's man, a belly-crawler.[19]

JENNY: Shut up!

BOB: I ken him, Kate, for I worked beside him.

KATE: (To break conversation) Where's your faither, Jenny?

JENNY: (Jerking her thumb towards room) Oh, lyin' in there wi' a fat heid ... D'ye ken what he did yesterday?

KATE: No.

JENNY: He backed a double and came hame as drunk as a lord, singin' like a canary.[20] And no' a crust in the hoose. He met in wi' some auld pal that's here on holiday frae America — so he says — and didna come oot the pub till the double was spent.

KATE: Was your mither wild?

JENNY: Wild! she was mad. I bet ye she put the singin' oot o' his heid.

KATE: Is your mither no' in?

JENNY: No, she's awa lookin' for grub. That auld McIntyre the grocer wouldna gi'e her ony things this mornin'. "I'll gi'e ye plenty," says he, "if you send your man back to his work!"

KATE: Eh! And what did she say to that?

JENNY: She spat in his face.

---

18 I.e., do you think I'm that gullible? Do you take me for a fool?

19 Ay (Sc.): always; gaffer: foreman.

20 Backed a double: placed an accumulating bet on the outcome of two successive horse-races.

KATE: That's the stuff to gi'e them. I canna undersand the tradesmen aboot here, they're a' up against the miners, but bad conditions for the miners means bad conditions for them, tae. They'll mebbe learn that some day when they're puttin' up their shutters ... Let me see your sums, Lizzie.

(LIZZIE goes to her with hook and pencil.)

BOB: Don't dae them for her, Kate.

LIZZIE: You mind your ain business.

BOB: I'll wallop your ear for ye if you set up ony auld gas to me. *(To KATE)* She's as thick in the heid as a wudden leg. I wouldna dae them for her, I would let her get the strap.

LIZZIE: You couldna dae them onywey. A' you can dae is play cairds and toss up pennies at the street corner — and swear.

BOB: Mind, I'll melt ye!

JENNY: That'll dae, noo, we a' ken hoo clever you are.

BOB: Would you like to hear a tune on my gramophone, Kate?

KATE: Ay, put it on, Bob, we're needin' something to cheer us up.

JENNY: *(Nodding towards room)* You'll wauken him.

BOB: What dae I care for him!

(Puts the gramophone on the table and takes some records from a drawer in the dresser.)

KATE: Here you are, Lizzie; I think that's richt.

LIZZIE: I wish you had been my sister, Kate, Jenny's just a dunce.

BOB: *(To KATE)* By gee! you're a right mug, I would let her get the strap.

(Lizzie puts out her tongue at him as she packs her books in her bag.)

BOB: What d'ye want? Danny Boy?

KATE: Oh, for God's sake, put on something cheery, and let Jenny and me get a dance.

(BOB starts the gramophone. KATE takes a hold of JENNY, and they begin to dance. BOB watches them for a time, then he grabs hold of LIZZIE. BOB and LIZZIE are footing it at the room door when it opens, and JOCK SMITH, a typical miner, in his shirt and trousers and stockinged feet, enters. He brushes BOB and LIZZIE aside in an irritated manner, and goes directly to water pail. He drinks greedily two 'Tinnies' full. Then he makes for fireside.)

JOCK: Oh! stop that damned thing!

(BOB jumps and puts the gramophone off. KATE winks at JENNY.)

JOCK: What kind o' dance d'ye ca' that?

KATE   That's what you ca' the Charleston, John.[21]

JOCK: God kens what the world's comin' tae. Nae wonder you're a' knocked-kneed and in-taed gettin'.[22]

KATE   Wha's in-taed?

JOCK: The half o' ye are gaun aboot like a lot o' hens. *(To JENNY, curtly)* Did you get a paper the nicht?

JENNY: *(Just as curtly)* You're sittin' on it. *(JOCK rises and gets paper under cushion)*

JOCK: *(Opening paper)* You're damned lucky that can think aboot dancin', that's what I have to say. *(Irritably)* Where's the racin' page? ... Ay, damned lucky that can think aboot dancin'.... *(Looking at race results)* Weel, I'm damned if that's no' hard lines.

BOB: It'll be a' the same to us.

---

21 From its African-American origins, the Charleston became an international dance craze from late 1923.

22 In-taed: in-toed, i.e. with feet pointing inwards.

JOCK: *(Making a rush at him)* I'll warm your ear for you, my lad.
(BOB scoots out.)
LIZZIE: He's a cheeky devil that.
JOCK: *(To JENNY)* Where's your mither?
JENNY: She's awa' seein' where she can get something to fill hungry bellies till we get
          some money frae the pairish: awa' beggin', and lowerin' herself again. And
          there was nae need for it if you had played the game yesterday.
JOCK: If the double had went doon what difference would it have made?
JENNY: But the double came up, and you gied the winnin's to the publican to help
          him to buy anither motor car.
JOCK: Hoo would you like to be me, Kate?
KATE: Onything fresh in the paper aboot the strike?
JOCK: To hell wi' the strike. It should never have happened. I'm payin' nae mair
          Union money after this.[23] I've got enough o' it this time. For thirty years I ha'e
          peyed it, but never anither penny will they get frae me.
KATE   What?
JOCK: Oor leaders. It's easy seen that this has a' been planned in Russia.[24]
KATE   *(With a smile)* What makes you think that, Jock?
JOCK: Look at the papers and you'll see pages aboot it every nicht. It's the Socialists
          to blame ... I ken what they want, it's a revolution they want.
KATE: D'ye mean to tell me, Jock, that you've been locked oot for six months and
          doesna ken ony better than that?
JOCK: It's you that doesna ken ony better ... I was makin' a pound a shift before they
          broucht us oot on strike, Jenny there'll tell you that.
KATE: You must have been well in the know. My faither wasna makin' as much as
          feed a canary.[25]
JOCK: Twenty white shillin's a shift *(Going to pail for another drink)* and the best o'
          conditions at that.
KATE: Are ye a Mason?
JOCK: No, I'm no' a Mason.
KATE: It's a mystery to me.
JOCK: God, but I'm dry ... Make a drink o' tea, Jenny.
JENNY: The caddie's empty.
JOCK: *(Drinks and returns to chair)* No, this strike! strike! strike! idea'll no' dae.
KATE: But it couldna be helped.
JOCK: Hoo could it no' be helped?
KATE: Weel, the maister wanted to reduce your wages and make you work langer
          'oors, what else could you dae but strike?
JOCK: We could have knuckled doon.

---

23 Jock's union is the Miner's Federation of Great Britain, which in 1926 had well over half a
    million members. It was founded in 1889, so Jock has been a member for most of its history.
24 The Miner's Minority Movement, a union under Communist control (and thus ultimately
    taking direction from Moscow) had been founded in 1924, but the MMM had no particular
    influence on the decisions to call or continue the strike, and in any case its 'attention was
    directed ... to short-term industrial ends' rather than revolution (G.A. Phillips, *The General
    Strike* [1976] p.44). It's not clear that Jock is referring to anything as specific as the MMM:
    he is more likely to have accepted the continual accusations in the right-wing press that all
    working-class activism was being directed from Moscow.
25 Kate has reason to be sceptical. In Scotland, the average rate per seven-hour shift before the
    strike was 10s 4d, a bit more than half what Jock claims to have been earning (Phillips, p.107).

KATE: But you're a Scotsman, Jock.

JOCK: I am, and prood o' it.

KATE: It doesna say much for Scotland.

JOCK: No, of coorse, no', it says mair for Russia. I ken what I would dae if I was the Gover'ment. I'd get a boat and ship the hale damned lot to Russia.

KATE: Wha, the coalmaisters?

JOCK: No, thae Socialists and Communionists.

KATE.:   But they didna reduce your wages?

JOCK: I ken that fine.

JENNY: And if ye ken that fine, what is the argument aboot?

JOCK: What I'm sayin' is, that we'd been far better if we had knuckled doon. I kent we were gaun to be defeated.

KATE: (Jumping) Who said we were defeated!

JOCK: I ken we are defeated.

JENNY: D'ye ken onything aboot backin' doubles and gi'en the winnin's to the publican?

JOCK: Oh, here! we've heard enough aboot that, give it a rest ... Bring me a drink, Lizzie.

LIZZIE: What kind o' drink, daddy?

JOCK: Ha'e some savvy.

(LIZZIE goes to pail. WULL BAXTER enters.)

WULL: Hullo, Kate. And how's the health?

KATE: Not too bad, considerin' we're slowly fadin' away.

WULL: That's a fine nicht, John.

JOCK: Is it?

(He takes 'tinnie' from LIZZIE and drinks.)

WULL: You're lookin' raither wild like, John. What's wrang?

JOCK: Oh Kate and me have been ha'ein' an argument.

WULL: Ay. What's the trouble?

JOCK: The strike.

WULL: We're a' thinkin' gey seriously aboot it noo[26] ... We werena expectin' it to last as lang as this.

JOCK: A piece o' damned nonsense and thrawnness. I've been tellin' her that I've payed my last penny to the Union.

WULL: I'm finished wi' the Union tae.

KATE: What's that you say, Wull?

WULL: The Union has failed us, Kate. They ken damned fine the battle's lost long ago, and they should have cried the strike off.

KATE: We've naething to lose noo, and we may as well fight to a finish.

WULL: If we saw ony signs o' the finish it wouldna be sae bad. But it's likely to go on for months yet, if it's left to oor leaders.

KATE: Weel, let it go on. The coalmaisters'll mebbe no' be sae keen to lock us oot again.

WULL: We dinna ha'e a very guid case, either. We can see noo that the pits havena been payin'.

KATE: Havena been payin'! But has that no' ay been their cry? Was that no' their cry when the women worked doon the pits?

WULL: There wasna mony women worked doon the pits.

---

26 Gey seriously (Sc.): pretty seriously.

JOCK: They were in the pits, Wull. My faither was born doon the pit.[27]
WULL: Born doon the pit.
JOCK: Ay, born doon the pit ... It's no' everybody that can bum aboot that.[28]
KATE: Something to bum aboot: a woman workin' doon the pit till the very minute
          o' confinement ... And still the pits didna pay.
JOCK: Ay, my grannie carried coal up the auld stair pit for mony a lang day. What's
          mair, she helped to lift the stane off my grandfaither when he was killed.
WULL: Is that true, Jock?
JOCK: Helped to lift the stane off him; helped to cairry him hame a corpse ... And
          you're grumblin', Kate, but you dinna ken you're alive. Frae daylicht to dark
          they had to work then; the only time they saw daylicht was on the Sunday.
KATE: And still the pits didna pay.
JOCK: I ken that fine, you didna need to tell me that.
KATE: And if the miners hadna foucht against it your women micht have been
          workin' in the pits yet.
JOCK: I ken that fine!
KATE: They had to fight to make things easier for you.
WULL: We're fightin' a losin' fight, Kate, you canna deny that.
KATL: We are, if a' the men are like you. But they're no', and we're gaun to win yet.
WULL: It's too late in the day to win noo. And the sooner it comes to an end the better
          for everybody concerned.
KATE: Mebbe you're yin o'them aboot the place that wants to bring it to an end.
WULL: I have been thinkin' aboot it, but I havena made up my mind yet.
KATE: If you've been thinkin' aboot it, Wull, you've made up your mind.
WULL: Well, to tell you the truth, I didna see the use o' carryin' on much langer.
KATE: Then you're no' the man I thoucht you were.
WULL: No?
KATE: No, you are not. I never thoucht you would stoop sae low as split on us.
WULL: I'm no' splittin'. But when word comes that the Parish Cooncil is no' payin'
          ony mair relief, it's time something was done to bring it to an end.
KATE: No' payin' ony mair relief! Wha tellt you that?
(They are all attentive)
WULL: The cooncil had a meetin' the noo, and that's their decision.
KATE: I've been expectin' it.
JOCK: That'll put us in a nice mess.
WULL: It's as weel it has come to that, Jock, for it'll bring the issue to a heid. It'll end
          the strike here.
KATE: Starve the women and bairns to force the men back to their work. *(Rising and
          facing WULL)* And you agree wi' that policy.
WULL: There's nae ither way that I see.
KATE: I have only yin answer for you, and it's THIS!
(She hits WULL a severe slap on the face. WULL staggers. They all rise excitedly)
JOCK: Kate!
WULL: *(Rushing at KATE, who stands her ground)* You flamin' tinker! Ye ...
JOCK: *(Holding WULL back)* Never heed her, man!
(JENNY goes to room crying)

---

27 Women were banned from working underground by the Mines Act of 1842, so this is histori-
    cally possible.
28 Bum (Sc.); brag (*SND* 4).

KATE: Keep your hands off me, ye blackleg ...
JOCK: Kate!
KATE: *(To WULL)* Ye traitor.
(BOB enters excitedly)
BOB: That's it noo; nae pairish money the morn, and a hunner polis in at the pit to smash up the pickets.[29]
KATE: *(With a hysterical laugh)* And Britons, never, NEVER shall be slaves.[30]
BOB: It's a revolution that's needed here.
JOCK: See here! If I hear tell o' you gaun to ony mair o' thae Bolshie meetin's I'll scud your ear for ye.[31]
WULL: I'll be in later, John, I want to ha'e a talk wi' ye.
KATE: Ay, awa' oot o' the sicht o' decent folk — ye scab![32]
(WULL, would return to her, but JOCK signs to him to go out)
BOB: Was he sayin' he was gaun to his work in the mornin'? He has been in the office wi' the manager, and his mither has been gettin' his pit buits mended at the store. By gee! if he goes to his work in the mornin' there'll be nothing left o' him but a big bubble.
JOCK: Did you see your mither doon the street?
BOB: No, I've mair to think aboot than look for my mither ... A flamin' worm like that ...
JOCK: Awa' and look for your mither!
BOB: He's worse than a worm, he's a dirty rotten blackleg.
JOCK: D'ye no' hear me speakin' to ye!
BOB: If he goes to his work I'll flatten his face wi' a half brick.
(JOCK rushes at him, and he scoots out)
JOCK: Nae pairish relief, Kate. Hoo dae they think we're gaun tae live?
KATE: It's murder, Jock. And the likes o' Wull Baxter, a workin' man, agreein' wi' it. I canna understand it. It's laughable.
JOCK: Something to laugh at; no' a crust in the hoose the nicht, and nae hopes o' gettin' ony the morn. Ach, I'm fed up wi' the hale blasted thing.
(He goes to room)
LIZZIE: Is that the strike finished noo, Kate?
KATE: No, it's no' finished, hen, it's just startin'.[33]
LIZZIE: I wish it was finished till I get my new frock.
(JENNY enters)
KATE: What d'ye think o' that, Jenny?
JENNY: I canna understand him, Kate, I didna think he was yin o' thae kind.
KATE: Neither did I. But dinna break your he'rt ower him, he's a guid riddance. *(JENNY sobs)* Noo, noo, Jenny, dinna greet;[34] thank your lucky stars you ha'e got rid o' him.
JENNY: We were to get mairrit when the strike was finished.
KATE: The dirty swine!

---

29 Hunner (Sc.): hundred.
30 Kate is of course quoting from the song 'Rule Britannia', written by the Scottish poet James Thomson in 1740: 'Rule Britannia, rule the waves; / Britons never will be slaves.'
31 Bolshie: Bolshevik, used in the period as a synonym for Communist. The Bolsheviks were the victorious party in the Russian Revolution of 1917.
32 Scab: strikebreaker, blackleg.
33 Hen (Sc.): a term of affection like 'dear' or 'love', specific to industrialised central Scotland.
34 Ower: here, over; greet: weep (both Sc.).

(The door opens and TAM PETTIGREW enters, standing at door)

TAM: *(To KATE)* Are you gaun to stay here a' nicht?

KATE: What d'ye want?

TAM: Your mither's in her bed, and I want you to get my pit claes ready.

KATE: Your what?

TAM: My pit claes; I'm gaun oot to my work.

KATE: Oh, are ye! And are we to have nae say in this?

TAM: Wha?

KATE: My mither and me?

TAM: What the hell have you to do wi' it?

KATE: D'ye think I could walk through the streets o' Carhill again if you blackleg? D'ye think my mither could speak to the neebours again?

TAM: It'll soon be forgotten.

KATE: Blackleggin' is a thing that can never be forgotten.

TAM: But, Kate, we're in utter starvation, that's what has put your mither to her bed ... And there's nae pairish money the morn.

KATE: If you march a thousand strong to the parish offices they'll pay oot the money.

TAM: The polis are here to keep us frae marchin'.

KATE: It takes mair than polis to stop a hungry mob.

TAM: I'm gaun oot tae my work.

KATE: If you go to your work you'll come hame to an empty hoose. I'd rather tramp the country and beg my crust than stay in the same hoose as a blackleg.

TAM: But something has to be done, Kate.

KATE: Fight on to the finish, that's what can be done.

(Enter JOCK)

JOCK: Did onybody see my pipe?

LIZZIE: It's on the fender, daddy.

(She goes for it)

JOCK: Weel, Tam!

TAM: Weel!

JOCK: What are we gaun to dae about it noo?

TAM: God knows.

LIZZIE: You'll need to go back to the pit, daddy.

JOCK: The pit'll come to me before I go to the pit. I'll stay awa' frae it noo, just for spite. Stop the pairish relief, what the hell'll be their game?

KATE: There'll be a riot here the morn if they try to stop it.

JOCK: A lot o' guid that'll dae.

TAM: Ay, a lot o' guid that'll dae, Jock; half o' us clouted wi' a polisman's baton, and landed in the jile.[35]

KATE: It's mair honourable to be clouted wi' a polisman's baton than clouted wi' a miner's fist, and that's what'll happen to the men wha try to blackleg.

JOCK: *(Looking at pipe)* No' a smoke either, Kate. It's a wash-oot!

KATE: *(Donning her coat)* Keep up your pecker, Jock, there's a guid time comin' yet.

JOCK: It's been comin' a' my time, but it's a damned sicht farther awa' noo than ever it's been.

TAM: Ay, a body would be better deid.

KATE: Did you ever hear such a crowd o' men? And they wonder why they're losin' the strike.

---

35 Jile (Sc): jail

TAM: It's a richt for you speakin', you havena the responsibility o' a hoose on your heid.

JOCK: Ay, they're young, Tam, and doesna ken what it means to the likes o' us.

KATE: Puir sowls, without your baccy and your beer you're no' much use.[36] (To JOCK) Stick oot your chest, man! Let them see you're a Scotsman and a man. Fight like hell, and never say die till a deid horse kicks ye.

JOCK: It's no' easy for a hungry man to stick oot his chest.

TAM: It is not, Jock.

KATE: Well, stick your fingers to your nose at them. Guid nicht.

JOCK: Guid nicht.

(KATE and JENNY go out)

JOCK: God kens what's to be done. For thirty years I have worked in the pit, and have come through many a hard time o't, but never the likes o' this.

TAM: I wouldna have troubled mysel' sae much, but the wife's no' keeping weel ava:[37] that cough o' hers is gettin' worse.

JOCK: She'll need to take care o' hersel', Tam.

TAM: Tak' care o' hersel'! and hasna had a meal the day! I'll need to do something, Jock, I canna let things go on like this.

JOCK: But what can you dae?

TAM: I can go to my work. It's the only thing I can dae.

JOCK: It's a problem, Tam. I wish I could help ye, but I'm needin' help mysel'.

(The sound of singing can be heard faintly. We'll hang every blackleg...)

TAM: Ach, to hell, I dinna ken what to dae.

(He goes out)

JOCK: Ay, it's a problem. Tam.

LIZZIE: Will my mammie be long, daddy?... Does she no' ken I'm hungry? ... I wish the strike was finished, I'm needin' a new frock ... see, I'm in rags ... And I'm needin' shoon tae, my feet are ay wet.

(JOCK is sitting gazing into the fire)

LIZZIE: My mammie was greetin' when I came hame frae the schule the day... Gimmie a piece, daddy.[38]

(Enter JEAN, wearily, an empty basket in her hand. She is followed by JENNY. LIZZIE runs to her mother, but JEAN takes no notice of her. She puts the basket on the table, takes off her shawl, and sits down at table side, as if she was exhausted)

JOCK: Hoo did you get on, wife?

JEAN: I'm beat, Jock, there's no' a grocer or a baker in the toon'll gi'e me a crust.

JOCK: (Rising) Get oot my pit claes.

JEAN: (Rising) No, you're no' dain' that.

JOCK: What else can be done?

JEAN: You came oot wi' your neebours, and you'll go back wi' them.

JOCK: And have we to dee o' hunger?

JGAN: Something'll turn up yet.

JOCK: Oh! for God's sake ha'e some sense. What can turn up?

(JEAN sits and breaks down)

JENNY: (With her hand on JEAN'S shoulder) Ha'e ye nae he'rt! barkin' at my mither like that when you ha'e mair need to be comfortin' her. For six months she

---

36 Sowls (Sc.): souls; baccy: tobacco.

37 Ava (Sc.): at all.

38 Piece (Sc.): usually, in this period, bread and jam (or similar).

has scraped through, and you've never kent what it was to want a bite or a smoke till the nicht; lowered hersel' mony a time to keep things gaun, and noo, when she's beat, you can only bark at her.

JOCK: I dinna mean it, Jean.

JEAN: I ken that, Jock, I'm no' worth a haet gettin'.[39]

JENNY: Mebbe my uncle, Bob, would help us?

JEAN: Supposin' we should dee you're no' gaun near him.

JOCK: Bob would help us if he kent we were in this hole.

JEAN: He's a blackleg, and we're no' askin' help frae him.

JOCK: Weel, something has to be done ... Can we no' sell that gramophone?

JEAN: No, it's the laddie's.

JOCK: But something'll need to go, Jean?

JEAN: That gramophone's no' gaun. The laddie boucht it wi' the first pocket-money ever he earned; he'd break his he'rt if he were to lose it.

JOCK: Right o! I'm gaun to the pit, for I'll starve for nae white man.

JEAN: *(Rising and going to room)* You're gaun to drive me mad yet.

(LIZZIE follows her mother)

JENNY: For God's sake, faither, ha'e some sense.

JOCK: It's your mither that has nae sense. I'm shair that gramophone's no' needed at a time like this. And you'd starve rather than hurt his feelin's. I canna understand it.

JENNY: If you were a woman you would understand it, you men ha'e nae he'rts.

JOCK: It's past the time for silly sentiment. We're up against it Jenny, and some o' us have to make a sacrifice.

JENNY: Weel, you should have sacrificed your beer yesterday. This wouldna have happened if you had played the game yesterday.

JOCK: I ken that fine, you dinna need to tell me that, but it's past and canna be helped noo. Hoo are we gaun to get a crust o' breid, that's the question ... Folk that ha'e toiled and battled a' their days, workin' frae hand to mooth, even in the best o' times, slaves, if ever there were slaves, and to think we've to go back to that pit on worse conditions! It's hellish to think o' it. It would be a God's blessin' if the roof came doon the first day and crushed the life oot o' us, they'd be responsible for oor wives and bairns, and we'd be awa' frae a' the bloody sufferin'.

JENNY: That's a selfish wey oot o' it, and it's selfishness and greed that's the cause o' a' the sorrow and sufferin' the day.

(LIZZIE enters from room)

LIZZIE: Jenny, my ma' wants ye.

(JENNY goes to room. LIZZIE follows. JOCK sits to put on his boots. WULL BAXTER enters)

WULL: Weel, that was some row the nicht, John ... She's a right tartar, isn't she?

JOCK: Ay, she has a temper.

WULL: Ye ken, it's the women o' this place that's keepin' the strike gaun on.

JOCK: They seem to ha'e got their birz up.

WULL: Hoo are things wi' you the nicht, John?

JOCK: No' too bad, we've been worse mony a time.

WULL: The morn'll tell a tale when there's nae pairish relief.

JOCK: It'll tell a tale someway or ither.

WULL: I'm thinkin' aboot tryin' to get oot to Canada. There's naething here for a

---

39 No...a haet (Sc.): damn all; but this construction is obscure.

young chap.

JOCK: It's no' easy gettin' out there.

WULL: I'll manage ... The men that are startin' the morn are gettin' a guid chance.

JOCK: Are they?

WULL: Five pounds when they make a start, and a pound a day.

JOCK: That's the stuff, eh!

WULL: Isn't it. It's no' often the miner get a chance like that.

JOCK: No, I can hardly believe it.

WULL: You can take it frae me, Jock, it's the truth ... What about it?

JOCK: What aboot what?

WULL: Makin' a start in the mornin' wi' the rest o' us?

JOCK: Eh! D'ye mean to tell me your canvassin' for blacklegs?

WULL: It's no' blackleggin'. You ken as weel as me that if it's left to the leaders it'll never be finished. The place is in ruination: if the pit doesna open soon it'll never open ... A week's work would put you on your feet again.

JOCK: Would put wha on their feet?

WULL: Don't be silly, John, this chance only comes yince in a lifetime.

JOCK: Wull, I'm hungry, richt enough, and money o' ony kind is a big temptation, but before I would touch their blood money I would eat grass at the roadside.

WULL: Are you feart for the Socialists and the pickets?

JOCK: I don't want ony insults, Wull.

(JENNY makes to enter, but when she sees WULL she returns)

WULL: *(Rising)* I thought you had mair pluck than that, Jock.

JOCK: *(Rising and gripping him)* Ye flamin' twister! if ye insult me like that I'll choke the life oot o' ye.

(JENNY and JEAN come to door)

WULL: I thought the wey you were speakin' ...

JOCK: Oot o' my sicht, ye traitor! *(Throws him from him)* And if ever I see Jenny speakin' to ye again, I'll cut the tongue oot o' her heid. *(JEAN returns to room)* Oot o' that door, I say!

(WULL goes out)

JOCK: Blackleg! No, I'm damned sure though it was a hunner pounds a shift ... Jenny, I came oot like a man, and I'll go back like a man; it'll never be said that Jock Smith was a blackleg.

(Enter BOB)

BOB: Was Wull Baxter in here?

JOCK: Ay.

BOB: Was he wantin' you oot to your work?

JOCK: Never you mind.

BOB: If you go to your work I'll leave the hoose.

JOCK: Is there a meetin' the nicht?

BOB: There's a meetin' the noo to get pickets.

JOCK: Awa' to the meetin' and let me ken what gangs on. I'll let you go this time.

(BOB is at door when JOCK speaks)

Bob! come here a minute.

(BOB returns)

We're up against it the nicht, Bob. Would you be vexed if we sellt your gramophone?

(BOB is silent)

We'll get you anither yin when the strike's finished.

(BOB is on the verge of tears)

We're at oor wit's end. Your mither has been in every shop in the toon, and canna get a crust withoot the money. And Wull Baxter was in here the noo offerin' me a pound a shift if I went to my work. I dinna want to go, Bob, but if we have to starve, weel ...

BOB: You can sell it, faither.

JOCK: Your mither doesna want to pairt wi' it.

BOB: I'll tell her.

(He goes to room)

JENNY: They've even to draw the blood frae the he'rt o' the bairns.

JOCK: I didna think I was sae sentimental.

(Re-enter BOB)

BOB: It's a richt, faither, I tellt her I was tired o' it. *(Going off)* I ken what's needed, it's a revolution that's needed.

JOCK: I'll need to get a breath o' fresh air, this nicht has me about suffocated.

(He dons muffler and jacket. A knock comes to the door. JENNY goes to answer)

JENNY: It's Tam Anderson.

JOCK: Come in, Tam!

(TAM enters, and JENNY goes to room)

TAM: Was Wull Baxter in here soundin' you aboot gaun to the pit in the mornin'?

JOCK: He was.

TAM: Are ye gaun, Jock?

JOCK: Am I hell!

TAM: Isn't he a richt traitor? Did you think he was yin o' thae kind?

JOCK: No, or he'd been coortin' some ither place ... D'ye think there'll be mony that'll try to go oot, Tam?

TAM: I couldna say. I heard that Tam Pettigrew was thinkin' aboot it, tae.

JOCK: I dinna think Tam'll be there, though Tam's up against it the nicht ... If the pairish doesna pay ower the morn I doot there'll be a big breakawa'.

TAM: The pairish'll pay ower, Jock, or we'll tear doon the buildin'. We're formin' pickets for the morn, Jock, will you gi e us a hand?

JOCK: I will, and if that Wull Baxter tries to pass me it'll be a face withoot a nose. Is there onything I can dae the nicht?

TAM: We're ha'in' a secret meetin' to discuss the plans for the morn, you can come if you like.

(JOCK claps his hand. Then singing can he heard, the tune is 'The Red Flag.')[40]

JOCK: That's the stuff to gi'e them! Blaw their blasted pits in the air, and the blacklegs wi' them. *(As they go out)* A pound a shift! No, I may sell my muscle; but I'll never sell my soul.

(The singing fades away. LIZZIE enters)

LIZZIE: That's my daddie awa' oot, ma!

(JENNY enters with her coat on. She lifts gramophone, and is near door when JEAN enters)

JEAN: Jenny. We canna sell that gramophone yet. Tak' this ring instead.

(She takes the ring from her finger)

JENNY: You canna sell that ring, mither. Bob wouldna let you pairt wi' that.

JEAN: I can pairt wi' it easier than the gramophone. Noo, Jenny, dinna argue aboot

---

40 'The Reg Flag': the international socialist anthem, sung by e.g. the British Labour Party, to the tune of 'O Tannenbaum'.

it. Hurry, and bring up some groceries, you're a' hungry. Hurry, Jenny.
(JENNY goes out. JEAN puts the kettle on the fire, then she sits)
LIZZIE: *(After a pause)* Maw!
JEAN: What is it, dearie.
LIZZIE: I'm sleepy.
(JEAN takes her on her knee. LIZZIE lays her head against her mother's breast. There is a short pause, then JEAN speaks dreamily)
JEAN: We were a prood pair that day, Jock, a prood pair. Blue skies and sunshine, and the birds singin' on every tree. But that was lang, lang syne ... nae struggle then, and nae tears, just sang and laughter. *(Sighs)* Ay, changed days noo, Jock.
(LIZZIE looks up in her mother's face. They kiss as the curtain falls)

ACT TWO

(The same as Act One. The following day, afternoon. The canary in the cage at the window sings merrily. JOCK sits at the fireside reading a racing paper. JENNY sits at the table side, in centre of floor, trying to knock a few tackets in her shoes.)[41]

JOCK: Canaries are like human bein's, Jenny, they canna sing when their stomachs are empty.
(JENNY makes no answer. JOCK takes a stump of pencil from his pocket, wets it in his mouth and begins to write the names of horses on a slip of paper which he also takes from his pocket)
If thae three dinna make the bookie squeal the day I'll never look at a horse in the face again. *(Puts paper in his pocket, rises and goes to the window)* I wonder wha it is that's workin' the day? I could bet you a thousand pounds it's that Wull Baxter. The dirty swine, if ever he comes aboot this hoose again I'll swing for him.
(Enter JEAN)
JEAN: There's nae pairish money the day yet.
JOCK: What! Are they no' payin' oot?
JEAN: No, there's a deputation awa' to Edinburgh, to see the Board o' Health, wha'ever he is. I thoucht your mairch to the Parish Council wouldna frighten them.
JOCK: Weel, I could have sworn they were gaun to pay oot, for they had the wind up properly.
JEAN: It was a' in the game, to get you awa' hame again. They ken fine that if they diddle you the first time, you'll no' get the same crowd to mairch a second time.
JOCK: I believe you're richt, Jean.
JEAN: Did you ever see me wrang?
JOCK: We ha'e a lot to learn before we win a strike.
JEAN: I hear them sayin' that Tam Anderson's likely to be arrested for the speech he made. What did he say?
JOCK: He made a great speech, Jean. He had the blood boilin' in my veins. "Fellow

---

41 Tackets: hob-nails.

workers!" he says, "are ye gaun to stand and see your wives and bairns starve to death before your e'en? Are you content to dae this and ca' yoursel's men? Fellow workers! we have been far ower meek in the past,[42] the time has come when we've got to be prepared to let them see that we're prepared to die ..."

JEAN: *(Interrupting)* Some hope.

JOCK: D'ye think I wouldna shed my blood for you?

JEAN: You'll no' shed your hair for me, let alane your blood.

JOCK: Just wait till the time comes and I'll let you see ... Have you heard wha it is that's workin'?

JEAN: Ay, it's Wull Baxter.

JOCK: I thoucht that. Hoo did he get through the pickets?

JEAN: He was at his work before the pickets were oot o' their beds. Some pickets!

JOCK: Weel, God pity him when he tries to get hame, he'll be torn frae limb to limb.

(JENNY rises and goes to room)

JEAN: Would you ha'e thoucht it o' him?

JOCK: I ay had my suspicions o' him; he was too damned nice and too damned wise, beware o' thae kind every time.

JEAN: If he had been a mairrit man wi' a family there would have been some excuse, but he has naebody to keep but that auld tinker o' a mither o' his. He's made a fine fool o' Jenny onywey.

JOCK: She'll soon forget aboot him.

JEAN: It's no' sae easy forgettin', Jock. They were to be mairrit after the strike, and she has been layin' by wee bits o' things for a while.

JOCK: There's nae weddin' takin' place noo.

JEAN: It's that mither o' his that's to blame, she's been nagging at him to start to his work.

JOCK: It's no' her to blame ava', he wants to make a wheen pounds and slip off to Canada,[43] I saw that was in his mind last nicht when he was in here.

JEAN: Jenny has been speakin' aboot Canada tae.

JOCK: Ay, a fine thing that would be, a douchter o' mine gaun to Canada on blood money. Jean, if he ever comes aboot this hoose again I'll leave him deid on that floor.

(Enter AGNES)

JEAN: Hullo! Agnes, I thoucht you were in your bed?

AGNES: I canna lie, Jean.

JEAN: Did you get a sleep last nicht?

AGNES: *(Hopelessly)* No.

JOCK: You'll need to see the doctor, Agnes, you're lettin' it gang ower far.

JEAN: The doctor's comin' the day, Jock, I'm sendin' for him mysel', we're standin' nae mair o' this nonsense.

AGNES: But, Jean, what's the use o' sendin'...

JEAN: *(interrupting)* He's comin', and that's a' that's aboot it. D'ye ken you're like a ghost?

AGNES: There's nae Pairish money the day.

JEAN: No. God kens what we'll dae, Agnes.

JOCK: I ken what I would dae, I would get the miners to mairch to London and blaw Parliament in the air.

---

42   E'en: eyes; ower: here, too (both Sc.).

43   A wheen (Sc.): a few.

JEAN: And where'll we be by the time you get to London?

AGNES: I dinna ken what to do, Jean. I'm just about mad.

(AGNES begins to cry)

JEAN: Wheesht! Agnes, I'll see if I can dae anything for ye.

AGNES: The weans are a' greetin' for something to eat, and I ha'e naething.[44] God, but I'm weary. I just want to lie doon and dee.

(She has a fit of coughing. JENNY enters)

JEAN: *(Taking her kindly by the shoulders)* Come doon wi' me, Agnes, and get to your bed. I'll see that you get something to tide ower till they pay out the Pairish money.

AGNES: *(Holding her brow)* I'm tired, Jean ... tired ... tired ... tired, but there's nae rest.

JEAN: I'll see that you dae get rest, supposin' I should sit at your bedside till you fa' asleep.

AGNES: It's no sleep, Jean, it's....

(She had another fit of coughing, and JEAN leads her out, shaking her head sadly at JOCK as she goes)

JOCK: You better go for a doctor, Jenny, there's something gey far wrang wi' Agnes.

JENNY: It's hunger that's wrang. I don't believe she has tasted a bite for days.

JOCK: It's hellish! And we can dae naething tae help, naething ava. And they wonder why we mairch in oor thoosan's wavin' the red flag. If they could only suffer oor lot for a week they wouldna wonder sae much. And that Wull Baxter oot workin'! cutting our very throats.

JENNY: I didna ask him to gang, faither.

JOCK: I ken, Jenny, and I'm vexed for ye. But the first time I'll meet him I'll take it oot o' his hide, the traitor.

(JENNY dons her coat)

JOCK: Forget aboot him, Jenny.

JENNY: I canna understand him, it was the last thing in the world I was expectin'.

JOCK: Ay, ay, but things'll come a' richt for you yet, lass.

JENNY: I was lookin' forward to happy days, but everything has a' gane crash and in the yin day.

JOCK: There's naebody escapin' the strike, Jenny, we're a' gettin' a blow o' some kind. But we're learnin' and some day we'll mebbe get oor ain back.

(JEAN enters, followed by LIZZIE)

JEAN: *(To JENNY)* Awa' and get the doctor, Jenny. And bring up a gill o' whusky when you're doon, that woman'll need to get a sleep or she'll be deid in the mornin'. You'll get a bottle in that end drawer.

(JEAN takes money from her purse)

JEAN: *(To JOCK)* Thae weans are in utter starvation.

JOCK: Can you help her, Jean?

JEAN: I'll gi'e her the half o' what I ha'e, I can dae nae mair.

(She gives JENNY the money for the whisky)

JEAN: *(To JENNY)* If Dr. Morrison's no' in, go for the ither yin; the sooner we ken what's what, the better.

(JENNY goes out. JEAN begins to put food in the basket)

JEAN: God be thanked we ha'e oor health and strength.

JOCK: If she could get a sleep she would be a' richt; though I dinna like that cough, Jean, it's something deeper than a cauld.

---

44 Weans (Sc.): children.

JEAN: I dinna ken, but we'll need to watch her weel, or she'll no' last long.

(TAM enters)

TAM: Is Jenny awa' for the doctor?

JEAN: Ay, he'll no' likely be long till he's up, Tam. I'm puttin' something in this basket for the weans. When had you onything last?

TAM: Yesterday mornin'.

JEAN: And Agnes?

TAM: I dinna ken ... she's had naething the day.

JEAN: And what wey did she no' come and tell me?

TAM: She's no' a guid moocher, Jean, she would dee before she would ask onything.[45]

JEAN: I'm sure she kens she needna ha'e ony fears o' comin' here.

TAM: She's ay been queer that wey.

JOCK: *(To TAM)* Was you in the mairch to the Pairish Council this mornin'?

TAM: No, I was not; you'll no' get me takin' pairt in any o' your Bolshie slunts.

JOCK: No, but you'll take the Pairish money when it comes.

TAM: Ay, WHEN it comes.

JOCK: We'll never get it sittin' at the fireside or lyin' on the grass ... Were you no' on the pickets this mornin' either?

TAM: No, I think mair o' my bed.

JOCK: Ay, but strikes are no' won in bed.

JEAN: Nor in the pub, either?

TAM: *(To JOCK)* Was you on the picket?

JOCK: Too true I was. Up at the pit at five o' clock.

JEAN: He's been singin' 'The Red Flag' since he came hame.

JOCK: This country's gaun to be a wee Russia if this s t r i k e lasts much langer.

TAM: And would you like to see it a wee Russia?

JOCK: Yes! and the sooner the better.

TAM: You had ay plenty to say against the Bolshies and Russia before.

JOCK: Ay, but my brains seem to be in my stomach.

TAM: Weel, I don't want to see this country made into a wee Russia, it would bring it to ruination.

JOCK: Ruination! That's the worst o' havin' a three course breakfast, it makes a man a hunner per cent Britisher.

TAM: If there's nae Pairish money the morn I'm gaun to work.

JOCK: A man that's feart to mairch to the Pairish Council, doesna ha'e the pluck to face the pickets. You'd been at your work this mornin' if you hadna been feart.

TAM: I ken, and so would anither hunner men in the place. It's the damned Bolshies that's keepin' us frae s t a r t i n'.

JOCK: And here's luck to them, says I.

TAM: And it's them that dinna want to work that's on the pickets.

JOCK: D'ye mean that I dinna want to work?

TAM: I never mentioned you.

JOCK: I was on the picket, and I'm damned sure I'll work beside you ony day.

TAM: Did I say you couldna?

JOCK: No, and you better no'.

JEAN: You look like a pair that'll dee wi' the shovel in your hand. *(To TAM handing him the basket)* Here! take this doon, and look slippy.

---

45 Moocher: scrounger, cadger.

TAM: Did I say he couldna work, Jean?

JOCK: Of course you did.

TAM: I did naething o' the kind.

JEAN: Did I tell you to look slippy?

TAM: *(As he goes out)* Oh, ay, take his pairt.

(He shuts door rather loudly)

JOCK: Isn't he an agitator? Ay talkin' aboot work, and has never worked a' his days; he has starved his wife off the face o' the earth.

JEAN: I've lost about ten stane mysel' since I got mairrit.

JOCK: You're a delicate lookin' cratur.

(JEAN pours out tea into a 'tinnie' and gives it to LIZZIE with a piece of bread. LIZZIE sits on fender)

JEAN: If it wasna for my guid nature I'd been a walkin' skeleton.

JOCK: *(Puttin' on his coat)* There's yin thing I admire aboot ye, Jean, and that's your pluck.

JEAN: I'm glad you appreciate it.

JOCK: I do, and I thank my lucky stars mony a time that I got the wife I did.

JEAN: Weel, what's the use o' continually grumblin' and grousin'; it does nae guid.

JOCK: Not a bit. D'ye ken, Jean, I'm prood o' ye.

JEAN: *(Looking at hint in surprise)* Ay!

JOCK: I am, as prood as Punch. *(Coughs)* Can you spare eighteenpence for a three-cross double?

JEAN: I kent there was something comin'. No, I can not. I ha'e mair need o' eighteenpence than gi'ein' it to the bookie.

JOCK: They're three solid pinches, Jean, I could stake my shirt that twa o' them'll win.

JEAN: Weel, you can stake your shirt.

JOCK: Can you no' spare ninepence then?

JEAN: Ninepence gets a loaf, and there's a family doon there in starvation.

JOCK: If it comes up I promise to gi'e ye every penny ... If you don't speculate, Jean, you'll never accumulate ... If I don't win money wi' this line the day, I'll list in the Salvation Army.

JEAN: *(Taking coppers from her purse)* Oh! here! there's a bob, you can get a glass o' beer wi' the extra threepence.

JOCK: *(Taking money)* You're a sport, Jean.

JEAN: I look it! that's a' you're gettin'.

(JOCK is on his way out when BOB enters, boisterously bumping into him)

          Here! Can you no' watch where you're gaun, ye muckle nowte![46]

BOB: It was you that wasna watchin' where you were gaun.

JOCK: If you gi'e me ony o' your lip I'll slap your ear for ye.

JEAN: *(To JOCK)* Awa' you and attend to the bookie.

JOCK: He's daft, that's what's wrang wi' him.

(JOCK goes out)

JEAN: *(To BOB).* Where ha'e you been?

BOB: Washin' tatties at the soup kitchen. Is there onything for me to eat?

JEAN: See here! you'll need to try to control your belly a bit, it would take a Carnegie to keep this hoose gaun the noo.[47]

---

46 Nowte (Sc.): ox.

47 Carnegie: Andrew Carnegie (1835 –1919), the fabulously wealthy Dunfermline-born Ameri-

BOB: Eat when you can get it, and when you canna get it, weel, you canna eat.

LIZZIE: I heard him swearin' the day, maw.

BOB: Wha heard me swearin'?

LIZZIE: Me.

BOB: You're a flamin' wee liar. Where did you hear me swearin'?

LIZZIE: At the street corner.

BOB: What did I say?

LIZZIE: You just want me tae swear tae, but I'm no'.

(She puts out her tongue at him. He makes a rush at her)

BOB: I'll warm your ear for ye.

JEAN: Here! That'll dae!

BOB: She's a flamin' wee liar.

JEAN: That'll dae I'm sayin'!

BOB: Just wait till I get her ootside, I'll bump her.

JEAN: D'ye want ony tea?

BOB: Is there ony ham left?

JEAN: No.

BOB: Never mind tea, then, just gimmie a piece in my hand.

(JEAN spreads bread with treacle)

BOB: I'm fed up wi' this treacle, I'll soon be like a darkie.

JEAN: Be damned thankfu' you're gettin' treacle. If the Pairish doesna pay oot you'll be doon on your knees on the grass.

BOB: Ha'e you heard the latest?

JEAN: No, what is it?

BOB: Tam Anderson's coortin' Kate.

JEAN: That's auld news.

BOB: Did you ken?

JEAN: Surely I kent when it was me that gi'ed him the wink that she had a notion o' him.

BOB: Can you no' gi'e somebody the wink to tak' a notion o' me?

JEAN: Wha would tak' a notion o' you?

BOB: What's wrang wi' me?

JEAN: There's a lookin' glass there.

(Enter JENNY)

JEAN: Did you get the doctor?

JENNY: He's comin' doon after he gets his dinner.

(She hands her mother the whisky)

JEAN: You'll rin doon wi' this to your auntie's, Bob, and tell Kate that I'll come doon when the doctor comes.

BOB: *(To JENNY)* That Wull Baxter o' yours is gaun to get a maulin' when he comes up the pit; a' the women o' the place are gaun to be there; they'll skin him alive.

JEAN: *(To BOB)* Tell Kate to make the half o' that into toddy, and gi'e it to her mither.

BOB: He's just a flamin' reactionary, but just wait till he gets a taste o' the dictatorship o' the proletariat.[48]

---

can steel magnate. Scotland benefited greatly from the philanthropic largesse of his later life in terms of libraries and other educational benefits. But he was also notorious among working people for the sometimes brutal tactics used in his steel plants to crush union activity.

48 This phrase is used in a couple of places by Marx to name the type of state to be established immediately after the overthrow of capitalism, in order to make possible the transition to a genuinely classless society (communism) in which the state would 'wither away'. It was used

JEAN: Here! chuck that Bolshie stuff and rin doon wi' that whisky.

BOB: *(Going off)* There's nothing like direct action for the revolutionary movement.

(He goes out)

JEAN: I wouldna worry mysel' ower Wull Baxter, he's no' worth it.

JENNY: I'm no' worried, mither, just disappointed.

JEAN: Was he speakin' aboot gaun to Canada after the strike?

JENNY: We were baith gaun there.

JEAN: That's the reason he's workin' Jenny.

JENNY: I canna understan' it, mither.

JEAN: He'll get his deserts yet, Jenny, just bide your time. Every dog gets its day.

(JENNY looks out window wearily)

LIZZIE: *(Rising and handing her mug to JEAN)* Read my cup, maw.

(JEAN takes mug and looks into it with a serious air. LIZZIE is serious too)

JEAN: There's a new frock comin' to you, dearie ... but I doot it'll no' be till the strike's finished.

LIZZIE: Nae stockin's?

JEAN: Ay, there's stockin's and shoon tae.

LIZZIE: Nae money?

JEAN: No, there's nae money, daurlin'.

LIZZIE: And hoo will I get a new frock, and shoon, and stockin's withoot money?

JEAN: Rin awa' for a pail o' water, darlin', and I'll mebbe be able to tell you when you come back.

(LIZZIE goes for pail)

LIZZIE: *(Going out)* This should be Bob's work, no' mine. Nae wonder I'm gettin' grey heided.

(The canary sings)

JEAN: I wish I'd been a bird.

(KATE enters)

KATE: Is Jock in, auntie?

JEAN: No. What d'ye want wi' him, Kate?

KATE: Will there be ony chance o' me gettin' some money if I go to the Pairish clerk? I'll need to get some nourishment for my mither ... she's beginnin' to rave noo ... Oh, Jean! I dinna ken what to dae.

JEAN: Where's your faither?

KATE: He's sittin' at her bedside.

JEAN: It's him that'll need to go to the Pairish, Kate, they'll no' listen to you.

KATE: He'll no' gang.

JEAN: He'll gang if I go doon to him, and in a hurry.

(Enter LIZZIE, with water)

JEAN: Is her cough ony better yet?

KATE: Ay, she's no' coughin' noo, just ravin' aboot the weans.

JEAN: The doctor'll gi'e her a bottle that'll make her sleep, and she'll be like a new woman in the mornin'. She's been worryin' hersel' ower much, that's a' that's wrang wi' her. You should have had the doctor lang syne, Kate. But that's what's wrang wi' the working women, they want tae dee on their feet[49] ... Tam Anderson would tell you what was the best thing to do to get some

---

much more often by Soviet leaders such as Lenin, who had no intention of allowing their state to wither away.

49 Lang syne: long since; dee: die (both Sc.)

money frae the Pairish.

KATE: I hear them sayin' that he's likely to be arrested if he takes pairt in the demonstration against Wull Baxter.

JEAN: If I see him, Kate, I'll ha'e a talk wi' him aboot it. He canna afford to take the risk o' gettin' the jile noo when the strike's aboot finished.

KATE: If he has his mind made up, Jean, you'll no' put him off it ... Everything seems to be gaun wrang thigither ... I'm fed up.

(She buries her head in her hands at table and sobs)

JEAN: *(Comforting)* It'll no' dae to lose he'rt, Kate. When things go against us we've still got to battle. Lyin' doon to things doesna help ony. Na, na, let us keep up oor he'rts ... Wheesht! lass, things'll come a' richt for us yet. Awa' doon to the hoose and get your faither to go to the Pairish clerk; if he doesna get onything I'll go for Tam Anderson and see what he has to say aboot it. Go doon and attend to your mither, gi'e her the rest o' the toddie till the doctor comes, then I'll come doon and see what's trumph.[50]

(KATE rises)

JEAN: That's the spirit, hen, keep up your pecker ... Go doon wi' her, Jenny, and keep her company till the doctor comes ... Your mither will be a' richt the morn', Kate, dinna worry aboot that.

(KATE and JENNY go out)

JEAN: Puir sowl, she hasna had much pleasure in life to be a young lass.

LIZZIE: What's wrang wi' my auntie, maw?

JEAN: Hunger, dear, that's what's wrang.

LIZZIE: What wey are folk hungry?

JEAN: Because some are ower fu' fed.

(TAM ANDERSON knocks and enters)

JEAN: Did you meet Kate and Jenny, Tam?

TAM: I dinna want to meet them, Jean.

JEAN: She's lookin' for you.

TAM: Is her mither nae better?

JEAN: She's wantin' to ken hoo she'll get some money frae the Pairish clerk; they're in utter starvation.

TAM: If she gets a line frae the doctor I'll see that she gets something. Tell her that, will ye?

JEAN: What wey dae you no' want tae see her?

TAM: I'm likely to be arrested the night, Jean.

JEAN: Hoo d'ye ken?

TAM: The sergeant o' the police warned me that if I took pairt in the demonstration against Wull Baxter I'd be arrested.

JEAN: And are ye?

TAM: If we let him get hame withoot a demonstration there'll be mair men oot the morn. We've got to nip it in the bud, Jean.

JEAN: Is it worth it, Tam? It means the jile for ye, and the breakawa'll take place some time or ither. You nor onybody else can stem it, and you ken that, for it has happened before in your time.

TAM: And it'll happen again, Jean, and will happen till the workers control their ain destiny. But we've got to fight till the last ditch every time, whether it means the jile or no'.

---

50 See what's trumph (Sc.); see what's happening.

JEAN: It'll hurt Kate, Tam.

TAM: I ken it will, but there's nae escape. I'll no' likely get ony mair than three months, and it'll be worth the sufferin' to come back again and ken that I did my bit.

JEAN: And you'll get a' your thanks for it in the yin day. The miners are a queer crowd, they forget about the fight when they get their first week's pay in their hand. You ken the trouble you had after the last strike collectin' money to pay the debts: you had to pawn your ain watch to help.

TAM: I ken a' that, Jean, but it has a' to be suffered, there's never onything won withoot a struggle ... But I didna come up to argue wi' ye, Jean, I want you to take a message to Kate. I'm no' likely to see her for a while noo.

JEAN: What d'ye want?

TAM: Will you ask her to stick to me, Jean?

JEAN: You needna ha'e ony fear o' that, Tam. But would you no' be better to ha'e a talk wi' her yoursel'?

TAM: I'm feart she micht put me aff takin' a pairt in the demonstration, you ken what women are, and she micht keep me back; at least we micht quarrel aboot it, and I dinna want that to happen ... Tell her, Jean, that whenever I get oot we'll get marrit ... And, Jean, I want you to gi'e her this; it'll mebbe tide them ower the strike.

JEAN: What is it?

TAM: *(Holding out his hand)* Three pounds, a' I ha'e left o' my savin's. It's no' much, but it'll ay help a wee thing. I'll no' need it, I'll be gettin' free digs where I go. *(He smiles)*

JEAN: I wish you would put this affair off, Tam. No, I dinna wish it either, laddie, for if you did you wouldna be Tam Anderson. But, Tam, you'll no'dae very weel in the jile, you're no' the jile bird type.

TAM: If my health doesna break doon, Jean, I dinna care, but this strike has been a tryin' time, and my nerves are a' knocked to bits. But never mind, auld yin, we'll come through it. You'll keep Kate's he'rt up till I come back?

JEAN: She'll be waitin' on ye comin' back, Tam, ha'e nae fear o' that.

TAM: Weel ... Guid bye! Jean.

(He holds out his hand)

JEAN: Guid bye! Tam ... This strike's gaun to break a' oor he'rts. *(She sobs)*

(TAM wants to say more, but is not able. He goes out rather suddenly. JEAN sits at tableside. BOB enters)

BOB: By gee, there's gaun to be some fun when that worm, Baxter, comes up the pit; a' the women o' the place are getting ready for him. They're no' half wild because there's nae pairish money the day. And the polis are comin' in their hunners.

JEAN: You'll keep awa' frae it.

BOB: You surely think it! I'm gaun to be in at the death.

JEAN: You're keepin' awa' frae it, I'm sayin' − and leavin' it to the men.

BOB: Leave it to the MEN! What am I?

LIZZIE: A mug.

BOB: I'm no' gaun to warn you again.

LIZZIE: You're worse than a mug, you're a ...

BOB: A what?

JEAN: That'll dae, the pair o' ye.

BOB: What am I?

JEAN: *(Angrily)* That'll dae, I'm sayin'!

LIZZIE: *(Running out)* You're a puddin'.

(BOB chases her the length of door)

BOB: I'm wantin' a lend o' that poker.

JEAN: What for?

BOB: A man's nae guid wi' his bare fists against a polisman wi' a baton.

JEAN: Your faither'll be gaun, and that's plenty oot o' the yin hoose. I dinna want two o' ye to get the jile.

BOB: The jile! Will we get the jile?

JEAN: Certainly you will.

BOB: I didna ken that. Will I get another piece?

JEAN: You'll get your tea at tea time.

BOB: By gee! when this strike's finished I bet ye I'll have yin solid tightener, I'll no' be able to eat onything for a week efter it. What aboot tuppence for a packet o' Woodbines?[51]

JEAN: I dinna ha'e tuppence; you're smokin' ower much onywey.

BOB: *(Going out)* I ken what's needed, it's a revolution that's needed.

(JEAN goes to cage and gives the bird some seed. Then JOCK bursts in)

JOCK: That's twa o' my horses up, Jean! Thirty-five bob!

(He catches hold of her and swings her round the room)

JEAN: Thirty-five bob!

JOCK: Thirty-five bob! and, if the ither horse comes up, you'll ha'e twa pound ten.

JEAN: When will you ken aboot it?

JOCK: No' till the mornin', but the thirty-five bob is as safe as the bank.

JEAN: You'll see and come hame wi' it, Jock, and no' dae as you did the last time.

JOCK: I'm safe enough noo, Jean, I got a lesson last nicht I'll no' forget in a hurry. *(Sits and lights pipe)* A bit win like that fairly lifts a body's he'rt, doesn't it?

JEAN: It tak's something to lift up oor he'rts nooadays. I had Tam Anderson in the noo; he's to be arrested if he tak's pairt in the demonstration.

JOCK: So I heard doon the street. But Jean, if they arrest Tam Anderson there'll he a riot.

JEAN: Mebbe! I ken the Carhill miners; they're gey feart o' their ain skins whiles.

JOCK: That's right enough tae. Let them sit on their hunkers at the street corner, and let the likes o' Tam Anderson risk everything for them.

JEAN: Are you gaun to the demonstration?

JOCK: There'll be plenty there withoot me. *(Then, to break the conversation)* We'll get oot your weddin' ring wi' the bookie's money.

JEAN: Let it stay where it is, we ha'e mair need o' the money than a ring on the finger.

JOCK: I wouldna care if the strike was finished, it's been a hell o' a time.

JEAN: You're no' gaun to be much better if you've to go back to the pit on the maister's terms. It's been a hard time, richt enough, and mony a nicht I have lain doon wonderin' where oor breakfast was to come frae, but, Jock, it's nae mair he'rt-rendin' than watchin' thae wheels turnin' every day, and never lookin' oot the windie but dreadin' to see some o' ye cairrit hame a corpse or maimed for life. There are plenty o' women never bother their heids, they have seen that much and come through that much, that they have got hardened to

---

51 A very popular brand of cigarette in the early 20th century.

it. But I havena reached that stage yet, na, thae wheels are ay between me and the sun, throwin' their lang, black shadows on the doorstep. It's mebbe been a time o' want since the strike started, but it's been a time o' peace; I was ay sure o' you and Bob comin' hame at nichts; but there's nae such faith when the wheels are turnin'. But you men dinna think o' thae things, you'll likely laugh at us when we tell ye aboot it?

JOCK: It's a fact, Jean, we put nae value on oor lives.

JEAN: You talk aboot a weddin' ring! I would gi'e the very he'rt oot o' my breist if I thought it would keep ye awa' frae that Hell.

JOCK: I'll need to try and get you awa' frae the pits, Jean, but it'll no' be easy noo they ha'e us gey weel chained, and I doot there's naething else for us but the same auld grind. Seven months' rent on oor heids noo, and we're a' needin' buits and claes. Ach. Christ kens what it'll be like.

JEAN: Ay, but keep up your pecker, Jock, there's a silver linin' to every cloud.

JOCK: So it says in the school books.

(Enter JENNY)

JENNY: Mither, that's the doctor here, and he's takin' my auntie awa' to the hospital.

JEAN: The hospital! what's wrang?

JENNY: I dinna ken, she has to go through an operation.

JEAN: Good God! it's surely gey serious.

JOCK: Did the doctor no' say what was wrang?

JIiNNY: No, he wouldna tell me.

JEAN: *(Putting on shawl)* Puir sowl, I thocht there was something gey far wrang wi' her.

(JEAN goes out, followed by JENNY)

JOCK: Starvation! And they write to America to say that there's nae distress in the coalfields. Christians! I wonder what Christ would think o' them if He was here?

(BOB enters)

LIZZIE: I heard him swearin' the day, daddy.

BOB: I'll warm your ear for you if you say that again.

LIZZIE: *(Runnin' out)* So you were, I heard ye.

(BOB chases her to door)

BOB: Where's my mither?

JOCK: Awa' wi' the lodger.

BOB: I could dae wi' something to eat.

JOCK: Weel, get it yoursel'. God knows where some o' ye get the appetites. Are ye aye hungry?

BOB: I can ay eat mair than I get.

(He goes to dresser and puts bread and margarine on the table)

BOB: *(Cutting bread)* There's gaun to be some fun at the pit when Wull Baxter gets up. Are you gaun up?

JOCK: What am I gaun to do there?

BOB: Feart you get the jile?

JOCK: No. I'm no' feart I get the jile.

BOB: What wey are you no' gaun then?

(Spreads margarine on bread)

JOCK: Hey! that's butter, and there's a strike on.

BOB: That's no' butter, that's margarine.

JOCK: Weel, ca' cannie wi' it.[52] If you want tea you'll need to put water in the teapot.

BOB: *(Going to fire to fill teapot)* Fancy oor Jenny engaged to a worm like Wull Baxter. I'm ashamed to go doon the street.

(Sits down and puts sugar in his cup)

JOCK: *(At third spoonful)* Here! ca' cannie wi' that sugar.

BOB: Don't get excited. Where did you say my mither was?

JOCK: Your auntie has to go to the hospital.

BOB: Oh, what's wrang wi' her?

JOCK: If you kent that you'd be as wise as me, wouldn't ye?

(JOCK lights his pipe)

BOB: My uncle, Tam, was up at the Pairish tryin' to get some money, but he didna get it.

JOCK: No.

BOB: No, the clerk tellt him he heard his yarn before. But he'll get it noo if the doctor says it.

JOCK: Ay, he'll get it noo when it's mebbe ower late. *(There is a short pause)* I ha'e twa horses up the day, Bob.

BOB: By gee! your jam's fairly in the noo.

JOCK: Thirty-five bob. And, if the ither yin comes in, I'll ha'e aboot three quid.

BOB: That's the stuff to gi'e them. If you had that every day you'd be a richt, eh?

JOCK: Ay, IF. If the Lakes o' Killarney were in Hell you'd get a shillin' a gallon withoot any trouble.

BOB: Would ye?

JOCK: Ay, if!

BOB: If what?

JOCK: Thick heid! Did you no' hear me say that if the Lakes o' Killarney were in Hell you'd get a shillin' a gallon!

BOB: What for?

JOCK: For the water, of coorse!

BOB: Oh, ay. IF! *(Spreading margarine on bread)* IF you hadna went into the pub wi' the last bookie's money …

JOCK: *(Interrupting)* Ca' cannie wi' that margarine, I said!

BOB: I'm doin' that, sir, it's no guid onywey.

JOCK: Be damned gratefu' you're getting' it.

BOB: I'm no' grumblin'. *(Pause)* Did you hear aboot Sam Lindsay?

JOCK: What Sam Lindsay?

BOB: Sam Lindsay, the bookie.

JOCK: No, what aboot him?

BOB: He was pinched on the street the noo.

JOCK: *(Jumping)* Eh?

BOB: The polis pinched him takin' bets on the street.

JOCK: *(Almost in tears)* I had my bet on wi' him.

BOB: Weel, you can say ta! ta! to your money, the polis took a' the slips off him.

JOCK: Cripes! that's a blow. Here! ca' canny wi' that breid, are you aware that's a' we ha'e in the hoose?

BOB: Listen! That's them singin' 'The Red Flag'. By gee! there's gaun to be some fun here the day! it'll be anither Waterloo! Can YOU sing 'The Red Flag' yet?

JOCK: Oh, shut up! It's bad enough backin' losers, but it's a damned sicht worse

---

52 Ca' cannie (Sc.): be careful, go easy.

281

backin' winners, and no' gettin' payed ower.

BOB: I ay tellt ye it was a mug's game.

JOCK: Shut up, I tell ye! And get thae things off the table. I thought Sam Lindsay had mair savvy than get pinched on the street. If I'd only put my bet on wi' Peter.

BOB: Ay, IF!

JOCK: I want less gab frae you, see! But if there's nae pairish money the morn that gramophone o' yours'll need to go to the pawn.

BOB: My mither'll ha'e a say in that.

JOCK: Wha's boss in here, me, or your mither?

BOB: My mither, of course.

(JEAN enters; she is crying. LIZZIE follows, much concerned)

JOCK: What's the maitter, Jean?

(JEAN is too much upset to answer)

JOCK: What has happened?

JEAN: Oh, Jock, she's deid!

JOCK: Deid! Good Lord!

JEAN: Oh, Jock, that's an awfu' sicht doon there; a' the weans greetin' like to break their wee he'rts, and Kate tearin' her hair and cryin' on her mither to speak.

JOCK: Where's the faither?

JEAN: He's awa to the Pairish wi' the doctor's line. But it's ower late noo. Oh, Jock, she's worn awa' tae nothing, lyin' yonder wi' her thin, white face.

JOCK: Is there onything I can dae, Jean?

JEAN: Naething ava', Jock.

JOCK: Christ knows what it's comin' tae.

JEAN: Puir wee things, they'll miss their mither. Gi'ed the bite oot o' her ain mooth, puir sowl. What can God be thinkin' aboot when he lets the like o' this happen.

JOCK: If it's God's will that has ta'en awa' puir Agnes He's a gey queer God, and doesna ha'e much o' a he'rt for the weans it seems.

(JEAN rises)

JEAN: Fill the kettle, Jock, I'll need to go doon beside them the nicht. I'll leave Jenny wi' them the morn's nicht.[53]

JOCK: Right o!

JEAN: *(going out)* Puir wee things. …

(JEAN goes out, LIZZIE following. Jock fills the kettle with water, spilling some on the floor. He puts kettle on fire then goes to scullery, returning with a cloth. He wipes floor awkwardly, and carries cloth away, as if it were a dead rat, by the tail, letting it drop on the way, and has to clean up another mess. He chucks cloth through scullery door. He then lifts floor brush and sweeps the floor, making the best of a bad job. He puts table nearer the window to hide the mess. Then he sits at fireside. Through the silence the booing of a crowd can be heard at intervals. He goes to window and looks out. BOB enters excitedly)

BOB: That's Wull Baxter up the pit, and he's comin' hame between twa regiments o' polis!

JOCK: Are there mony women there?

BOB: Hunners, did you no' hear them booin'?

JOCK: Could they no' stay in their hooses and leave it to the men?

---

53 The morn's nicht (Sc.): tomorrow night.

BOB: Leave it to the men! There's mair fecht in twa women than there is in a hunner men. *(The booing is heard again)* Listen! Are you comin' to see the fun?

JOCK: I ha'e mair to think aboot.

BOB: You're feart you get the jile, I'm no'.

(He runs out. JOCK peers through window. The sound of disorder gets louder. There is one loud 'Boo!' then JENNY hursts in)

JENNY: Oh, faither, there's a riot started doon the street!

JOCK: I kent it would happen. Could thae blasted women no' kept to their hooses onywey. *(Draws aside curtains of window)* God Almighty! there's the crowd has got Wull Baxter awa' frae the polis! They'll lynch him. … Jenny! shut that door, he's making for here.

(JENNY stands undecided. JOCK makes to lock door. JENNY holds him back)

JOCK: Oot o' my road woman!

(JENNY struggles. JOCK loses his temper, and thrusts her aside as the door bursts open, and WULL BAXTER almost falls in, locking the door behind him. The mob is at his heels, shouting madly. A stone crashes through the window)

JOCK: Oot o' this hoose!

WULL: They'll kill me, Jock!

JOCK: Oot o' here, you traitor!

(JOCK makes to eject him when the sound of a police whistle is heard and the screaming of women. Then a stampede, and then silence)

JOCK: *(At window)* Bloodshed! Bloodshed ower the heid o' you! Oot o' here before I crush the life oot o' ye!

(WULL looks pitiously at JENNY. She hesitates a second, then she goes to door, unlocks it, and opens it. He goes out, and she shuts the door again)

JOCK: Bloodshed ower the heid o' a worm like that! a traitor! a bloody skunk. And you would …

JENNY: *(Burying her head in her hands against the door)* Oh! faither!....

(He looks at her sympathetically as the curtain falls)

ACT THREE

(The same as Acts One and Two. A week later. At rise of curtain, BOB sits at table side with a soup bowl on his knees, playing on it with two spoons as he would a kettle drum; he whistles a bagpipe tune. JOCK enters from room: jacket off)

JOCK: Is it no' time you were awa' to the soup kitchen?

BOB: I'm waitin' till the last the day, it's aboot time noo I was gettin' some o' the thick stuff.

JOCK: Ay, wait till the last, and, when you get doon, there'll be nane left.

BOB: That'll be MY funeral.

JOCK: Ay, but you'll be guzzlin' the dinner in here.

BOB: Some hope when YOU'RE there.

JOCK: I don't want ony lip, see!

(BOB rattles on the bowl and whistles)

JOCK: Oh, for God's sake stop that, it gets on my nerves.

BOB: I think I'll join the pipe band.

(Has another rattle)

JOCK: You'll break that flamin' bowl.

BOB: No fear, sir. *(Rattles still)*

JOCK: *(Rising)* Are you gaun to stop it?

(BOB stops)

BOB: It's high time we had the dictatorship o' the proletariat here.

JOCK: Did you hear ony word o' Tam Anderson when you were doon the street?

BOB: There's word comin' ower the telephone whenever the trial's finished.

JOCK: *(Half to himself)* I wonder hoo he'll get on?

BOB: Ten bob, or thirty days.

JOCK: They're no' tryin' him in the High Court before a jury o' auld farmers and grocers and butchers to let him aff wi' a fine. I wouldna be surprised if he gets six months.

BOB: Away and don't haver! Six months! You're a reactionary. What would he get six months for?

JOCK: If you had seen the summons you wouldna say that; they're just aboot chairgin' him wi' startin' a rebellion.

BOB: But it was Wull Baxter that was the cause o' it, no' Tam Anderson.

JOCK: Ay, but Wull Baxter was helpin' the maisters, he was dain' richt as far as they were concerned.

BOB: But the maisters are no' tryin' him.

JOCK: Are they no'? You ha'e a lot to learn aboot your revolutionary movement.

BOB: I ken mair than you ken; it's a revolution that's needed, and you dinna ken that.

JOCK: I ken that when the revolution comes you'll be fillin' your belly some place.

BOB: When the revolution comes, sir, I'll be in the thick o' the dictatorship o' the ...

JOCK: Oh! shut it!

(JEAN enters carrying a basin containing potatoes which she puts on the table and begins to pare.)

JEAN: Is it no' time you were awa' to the soup kitchen, Bob?

BOB: I'm waiting on the thick stuff the day.

JEAN: Ay, and you'll likely wait till it's finished.

JOCK: I've just been tellin' him that, but you may as weel speak to the Bass Rock noo as speak to him.

BOB: I dinna ken what you're a' worryin' yoursel's aboot. If I dinna get ony soup it'll be me that'll be hungry, no' you.

JOCK: I dinna want ony backchat, see!

BOB: *(Rising)* If there's nae soup left for me there'll be a revolution doon there.

JOCK: Revolution! and if onybody was burstin' a paper bag at your back you'd dee wi' the fricht.

BOB: Oh, you're just a reactionary, when the revolution comes you'll be usin' propaganda for the bourgeois. *(Going out door)* Three cheers for the dictatorship o' the ...

(JOCK rises in a hurry, and BOB scoots)

JOCK: They damned Bolshies are settin' the young yins off their heids.

JEAN: He's only a laddie, man. You're worse than him that pays ony attention.

JOCK: Dictatorship o' the proletariat! and, if you asked him what it meant, he couldna tell ye.

JEAN: Do you ken what it means?

JOCK: Ay.

JEAN:	What?
JOCK:	It means … it means … weel, it means if … it means a revolution that's what it means.
JEAN:	Ay, you ha'e a lot tae learn yet tae, I doot … Hoo d'ye think Tam Anderson'll get on the day?
JOCK:	Six months!
JEAN:	Six months! He'll no' get off as easy as that.
JOCK:	Then, if you ken, what are you askin' for?
JEAN:	Just for fun. They're sayin' doon the street that they'll no' be ower hard on him seein' that the strike's aboot finished. But there's no' much sympathy wi' lawyers and judges, it's hard facts wi' them a' the time, hard, cauld facts; staring you through and through wi' their cauld, grey e'en seein' a' the bad points, but very few o' the guid yins.
JOCK:	It's true, Jean. Mebbe eighteen months for him, and the strike likely to be finished the day; it's hard lines … Ay, it's bad when you think aboot it, oot for seven lang months, hungered and starved just aboot off the face o' the earth, and to go back defeated.
JEAN:	Ach! you men dinna ken hoo to strike onywey; you throw doon your tools, come oot the pit, and stand at the street corner till you starve yoursel's back to the pit again. And, when you DAE go back, instead o' strikin' oot for mair on your rate, you fill mair hutches, and would cut each ither's throat to get them.
JOCK:	I ken there's a good wheen o' thae kind.
JEAN:	You're yin o' thae kind yoursel'. And you're grousin' aboot the langer 'oors you'll need to work, but you'll be awa' to the pit an 'oor before the time, and be an 'oor later in comin' hame frae it. Ach! you dinna ken the first thing aboot strikin', for as often as you've been on strike.
JOCK:	D'ye want us to blaw the pits in the air, or what?
JEAN:	If you'd slip oot the road and play cricket, and leave it to the women you'd dae mair guid.
JOCK:	You ha'e plenty o' gab, if that would win a strike. I was at yin women's meetin', and I couldna hear a word for a week efter it, gab-gab-gab!
JEAN:	We ha'e mair than gab, we ha'e courage, and that's what you men dinna ha'e.
JOCK:	I'll bet you the next strike'll no' be sae quiet.
JEAN:	*(Sarcastically)* The next strike! and you'll be breakin' your necks rinnin' up to the pit to get your jobs before the strike's finished.
JOCK:	What else can we dae?
JEAN:	Huh! I tellt ye. Some men to win a strike.
JOCK:	The men were richt enough, it was the leaders that let us doon.
JEAN:	And wha put the leaders there? Hoo often dae ye attend the Union meetin's? You tak' nae interest in your affairs till there's a strike on, then you find oot that you want new leaders. You just get the leaders you deserve.
JOCK:	There's a lot no' interested, right enough: of coorse it's a' for the want o' sense.
JEAN:	It's the want o' sense that makes a man buy that paper you're readin', tae, after a' it has said aboot ye since the strike started.
JOCK:	Eh?
JEAN:	That's a coalmaisters' paper you're readin'.
JOCK:	I ken that fine, you dinna need to tell me that.

JEAN: Then what dae you buy it for?

JOCK: Oh, just for the sake o' the pictures.

JEAN: You'd be as weel to stop it, then, and buy 'Comic Cuts'.[54]

JOCK: Where's Jenny?

JEAN: She's doon at the soup kitchen, gi'en them a hand.

JOCK: They tell me they're on their last bag o' tatties.

JEAN: Ay, and as mony tattie pits aboot the place. It doesna say much for you men.

JOCK: I think you want to see us in the jile.

JEAN: The jile! You'd rather lie doon on a tattie pit and dee wi' an empty belly than risk the jile. I canna understand you men.

JOCK: Where did you get THAE tatties?

JEAN: When you were studyin' the form o' the horses.

JOCK: Wull Baxter was doon the street yesterday, I hear.

JEAN: Ay, he was in the toon, at the shippin' office.

JOCK: Gaun off to Canada likely?

JEAN: Ay.

JOCK: Does Jenny ken?

JEAN: He sent a letter to her yesterday.

JOCK: Oh? did he! And what was in it?

JEAN: Wantin' her to go to Canada wi' him.

JOCK: Well, I'll be damned! Did you ever hear sic' neck? What did he say?

JEAN: He's vexed for everything that's happened. Says it was for Jenny's sake he blacklegged — wanted to get as much as take them awa frae here.

JOCK: If you dinna watch her she'll slip off wi' him, that's what you'll see.

JEAN: I'm kind o' vexed for him tae, Jock.

JOCK: I tellt ye. See here, Jean, there's to be nae damned nonsense aboot this. Wull Baxter's gaun to Canada HIMSEL'! What would the neebours say aboot a thing like this?

JEAN: To hell wi' the neebours! they dinna concern me, Jock.

JOCK: It's no' happenin', see!

JEAN: Wha said it was happenin'? I just said I was vexed for him.

JOCK: Ay, but you're fishin' to get roon' the saft side o' me. I see the game a' richt.

JEAN: You'd think you were boss in here the wey you're talkin'. The saft side o' YOU. You havena had ony drink this mornin', ha'e ye?

JOCK: There's something in the wind when you're beginnin' to pity him noo. Vexed for him! and Tam Anderson likely to get the jile ower the heid o' him.

JEAN: He made a mistake, that was a'. And that tinker o' a mither o' his made him go.

JOCK: Where's his letter?

JEAN: She says she burnt it.

JOCK: Then she has mair sense than you.

JEAN: Ay, she tak's it off her faither.

(JENNY enters, almost in tears)

JENNY: Ha'e you heard aboot Tam Anderson?

JOCK: No, hoo did he get on?

JENNY: Oh, faither, he's got three years.

JOCK: Three years!

JENNY: Three years! That canna be true, Jenny.

---

54   A comic-strip magazine, published 1890–1953.

JENNY: Ay, it's true, mither, he's awa' to the jile for three years.

JOCK: Good God! that's cruel. Three years! as quiet a laddie as ever stepped in twa shoon.

JEAN: This'll send Kate mad. Puir sowl, she's hain' her fill o' sorrow the noo. Does she ken, Jenny?

JENNY: No. Will you go doon and tell her, faither?

JOCK: Will I go doon, Jean?

JEAN: (At window) Here she's comin'. You'd better go to the room, Jenny.

(JENNY goes to room)

JOCK: This is a bad job, Jean.

JEAN: Oh, this strike's gaun to break a' oor he'rts before it's finished.

(KATE enters. She is very pale and worn-looking)

KATE: (Holding out her hand) Here, Jean.

JEAN: What is it, Kate?

KATE: Some money.

JEAN: What is that for?

KATE: Just a wee bit help, Jean.

JEAN: I dinna want it, Kate, you ha'e mair need o' it than me.

KATE: I got the insurance money the day, Jean.[55] Tak' it, noo, or I'll be angry.

JEAN: I'll tak' it, Kate, but I'll pay it back when the strike's finished.

(She takes the money)

KATE: Ha'e you seen my faither this mornin', Jock?

JOCK: No' me, Kate.

KATE: He went oot after breakfast time, and he's no' hame yet. He cam' hame gey fu' yesterday.

JOCK: So I suppose.

KATE: D'ye ken, Jean, I'm weary.

JEAN: I'm sorry for you, Kate, but you'll no' need to lose he'rt.

KATE: Hoo d'ye think Tam'll get on the day, Jock?

JOCK: I dinna ken, Kate, I don't think they'll be too hard on him.

KATE: Will he get off, d'ye think?

JOCK: I doot he'll no' get off, Kate.

(He looks at JEAN, KATE sees him)

KATE: Is the word in?

JOCK: I dinna ken, Kate, I havena heard onything.

(He hangs his head)

KATE: You HA'E got word. Tell me, Jock. Tell me, Jean. Oh! for God's sake tell me!

JOCK: (Pulling his hand on her shoulder) Kate, … I ha'ena very guid news for ye…. you'll need to bear up … They ha'e him awa' for … three years.

KATE: (In whisper) Three years! … three years! … Oh! Jock.

(She buries her head on his shoulder)

JEAN: (Going to her) Kate, dearie.

(KATE cries bitterly)

JEAN: Puir lass, I'm sorry for ye.

KATE: Three years! Oh, Jean … Jean!

JEAN: Come awa' doon wi' me, Kate. Puir Tam!

(They go out, and JENNY enters)

JOCK: Three years, and we live in a civilised country. If this is civilisation put me in

---

55 Presumably life-insurance money on her mother.

among the savages. You better go doon and keep her company a wee while, Jenny.

JENNY: *(In a hysterical kind of way)* Three years? and the miners are feart for revolution. Ha! ha! ha!

(She goes out. JOCK takes his pipe from his pocket; it is empty. He looks towards door, then hurries to the tea caddie on mantleshelf. He fills pipe with tea, and is seated, puffing merrily when JEAN enters)

JEAN: Puir lass, she's in an awfu' state.

JOCK: *(Puffing)* She's gettin' HER share o' the strike, Jean.

JEAN: God kens she is. And that faither o' her's awa' boozin', I suppose. You'll need to ha'e a word wi' him; that kind o' conduct'll no' dae at a time like this; he'll break that lass's he'rt.

JOCK: He has aye been the same, a washout: the least excuse and off on the beer. He had the best wife in the country, tae, but didna seem to ken it.

JEAN: He'll ken noo, when she's awa'.

JOCK: I'll ha'e to talk wi' him and see if I canna put some sense into his fat heid. *(Puffs)* What ha'e you for the dinner the day?

JEAN: Tatties and onions.

JOCK: Stovies?

JEAN: Ay. *(Coughs)* What kind o' baccy is that you're smokin'?

JOCK: Eh! It's … it's some fag ends I got frae Bob.

JEAN: It's surely that, that's an awfu' smell.

(BOB enters carryin' his bowl, which he puts on table)

JEAN: Hullo! did you no' get your soup?

BOB: I was ower late.

JOCK: I tellt ye, didn't I?

BOB: *(To JEAN)* Ha'e you ony dinner, mither?

JEAN: Stovies and onions.

BOB: Some feed!

JEAN: It's better than nane.

BOB: No' much. … Is it true that the strike's aboot finished?

JEAN: Ay, ham and eggs every Sunday mornin' noo.

BOB: If we had eggs, we could ha'e ham and eggs the noo, if we had ham.[56]

JOCK: Eh?

BOB: I'm sayin', if we had eggs, we could ha'e ham and eggs.

JOCK: What the flames are you talkin' aboot?

BOB: *(Snuffing)* What kind o' baccy is that you're smokin'?

JOCK: What was wrang, there was nae soup?

BOB: Nae money left in the funds.

JEAN: Did you hear aboot Tam Anderson, Bob?

BOB: No, hoo did he get on?

JEAN: Three years.

BOB: Three years! I ken what's needed, it's a revolution that's needed.

JOCK: Oh, for God's sake gi'e that revolution a rest.

BOB: What kind o' baccy is that you're smokin'?

JOCK: *(Coughing)* It's fag ends.

---

56 This expression of comic despair seems to originate from Eastern Europe, but also seems to first appear in English in the U.S., presumably via the large-scale immigration of the late 19th and early 20th centuries.

BOB: *(Jumping)* Where did you get them?

JOCK: Never you mind.

BOB: I havena had a smoke the day. By Gee! When the strike's finished I'll smoke till I'm sick.

JEAN: *(Putting on shawl)* I'm gaun doon for something to eat. *(Lifting basket)* Lift off that pot, Jock, you're bound to be tired o' stovies. We'll ha'e ham and eggs the day, supposin' we should never ha'e them again.

(She goes out)

BOB: *(Shouting after her)* Bring me a packet o' Woodbines, mither. Ay, if we had eggs, we could ha'e ham and eggs the noo …

JOCK: *(Interrupting)* Oh! shut up.

BOB: Where did you get the fag ends?

JOCK: I forgot to tell your mither I was needin' baccy.

BOB: She'll mebbe forget the ham and eggs, but she'll no' forget your baccy.

JOCK: You better rin efter her and tell her.

BOB: She'll mind richt enough.

JOCK: It's high time the wheels WERE gaun roond; wheen o' ye'll soon no' be able to walk wi' laziness.

BOB: I'm tired.

JOCK: What dain'?

BOB: Rinnin' back and forrit to that soup kitchen on an empty belly. *(Suddenly)* I wonder if she'll mind my Woodbines? *(He jumps and rushes off. JOCK watches him go, and shakes his head. He sits repeating:* If we had eggs, we could ha'e ham and eggs the noo, if we had ham, *in a baffled way. He gives up. Then he lifts pot from fire and takes it to room. LIZZIE enters from school. She takes off her schoolbag, then looks into the cupboard of dresser. JOCK enters.)*

JOCK: What are you lookin' in there for?

(LIZZIE is startled)

LIZZIE: I want a piece, daddy.

JOCK: You'll need to wait till your mither comes hame.

LIZZIE: Where is she?

JOCK: Awa' for ham and eggs.

LIZZIE: Ham and eggs!

JOCK: Ay, if we had eggs we could ha'e ham and eggs the noo … no, I'm damned if I can get that.

LIZZIE: Eh?

JOCK: Naething.

LIZZIE: I couldna tak' my dinner at the schule the day, daddy.

JOCK: What was wrong wi' ye?

LIZZIE: I got the strap frae the maister, and I was sick.

JOCK: What did you get the strap for?

LIZZIE: Because I dinna ha'e my hame-sums richt … See, daddy.

(She holds out her little hand)

JOCK: Puir wee sowl, you had mair need o' a guid diet the day than the strap. Ower fu' fed, and get their money ower easy, that's what's wrang wi' them. But I'll see him the morn, Lizzie, and he can tak' what he gets frae me, the dirty swine.

LIZZIE: I ken what's needed, daddy, it's a revolution that's needed.

(BOB enters)

JOCK: Did you tell her aboot my tobacco?

BOB: No' me, she kens to get your baccy richt enough.

JOCK: No, but you would tell her aboot your Woodbines?

BOB: That's what I ran efter her for. That's a fine state o' affairs doon there noo!

JOCK: What's wrang?

BOB: Oh, they're flockin' up to the pit in their hunners to get their jobs back.

JOCK: What are they dain' that for?

BOB: There's a notice up at the pit that every man has to go before the manager before he gets his job back.

JOCK: What's the big idea?

BOB: Every man has to promise to chuck up the Union.

JOCK: Oh! and if we DINNA promise?

BOB: Well, you'll no' get your job back.

JOCK: So that's the wey o' it, they've got their foot on oor necks, and they're gaun to put on the screw. Chuck up the Union! The men'll never agree to that.

BOB: What else can they dae?

JOCK: They can go on the 'dole'.[57] We micht be better on the 'dole' onywey.

BOB: By gee! that's a good idea, I never thoucht o' that. Dinna go near the pit, faither, we ha'e nae buits or claes to start oor work wi' onywey. *(At mirror)* My face is no' half broon, faither.

JOCK: They'll soon take the broon off your face: they'll soon make a mushroom o' ye. It's a hell o' a job, hunger and rags, water and bad air, and up at fower o' clock on the cauld, snawy mornin's, and under the heel o' a set o' tyrants for starvation wages. And what can we dae, just suffer it oot and say naething.

BOB: I ken what's needed …

LIZZIE: It's a revolution that's needed, Bob.

JOCK: *(To BOB.)* Did you see any signs o' Tam Pettigrew when you were doon the street?

BOB: Ay, he was comin' oot the pub. As drunk as a sodger.

JOCK: I'm gaun to gi'e that yin a thick ear, that's what's gaun to happen.

BOB   *(At window)* Here he's comin', faither. he's comin' here. Will I lock the door?

JOCK: No, let him come in, I'll mebbe sober him up a bit.

BOB: That booze is just a curse, the pubs should be a' shut.

(TAM PETTIGREW passes the window singing)

TAM: *(Off)* Are ye in?

JOCK: Come in!

(TAM enters, and stands at door)

TAM: I'm up to gi'e ye a dram, Jock. I'm Tam Pettigrew, I gi'e a dram to wha I like and I take a dram … when I like … that's me!

JOCK: Are you no' ashamed o' yoursel', Tam?

TAM: Ashamed o' mysel'! What the hell ha'e I to be ashamed o'? I take a dram when I like … and gi'e a dram to wha I like … that's me … and always has been me … see!

(JOCK goes to help him to chair. TAM pushes him from him)

---

57 That is, National Unemployment Insurance, for which all workers and employers paid regular contributions from its introduction in 1911. A later historian agrees with Jock's estimation of the pay awaiting the Scottish miners after the victory of the mine-owners: 'For a former élite, it was a terrible defeat, with wages and status reduced to a level little above that of the unemployed' (Christopher Harvie, *No Gods and Precious Few Heroes: Scotland 1914–1980* [1981] p.94).

TAM: You surely think I'm drunk. I can manage to the chair myself. *(Walks unsteadily to chair)* I'm Tam Pettigrew … I take a dram when I like … and gi'e a dram to wha I like … that's me!

(He sits down)

TAM: Gimme a glass, Jock, and I'll gi'e ye a dram.

JOCK: *(To BOB)* Rin doon and tell Kate he's here; she'll likely be anxious aboot him.

TAM: What's that? anxious aboot me? I know what I'm dain', there's naebody need to be … anxious aboot me … Bob! here's something for fags.

BOB: *(At door)* You shairly think I'd take money frae you. If I was Kate …

JOCK: Rin awa' doon.

(BOB goes out, LIZZIE following, looking at TAM, half afraid)

TAM: Anxious aboot me! aboot ME! Here, Jock, are you tryin' to be funny? … if you are, it's no' gaun to work, see? I'm Tam Pettigrew, and there's nae man tryin' to tak' his nap aff me, see!

JOCK: D'ye think you're playin' the game, Tam?

TAM: D'ye want a dram, or dae ye no'?

(JOCK loses his temper and snatches the bottle from TAM's hand)

TAM: *(Rising)* Here! … what's the game?

(JOCK forces him to his seat)

JOCK: Sit doon, see? I ha'e something to say to you.

(TAM struggles, and JOCK has to raise the bottle to strike him)

JOCK: SIT DOON!

(TAM sits, afraid, and much sobered)

JOCK: A fine sicht you to cheer the he'rts o' your bairns, a lot o' he'rtnin' a drunk faither'll gi'e them. See here, Tam, this conduct'll no' dae: you've got to pull yoursel' thigither; be a man, it's only cowards that droon their sorrows in the pub. Ha'e some respect for the wife you laid to rest.

(There is a pause)

TAM: Jock, my he'rt's broken.

(He buries his head in his hands)

JOCK: Your's is no' the only he'rt that's broken, there's a hoosefu' doon by. And Kate's needin' a' the help you can gi'e her, or there's gaun to be anither death in the hoose.

TAM. I'll never get the better o' this Jock. … Died o' starvation. … Them and their strike … They've killed her.

JOCK: Noo, noo, Tam, it'll no' dae to lose he'rt that way, it canna be helped noo, and you'll need to put a stout he'rt to a stey brae.[58]

TAM: It COULD ha'e been helped! Them and their bloody strike! The best woman that ever lived. Hoo can I get ower it?

JOCK; You'll never get ower it if you're gaun to boose. You ha'e your bairns to care for noo. YOU'VE got to take the mither's place, and you'll need to get ower it for their sakes. D'ye think the wife would rest in her grave if she kent o' this cairry on the day?

TAM: Them and their strike … Oh! Jock …

(Enter KATE, followed by JENNY and BOB)

KATE: Come awa' doon, faither.

TAM: *(After a pause)* Are you angry wi' me, Kate?

KATE: No' me. Come awa' doon and we'll ha'e a cup o' tea.

---

58 Proverbial: put a stout heart to a steep slope.

TAM: Kate, lass, I'm no' playin' the game. Tell me you're no' angry wi' me.
KATE: No, I'm no' angry wi' ye. Come awa doon, the weans are wearyin' on ye.
TAM: Kate, I'm no' playin' the game.
(JOCK helps Kate to get TAM on his feet)
TAM: Jock, she likes her mither.
JOCK: Ay, ay, Tam. Awa' doon wi' her and get a cup o' tea and you'll soon be as richt as the mail.
TAM: YOU'RE no' angry wi' me, Jock?
JOCK: No' me, Tam.
TAM: *(Going out with KATE)* Them and their strike ... them and their bloody strike!

...

(JENNY follows)
JOCK: God guide ye, Kate, for you ha'e a big battle in front o' ye.
BOB: The boose is just a flamin' curse.
JOCK: It's a pity for him tae, Bob.
BOB: It's NAE pity for him, he's a washoot. May I choke mysel' stane deid the first time I put that stuff in my mooth.
JOCK: It's easy speakin', but we're no' a' made o' steel. You're young yet, Bob, and you ha'e a lot to come through before you can say what you can dae.
(JOCK sits at fire)
BOB: Kate's far too saft wi' him, it's a slap on the kisser he needs.
JOCK: Awa' and meet your mither, she'll be on her road noo.
BOB: I ken what should be done wi' it a'.
(He lifts bottle from table, and, unseen by JOCK, goes out and smashes it against wall. JOCK jumps on hearing the crash. BOB enters, rather proud)
JOCK: What the flames was that?
BOB: That's the stuff to gi'e them, poor it doon the street.
JOCK: *(Looking at table)* Here! is that you broken that bottle o' whisky?
BOB: Too true, it's a pity there's only yin.
JOCK: Well, I'll be damned. *(Loudly)* Are you aware a bottle o' whisky costs thirteen shillin's, and here you've sent it sailin' doon the street. Ye flamin' imp!
BOB: *(Retreating)* But I thoucht you said ...
JOCK: What did I say! WHAT DID I SAY! Thirteen shillin's worth runnin' doon the street.
BOB: Was you wantin' to pour it doon your ain neck?
JOCK: Shut up, ye flamin' agitator, before I lose my temper wi' ye. Thirteen white shillin's worth rinnin'. Oot my sicht, see! before I mulligrize ye!
BOB: By gee! it's great, richt enough: tellin' a man aff because he was drunk, and shootin' oot your neck because you canna get the same chance.
(JOCK makes a mad rush after BOB, who scoots)
JOCK: Never heard tell o' such a dirty trick a' my flamin' days. Thirteen white shillin's worth ... ach! It's enough to break a body's he'rt.
(JENNY enters)
JENNY: Faither, you'll need to go doon beside that man, he's still ravin' aboot the strike.
JOCK: *(Putting on coat)* A damned guid thumpin' is what HE'S needin'. *(Going out)* Thirteen white shillin's worth rinnin' doon the street.
(JENNY sits at fire side, and, after lookin' into the fire for a while, takes a letter from her bosom. The canary sings merrily in the quietness. LIZZIE enters and JENNY

hides the letter again in her bosom)

LIZZIE: Jenny, Wull Baxter wants to see ye.

JENNY: Where is he?

LIZZIE: He's standin' roon' the corner o' the hoose.

JENNY: Tell him to come in.

(LIZZIE goes out. JENNY walks nervously round room. She is facing the fire when WULL enters. He halts at door)

WULL: *(Softly)* Jenny.

(JENNY turns and straightens herself)

JENNY: What d'ye want here, Wull?

WULL: I'm gaun awa' the morn, Jenny.

JENNY: Weel!

WULL: I canna go withoot sayin' Guid-bye!

JENNY: There was nae need, Wull.

WULL: You're gey hard, Jenny.

JENNY: No, Wull, I'm no' hard, you played a gey hard game wi' ME.

WULL: I thoucht I was daein' richt, Jenny. I thoucht the men would make a start if somebody look the lead.

JENNY: And you stabbed them in the back; the neebours you ha'e lived wi' a' your days, the men you ha'e kept company wi', the men you ha'e sported wi' … ye traitor!

(WULL is stung by the thrust, and JENNY relents)

JENNY: Oh, Wull, what made you dae it? We were happy … ower happy … and noo …

WULL: We can be happy yet, Jenny. Let us gang awa' thegither … awa' frae here … awa' where nobody kens me … where we'll get peace.

JENNY: It's ower late, Wull, I canna forgi'e ye.

WULL: It was to let us get to Canada, Jenny. It was for your sake.

(JENNY looks into the fire. but makes no answer)

WULL: I made a mistake, Jenny. I see that noo, but it's no' ower late to forgi'e me, and let us start a new life. … The auld days were happy days, Jenny, I could go about wi' my heid in the air, and everybody had a smile for me. But noo … everybody has a scowl and a curse. … God, but I have come though hell.

(There is a pause)

WULL: It was the strike to blame, Jenny.

JENNY: *(Still looking into fire)* Ay, the strike … the strike … shattered hopes and broken he'rts.

WULL: We can be happy yet, Jenny.

JENNY: It's ower late, Wull.

WULL: The strike'll soon be forgotten.

JENNY: Ay, but you failed me, failed us a', THAT can never be forgotten.

WULL: If I was to send for you after a while, Jenny …

JENNY: It's ower late, Wull … *(Holding out her hand)* Guid bye!

WULL: Think it ower for a while …

JENNY: Guid bye!

(He shakes hands with her, and then goes slowly away. JENNY looks into fire. WULL halts at door, watches her for a second or two, then goes out. The bird sings blythly. After a pause, BOB enters)

BOB: Here! was that Wull Baxter in here?

(JENNY makes no answer)

BOB: What was he dain' in here, I'm askin'?

(Then he sees that she is upset)

BOB: What's wrang wi' ye, Jenny? Are ye vexed because he's gaun awa'? I wouldna be vexed; he's just a dirty, rotten blackleg.

JENNY: For God's sake, Bob …

BOB: I wouldna vex mysel' like that.

JENNY: Ay, you would vex yoursel' tae, Bob; hunger and rags we can get ower but no' the likes o' this. … Every dream and every hope shattered into a thousand bits. Oh! is there to be nae peace … ha'e we ay to be crushed, and crushed, and never get a chance to live! Ha'e we ay to be gropin' in the darkness? nae sunshine ava! Oh, God, dae something to tak' the load off oor shouthers or we'll gang mad![59]

(She goes to room. BOB watches her go in wonderment. Then JEAN and JOCK and LIZZIE enter, JEAN carrying a laden basket)

JEAN: If we had eggs, we could ha'e ham and eggs the noo, if we had ham, eh, Bob?

BOB: Did you mind my Woodbines?

(JOCK cuffs his ear off easy chair; JEAN hands BOB his Woodbines)

LIZZIE: Is the strike finished, Daddy?

JOCK: *(Taking her on his knee)* Finished, dearies, and we ha'e got knocked oot again.

JEAN: *(Putting groceries out on table)* Ay, but we're no' gaun to lose he'rt, Jock; we'll live to fight anither day; there's life in the auld dog yet.

(Then the sound of voices can be heard singing in the distance, the tune is 'The Red Flag'. A look of pride comes into JEAN's eyes, and she listens. Then she speaks, as if inspired by some great hope)

JEAN: That's the spirit, my he'rties! sing! sing! tho' they ha'e ye chained to the wheels and the darkness. Sing! tho' they ha'e ye crushed in the mire. Keep up your he'rts, my laddies, you'll win through yet, for there's nae power on earth can crush the men that can sing on a day like this.

THE END

---

59 Shouthers (Sc.): shoulders.

Willa Muir, 'Clock-a-doodle-doo'.[1]

They were all wag-at-the-wa' clocks,[2] but of every conceivable size and shape, and they covered three walls of the room, which had a fourth wall of clear glass as if it were an enormous show-case. Every day a Woman opened a little side-door and came in to wind up any weights that had run down. She always came in just when the sunlight, having fingered its way round half the room, touching clock after clock, had withdrawn for a siesta on the floorboards before creeping back to finger the clocks on the other half of the walls. She handled the weights lovingly as if she liked feeling them, and the clocks were excited and glad to see her, so that they whirred and chimed in unison no less than twelve strokes, the maximum effort of which they were capable. A great deal of their tick-talking and clock-clacking was concerned with her and her doings, yet she never showed the least interest in their mechanism, except for the weights, and the clocks, who were proud of the cog-wheels inside their heads, especially when daylight failed and they could not see each other, were puzzled by her indifference. In the dark they lived only in their cog-wheels and so the shadow that hid each clock from its neighbour was also a shadow of fear, for if a wheel were to fail in the night or a spindle break the damaged clock could not ever show a face to the world but was as if annihilated. In the dark, therefore, they were resentful of the Woman's indifference, but they did not discuss her except to accuse her of stupidity, for they were eager to forget their fear by speculating on the nature of cog-wheels and propounding theories for their repair. Every night the discussion waxed in liveliness until the defiance of the clocks culminated in striking midnight, after which they relapsed contentedly into the hum-drum routine of the small hours where little effort was needed.

On moonlight nights, however, the liveliness continued as long as the moonshine lasted. And on these occasions they speculated about the moon, arguing that it must be a super-clock, permanently lit-up and delivered from the fear of darkness, not to speak of its power to move freely, if erratically, across the wall of the sky. One very grandfatherly clock, reputed to be the oldest inhabitant, sought in vain to discourage what he called the heresy of revering the moon; the other clocks were tired of hearing his admonitions to honour the punctual sun, which was, he said, the Author of their Being: 'He is like ourselves, only greater. He too vanishes from sight in the darkness. He too is regular in his movements — does he not visit us daily, each in turn, to watch over our welfare and to remind us that we belong to the great cosmic rhythm of Time? Your moon is no clock-face, your moon spins round until only its edge is visible, your moon is merely the sun's pendulum.'

'Bah!' said the young, impatient clocks, and they said it loudly ten times so that the wheezing, grandfatherly clock was quite inaudible. 'Of course the moon is a clock-face. Can we not see the signs upon it although they are difficult to read?'

'Use your cog-wheels, old fool, use your cog-wheels,' added a very Clever Clock, who claimed to have twice as many cog-wheels as any of the others. 'It's face-values you're trying to foist on us, face-value wrapped up in pious sentimentality. If the sun takes the trouble to visit us it's because he thinks it worth his while. And as for you,' he addressed the young clocks, 'it's face-values you're serving too, the whole clacking of you, when you say that you admire the moon *although* you can't read its face! Admire it rather *because* it is illegible, because its meaning lies hidden in its private cog-wheels, because it is an intricate and baffling piece of mechanism, unlike your hum-drum, bourgeois sun.'

---

1 First published in *The Modern Scot* 5 (June 1934).
2 A 'wag-at-the-wa'' clock is a wall-mounted one with an unencased pendulum.

The moon shone straight in upon the Clever Clock. 'Ah! I am lit-up too!' he cried. 'Now I shall tell you the truth. The numbers on our faces are only a device to keep us marking time, to prevent us from inquiring into the nature of reality —'

He had to break off to strike Eleven, and this made him furious; besides, in spite of his multifarious cog-wheels, his voice was not the loudest in the room. A much simpler-looking clock on his right had a fuller, more resonant chime, and the Clever Clock, aware of his superior intricacy, kicked his pendulum petulantly as far as it would go.

'I appeal to my friends on the left,' he exclaimed, as soon as the echoes had died away. 'What is this so-called Time to which we are bound in slavery? Can anyone define it? Is it anything but an ideological figment?'

These words impressed the young clocks. And when the Clever Clock went on to point out that the Truth of things lay inside their own heads, and was to be discovered only by the study of their own cog-wheels, they were interested. But when the Clever Clock said that a knowledge of the springs of their own conduct would enable each of them to detach himself from routine and become an independent moon, they were elated.

'Let us make a beginning — any beginning!' they cried.

'Good,' said the Clever Clock, 'Watch me.'

He shrugged and twisted himself until he had dislocated the numbers on his face, so that they were all in the wrong places.

'That is the first step towards illegibility,' he announced, 'the first step on the road to freedom. *A nous la liberté!*'[3] And he struck Twelve on a high, tinny note of exultation, with both his hands pointing to the number One. 'Now I shall withdraw into myself and meditate on my cog-wheels,' he said. 'I have already made several important discoveries —'

'Do tell us,' buzzed the clocks. But at that moment the moon fled behind a cloud-bank and the clocks began to be a little fearful at the return of darkness. The Clever Clock felt their fear creeping into him, and muttered 'Fools!' so savagely that the clocks did not dare to address him again that night.

Now the Clever Clock had really discovered something. By listening very intently to himself he had discovered that his cog-wheels were interlocking and moved each other. But which of them was the *primum mobile*?[4] He groaned in private over the difficulty of his task. 'If I could only be quit of this nonsense of striking the hours!' he reflected. 'What I want is Pure Horological Thought. ...'[5] He fell into a kind of trance, murmuring to himself: 'I am I. I am my cog-wheels.' This so refreshed his self-conceit that on the morning after, when the other clocks looked uneasily at his face, wondering what the Woman would say, he tick-tocked and clack-clacked more arrogantly than ever. 'She won't dare to say anything. She is a mere servant of the cog-wheels. Does she not handle our weights simply and solely to minister to the cog-wheels?' he declared, and was proved right, too, for the Woman did not look at his face at all. He was a clock

---

3   *À nous la liberté!* ('Freedom for us!') is a film by René Clair from 1931. It is the story of two convicts, forced to work on an assembly line, one of whom escapes and becomes a factory-owner himself. It ends with the friends abandoning industrial society for the freedom of the open road as tramps.

4   *Primum mobile* ('first moved'): a term from pre-Copernican cosmology, this was the outer-most of the moving spheres that surrounded the earth, containing the stars. It is possible that Muir has in mind instead the *primum movens* ('first mover') of Aristotelian philosophy: the 'first cause' which makes other things move without being moved itself (and equated in Christian and Islamic thinking with God).

5   Ellipsis in original.

who could run for months at a time without her, and she disregarded him. 'In any case,' said the Clever Clock, after she had gone, 'she is stupid. And so are most of you – all of you. Marking time is all you're fit for. Not one of you is capable of becoming a free agent, except myself. However, when I am a moon I shall be lit-up for ever, and I shall be famous when you are all on the scrap-heap.'

'No, no!' cried several young clocks, so young that they were almost watches. 'We want to be lit-up too!'

'How can you take him seriously?' growled the grandfatherly clock.

The Clever Clock interrupted him. 'We must free our terminology from the materialism of content, if we are to discover the laws of Pure Horological Thought,' he said rapidly, impressing his audience once more.

At that moment the finger of the sun touched him, giving him a warm, tickling sensation which was so pleasant that, even while reminding himself how much he despised sensation, he forgot momentarily to continue talking. As the sun slid over him the carved detail on his case stood out clearly, and one could see what a very fine clock he had been meant to be. Twelve little wooden figures stood in niches around the clock-case, and an angel with a little trumpet was perched on the very top. There could be no doubt that his intricate machinery had been planned to set these figures in motion, but something must have gone wrong, for they were gathering dust, and looked a little forlorn. And the Clever Clock, pondering his cog-wheels, had never even suspected that what they really needed was the adjustment of a minute pinion to set the little figures dancing. There was a tiny screw loose in the Clever Clock, but he was too busy boasting and studying Pure Horological Thought to observe anything of the kind.

He felt restless again when the finger of the sun left him. The Daily Dope! he muttered to himself, sneering at the travelling beam of light. And he shrugged himself so hard that his numbers fell into confusion; one of them even came off and tinkled on to the floor. That delighted the Clever Clock.

'Now I am well on the way to become unintelligible,' he said. 'I am unique among clocks!'

'But you are still marking Time,' retorted the grandfatherly clock, for at that moment the Clever Clock had to strike Two along with all the others. This so exasperated him that with a violent kick he dislodged the balancing weight from his pendulum.

'Now I am Really Unique,' he gasped, somewhat out of breath, since his pendulum was clacking wildly. 'Now I can swing from one extreme to the other as much as I like! There is no other clock like me in the whole universe. Clack-clack! Clack-clack! CLACK! Not one of you can do this! Clack-clack-clack-clack!!'

'Oo-oo-oh!' cried the young clocks, feeling excited. 'What marvellous high-kicking!'

And that night, when he was lit-up, the Clever Clock set all the others to shrugging and kicking in imitation of him, crying at top-speed:

'This is – clackety-clack – this is the Horological Renaissance!'

When the Woman came in the next day her foot struck against a little pile of discarded numbers and a pendulum balance. Also, she could hear the Clever Clock clack-clacking at furious speed. She reached up and took him from the wall and blew the dust off the little wooden figures.

'Watch me!' said the Clever Clock to the admiring young clocks. 'Now I move from the wall as I promised you. This Woman is the servant of my will.'

And he went out in her arms and the door shut behind them.

www.ingramcontent.com/pod-product-compliance
Lightning Source LLC
Chambersburg PA
CBHW080952020726
47505CB00009B/2176